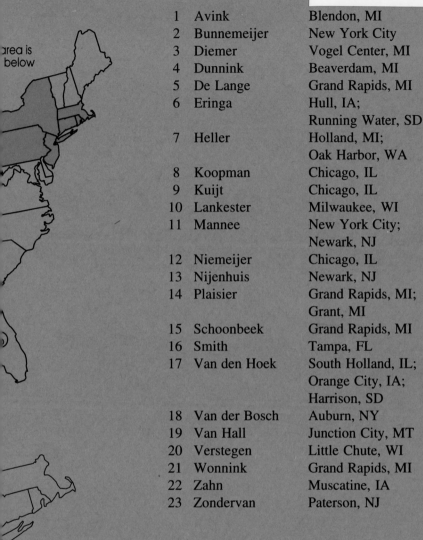

area is
below

1	Avink	Blendon, MI
2	Bunnemeijer	New York City
3	Diemer	Vogel Center, MI
4	Dunnink	Beaverdam, MI
5	De Lange	Grand Rapids, MI
6	Eringa	Hull, IA; Running Water, SD
7	Heller	Holland, MI; Oak Harbor, WA
8	Koopman	Chicago, IL
9	Kuijt	Chicago, IL
10	Lankester	Milwaukee, WI
11	Mannee	New York City; Newark, NJ
12	Niemeijer	Chicago, IL
13	Nijenhuis	Newark, NJ
14	Plaisier	Grand Rapids, MI; Grant, MI
15	Schoonbeek	Grand Rapids, MI
16	Smith	Tampa, FL
17	Van den Hoek	South Holland, IL; Orange City, IA; Harrison, SD
18	Van der Bosch	Auburn, NY
19	Van Hall	Junction City, MT
20	Verstegen	Little Chute, WI
21	Wonnink	Grand Rapids, MI
22	Zahn	Muscatine, IA
23	Zondervan	Paterson, NJ

The Pius XII Library

SAINT JOSEPH

COLLEGE

West Hartford, Connecticut 06117

DUTCH
AMERICAN
VOICES

DOCUMENTS IN AMERICAN SOCIAL HISTORY
A series edited by
Nick Salvatore

A full list of titles in the series
appears at the end of this book.

DUTCH AMERICAN VOICES

Letters from the United States, 1850–1930

EDITED BY

Herbert J. Brinks

CORNELL UNIVERSITY PRESS

ITHACA AND LONDON

Cornell University Press gratefully acknowledges a subvention from
the Friends of the Calvin College Archives Endowment Fund,
which aided in bringing this book to publication.

Printed in the United States of America

Library of Congress Cataloging-in-Publication Data

Dutch American voices : letters from the United States, 1850–1930 /
edited by Herbert J. Brinks.
p. cm.—(Documents in American social history)
Includes bibliographical references and index.
ISBN 0-8014-3063-1 (alk. paper)
1. Dutch Americans—Correspondence. 2. Dutch Americans—History—
Sources. I. Brinks, Herbert J., 1935–   . II. Series.
E184.D9D87   1995
973'.043931—dc20   94-24168

For Ruth, our children,
and our grandchildren

CONTENTS

[vii]

ILLUSTRATIONS

MAPS

LETTER FACSIMILES

PHOTOGRAPHS

PREFACE

The Calvin College Library Archives, which have assembled the Dutch Immigrant Letter Collection, stem directly from institutions founded by nineteenth-century Dutch immigrants. Calvin College and its sponsoring denomination, the Christian Reformed Church, date respectively from 1876 and 1857. The archives, begun in 1961, contain a wide spectrum of institutional and personal papers from the Dutch Reformed community and include four thousand linear feet of manuscripts together with a selected seven-thousand-volume collection of books, pamphlets, and periodicals to accommodate a wide variety of Dutch American studies. Although the archives' holdings conform generally to the social and institutional shapes of nineteenth-century Dutch Calvinism in North America, the Dutch Immigrant Letter Collection includes a wider spectrum of Dutch immigrant experience—Protestant, Catholic, and secular—and it is the only major collection of its kind.

To assemble the Immigrant Letter Collection the archives conducted four major manuscript collection campaigns in the Netherlands and the United States between 1976 and 1990. These efforts accumulated at least eight thousand items—letters, travel accounts, immigrant memoirs, and photographs. Of the 4,970 letters gathered (1838–1930), 2,793 were American postings and 2,179 were from the Netherlands to the United States. Half of the letters from immigrants cluster between 1873 and 1893, accurately reflecting the numerical configuration of Dutch immigration. Moreover, immigration peaks in 1848–1857, 1867–1888, and 1892–1915 are followed a year or two later by peaks in correspondence. Unfortunately we acquired no useful examples of two-way correspondence. Furthermore, the immigrant letters represent at best 0.0032 percent of an estimated 889,000 letters mailed from the United States to Holland between 1820 and 1930.[1] Of all these letters the most pertinent

[1] Based on calculations using Robert P. Swierenga, "Dutch International Labour Migration to North America in the Nineteenth Century" in *Dutch Immigration to North*

for this publication are those of 482 correspondents who wrote between 1850 and 1930.

Nearly half of these correspondents are represented by one or two letters, which, because of their short time spans, disclose little about ongoing acculturation. Consequently, this book's letters were taken primarily from the 263 correspondents who wrote three or more letters. Nineteen of the more lengthy correspondence series and four single and double letter collections have been reproduced for this book. The series range from three to thirty-five letters, with an average of twelve letters covering twenty-one years. One series spans fifty-seven years; two others persist for only three years. The correspondents who appear in this book represent every major category of nineteenth-century Dutch immigration, and their letters represent every decade. There are three from the 1840s, three from the 1850s, two from the 1860s, three from the 1870s, two from the 1880s, five from the 1890s, three from the 1900s, one from the 1910s, and one from the 1920s.

The criteria for selecting the contents of this volume are, first, that the correspondents represent typical sending and receiving communities and, second, that the writings traverse sufficient blocks of time to disclose patterns of acculturation. Then, when alternatives were available, those who wrote with attention to significant and interesting detail received preference. Fortunately, correspondence by women is readily available within these guidelines. The major exclusions are letters published specifically to encourage immigration—and that category includes flagship accounts written and published by such colonial founders as the Reverend A. C. van Raalte, the Reverend H. P. Scholte, and others. These pamphlets have been publicly available since the 1850s and have heavily influenced interpretations of the Dutch American experience. The private correspondence in this book, directed to families and friends, provides a candid expression of the immigrants' experience, and should promote a reassessment of traditional interpretations.

The primary objective of this book is to provide English-language sources that can personify the considerable accumulation of recent Dutch ethnic scholarship crafted principally from computer-assisted research,

---

America, ed. Herman Ganzevoort and Mark Boekelman (Toronto: Multicultural History Society of Ontario, 1983), p. 2, which indicates that about one-third of the immigrants were letter-writing household heads or single adults, so that out of 380,000 immigrants about 127,000 probably wrote letters. Estimating that each correspondent wrote seven letters (the average series in our Immigrant Letter Collection is five), the total number of letters would be 889,000. Also see Annemieke Galema, "Now I Will Write You Something about America," in *Images of the Nation: Different Meanings of Dutchness, 1870–1940*, ed. A. Galema, B. Henkes, and H. te Velde (Amsterdam: Rodopi, 1993), pp. 105–31.

pioneered by Robert P. Swierenga and several of his doctoral students. These studies have identified more precisely than ever the various religions, occupations, geographic mobility patterns, and vital statistics of the nineteenth-century immigrants. Their findings have made it possible to translate and publish an accurately representative selection of immigrant letters.

Furthermore, because so few scholars in history and the social sciences read Dutch, the English translations in this book are intended to facilitate a growing interest in comparative ethnic studies. Moreover, Dutch Americans in general cannot read their ancestral language, and this collection of letters will enable them to rediscover their own past.

The translations are relatively free, that is, they are ordinary sense-for-sense translations. I have avoided literal renditions because they are almost always awkward and frequently misleading. Rather, I have attempted to retain the general style of the originals by reproducing either their simple or more complex syntax. In most cases punctuation has been inserted or modified to clarify meanings. I have followed the Dutch convention in the capitalization of surnames.

Many of the correspondents spelled phonetically in their regional dialects. Unfortunately, there is no way to capture these interesting variations in translation, and linguists will not be well served. Still, several original manuscripts have been reproduced to exemplify this phenomenon. Doubtless anyone who wishes to retrace the translation process will discover some ambiguities or prefer alternative translations, but my guiding rule has been to provide the clearest and most direct meanings of each correspondent. Some letter segments were simply undecipherable, and other short passages were eliminated because they were repetitious. These instances have been identified by three ellipsis points. Several correspondents, especially Teunis van den Hoek, H. Koopman, and Klaas Niemeijer, penned lengthy and redundant passages, frequently of a pious nature. Some of these have been omitted, the elision indicated by three asterisks. In general, predictable salutations and closings are not repeated after the first letter in each series.

Both the acquisition and the translation of the immigrant letters have required an extensive network of volunteers in the United States, Canada, and the Netherlands. In each of three major European projects Jan Niemeijer, an author and journalist, directed me to proper media personnel to gain effective publicity. During a three-month campaign in 1990 Annemieke Galema organized a nationwide effort involving contacts with provincial archives and local historical societies, television coverage, and radio and newspaper interviews to reach all sectors of the Netherlands. Arie Bor and Caroline Bor, both Dutch-language professionals, and Hans

Krabbendam from the Roosevelt Study Center in Middelburg teamed with Dr. Galema throughout the 1990 campaign. The Bor family provided a home base for me during the three-week culmination of this project. The hundreds of Netherlanders who responded to this and two earlier letter-collection campaigns are too numerous to list. In the vast majority of cases we photocopied the original letters for deposit and research in the Calvin College Archives.

At least sixty persons have assisted in the translation of the immigrant letters. George Kamp, Jan Driesten, G. H. Ligterink, Charles Greenfield, David van Vliet, Egbert Post, and John Dahm Sr. are now deceased. Archivist Zwanet Janssens has organized and administered the ongoing translation of the Immigrant Letter Collection while also providing indispensable advice in many instances of linguistic ambiguity. Dutch students attending Calvin College have also helped with translation. In addition a cadre of about twenty volunteers, mostly post–World War II Dutch immigrants in Canada, have translated dozens of letters. In particular, Leonard Sweetman, Maria de Groot, Peter de Gelder, Henry Baak, Suzanne Sinke, George Harper, Peter de Klerk, and Jacoba Dahm have been overwhelmingly generous with their time and talents. Appendix A is a list of those translators who were extraordinarily helpful.

With consummate skill and even greater patience, Hendrina Van Spronsen prepared the complicated manuscript for publication. Conrad Bult, a librarian who loves rare books, neglected nothing to obtain obscure books and pamphlets from distant libraries. I have benefited much from the advice of Annemieke Galema, James Bratt, Leonard Sweetman, Robert P. Swierenga, Yda Schreuder, and Rob Kroes, who graciously consented to read segments of the manuscript.

Research leading to the establishment of the Dutch Immigrant Letter Collection began in 1976 with combined assistance from the Bentley Historical Library of the University of Michigan, the Earhart Foundation in Ann Arbor, and a Calvin College sabbatical. The National Historical Publications and Records Commission funded my 1978 proposal, "Acquisition and Preservation of Correspondence from the Netherlands to American Immigrants, 1840–1930." In 1981 the Fulbright-Hays Council funded my research in the Netherlands, and a Calvin College sabbatical followed in 1986. The last acquisition campaign (1990) had the assistance of two foundations, Meijer Inc. and Russel and Julia Bouws. Witte Travel and the Dutch International Society also contributed to the 1990 effort. Over these many years Calvin College has consistently funded the programs of the archives, and this book is a tribute to that support.

HERBERT J. BRINKS

Grand Rapids, Michigan

DUTCH
AMERICAN
VOICES

1	Avink	Borculo, GLD
2	Bunnemeijer	Naarden, NH
3	Diemer	Hoogeveen, DR
4	Dunnink	Staphorst, OV
5	De Lange	Deventer, OV
6	Eringa	Spannum, FR
7	Heller	Ulrum, GR
8	Koopman	Borger, DR
9	Kuijt	Amsterdam
10	Lankester	Middelburg, ZLD
11	Mannee	Zierikzee, ZLD
12	Niemeijer	Middlestum, GR
13	Nijenhuis	Winterswijk, GLD
14	Plaisier	Ridderkerk, ZH
15	Schoonbeek	Nieuwolda, GR
16	Smith	Finsterwolde, GR
17	Van den Hoek	Noordeloos, ZH
18	Van der Bosch	Gendrigen, GLD
19	Van Hall	Huissen, GLD
20	Verstegen	Zeeland, NB
21	Wonnink	Geesteren, GLD
22	Zahn	Amsterdam
23	Zondervan	Firdgum, FR

The Netherlands

INTRODUCTION

An Overview of Dutch Immigration, 1850–1930

The earliest letter in this collection follows by over two hundred years Henry Hudson's 1609 exploration of New York Harbor and the subsequent founding of Forts Orange and New Amsterdam. The entire New Netherland colony persisted only until 1664 when Governor Pieter Stuyvesant capitulated to British invaders. Thereafter, immigration from the Netherlands virtually stopped until the post-Napoleonic era, finally surging again in 1846–1847. Then, along with Germans, Irish, and other Northern Europeans, the Dutch began to leave their homeland in significant numbers, and the vast majority, over 90 percent, came to the United States.

Already during the French occupation of the Netherlands, 1810–1814, Jewish merchants from Amsterdam, hampered by trade embargoes, were migrating to London, and some of these sailed farther west to settle in New York and Philadelphia. After 1815, working-class Jews migrated directly to New York and other cities where their coreligionists were well established. Although among the first to emigrate, these Dutch Jews did not establish a model for the vastly larger group of Christians (about 90 percent of 380,000) who came to the United States between 1820 and 1930.

Almost all Jews were moving from city environment to city environment, singly or in family groups. By contrast, both the Catholics and a segment of ultra-Calvinist religious seceders initially immigrated in large groups led by ministers. Both were disaffected with the privileged Dutch Reformed (Hervormde) church and the governmental policies that favored it. Despite a history of civil and social discrimination against Catholics, most church officials in the Catholic provinces, Limburg and Noord Brabant, to protect the religious and social cohesion of their parishes, discouraged emigration. Consequently, only one priest, Father Theodorus van den Broek in Little Chute, Wisconsin, sponsored a major

Catholic colony. Catholic immigrants constituted only 17 percent of the 1835–1880 immigration, even though they made up 38 percent of the Dutch population in 1849. Furthermore, only about 10 percent of them settled in or near Little Chute. The balance, about nine thousand, was scattered across the United States, most selecting homes in places such as St. Louis, where German and other Catholic parishes were prominent.

Protestants of various sorts made made up about 70 percent of the Dutch immigration. The conservative Calvinist seceders established the first two colonies, in Michigan and Iowa (1846–1847). These original settlements and at least six others like them were organized and tended by pastors who immigrated with their parishioners and other adherents before 1860. They aimed to create predominantly Dutch Calvinist set-tlements and were successful enough to inspire the establishment of over one hundred similar villages in the Midwest and across the northern tier of states between 1848 and 1900. Even though religious seceders initiated this cultural pattern, the wider spectrum of Reformed church members who later dominated immigration usually joined the original immigrants in their communities and churches.[1]

The founders of the two earliest settlements, Holland, Michigan, and Pella, Iowa, maximized ethnic solidarity by selecting sites that were thinly populated and nearly void of institutions. In each case the immigrants acquired exclusive possession of the available real estate and established regional schools and churches. The structure of these first colonies then became paradigmatic for those that followed, and the model persisted into the twentieth century. Each new community dominated a chosen landscape of contiguous farms and a village center with Reformed churches and district schools. Successful settlements attracted successive

[1] The three standard surveys of Dutch American history are Henry Lucas, *Netherlanders in America: Dutch Immigration to the United States and Canada, 1789–1950* (Ann Arbor: University of Michigan Press, 1955); Gerald F. De Jong, *The Dutch in America, 1609–1974* (Boston: Twayne, 1975); and Jacob van Hinte, *Netherlanders in America: A Study of Emigration and Settlement in the Nineteenth and Twentieth Centuries in the United States of America*, ed. Robert P. Swierenga (Grand Rapids, Mich.: Baker Book House, 1985). See also Robert P. Swierenga, "Dutch," in *Harvard Encyclopedia of American Ethnic Groups*, ed. Stephan Thernstrom (Cambridge: Harvard University Press, 1980), pp. 284–95; Herbert J. Brinks, "The Dutch," in *Encyclopedia of American Social History*, ed. Mary K. Cayton, Elliott J. Gorn, Peter Williams (New York: Scribner's, 1993), 2:711–18.

For specific treatment of the Jewish and Catholic experience, see Robert P. Swierenga, "Dutch Jewish Immigration and Religious Life in the Nineteenth Century," *American Jewish History* 80 (1990): 56–73; Swierenga, "Religion and Immigration Behavior: The Dutch Experience," in *Belief and Behavior: Essays in the New Religious History*, ed. Robert P. Swierenga and Philip R. Vandermeer (New Brunswick: Rutgers University Press, 1991), pp. 164–88.

waves of new immigrants and, in all, absorbed nearly three-quarters of the Netherlanders who arrived between 1847 and 1900.[2]

In contrast to those who joined enduring ethnic strongholds, other immigrants, typically of common geographical origin, organized transitory communities in places such as Franklin, Wisconsin, Muscatine, Iowa, and Friesland, South Dakota. Either these communities did not prosper sufficiently to support ethnic churches or, as in the Friesland case, agricultural failures forced the settlers to move elsewhere. Nonetheless, during the early stages of cultural adjustment, these ephemeral enclaves provided attractive economic opportunities and the comforts of familiar associations. When these communities dispersed, many of the residents relocated in more flourishing Dutch ethnic centers, and those who resettled in "American" surroundings were better prepared to adjust to novel cultural structures.

The enclaved immigrants, whether in permanent or passing communities, acculturated differently from those who settled directly in strange surroundings. Of these, although they may constitute as much as 10 percent of the total immigration, relatively little is known.[3] Links with their native places were not kept strong by ethnic cohesion in the United States, and partly on that account, their letters were fewer and less persistent than the writings of the enclaved immigrants. More than families, unmarried persons were inclined to settle apart from ethnic centers, and when these single immigrants married they were usually absorbed into their spouses' communities. They found, in other words, surrogate in-groups from which communal news was largely irrelevant in the Netherlands.

In contrast, the ties between Dutch American population centers and their sending communities were complex and enduring because chain migrations flowed persistently from specific regions in the Netherlands to ethnic concentrations in the United States. In fact, nearly 75 percent of all the arrivals (1835–1879) originated from 12 percent of the *gemeenten*[4] in the Netherlands. And in 1870, 56 percent of the Dutch immi-

[2] Throughout the period from 1850 to 1900 the U.S. Census records indicate that 74 percent of the foreign-born Dutch were concentrated in the seven states (Illinois, Indiana, Iowa, Michigan, Minnesota, New Jersey, and Wisconsin) that contained the major Dutch American enclaves. As late as 1920, 67 percent of Holland-born Americans lived in these states. Lucas, *Netherlanders in America*, Appendix, Table II.

[3] Assuming that Jews and most Catholics (27 percent of the total immigrants) settled in religiously compatible surroundings and that at least 65 percent of the Protestant balance joined existing enclaves or established new communities, only about 8 percent of the Dutch immigrants (1835–1879) jumped directly into mainstream American culture.

[4] The term defies precise translation into English. The *gemeente* is a city or town that

grants were located in just eighteen U.S. counties.[5] Consequently, news of births, deaths, and marriages along with special attention to religious leaders remained of interest in both the sending and receiving communities for up to three generations. Pastors received exceptional notice because the earliest communities (1847–1857) were either founded by clergymen or profoundly shaped by them. And throughout the century, the ethnic churches sought both pastors and schoolteachers from the homeland; these leaders brought infusions of Netherlandic culture by carrying news from Old World villages and updating ecclesiastical and theological concerns. In addition, the establishment of Dutch-language periodicals in the major ethnic communities reinforced social solidarity with news and information about the homeland and about the spectrum of Dutch settlements in the New World.[6]

It seems clear enough that the immigrants' choice of residence implied a strategy of cultural adaptation, which is also reflected in the character of their correspondence. The inclusion in this volume of letters from inside and outside enduring ethnic clusters should facilitate the study of Dutch American acculturation patterns and also provide a basis to analyze the effects of modernization on the immigrants' behavior. In every context, whether in or out of ethnic clusters, whether consciously or intuitively, the migrants were reacting to the social, economic, and religious components of modernization; just as they left ancestral communities amid perceived threats to their well-being, they also sought employment, with suitable social and religious connections, in the United States to maximize the realization of their values and objectives.[7]

Recent reexamination has augmented the standard accounts of Dutch American history to create a full and precise narrative. The general con-

---

performs the functions of a U.S. county seat and provides services to a number of towns and villages in the surrounding region.

[5] Robert P. Swierenga, "Dutch Immigration Patterns," in *The Dutch in America: Immigration, Settlement, and Cultural Change*, ed. Swierenga (New Brunswick: Rutgers University Press, 1985). This collection of thirteen essays by leading scholars of Dutch American history incorporates much of the recent scholarship. See also Swierenga, *The Dutch Transplanting in the Upper Middle West* (Marshall, Minn.: Southwest State University Press, 1991), 20 pp.

[6] Lucas, *Netherlanders in America*, pp. 89–320, provides the best account of Netherlandic enclave formation, 1846–1870.

[7] The most influential studies of acculturation and the implications of modernization for ethnic scholarship are Milton Gordon, *Assimilation in American Life: The Role of Race, Religion, and National Origins* (New York: Oxford University Press, 1964); John Bodnar, *The Transplanted: A History of Immigrants in Urban America* (Bloomington: Indiana University Press, 1985); Charles Tilly, "Transplanted Networks," in *Immigration Reconsidered: History, Sociology, and Politics*, ed. Virginia Yans-McLaughlin (New York: Oxford University Press, 1990), pp. 79–95.

tours of the story indicate that, with the close of the Napoleonic era in
1815, Dutch emigration began as a small trickle. It accelerated noticeably
in 1847 and thereafter followed the typical pattern of migration from
Northern Europe, except that the Dutch émigrés were overwhelmingly
of rural origin. Throughout the whole era, with three numerical peaks
between the Civil War and World War I, the immigrants came largely
(up to 80 percent), from the agricultural provinces that encircle the western urban core of the Netherlands. Yet the total for the whole century
(1820–1920) was fewer than 400,000, a number the Irish easily surpassed
in nearly every decade of that era.

The relatively small number of Dutch emigrants (they ranked tenth
on the list of European sending countries), relates partly to the late economic modernization of the Netherlands, which lagged at least fifty
years behind its industrializing neighbors. Steam power applied to transportation and mass production became a common feature of the Dutch
landscape only after the turn of the century. Thus, emigration did not
stem from massive economic dislocations following in the wake of urban
industrialization. Still, like much of Northern Europe, the Netherlands
did experience a long cycle of population growth, which created surplus
labor to fill high-wage industrial workplaces in the United States and to
till its huge reservoir of arable acreage. The Dutch preferred farms to
factories.[8]

The initial cluster of immigrants came from the economically stagnant
region of Drenthe, Gelderland, and Overijssel, whose sandy soil supported only small marginal farms and where manufacturing was limited
to locally marketed handicrafts and some cottage industry. In general the
prospects for agricultural expansion or increased trade were minimal in
these areas. The introduction of commercial fertilizers and the construction of better transportation networks changed these conditions in the
second half of the century, but until then, emigration was appealing.
Consequently, the original settlers of Holland, Michigan, and many of
its satellite communities (1846–1860) came primarily from the sand-soil
regions of the outer provinces. Thereafter chain migration from this area
amounted to about one-third of the entire emigration.

[8] Robert P. Swierenga, "Dutch International Labour Migration to North America in
the Nineteenth Century," in *Dutch Immigration to North America*, ed. Herman Ganzevoort
and Mark Boekelman (Toronto: Multicultural History Society of Ontario, 1983), pp. 1–
34. Izaak J. Brugmans, *De arbeidende klasse in Nederland de 19e eeuw 1813–1870* (The Hague:
Martinus Nijhoff, 1925); J. H. van Stuijvenberg, *De economische geschiedenis van Nederland*
(Groningen: Wolters-Noordhoff, 1977), pp. 201–59; Hille de Vries, "The Labor Market
in Dutch Agriculture and Emigration to the United States," in *The Dutch in America*, ed.
Swierenga, pp. 78–101.

Another cluster of early (1847) immigrants came from Zuid Beveland on Zeeland's principal island. The commercial agriculture that dominated this region's economy divided the populace between large landholders and dependent laborers. With financial assistance and direction from one wealthy farmer, Jannes vande Luyster, over four hundred farmhands left the area to found the colony of Zeeland, near Holland, Michigan. The neighboring Zuid Holland island, Goeree-Overflakkee, had the higest per capita emigration of any Netherlandic area (4,200 between 1835 and 1880). Impoverished by the collapse of markets for the region's main crop, meekrap (a root used to produce red dye for fabrics), and with no assisting sponsor like Vande Luyster, the Goeree-Overflakkee immigrants probably lacked the funds to travel west from the Castle Garden terminal. They settled nearby, founding a persisting Dutch American subculture around Paterson, New Jersey. Between them, the Zeelanders and Zuid Holland islanders provided the largest regional percentage of immigrants to the United States during the last century.[9]

The major clay-soil regions of Friesland and Groningen on the North Sea provided about 40 percent of all the emigrants to the United States, but that movement did not accelerate rapidly until the 1870s. In the Netherlandic agricultural crisis (1875–1895), available homestead land in the United States offered a powerful inducement for the immigrants who came to the States between 1880 and 1900. Nearly 75 percent of these eighty thousand immigrants were reacting to agricultural disruptions in regions that traditionally produced wheat and other grains. Alternate cropping and mechanization combined to create a labor surplus, and, although other employment was available in new agricultural processing plants or in the industrial sectors of Germany and the Netherlands, a general preference for farming together with encouraging reports from the United States drew many farmers and day laborers from the clay soils of the Netherlands to American prairies and plains. As one historian concluded, "Emigration to America took advantage of the resistance of Groningers, Frisians and Zeelanders to the industrial way of life."[10]

Most of these rural immigrants came from economic groups with sufficient means to transport themselves and acquire basic farm tools and some livestock. Those of lesser means, single men in particular, worked as farmhands to accumulate savings before beginning as sharecroppers or homesteaders. The wealthiest immigrants acquired well-developed farms on the best land available. In some instances the lure of successful

---

[9] Robert P. Swierenga, "Local Patterns of Dutch Migration to the United States in the Mid-Nineteenth Century," in *A Century of European Migrations, 1830–1930*, ed. Rudolph J. Vecoli and Suzanne Sinke (Urbana: University of Illinois Press, 1991), pp. 134–57.

[10] Hille de Vries, "The Labor Market," p. 93.

agriculture led both immigrants and Dutch American migrants from the Midwest to the Far West to settle in places such as Lynden, Washington, and Ripon, California.[11]

Because Dutch emigration was predominantly rural the selections in this book are weighted in that direction. The exit from villages in sand-soil regions, which characterized the first immigration wave, is exemplified by Jacob Harms Dunnink, who left Staphorst, Overijssel, in 1848 and found better but unbroken soil near Zeeland, Michigan. Many Staphorsters had preceded him to that region, and his letters home regularly report on the fortunes of his transplanted neighbors from Staphorst. One of his daughters married a farmer from a neighboring village; another married a brickmason in Grand Rapids, twenty-five miles away. She probably met him while working as a housemaid and attending an ethnic church in that city. Her experience typifies the accumulating migration that made that city a major Dutch American population center.[12]

By the 1870s Grand Rapids, Michigan, had attracted about three thousand foreign-born Netherlanders, amounting to 18 percent of the urban population. With several churches and schools the ethnic community established a foundation for persistent growth and high visibility.[13] With its West Michigan hinterland, the city has become the current population and institutional center of ethnic Dutch in the United States. Jan Wonnink, an immigrant from the sandy soils of Geesteren in Gelderland, joined the Grand Rapids enclave in 1873. Despite his rural background, Wonnink worked in a furniture factory, and his correspondence provides a wide-ranging description of the city, its churches, and the ethnic community. Unlike Aart Plaisier, who moved from a Grand Rapids factory to a farm in Grant, Michigan, Wonnink remained in the city to establish a small woodworking business.[14]

Agricultural workers from the clay-soil regions, who dominated emigration from 1880 to 1900, are accurately represented by Ulbe Eringa who, after leaving Friesland in 1892, advanced by 1899 from the status of farmhand in Hull, Iowa, to independent farmer in Running Water, South Dakota. He married an immigrant from Friesland and achieved sufficient means to acquire a family estate of 320 acres. Ulbe's life re-

---

[11] Lucas, *Netherlanders in America*, pp. 253–459, Swierenga, "Dutch Immigration Patterns," pp. 25–36.

[12] J. H. Dunnink Correspondence, 1848–1865, Immigrant Letter Collection, Calvin College Library Archives, Grand Rapids, Mich.

[13] David G. Vanderstel, "The Dutch of Grand Rapids, Michigan, 1848–1900" (Ph.D. diss., Kent State University, 1984), p. 50.

[14] Jan Wonnink Correspondence, 1871–1873; Aart Plaisier Correspondence, 1910–1916, Immigrant Letter Collection.

volved around his farm, family, and church. Culturally he was never adrift in utterly strange social or religious circumstances.[15]

In some instances migrations that began in the Netherlands can be traced across North America as family groups moved from one location to another. Teunis B. van den Hoek's family, for example, left Noordeloos near the Lek River in 1866 to join family and friends in South Holland, Illinois. After purchasing, improving, and then selling a farm, the Van den Hoeks moved to Orange City, Iowa, in 1882. Two years later, accompanied by family and friends, the Van den Hoeks moved to Harrison, South Dakota, where they helped organize a new Dutch American community. With that, the Van den Hoeks were no longer followers but colony builders. Yet, at each location they and their cohorts preserved social networks that stretched across the United States and back to their native villages in the province of Zuid Holland.[16]

Other immigrants from clay-soil regions resettled in cities. Marten Schoonbeek, for example, moved directly from Nieuwolda in Groningen to Grand Rapids in 1873, but one year later his death cast his wife and six children into utter poverty. Local charity helped keep the family from total disintegration, but their marginal existence also exposed them to the stern realities of urban poverty. Driven by economic necessity, the children married early and some scattered across the national landscape.[17]

After 1900 and on through the 1920s, the pattern of emigration shifted, and the number of emigrants leaving urban and industrializing provinces bounded upward. Departures from Noord and Zuid Holland surpassed those from the clay-soil regions between 1900 and 1904, and during the next five years emigration from the urban region nearly equaled the combined emigration from the other eight provinces. But 44 percent of the urbanites chose destinations within the Dutch colonial empire, and those who immigrated to the United States continued to be relatively more rural than urban. Nonetheless, the quickened pace of Netherlandic industrialization restructured economic options in the homeland and migration for employment in Netherlandic cities competed with the possibility of relocating in U.S. cities.[18]

Those who crossed the Atlantic after 1900 generally settled in Chicago, Paterson, New Jersey, and Grand Rapids, Michigan. Each of these locations contained well-defined contingents of Dutch Americans who had never settled on farms. Although these early urbanites may have preferred agriculture, they remained in the cities, where high wages, to-

[15] Ulbe Eringa Correspondence, 1892–1918, Immigrant Letter Collection.
[16] Teunis B. van den Hoek Correspondence, 1866–1895, Immigrant Letter Collection.
[17] Marten Schoonbeek Correspondence, 1873–1930, Immigrant Letter Collection.
[18] Hille de Vries, "The Labor Market," p. 94.

gether with the possibility of homeownership and the potential of capital
accumulation, offered an attractive alternative to farming. By 1900, because the best homestead lands were occupied, farming was becoming
less attractive. Like their agricultural compatriots, urban immigrants reported economic prospects to family members and friends in great detail.
Wages, rents, food costs, and property values in Chicago or Grand
Rapids were carefully described for prospective immigrants, who, when
they decided to leave, had already selected precise destinations based on
firm knowledge of employment options and specific social networks.

Klaas Niemeijer, who immigrated from Groningen to Chicago in
1904, is a case of this sort. The Niemeijers traveled directly to Chicago,
where they found temporary shelter with another Dutch family. Within
four days they had rented an apartment at seven dollars per month and
Niemeijer had begun work as a teamster, hauling trash from Chicago at
ten dollars per week. They stayed on and settled into the community.
Their children attended the Holland school, for which Niemeijer paid
$1.50 per month. At the Dutch church the family enjoyed sermons in
their native tongue and drank coffee with fellow parishioners after the
services. They traveled to other Dutch neighborhoods in the city to meet
acquaintances and friends from the Netherlands, and they read the
Dutch-language newspaper, *Onze Toekomst*, which informed them of
events in the Netherlands as well as in America.[19]

Urbanites, often business people or professionals, made up less than
15 percent of the Dutch immigration before 1880, and they preferred to
relocate in cities. Almost all Jews and some Catholics fall into this category. The poorest Jews left the Netherlands after 1815 and selected
New York, Philadelphia, and Boston as their favored destinations. In
each of those cities they established enclaves centered around Dutch tem-
ples and rabbis, and it is clear that these neighborhoods attracted chain
migrations from Jewish ghettos in Amsterdam and Rotterdam. Because
Dutch Jews were virtually exterminated during World War II, however,
the family correspondence they might have preserved has generally disappeared.[20]

Dutch urbanites were a small minority of the general immigration and

[19] Klaas Niemeijer Correspondence, 1904–1930, Immigrant Letter Collection.
[20] Robert P. Swierenga, "Jews First, Dutch Second, Americans Third: Dutch Jewish
Settlement and Life in the United States in the Nineteenth Century," in *The Dutch in
North America: Their Immigration and Cultural Continuity*, ed. Rob Kroes and Henk-Otto
Neuschafer (Amsterdam: Free University Press, 1991), pp. 391–403; Th. Deeleman, *Opdat
wij niet vergeten* (Kampen, Netherlands: J. H. Kok, 1949), pp. 70–218, estimates that 80
percent (190,000) of Dutch Jews were transported to Nazi death camps; Louis de Jong,
The Netherlands and Nazi Germany (Cambridge: Harvard University Press, 1990), pp. 3–
25.

their letters have survived in proportionately fewer numbers than those of their rural compatriots. Nevertheless, apart from the Jewish case an adequately illustrative number of urban letter collections has been preserved. Two of these, dating from before the Civil War, illustrate the experiences of businessmen prior to industrial modernization. Jan George Zahn, for example, immigrated in 1856 from Amsterdam with a stock of tobacco and opened a shop in Muscatine, Iowa. Whereas Zahn, who traveled first class, was relatively well-to-do, Cornelis Mannee immigrated to New York City in 1846 to escape poverty and growing indebtedness. He established a shoemaking business in the city and managed to accumulate enough assets to own a home and a business. But it is unlikely that he ever repaid the debts he owed to family members in his native city, Zierikzee. His letters (1847–1873) disclose Mannee's migrations within the city and to Long Island. His widow, Jacoba, spent her last years near relatives in Newark, New Jersey.[21]

Established urban enclaves such as Grand Rapids and Paterson also attracted immigrants from outside the ultra-Calvinist religious networks for whom the general use of the Dutch language and the prevalence of other ethnic customs were sufficient attraction. Often such newcomers conformed to the host community by joining its churches and other institutions, forging links to employment and securing poor relief in hard times. Anecdotal evidence suggests that the percentage of these cultural conversions was considerable. The Marten J. Schoonbeek family letters in this collection illustrate that pattern.[22]

Available sources disclose few examples of immigrants who lived totally apart from ethnic networks; those who did were either exceptional adventurers or socially detached by flight from military, marital, or economic obligations. For this behavior the letters of I. M. L. Bunnemeijer (1882), J. W. Nijenhuis (1908), H. Koopman (1892–1922), and Anna Kuijt (1909–1918) illustrate both the loneliness and the economically precarious circumstances such immigrants were likely to experience.[23]

Because they continue to thrive, such major urban enclaves as those in Grand Rapids and Chicago have, quite properly, received steady attention from historians and other scholars. Ethnic communities that did not flourish and survive, such as Franklin, Wisconsin, however, have attracted little attention. Yet, the pattern of Franklin's inception and early development varied little from those of the successful communities.

---

[21] Jan George Zahn Correspondence, 1856–1858; Cornelis Mannee Correspondence, 1847–1873, Immigrant Letter Collection.

[22] Schoonbeek Correspondence.

[23] Correspondence by "socially detached" immigrants, I. M. L. Bunnemeijer et al. (1882–1916), Immigrant Letter Collection.

Pieter Lankester from Middelburg, Zeeland, was a prominent founder of Franklin in 1849, together with about twenty-five of his compatriots, and the community persisted until about 1900. By then, however, the principal founders and most of the original settlers had moved on. Pieter Lankester moved to Milwaukee in 1863 and then to Grand Rapids in 1869. Although he began his career in Wisconsin as an agriculturist, his urban proclivities lured him and his family to the opportunities of trade and business. His migrations, however, remained within the spectrum of Dutch ethnic enclaves. His last residence, Grand Rapids, was and continues to be the leading Dutch community in the United States.[24]

Many, doubtless a majority, of the immigrants arriving throughout the century, clustered in specific destinations because of their reputed Dutch characteristics, well publicized in the Netherlands in newspapers, pamphlets, and the correspondence of the participants. It was clear from the beginning that the original Dutch settlements in Michigan, Iowa, Illinois, and Wisconsin were designed to encourage ethnic isolation as a strategy for preserving family values and religious precepts. A major theme among the founding populace was that their particular cultural attachments were under siege in Holland. Their goals, then, were not to become mainstream Americans and absorb new values but to preserve old values and to remain, in their sense of it, more Dutch than the Dutch. The events which engendered these objectives were mainly associated with church history in the Netherlands.

The "golden age" for traditional Calvinists in the Netherlands harked back to the Synod of Dordrecht (1618–1619), which established rules for government of the national church and attempted to settle an international theological debate concerning divine election and free will. But Dordrecht's dogmatisms were incompatible with the rationalist views that gained prominence in most of the universities and pulpits of the Netherlands in the eighteenth century. Theologians trained prospective pastors to view both the Bible and denominational creeds as historical products with textual flaws and debatable claims. At the same time, ordination rites required the clergy to assert the veracity of Dordrecht's formulations along with the Heidelberg Catechism and the Confession of Belgium. Because they no longer subscribed to those confessional statements, the clergy generally ignored them but chafed under the enforced hypocrisy of their ordination vows.

Only a small minority of the church members offered vigorous opposition to the prevailing spirit of theological liberalism. Many who did protest met in conventicles where they read traditional sermons and stud-

[24] Pieter Lankester Correspondence, 1850–1867, Immigrant Letter Collection.

ied the Heidelberg Catechism as an antidote to the spirit of the age. Their discontents were exacerbated after 1815, when the newly crowned king, Willem I (1815–1840), assembled a national synod to restructure the church. For this, the first national synod since 1618, the administration bypassed local congregations and provincial bodies to recruit delegates whose views reflected the modern temper. With little debate the synod altered the oath of ordination, established a continuing executive body to administer church life, and reestablished the favored status of the Reformed church which had been diminished during the French occupation (1795–1813). Among the liturgical novelties instituted was the use of some hymn singing to augment the heretofore exclusive use of rhymed psalms. The weekly explication of the Heidelberg Catechism was no longer required.

Negative reaction to the synod's decisions smoldered in many quarters. Those intellectuals sympathetic to Willem Bilderdijk's[25] criticism of the French Enlightenment inveighed against the government's failure to support orthodoxy and decried the growing secularization of Dutch culture. Poets and publicists, Isaac De Costa and G. Groen van Prinsterer among them, were outraged that the king failed to dismantle the revolutionary institutions erected during the Napoleonic era. For example, elementary education remained religiously neutral under the supervision of a national commission, and the Catholic provinces, Noord Brabant and Limburg, retained equal status with the original Protestant provinces of the Dutch republic. Disaffected intellectuals attempted to divert the forces of modernization from within the church, but other folk, mainly from the lower social orders in rural areas, simply refused to comply with the new rules, and their public disruptions led to ecclesiastical schism. Without clerical leadership the discontented country people could have been ignored, and in fact, their unofficial conventicles had provided alternative religious exercises for decades without determined opposition. But in 1834, when their movement gained clerical leadership, public censure followed.[26]

On the agricultural fringes of the Netherlands, in the small village of Ulrum in Groningen, a young pastor, Hendrik de Cock, became the hero of the movement. His conventicled parishioners, those not attending regular Sunday services, persuaded him to reexamine traditional Calvinism, and when his commitment to the old precepts became evident in his

[25] A rough equivalent in the Netherlands to Edmund Burke.
[26] H. Algra, *Het wonder van de 19e eeuw: Van vrije kerken en kleine luyden* (Franeker, Netherlands: T. Wever, 1966); J. Reitsma, *Geschiedenis van de hervorming en de Hervormde Kerk der Nederlanden* (Groningen, Netherlands: J. B. Wolters, 1899). Together, these volumes provide a general overview of Reformed church history in the Netherlands.

preaching, his following multiplied astonishingly. Adherents from nearby and from across provincial borders filled the village streets with their wagons and taxed the capacity of the small church. They carried reports of De Cock's sermons to their own villages, where they undermined the authority of local pastors with invidious comparisons. Complaints led to official discipline and De Cock was censured, but before he could be defrocked he and his Ulrum followers seceded and organized an independent congregation. The Act of Secession signed by 137 members on October 14, 1834, declared, arrogantly enough, that the separatists were the true remnant of orthodox Calvinism in the Netherlands.

The secession spread. A second pastor, Hendrik P. Scholte, who had encouraged the Ulrum seceders during a visit there in 1834, initiated a similar act among his own parishioners in Noord Brabant. Four of Scholte's classmates, who were also recent graduates of the University of Leiden, followed his example. Scholte, De Cock, and the four others were stationed in six of the eleven provinces, and after their aberrant behavior led to disciplinary actions, they all became prophets of the secession. Within two years they organized over 125 separatist congregations. The movement also gained clerical support in Zeeland, where conventicles were common. Most of the seceded pastors trained and ordained disciples to serve the large number of newly organized congregations. Church officials, and the king too, viewed the secession with consternation. The national constitution tolerated a variety of religious practices, but it did not envision a revolt within the ranks of the Netherlands Reformed church. To stanch the dissident flow, a Napoleonic statute that forbade popular assemblies of more than twenty persons without permission, was used to hinder the separatists until 1840. During that period both pastors and parishioners were regularly penalized and occasionally imprisoned. De Cock spent three months in a Groningen prison, and in Zeeland the Reverend Hubertus Budding was fined heavily. When he refused to pay, he was imprisoned for a lengthy term. These events, coupled with a pattern of social and economic ostracism, provide the foundation for those who highlight religious persecution as the primary motivation for emigration in the nineteenth century.[27]

The official oppression of the separatists, however, ended six years before they massed for emigration in the late 1840s and could not, then, have been the immediate cause of their expatriation. Still, the memory of these trying times and some lingering social disapproval surely contributed to the disproportionately high representation of seceders among

[27] Algra, *Wonder*, pp. 107–43; J. Wesseling, *De Afscheiding van 1834 in Groningerland* (Groningen, Netherlands: de Vuurbaak, 1972), 1:30–98.

the early emigrants. Although they were only 1.3 percent of the total populace, they contributed nearly 50 percent to the first wave of emigration (1845–1849). Nevertheless, the most immediate cause of that movement was economic. Crop failures from potato blight (1845–1847) and rye rust (1846) bore heavily on the poor, for whom potatoes were a staple. Those disasters, coupled with general economic stagnation and an especially severe winter in 1846–1847, doubled the poor relief rolls and sparked a growing interest in emigration.[28]

To consider that option two separatist pastors, Albertus C. van Raalte and Anthony Brummelkamp, met with a number of parishioners in 1846 and organized the Society of Christians for Netherlandic Immigration to America. The society established contact with Reformed church officials in New York and collected funds to purchase transportation and land. In September 1846 Van Raalte accompanied the first group of one hundred emigrants. Another group of nine hundred traveled under the direction of Hendrik Scholte in the spring of 1847. By then Van Raalte's party had already selected western Michigan for its colony. Scholte's group traveled farther west to found Pella, Iowa. In the following years before 1860 six other pastors accompanied immigrant groups to Michigan, Iowa, and Wisconsin. Apart from Father Theodorus van den Broek, who directed about 350 settlers to Wisconsin's Fox River valley in 1848, the clergymen were all seceders connected with the 1834 schism.[29]

From 1846 to 1850 at least 6,400 Dutch immigrants entered the United States, and according to the 1850 census 4,800, or 75 percent of that number, could be found in Michigan, Iowa, and Wisconsin.[30] Because only a small fraction of these immigrants predated the 1846 movement, the vast majority of the midwestern immigrant community either founded the mother colonies or quickly affiliated with them. The precise religious views of each immigrant cannot be known, but obviously most of them were willing to join the followers of the seceded clergymen who either led or greatly influenced the midwestern settlements.

Before the Civil War two major Dutch American communities with religious characteristics similar to those of Pella, Iowa, and Holland, Michigan, took shape in Illinois and New Jersey. In the Chicago area the immigrants gathered in three distinct areas. Garden farmers clustered in Roseland on the South Side, and general farming engaged a group in South Holland, Illinois. Near the city's center another group, drawn to

[28] P. R. D. Stokvis, *De Nederlandse trek naar Amerika* (Leiden, Netherlands: Universitaire Pers, 1977), pp. 35–76; Swierenga, "Religion and Immigration Behavior," pp. 102–39.
[29] Lucas, *Netherlanders in America*, pp. 58–80, 217–25.
[30] Ibid., appendix, tables I and II.

the area by employment opportunities, found work as tradesmen, laborers, and in cartage.

The reasons for the settlement of the New Jersey community are less clear. One historian asserts that Dutch immigrants remained there because they could not afford overland transportation, and when they found gainful employment among the Jersey Dutch populace, with whom they could communicate, they remained on the East Coast.[31] Although the Chicago and Paterson, New Jersey, communities originated without clerical founders, they quickly linked their religious fortunes with the Michigan colony.

Religious, social, and economic discontents coalesced to unify the antebellum founders of the Dutch American community. Throughout the Midwest they gathered around church-centered villages in which a single spire symbolized religious uniformity and identified the focal point of daily life. Thus, the seceders who had been marginalized in their native villages, became dominant in their transatlantic settlements. In such places as Zeeland, Michigan, or South Holland, Illinois, the seceded church assumed a cultural authority that was much like that of the national church it had spurned in 1834. Local pastors and consistories shaped the community's social life and even arbitrated economic disputes. But religious uniformity prevailed for less than a decade. By 1857 religious disputes had already fractured nearly every immigrant community. Yet, even when competing church spires arose, the ethnic enclave persisted.

In their native language the disputants solemnly battered each other for at least sixty years, and since their contests were largely unknown beyond the hearing of their belfry bells, their grapplings only intensified cultural isolation. The esoteric history and terminology of their debates shackled them together. In general the dispute was rooted in differing religious loyalties established in the Netherlands, but in the United States these distinctions took shape as contrasting strategies for cultural adaptation. A major part of the community, influenced especially by Albertus van Raalte, moved from ecclesiastical independence to affiliation with the New York–based Dutch Reformed Church (later Reformed Church in America) in 1850. The English-speaking RCA had already established a theological school and adopted such Anglo-American religious practices as revivals, Sunday school, and a vigorous home mission program on the frontier. Because the RCA's seventeenth-century links with its mother

[31] Gerald F. De Jong, "Dutch Immigration in New Jersey before World War I," *New Jersey History* 94 (1976): 69–88; Hans Krabbendam, "Serving the Dutch Community: A Comparison of the Patterns of Americanization in the Lives of Two Immigrant Pastors" (M.A. thesis, Kent State University, 1989), pp. 55–77.

church in Holland had become largely vestigial, the ecclesiastical distinctions born of the 1834 schism in the Netherlands were functionally moot in the RCA. Those immigrants who regarded loyalty to the religious revival of 1834 as their spiritual cornerstone could not identify with the RCA and considered Van Raalte's coalition with it a betrayal. By 1857 their discontent resulted in the organization of the Christian Reformed Church (CRC).[32]

Although born in America, the new denomination identified almost wholly with its seceded counterpart in the Netherlands. The CRC's pastors, the instructors in its theological school (dating from 1864), and those who taught the Dutch language to the upcoming generation were all selected from the Netherlandic community of seceders. The dialogue between the CRC and its Netherlandic sister church has persisted to the present, but between 1857 and 1920 the U.S. church group looked almost exclusively to Holland for status and direction. Issues that concerned the Netherlandic separatists automatically gained the attention and energies of the CRC, and a profound religious quickening that altered the Dutch church in the 1880s also significantly changed the CRC.[33]

The religious quickening is generally associated with the person and ideas of Abraham Kuyper (1837–1920), who spearheaded a second secession (the *Doleantie*) from the Netherlands Reformed Church. Unlike the 1834 *Afscheiding*, the *Doleantie* attracted more adherents from the middle classes, and although Kuyper dubbed them "the little people," they were more at home in the shops and schools of Holland than in the day laborer's cottage. Whereas the *Afscheiding* is appropriately symbolized by rural villages, the *Doleantie* belongs more to Amsterdam and the urban heartland. The original seceders sought pious isolation, but Kuyper's followers helped him establish a university, a political party, and two newspapers. He urged his people to turn toward social engagement.

---

[32] The thesis that insular theological disputes preserve and even intensify ethnic solidarity is explored by Lawrence Taylor, *Dutchmen on the Bay: The Ethnohistory of a Contractual Community* (Philadelphia: University of Pennsylvania Press, 1983). Rob Kroes, *The Persistence of Ethnicity: Dutch Calvinist Pioneers in Amsterdam, Montana* (Chicago: University of Illinois Press, 1992), pp. 99–121, notes explicitly that theological conflict in Churchill, Montana, welded the Dutch together. Linda Pegman Doezema, *Dutch Americans: A Guide to Information Sources* (Detroit: Gale Research, 1979), pp. 167–248, provides a bibliograpy for much of the literature on the theological conflicts between 1857 and 1930.

[33] Henry Beets, *De Chr. Geref. Kerk in N.A.* (Grand Rapids, Mich.: Grand Rapids Printing, 1918); John Kromminga, *The Christian Reformed Church: A Study in Orthodoxy* (Grand Rapids, Mich.: Baker Books, 1949); Herbert Brinks, "The Christian Reformed Church and the Reformed Church in America: A Study of Comparative Cultural Adaptation in America," Great Lakes History Conference Paper, 1979, in Calvin College Library Archives.

By 1892 he drew the 1834 seceders into a fusion with the *Doleantie*, and together they reorganized as the Reformed (Gereformeerde) churches of the Netherlands.

Kuyper's movement flourished during the last two decades of the century, when several factors coalesced to make it influential among a major segment of the Dutch American community. Kuyperians, known generally as neo-Calvinists, were most heavily concentrated in Noord and Zuid Holland, the western urban center of the Netherlands, but the next largest cluster occurred in the clay-soil province of Friesland, where thirty-one neo-Calvinist congregations were organized between 1886 and 1887. This development occurred during the middle of the agricultural depression of 1878–1895, which affected Friesland and other clay-soil regions most directly. Friesland was also the province that sent the greatest number of emigrants to America between 1880 and 1899. Of these, most of Kuyper's so-called "little people" joined their fortunes with the CRC in Paterson, New Jersey, and the Midwest. Wherever they settled, the neo-Calvinists urged the adoption of Kuyper's "world and life view."

This rather complex social-religious program was rooted in the belief that every aspect of life—familial, educational, economic, and political—should be organized upon Calvinist principles. The practical implications of this ideal required the erection of Calvinist institutions distinguishable from those based upon other religions or secular values. These objectives were largely realized in the Netherlands, where Kuyper's adherents established Calvinist institutions for political activity, education, labor relations, social interaction, and dissemination of news. Kuyper himself became prime minister of the Netherlands in 1892. The U.S. Kuyperians, however, were heavily dependent on literature and examples from the Old World, and that dependence alone retarded the adaptation of their ideas to North American culture. Consequently, neo-Calvinism in the United States generally reinforced ethnic isolation.[34]

To a large extent the ethnic community established before 1880 was able to co-opt the Kuyperian newcomers. In their joint promotion of educational programs they created many Christian day schools, a liberal arts college, and some revisions in theological perspective. By 1920, however, the two major Dutch Reformed churches (RCA and CRC) had become deeply influenced by American church life. With the death of Van Raalte in 1876, the main immigrant contingent of the RCA, which

[34] James H. Bratt, *Dutch Calvinism in Modern America: A History of a Conservative Subculture* (Grand Rapids, Mich.: Eerdmans, 1984), pp. 14–105; Henry Zwaanstra, *Reformed Thought and Experience in the New World* (Kampen, Netherlands: J. H. Kok, 1973), pp. 132–239.

arrived between 1846 and 1880, lost its major tie with the Netherlandic theological community. Beginning in the 1920s, the issues that gained attention in the CRC were increasingly drawn from American rather than Netherlandic culture. Moreover, following the nativist assaults on foreign languages during the "Great" war, both church groups ceased to function as Dutch-language shelters.[35] Yet, throughout the whole era represented in this book, the retention of Old World religious loyalties must be regarded as a significant indicator of cultural adaptation.

Like their Protestant counterparts, Dutch Catholics also began to emigrate in clusters during the late 1840s and early 1850s, when they organized a major colony with clerical guidance. In 1848 Wisconsin's Fox River valley near Green Bay attracted about 350 immigrants coming largely from the sand-soil regions of northeastern Noord Brabant, an area characterized by subsistence farming and cottage industry along with an overwhelming (90 percent) adherence to Catholicism. From this region Father Theodorus van den Broek attracted the immigrants who joined him in Wisconsin.[36]

In a widely distributed pamphlet, *Reize naar Noord Amerika*, and in other published accounts Van den Broek reported that both land and employment at high wages were available around Little Chute, Wisconsin, the site of his work in the Menominee Indian mission until 1843, when the mission was dissolved. Father van den Broek returned to the Netherlands in 1847, circulated among his Dominican brothers in Noord Brabant, and proposed immigration for the poor of the area. That he could speak from experience heightened his credibility, for unlike the Protestant colonial leaders, Van den Broek had lived in America for fifteen years.

After the Menominee Indians had been forced to migrate to Lake Poygan, thirty-six miles west of Little Chute, land developers and other entrepreneurs in the Green Bay area were able to proceed with plans to build a canal around the Fox River rapids. The river provided a commercial power source and the canal was intended to link the Great Lakes with the Mississippi River via Green Bay and the Fox River. Canal construction provided employment for those who could not immediately afford the fertile river valley land which was available from the canal company, land speculators, and the state of Wisconsin. Van den Broek declared that Little Chute offered both well-paid work and the long-

---

[35] Arie R. Brouwer, *Reformed Church Roots* (Grand Rapids, Mich.: Reformed Church Press, 1977); Bratt, *Dutch Calvinism in Modern America*, pp. 187–221.

[36] Yda Schreuder, *Dutch Catholic Immigrant Settlement in Wisconsin, 1850–1905* (New York: Garland, 1989), pp. 43–61, 127–35.

term security of landownership. Given the well-known anti-Catholic sentiments that prevailed in the United States during the 1840s, the priest urged prospective immigrants to band together for social well-being and the preservation of their beliefs.[37]

The Fox River colony flourished from the beginning and has survived as the major Dutch Catholic community in the United States, but most Dutch Catholics immigrated to other places. Because the largest Catholic occupational group, skilled workers, was able to function in urban areas, many Catholic immigrants settled in Cleveland, St. Louis, and other cities. In such places they affiliated with established Catholic churches, none of which were exclusively Dutch American. The Dutch assimilated most easily with German Catholics and were likely to intermarry with them. Johan Philipsen's correspondence (1855–1877) illustrates this pattern. Catholicism's universal liturgy facilitated interethnic accommodations of various sorts, including marriage. Consequently the acculturation of Dutch Catholics was not notably marked by endogamous marriages over successive generations, and ethnic cohesion diminished more rapidly among them than among Dutch Protestants.[38]

It is evident that most Dutch immigrants sorted themselves out by religious affinity rather than social status or wealth. There is, for example, no record of Jews and Christians joining hands for any common objective. Dutch Catholics and Protestants also avoided official connections even in the large ethnic enclaves of Grand Rapids and Chicago, where Dutch Catholics were numerous enough to form a parish with Dutch-speaking priests.[39] All of them—Jews, Catholics, and Protestants—remained mutually independent if not suspicious of each other.

These intraethnic rifts can be explained in part as consequences of the Netherlands' most foundational cultural mythology, which pits Spain's ultra-Catholic Philip II (1527–1598) against the Dutch republic's national hero, Willem of Orange (1533–1584), and his victorious Calvinist armies. Willem's assassination and the gruesome military cycles of invasion, siege, starvation, and plunder embittered the cultural memory of the Eighty Years' War (1568–1648), and as is usual, the victors interpreted the events. Protestants governed the Netherlands and wrote its

[37] Henri van Stekelenburg, *Landverhuizing als regionaal verschijnsel Van Noord-Brabant naar Noord-Amerika, 1820–1880* (Tilburg, Netherlands: Stichting Zuidelijk Historisch Contact, 1991), pp. 82–110; Schreuder, *Dutch Catholic Settlement in Wisconsin,* pp. 69–82.

[38] Swierenga, "Dutch Immigration Patterns," pp. 15–42; Lucas, *Netherlanders in America,* pp. 444–59; Schreuder, *Dutch Catholic Settlement in Wisconsin,* pp. 141–59; Philipsen Correspondence.

[39] Swierenga, *Belief and Behavior,* pp. 164–88.

history until well into the nineteenth century, when the constitutional monarchy became increasingly more democratic.[40]

Constitutional reforms and the organization of political parties in the 1850s have eventuated in broadly based Christian political coalitions in the Netherlands at present, but for nearly a century (1870–1970) Dutch political parties were separated and identified by their religious loyalties. The most prominent of them, Abraham Kuyper's Antirevolutionary Party, attracted conservative Calvinists, and the Catholics rallied behind Hermanus Schaepman (1844–1903). Kuyper's separatist ideology was grounded in what the Dutch called a cultural "pillar"—churches, a labor union, schools, newspapers, and other institutions—which served their adherents from cradle to grave. This phenomenon was duplicated by the Catholic community, and even the socialists followed this pattern.[41] Consequently, until about 1970 and during the whole era of Dutch American immigration, nearly all of Dutch society was "pillarized." It is hardly surprising, then, that most Dutch immigrants also gathered in confessional groups.

In the Netherlands pillarization has virtually disintegrated at present, and it is also fragmenting rapidly among American Dutch Calvinists. Dutch Jews and Catholics did not create elaborate ethnic pillars in America because they assimilated readily and quickly with other Jewish and Catholic national origin groups. For the Calvinists, including six or more varieties of Reformed churches, separatism resulted initially from the formation of ethnically exclusive villages and neighborhoods where the Dutch language and worship patterns were preserved. Thereafter, beginning in the 1880s, a host of institutions—schools, a psychiatric hospital, homes for the aged, adoption agencies, mutual insurance groups, and even a labor union—recreated a major segment of the Kuyperian "pillar."[42] But since the 1970s, all these institutions, including the major Reformed churches, have endorsed and pursued multicultural strategies for membership growth or institutional survival. None are ethnically exclusive any longer either in theory or practice.

Several examples presented in this book illustrate the weakening of

[40] A. J. Barnow, *The Making of Modern Holland* (New York: Norton, 1944), pp. 63–102, provides an English-language account of this era with a mildly Protestant bias. Much closer to the mythic account is John L. Motley, *The Rise of the Dutch Republic: A History*, 2 vols. (New York: A. L. Burt, 1864).

[41] F. Gunther Eyck, *The Benelux Countries: An Historical Survey* (New York: Van Nostrand, 1959), pp. 61–68. Two books by William Shetter, *The Pillars of Dutch Society: Six Centuries of Civilization in the Netherlands* (The Hague: Martinus Nijhof, 1971) and *The Netherlands in Perspective: The Organization of Society and Environment* (Leiden: Martinus Nijhof, 1987), demonstrate the radical changes in Dutch society over the past two decades.

[42] Zwaanstra, *Reformed Thought*, pp. 132–239.

Dutch Calvinist cohesion. In the Eringa, Schoonbeek, Plaisier, and Lankester families, in which three or more generations can be traced, at least 50 percent of their last-identified descendants have moved into mainstream American social patterns. They have married out of the ethnic subculture; many worship in conservative mainline evangelical churches; and they live apart from ethnic enclaves.

Nonetheless, during the period treated in this book, 1850–1930, Dutch ethnicity was evident everywhere. For this era of Dutch American cohesion, when both Catholic and Protestant enclaves formed, when high birth rates, endogamous marriages, and fresh immigrant accretions expanded the borders and filled the empty corners of ethnic places, the correspondence published here captures the essential characteristics of Dutch immigrant life.

I

Rural to Rural: Sand-Soil Emigrants

Introduction

The four immigrants whose letters are reproduced in this part left sand-soil regions in Holland where there was little prospect of acquiring additional land or attaining economic independence. They represent about 30 percent of the Dutch immigration. Two of them, Arnold Verstegen and Jacob Dunnink, had farmed small holdings in the Netherlands, but the other correspondents, Frederik Diemer, a field hand, and the weaver Harm Avink, acquired their first farms in Michigan. Although their rural backgrounds certainly familiarized all of them with farming, success in the frontier woodlands demanded the adoption of new methods for the management of soil, crops, and livestock. Although the newcomers adapted quite readily, they did not become wealthy farmers. Arnold Verstegen, in Little Chute, Wisconsin, was the most successful of the four, but he began his career with more assets than the others and he inherited his brother's grain mill in Little Chute. All of them, however, reached goals that had been beyond their expectations in the Netherlands. They became independent farmers and passed debt-free estates on to their children.

The letters in this part encompass the chronological scope of the book. They include reports of tillage with oxen and hand tools as well as mechanized implements powered by steam and gasoline. Perhaps, because these settlers were relatively poor and lacked managerial power in the Netherlands, they were not committed to Old World methods. Instead, they embraced novel technology with enthusiasm, often reveling in their labor-saving cultivators and steam-driven harvesters.

Despite their quick adoption of new technology, these families remained rigorously loyal to their inherited religions. Dunnink, Avink, and Diemer, like the vast majority of Dutch Protestants, were Reformed and Calvinist, but they also supported particular versions of that faith both before and after immigrating. In Beaverdam, Michigan, for example,

Dunnink walked past at least two Reformed churches in order to affiliate with an independent congregation that maintained precisely the viewpoints and practices that had dominated his native village. In Blendon, Michigan, Avink and his two brothers were active members of their local branch of the Reformed Church in America, which, like their native church in Gelderland, had strong links with the Reverend Albertus C. van Raalte. The Avinks joined other Gelderlanders to construct a church building and support a pastor at considerable sacrifice. The Diemer family in Vogel Center, Michigan, exhibited a similarly sacrificial loyalty by helping to build and maintain a Christian Reformed Church along with a private Christian school. In 1893, when Frederik Diemer immigrated, these were the essential institutional requirements of Abraham Kuyper's vision for Calvinism. Verstegen's religious commitment, too, is obvious from his choice of residence. Unlike a majority of Dutch Catholics, he settled among his Old World village cohorts and encouraged his former neighbors in northeast Noord Brabant to join him in Little Chute's Catholic parish.

For all their varied ecclesiastical affiliations, the four correspondents expressed their pieties with similar fervor and frequency. They wrote enthusiastically about church life, priests, and pastors. Both the Catholic, Arnold Verstegen, and his Protestant counterparts attributed their good fortune to God's favor and resigned themselves to God's will under all circumstances. Traditionally committed to Bible reading, the Calvinists quoted the Psalms and other biblical texts more readily than Verstegen. All the letters, however, give evidence that they were written in the Christian, not the post-Christian, era. Secularism was of little consequence among them.

It is clear throughout the whole of this correspondence that the immigrants lived out their lives with few sustained relationships outside their ethnic subcultures. They worked, worshiped, married, and socialized almost exclusively with other Dutch Americans. Political and economic activities required some outside contacts, but these were temporary and infrequent. Because they gained majoritarian control of whole townships and even counties, civic duties did not require regular encounters with the dominant Anglo-American establishment. It is evident too that these self-contained subcultures in Michigan and Wisconsin largely duplicated the religious and social characteristics of village culture in the Netherlands.

1 Jacob Harms Dunnink and Lucas Vredeveld

To the present day the *gemeente* of Staphorst in Overijssel has preserved traditional customs that date from the Middle Ages. Clothing styles, jewelry, and architectural ornamentation together with rituals for courtship and worship distinguish this community in much the same manner as the Amish are identified in North America. Both groups have elevated social characteristics from the premodern era as norms for the preservation of virtue and social solidarity.

Staphorst was and remains a pervasively agricultural community. Its general dimensions, about thirty-four thousand acres, have changed little over the centuries, nor have its marketable surpluses—cattle, hogs and milk products. The supply of arable land has increased twelve times since 1847, but the number of its farms has remained constant. Meanwhile, the population has tripled and that increase, no doubt, contributed to the emigration bulge near the middle of the last century.[1]

Like the land in New England colonial towns, Staphorst's land was originally parceled out to provide each farmer with a town lot and equal shares of the fertile and poor soils in the jurisdiction. As peat digging exposed new farmland, it was also divided equally among the descendants of the founding families. Because they did not practice primogeniture, landowners solved the inheritance riddle by constructing two or more farmsteads (houses with connected barns on the Saxon model) on their village lots. Each of these could shelter up to three generations. Although living quarters could be enlarged or multiplied, the family acreage could only be divided in relatively equal shares. In the long run that process was bound to narrow the extended family's economic viability.

Considering the residents' obvious attachment to traditional values, it is remarkable that anyone emigrated from Staphorst. But during the 1840s, when the first wave of immigrants arrived in West Michigan, exceptional circumstances prevailed. The severe agricultural crisis of 1845–1848 was an obvious factor, but because Staphorst depended more on dairy products than on potatoes, the area was less severely affected than its neighboring province, Drenthe. Nevertheless, high prices for

These letters were donated by J. de Wolde in 1976 and first translated by Jacob Reedijk. The original letters were transcribed in the Netherlands.

[1] J. de Wolde, *Staphorst zoals het werkelijk is* (Staphorst, Netherlands: Gemeentebestuur, 1978), p. 93; A. J. van der Aa, *Aardrijkskundig woordenboek der Nederlanden* (Gorinchem, Netherlands: Jacobus Noorduyn, 1847), 10:663–67.

The main street of Staphorst, about 1880. From *Oud Staphorst in woord en beeld*
(The Hague: Boekencentrum, 1976), p. 16, reproduced with the permission of
the publisher.

food staples and markets restricted by general poverty brought hard times
to Staphorst.[2]

The ecclesiastical schism of 1834 with its attendant persecution is often
cited as a cause for Dutch emigration in the 1840s, and indeed the *Afscheiding* came quickly and vigorously to Staphorst, centered in Rouveen,
a village cluster and church located within the *gemeente*. By 1836 there
were seceders throughout that region, and persecution followed them.
The most dramatic instance involved the Hendrik E. Dunnink family,
relatives of Jacob Dunnink, whose letters follow. On September 25, 1836,
Hendrik Dunnink opened his farmstead to more than five hundred seceders who gathered illegally to attend religious services led by the Reverend Albertus van Raalte, a leading pastor in the *Afscheiding*. Later, when

[2] J. de Wolde, *Ontginning en verkavelingen in de gemeente Staphorst* (Staphorst, Netherlands: Gemeentebestuur, 1980), pp. 5–17; W. J. van Dedem, *Staphorst 100 jaar geleden*
(Staphorst, Netherlands: Heinen van de Rollecate, 1984), p. 48.

the mayor of Staphorst and his agents brought the principal violators to court, Van Raalte was sentenced to an eight-day imprisonment and Hendrik Dunnink was fined fifty guilders (twenty dollars).

Jacob Dunnink was certainly well aware of these events and understood that areas outside very traditional Staphorst were hostile to his religious sympathies, but he was not a seceder. Jacob's pastor, the Reverend J. A. Hartman, was among a small number of state church clergymen who sympathized with the *Afscheiding* without joining the schism. Hartman's congregation in the village of Staphorst understood his position, and consequently only a few of his parishioners seceded.[3] Nevertheless, when Jacob Dunnink and his family left in 1848, they went with a group led by the Reverend Hubertus Budding, a notorious secessionist.

Budding, a wealthy man and an independent pietist, sponsored a group from Zeeland, where he had served a number of churches. His group attempted to colonize Ravenna, Michigan, but though Budding was a charismatic preacher, he was a poor colonizer, and the effort failed miserably. He quickly left Ravenna and migrated from one Dutch settlement to another until he returned to the Netherlands in 1852.

The Dunninks—Jacob, his wife, Geertje, and their children—traveled with Budding's group but not as part of it. They were headed for Drenthe, in West Michigan, where their village cohorts had already migrated. These émigrés had lauded the religious freedom and economic opportunities to be found in their settlement.[4] Both were no doubt attractive to Jacob. Dutch records cite economic improvement as the reason for his emigration, but he was not a victim of poverty. Indeed, the same records list him as "well-to-do."[5] Jacob's correspondence reveals that he received a share of his inheritance just before emigrating, and in 1855 he received an additional 680 guilders (272 dollars). In West Michigan these assets enabled him to acquire an ample farmstead, whereas in Staphorst he could have expected only a future of diminished landholding for his children. As the second son born to Harm and Geertje Dunnink (1811), Jacob had already experienced a division of the family estate.

Among the Staphorsters who had preceded him to West Michigan, Jan Hulst had become prominent in the settlement at Drenthe, a village in Overisel Township, Michigan, and reports of his experience had been

[3] J. Wesseling, *De Afscheiding van 1834 in Overijssel* (Groningen, Netherlands: De Vuurbaak, 1984), pp. 207–46.
[4] W. Kappe, "Staphorsters in Noord Amerika," *'t Olde Staphorst* 1 (1980): 11–19.
[5] Robert P. Swierenga, *Dutch Emigrants to the United States, South Africa, South America, and Southeast Asia, 1835–1880: An Alphabetical Listing by Household Heads and Independent Persons* (Wilmington, Del.: Scholarly Resources, 1983), p. 79.

Dunnink family farmstead in Staphorst. From *Oud Staphorst in woord en beeld* (The Hague: Boekencentrum, 1976), p. 16, reproduced with the permission of the publisher.

circulated in Staphorst. The terrain was open for agricultural development as Jacob had expected. He selected land about five miles north of Drenthe to gain the price advantage of uncleared woodlands. Despite their distant location (a two-hour walk) the Dunninks worshiped with the Staphorsters in Drenthe. By 1851 the congregation acquired the services of the Reverend Roelf Smit, a native of Staphorst/Rouveen and a seceder, who had pastored a contingent of immigrants from his home area.[6]

The larger settlement of Zeeland, Michigan, about four and a half miles southwest of Beaverdam, provided markets for Dunnink's produce—butter at least weekly and livestock on the first Wednesday of the month. These patterns were much like those of Staphorst which sold its butter in Meppel and its animals in Zwolle. The Dunninks prospered on their Beaverdam farm after they adjusted to new agricultural practices—clearing heavily wooded land, working clay soils not common in Staphorst, planting between stumps, and traveling as far as Grand Rapids (about twenty-five miles) to mill their grain. Apart from Sunday and an occasional trip to Grand Rapids, most of Dunnink's associations were with the Zeelanders who founded Zeeland, Michigan. Dunnink found

[6] Lucas, *Netherlanders in America*, pp. 138–41.

them entirely wholesome. "I think," he wrote in his letter home on January 24, 1850, "that the Lord has brought many of his people to this place, because the language of Canaan [larding ordinary discourse with biblical references] is heard widely here. . . . It seems that the Lord has preserved this place for the Dutch people. Almost no Americans settle here and also no people with alien beliefs."

For the Dunninks and their Dutch American neighbors cultural assimilation was barely perceptible, for they had exceedingly little contact with "Americans." But they did encounter various Netherlandic provincial cultures more intimately than they had in Holland and therefore experienced a kind of intraethnic acculturation. In Drenthe, for example, the residents were divided over the naming of their settlement, which was originally called Staatsland. When the Drenthe majority carried the day, the Staphorsters posted a marker on their end of the village which proclaimed, "Staphorst begins here." More serious divisions broke out over religious practices. Already in 1853 Pastor Smit had organized an independent congregation in order to celebrate Old World religious holidays and to curb the influences of A. C. van Raalte, the founder of Holland, Michigan.[7]

The Dunninks were too distant from Drenthe to participate actively in its controversies or its daily routines, and perhaps it was their separation from the culture of that village which weakened their attachment to the customs of Staphorst. Although the children married into the larger ethnic structure, they did not marry Staphorsters. One daughter, Grietje, married Lucas Vredeveld from the province of Drenthe and another daughter married a Zeelander; she worked in Grand Rapids as a housemaid and remained there after marriage. Dunnink's youngest son died during the 1860s. By 1870 his oldest son, Jan, had established his own farm in a neighboring township. Meanwhile Jacob and Geertje continued to manage the Beaverdam farm with help from recent immigrants, a maid and a day laborer. By then the value of the family estate had risen to $4,300 from an 1850 evaluation of $300.[8]

For the Dunninks, immigration destroyed the social patterns they had learned in Staphorst. Multiple farmhouses on a single estate were no longer necessary in Michigan, and the Dunnink children were not clustered within walking distance of their parents. They no longer worshiped together in a single congregation, and Jacob's grandchildren could not easily participate in his daily routines. In short, the American nuclear

---

[7] Jacob van Hinte, *Netherlanders in America*, pp. 360–61.
[8] Robert Swierenga, *Dutch Households in U.S. Population Censuses, 1850, 1860, 1870: An Alphabetical Listing by Family Heads* (Wilmington, Del.: Scholarly Resources, 1987), 1:300.

family pattern replaced the tightly woven intergenerational social structure of Staphorst. Even though they continued to speak provincial dialects and associated exclusively with other Dutch immigrants, the Dunninks lost crucial aspects of their inherited traditions.

Jacob Harms Dunnink to Harm Dunnink Family
Beaverdam, Michigan, to Rouveen, Overijssel
September 1848

Dearly beloved Father, Mother, and family,
    We left Rotterdam on August 7 and almost all of us were seasick. . . . I was seasick nearly the whole time and spent most of the trip in bed. But now I am healthy again. The ship was one hundred and sixty feet long and thirty feet wide. We had food regularly and water every morning. Water was limited but sufficient. Inside the ship it was bed upon bed— two on top of each other and trunks next to the beds.
    The captain was very good and the ship's personnel were not unpleasant. We walked on deck every day, but we had continuous storms although they were not dangerous. On September 22 we ran into a rock but it caused no damage. It was a great relief when the pilot came aboard on September 24 [in New York Harbor to dock the ship].
    Reverend [Hubertus] Budding had no seasickness and he held prayer services every morning and evening—he read a selection from the Bible and we sang psalms. On Wednesdays he taught the children catechism and distributed books for that purpose. He was leading a group of twenty-seven persons and he paid for their passage. When the pilot came aboard the people were so excited that Rev. Budding took us below deck where we held a thanksgiving prayer service for the care which the Lord had provided to us. There were many good people in this group.
    [The trip from New York to Holland, Michigan,] cost eight dollars and fifty cents for each person over twelve years of age and we were allowed one hundred pounds of goods. We expect to reach Van Raalte's colony in ten days.
    Yes, Father and Mother, and all my friends, we are now separated. Only those who experience it can know what that means. My heart was heavy when I left my family and fatherland. My brother could not look me in the eyes, but my sister did. But I could not express my feelings. . . . And when we parted in Zwolle, Father, we could not look in each other's eyes. But be of good cheer, I hope that the Lord will be with us in the land to which we have come and that His will brings us to our destination.

* * *

Now I end with my pen but not with my heart,

Jacob Harms Dunnink

January 24, 1850

Dearly beloved Father, Mother, and other relatives,

We have not had a cold winter and my cows and calves have not been inside yet. I do not have to give them food and drink. I have carried the hay into a stack and built a fence around it so that the cows can reach through the fence opening. . . . We do not need to fertilize the soil around here.[1]

Many people from the province of Zeeland arrived here this year. Most are from the laboring class and others paid for their transportation. But there is not enough work for all of them in the colony so they have to earn their living by working among the Americans. It is good there, but because of the language they have difficulties in understanding each other and in worshiping.

Potatoes are planted on newly cleared land in this way. Two or three are placed together and then the soil is heaped up over them so that they look like mole hills. This is done among the tree stumps. The trees are cut off about three feet above the ground. Much corn is grown here. The stalks are about six to eight feet long and are good as cattle feed. The ears are even better. We use them to fatten the swine and to feed the oxen. The trees are cut off and then placed in fencerows. Between these are the clearings where spring planting is done. Farmers here use fat, ashes, and bones to make their own soap. Many people live in log houses. The space between the logs is filled with clay. They are comfortable and warm but not very attractive. There are no good roads here, but much work is being done on them. Farmers do that work themselves. Each contributes according to the amount of land he has, the amount of land already cleared, and the number of his oxen. Each person also has a specific day to do the work.

I hear that Hendrik Winkel has returned to Holland. That is not surprising. He lost his wife and children. Yes, friends, it is a difficult road here—no one in Holland has ever seen such huge trees. And it costs lots of money here. We use dollars here. Four dollars equal ten guilders. The people we meet most here are the Zeelanders because we sell our butter in their town.

We also gather for worship on Sundays and after the service the children recite their catechism. I think that the Lord has brought many of

A log house in northern Michigan, about 1910. Courtesy of Calvin College Library Archives, photo collection.

his children to this place, because the language of Canaan is heard widely here. The Bible is very prominent here. Of course there are other sorts here too, but they are in submission. It seems that the Lord has preserved this place for the Dutch people. Almost no Americans settle here and also no people with alien beliefs.

I hope that you receive this letter in good health, dear parents. . . . I also want to thank you, dear Father and Mother, for giving me my share of the inheritance. But we remember too that it is God who works in all and through all. We will probably not meet again on this side of the grave. But if we have the Lord as our portion all will be well. For we are all traveling to that great eternity.

* * *

You must write us about your situation. I believe that letters sent along with emigrants are more sure to arrive than mail sent the other way.

[Closing]

1. Dutch farmers collected manure in the barn to spread as fertilizer. Cows left to roam could not provide manure for fertilizer.

December 15, 1851

Dearly beloved Father, Mother, and other relatives,

Once again we want to tell you that we are well. We have received your letter through our minister, Rev. Roelf Smit. Until recently we have all been healthy but in September two of my children, Grietje and Jentje, had a fever for about three weeks. Our little son Harm has begun to walk at fourteen months but Albert remains very weak and thin. Otherwise he is in good health.

We have had poor crops this year. In the spring tremendous rains—day after day. Yes, it kept coming until the seed rotted in the ground. We also have a kind of pest here which you might call a squirrel [probably a chipmunk]. They are small, about like your squirrel. They have dug up a lot of seed so that we had to replant two or three times. When ·the wheat was ripe these same pests almost ruined it.

Our land has yielded very little this year, but we are not alone in this. The whole colony has had it.

My land lies rather high—about twelve feet above the normal water level. Flooding does us no harm. The hay land, however, has been under water much of the year but I was still able to harvest hay in the fall.

We now have fourteen cattle. Two are oxen which will be three years old in the spring. This year they will have to be broken in for the yoke. Sometimes this is difficult. We have tried it a number of times and usually we have to use a whip or a rod.

Our daughter, Grietje, hired out again this July. She earns one dollar each week. American women and girls do not work in the fields. The Dutch girls don't want to do it either and it really is not girls' work. My daughter Geertje would also like to start hiring out, but we really cannot spare her yet. There is still much work at home with the little ones. But fifty dollars per year is also a considerable sum.

* * *

I bought a new plow for six dollars and a new clock for four dollars. I bought my land from the government, which is the cheapest. The price of government land is ten shillings per acre [$1.25] everywhere. Where the others live [in Drenthe] land has been sold three and four times already. The land there is not any better, but they have the church and school nearby. We live about three hours from there by the road, but if we cut through one woods it is five miles. A mile is twenty minutes' walking—so less than two hours. I have talked with Rev. Smit and he was in good health. We shook hands and he said he was happy to see me. We talked together until midnight.

Now, my dear Father and Mother, it's as if we have buried each other before dying, because we will not see each other's faces again on this side of the grave. We are bound by these natural ties so we can't do without one another. But the time is coming when all natural love will cease and then we will appear before God. Oh, we hope then that He will be to us a reconciled Father in Christ so that our death will not overtake us as a death of horror.

[Closing]

October 9, 1853

Dearly beloved Father and brother,

When our letter which you received on September 2, 1852, was just on its way we learned that Mother was dead from the wife of Berend Boesenkool, who visited us. . . . I can clearly call to mind the scene on that afternoon when we heard the news of her death. That day we had a day laborer helping us with the hay and he is also an elder in the church. After we had eaten, read the Bible, and sung a psalm, that man prayed specifically for each of us. Then he proceeded to talk to each of the children who were home. It was a very refreshing hour for me and it reminds me of the saying, "blood creeps where it cannot go."[1]

* * *

The crops have been rather good this year. The hay and wheat good and the oats acceptable. The corn was also good. The potatoes on the high land were better than on the low land.

* * *

I have already plowed much of my land because without plowing nothing grows but weeds and more weeds. It takes about two years for the old grass and leaves to decay. In the third year the ground can be broken up, but you still can't plow close to the tree stumps. But that gets better every year. On the land which I cleared first I have already plowed out many small stumps. It is lots of work—not only the stumps but removing the roots. Then the cutting, moving, and burning. During two previous years we had very poor crops. One year was too wet and the next year too dry. We were not able to plow the ground properly. Until now we have always been able to pay our way—but of course we have our own potatoes, pork, beans, butter and milk. I have been able to earn enough cash making wooden shingles[2] to cover living expenses.

I don't know exactly how much land I have cleared—thirty acres I think. I have cleaned up about twelve acres. I have sown about eight bushels of wheat, and it is beginning to grow. Now that I am plowing my land I feel better about the soil. At times I thought it contained too much heavy clay, but I have now noticed some sand and black soil. Sand and black soil can stand the drought better than clay.

* * *

While I was writing this we have had an experience which made it impossible to continue writing. I have lost my little son, Albert. His sickness has interrupted my writing for a few days. We thought that he had a cold when he did not feel well for about four days. On his last day he could not eat, and the following night his chest was so congested that I went to the doctor at twelve o'clock to get some medicine. He used it but little, and at about nine o'clock on October 11 he passed away. He was thin and weak and unable to walk by himself or to talk. We have gone through much with him. His lungs were bad and he remained small so that he would never have become a robust lad. He lived just past his third year. This is the first child that I have had to give up. If I had not experienced it I would not have believed that one could become so attached. My wife is overcome by grief by the death of her child—a child that nursed at her breast for over three years. I hope that the Lord will support us in the way He has ordained in this matter.

Our son Harm [Albert's twin] continues to be healthy. He is developing so well that one cannot tell that he is one of the twins. Now I will close for this time with the wish that you may receive this letter in good health.

[Closing]

1. An expression indicating the powerful ties of blood relationships even at great distances.
2. Many farmers cut stumps into wooden shingles, which were marketed in cities such as Chicago.

November 26, 1855

Dearly beloved Father, brother, and family,

We have had a moderately good crop this year. We have had much rain and so our hay crop did not do well. But the potatoes and oats were good while the rye and wheat were only acceptable. But all the products bring good prices so that a farmer here has a decent living. We now have twelve cows and one horse. This summer we sold three cows for seventy-two dollars and a pig for fifteen dollars. We have bred the horse. My wagon is almost finished. It is supposed to cost fifty dollars. When we are all outfitted for summer and winter with both a wagon and sleigh the whole of it will cost one hundred and sixty-five dollars.

My daughter Geertje was married in March 1855. Her husband was born in Zeeland and they live in Grand Rapids where they have built a new house. He works for a bricklayer and earns ten shillings [$1.25] per day. A dollar is eight shillings. If they remain healthy they will have a good living. There is a large Dutch church in Grand Rapids with a minister from Zeeland [the Reverend Hendrik Klijn].

I have received the sum of six hundred and eighty guilders without difficulty by way of the Brouwers. It came on the first of November which I remember because that is the market day for cows, pigs, and horses in the town of Zeeland. . . . A brother-in-law of Jan Brouwer recently came to Zeeland from the Netherlands and brought the money with them. I have received it with joy and I gave them a tip of ten guilders. They were well satisfied with that.

* * *

Many people have arrived at the settlement [the Holland and Zeeland, Michigan, colonies] this summer. Some came from Europe, but many also came from New York, Albany, and Buffalo. These are people who could not travel farther at first because of their poverty. Land around here is getting to be rather expensive. It is already being sold for the second and third time. An acre now costs between six and ten dollars—and that is forest land solidly covered with trees.

We have not yet had winter this year and without snow we can do our daily chores nicely. The cows go into the woods to feed daily. Deer hunters are walking around in the woods a great deal too. During the fall the roads are very muddy so that we sometimes long for frost and snow. Then we can move our wagons with the sleigh because it is almost impossible to do that with the wagons.

We have bought a new stove for twenty dollars. It is rather big and our old one was worn out. Yes, in six or seven years a stove can be worn out.

Many houses are being built along the road between us and Zeeland. . . . During the summer six of them were already completed and many other people are beginning to clear the trees and are planning to come here to live.

There is a large congregation in Zeeland which I believe has about four hundred members. The building is already becoming too small. On Sundays thirty or forty people can't even get a seat.

Now, brother, it is my solemn duty to thank you for your faithful care and charity [probably a reference to the money sent from the family estate] to us. . . . May the Lord bless and protect you and yours. Yes, brother, it is a great privilege that we are able to speak to each other by means of paper and pen. So many of our fellow men must forgo this blessing.

* * *

Brother, . . . take care of Father as well as you can because you are nearest to him. Look after his interests. Brother, don't imagine that I do not trust you. Far from it. I say this because I feel a responsibility.

And now, Father, I hope you will have all that you need for time and eternity. Because eternity is at hand and all of us must move from here to the other side of the grave. May it please the Lord that you receive this letter in good health.

[Closing]

May 20, 1856

Dearly beloved Father, brother, and family,

* * *

My daughter Geertje has been ill much of this past winter. We and others feared for her life and the doctor did not want to give her heavy medication because she was pregnant. The minister even prayed for her in the church service. Our daughter Jentje spent eighteen weeks to help her and now she is in good health again. She has gained a young son.

* * *

I spoke to Jentje Visscher in Grand Rapids this week and she was in a happy frame of mind. She told me that her brother Jan would be coming over here with a large group. Yes, seventy people. . . . We have received your letter of January 1856. . . . Brother, I cannot tell you what is best for you—staying there or coming here. If it only concerned yourself I would say, stay. But if you are concerned about your descendants I would say, come. North America is a large and good country, but hard work is necessary.

* * *

For us everything was right for moving, but that is not yet the case for you. How can you do it? You must not and cannot leave Father behind. But I can't discourage Hendrik, who faces a possible military draft. Is he old enough to make such a trip by himself? If he comes here I will help him as much as I can. If Hendrik comes he should not bring much clothing, but lots of underwear. Also he should have a small chest which he can easily keep with him.

It is now spring again and the crops are beginning to grow. We keep getting rain, which is not to our liking for planting and burning wood. We have fourteen cows and three hogs. One we fatten for ourselves and another will have piglets. I sold my horse for one hundred dollars. It was a good horse but we had so little work for it that it was not worth keeping. I think we are going to replace it with an old horse. The cart just stands there idle and it is too light for the oxen. We have finished planting about seventeen bushels of oats, and we have seeded grass in the same field so that after the oats we will have hay to mow. Last year the oats were so good that we harvested over one hundred bushels. Horses and cows are expensive here. A decent cow is forty dollars and a team of six- or seven-year-old pulling oxen costs about one hundred and forty dollars.

[Closing]

December 27, 1857

Dearly beloved Father and relatives,

We had a decently good crop this year but in the fall we had a drought with such hot weather that we had to leave the field for a time to cool off in the shade. The potatoes also remained rather small. They grew but little in the fall.

My daughter Grietje is also married and in the town of Rev. Smit [Drenthe]. I think she has done well. He is an immigrant from [the province of] Zeeland and has a decent farm. He has adopted Grietje's child as his own. And Grietje also received one hundred dollars from the person who deceived her.[1] Rev. Smit has married them and he has also baptized the child. Grietje attends catechism instruction and plans to make profession of her faith.

My oldest daughter is still living in Grand Rapids. Her husband has continued in the same work for three years. She sees many other women there. I, and others too, think that the Lord is at work in her life with His spirit and grace. Her husband has made profession of his faith and has celebrated the Lord's Supper.[2]

Jentje, Jan, and Harm are here with us at home. I bought a three-year-old mare which cost eighty dollars, or two hundred guilders. . . . I also bought a saddle for seven dollars and a pulling harness for twelve dollars and fifty cents. Now I am having a small sleigh built for about twenty dollars. We have had an early snow and sledding has already started. When the roads are good there is a lot of horse-drawn sled traffic to have products hauled back and forth.

* * *

The Hollanders are doing quite well here. All farm products bring high prices because of the war in Europe [the Crimean War, 1853–

1856]. Every week the newspaper has war news and I also read that
Rouveen and Staphorst have suffered so much from mice that you had
to harvest green grain—a thing that only the very old had ever seen. I
also read this week that the seceded church of Staphorst/Rouveen has
called Rev. Eising from Emmelenkamp in the county of Bentheim [Ger-
many].

* * *

When you receive this letter write back quickly. Tell us how Father
is doing and what your situation is. Also tell us about the money because it has not arrived yet. I am advised that the best procedure is to
deposit the money [in Holland] so you are issued a draft [receipt].
Then in case the ship meets with an accident the draft could be presented and a second one could be sent out of Holland. I don't understand why the local government should have anything to say about
that. Many of these drafts arrive from Holland to America. I think that
is the best way to do it. Deposit the money and enclose a draft in a
letter to me. Do it as quickly as possible. For the rest we have to trust
the Lord's providence.

Land here is at a very low price and now the state [Michigan] has set
the price at fifty cents per acre. Many who still have some money went
to buy state land. But those who were not ready to go and live on the
land could not get any. They have to swear an oath that they intend to
go and live on it. If they have made no start in clearing the land after
three months they are put in prison and the land is taken back. It was
the state's purpose to help poorer people gain their own land.

We are enjoying life. We have a good living and enjoy many pleasant
associations with other Hollanders. But on Sundays, as you know, we are
far from the church [in Drenthe]. But we are intending to use our horse
to ride to church. In winter by sleigh and in summer by carriage. That
is our plan if the Lord wills and we live.

Many Hollanders continued to come to our settlement this summer.
Some from Europe but also many from New York, Albany, Buffalo,
Rochester, Detroit, and other places. Places where the Hollanders earlier remained because they were out of money. After earning some
money they still want to live among the Dutch. They also want to attend Dutch worship services. They don't yet understand English very
well.

When they first get here many find it difficult, but, after they have
been here for a couple of years and they are able to live from their own
crops, they feel differently. Some, like us, were happy to leave the fa-

therland. Our prospects there were dark and our bread would probably have been scarce.

[Closing]

1. Following common-law customs prevalent in Staphorst to the present, prenuptial intercourse was permitted to ascertain fertility. After pregnancy marriage was expected. In this case, as in Staphorst, the party breaking the marriage promise was penalized.

2. The pattern of religious development included a public profession of faith in the worship service, followed by full participation in the church's sacramental observances.

June 2, 1858

Dearly beloved Father, brother, sister-in-law, and children,

In your January 1858 letter we read that my sister passed away and that brother-in-law Jan Veyer is left with eight children. Yes, God's Word teaches us that we are here today and gone tomorrow. . . . Oh that death may not be a king of horror for us. . . . Oh, brother, may we spend our days wisely—the days which God may still allow to us in this world and in the pursuits of daily life. May He have pity on our undying souls, which are created for an undying eternity. Before long we too will have to put aside our traveler's staff.

* * *

As far as we know our daughter Geertje is in good health but we have not seen each other for three weeks. We live six hours apart. They are quite well off. He has a steady job. It is nice for us too that when we go [to Grand Rapids] to get our wheat milled they can put up our horse overnight and they have a bed for us to sleep in. On March 25, 1858, their family was enlarged by the birth of a son. They now have two children. The oldest is Jans and the second is Jacob. They spent about four days at our home this winter and my opinion is that she has got herself a good husband. I believe that both of them want to live for the Lord.

We have built a small schoolhouse in our neighborhood, which our Jentje and Harm attend. English is being taught there.

Right now it is very wet so that for weeks now we have not been able to do any work in the fields. We will probably have to reseed and replant the lowland crops. The wheat, however, is in rather good shape. Last year the crops were decent. These are poor days for cash income because the farm produce brings low prices. Trade is almost at a standstill. There is little employment for the laboring class and wages are being lowered.[1]

Last winter we had a huge amount of hay left over, which we traded for thirty-four dollars' worth of wood planks. Trading and bartering are common practice in this country. We came through the winter with ten cows, fourteen pigs, and the horse.

Hendrik Knol lives two miles away from here. He works at the sawmill. He requested that I send a note to say that he is in good health and that he has hired out his son to Berend Boesenkool. Please pass this along to Klaas Grit. As far as I know all the Staphorst/Rouveen people on this side of the ocean are still in reasonably good health.

[Closing]

1. It was the economic depression of 1857–1858, caused by overspeculation in railroads and land development.

Jacob Harms Dunnink to Friends
Beaverdam, Michigan, to Rouveen, Overijssel
January 18, 1859

Dear Friends,

We are in good health and hope the same for you. We had very poor crops this past summer. In the spring the rain continued until mid-June. The seed rotted in the ground and then we planted again. After that the Lord caused the torrential rains to stop, but then He gave us a terrible drought. The ground became unnatural. The clay soil was worse than the sand soil on our farm. It also pleased the Lord to strike the wheat crop with honeydew. This is caused by little yellow worms which sit in the ear. They eat the kernels—sometimes ten in one ear. Honeydew is more often found in flax plants here. Yes, our crops were so poor that I have not heard of any that were worse. We can eat hardly any of the wheat. And the potatoes were so few that we have to keep them for planting [that is, as seed potatoes for the next year]. Yes, friends, things look rather bad.

The year before was pretty good so that we have no needs. We fattened six pigs for sale and three for our own use last summer. At the present we have twelve cows and an old horse which I believe is carrying a colt. We also bought two new milk cows this fall. At first they gave a lot of milk but now it is tapering off because we have no extra food to give them unless we buy it. And butter doesn't bring much income at fifteen to sixteen cents per pound. We are having an exceptionally mild winter with little frost or snow so the sleigh trails are not yet in good shape.

The past summer we also had an epidemic of contagious disease [probably dysentery]. Mostly it affected the children—blood run and gall fever. Many people died from it. In some families as many as five. So far we and our neighbors have been spared. The Lord has also fulfilled your wish that we should receive your letter in good health.

And shouldn't we acknowledge that it is He who granted this wish? If only we would desire and ask more of the Lord. Then we would surely receive more from Him. . . . We did not deserve to receive your letter in good health and you were not worthy of having the Lord fulfill your wish. But this again demonstrates how the Lord deals with the undeserving.

Oh that our eyes were more fixed on Him who gives us life, breath, and all things. May we live only for the honor of His name, so that our lives may end with the salvation of our immortal souls.

*   *   *

Now I will end this letter because Hendrik Knol and I are going to mail our letters together in one envelope.

[Closing]

Lucas Vredeveld to Harm Dunnink
Overisel Township, Michigan, to Rouveen, Overijssel
May 2, 1865

Esteemed Uncle, Aunt, and cousins,

We thought you would like to hear from us. You don't know me but we have become friends through marriage because I married Grietje Dunnink. Thanks to the Lord's blessing we are in good health and we have six healthy children. We make a good living. We have five horses—two work horses and three young ones. We have twelve cows, eight of which are milk cows. We have twenty-five mature sheep and sixteen young sheep. And also five pigs. The winter crops [probably rye or winter wheat] are looking rather good. We have planted some, but not all of the summer crops. Daily wages are high—between one and two dollars per day. Those who hire out by the year get between one hundred and fifty and two hundred dollars [with room and board]. People who are willing and able to work have a good living here. But we don't use as many people on the farm as you do because much of our farm work is done with machines. Last summer we bought a machine that does the mowing. It is pulled by two horses.

The Civil War seems to be settled now. Many have been plunged into deep mourning because of this war. There are thousands, indeed tens of thousands, who have lost their lives on the battlefields. So we have reason to thank the Almighty because He has settled this matter and has not totally destroyed and exterminated us. Rather, He has been willing to look upon us in love.

I was drafted by the lottery twice, but by joining hands and combining the money of all the people, we have always bought men to take our place.[1] That did cost a lot of money, but because prices were high, income was also high. Our brother Harm Dunnink died on February 4. Two other immigrants from Staphorst and Rouveen also fought on the side of the North. They are Jan Dunnink and Jacob Kaiers.

On another matter, the nation has been cast into mourning again because the president of the country was murdered horribly by a bullet in his head. As far as we know the murderer has not yet been caught.

Regarding the church, there is a lot of division here. We attend the church of Rev. R. Smit and attendance is fairly good.

We have a good school too, which is located on our land. The children are taught English in winter and Dutch in the summer.

Well, friends we hope that the Lord grants that you may receive this letter in good health. May the Lord continue to preserve us, above all we pray that we may spend our days in His peace while living here as pilgrims and strangers. This world is but dust and our life passes like a flower of the field.

[Closing]

1. The township of Overisel collected money to establish a bounty fund which was used to find substitutes for married men such as Vredeveld. See Christine Jacobs, "Avoiding the War," *Origins* 6, no. 1 (1988): 23–26.

2   *Arnold Verstegen*

Arnold Verstegen's correspondence, which effectively illustrates the colonization of Wisconsin's Fox River valley by Dutch Catholics, was published in 1955 by Henry Lucas.[1] Henri van Stekelenburg reviewed the essential contents of Verstegen's correspondence in his doctoral thesis. Reporting that several of the original letters have been lost, Van

These letters were donated by Henri van Stekelenburg, 1993.

[1] Henry Lucas, ed., *Dutch Immigrant Memoirs and Related Writings*, 2 vols. (Assen, The Netherlands: Van Gorcum, 1955), has been out of print for decades and is now a very scarce item on the used book market.

Stekelenburg also noted that a comparison of the surviving originals with the published versions reveals "very free" translations "with many expatiations." Further distortions have arisen from a widely circulated Dutch-language version retranslated from the Lucas publication. Van Stekelenburg concluded that the Verstegen letters have been mishandled and linguistically polluted.[2] They are, however, the only letters available from the period of Little Chute, Wisconsin's settlement and early development. Thus, despite their deficiencies, I reprint four of the Verstegen letters from Lucas's *Memoirs*, along with the nine Henri van Stekelenburg photocopied in 1990. Apparently the originals of these nine letters have also been lost.[3]

In 1850 the Verstegen family from the village of Zeeland in northeastern Noord Brabant joined about sixty other households that abandoned the sandy heath lands of that area between 1848 and 1870 to seek economic opportunities in the Fox River valley. The first immigrants were mainly small farmers who, even before immigrating, had migrated within Noord Brabant to subsist on heath or peat lands. By the 1860s they were joined in Little Chute by an economically displaced populace of farmhands, linen weavers, and an assortment of other small craftsmen for whom an already vulnerable subsistence was further threatened by commercial agriculture and industrial modernization that increasingly displaced cottage industries.[4]

In Zeeland and its neighboring villages (Uden, Boekel, and Volkel) Father Theodorus van den Broek's 1847 invitation to organize the Little Chute colony attracted a positive response, and by 1850, when Arnold Verstegen immigrated, his brother Johannes had already established a general store in Little Chute. Unlike most of his immigrant cohorts, Arnold was financially well off, and he was able to purchase land immediately. His progress from farmer to landholder and mill owner is evident in his letters, and they also disclose the general growth and development of the Fox River area from 1850 to 1880.

The correspondence corroborates Yda Schreuder's analysis, which describes the evolution of the Fox River settlement (including Little Chute, Holland Town, De Pere, and Green Bay) from an agricultural to a commercial and industrial economy. This development increased land values and agricultural prosperity and also provided employment in flour mills,

---

[2] Van Stekelenburg, *Landverhuizing als regionaal verschijnsel*, pp. 112, 210–16.

[3] Nine of a reputed twenty originals have survived as seven complete letters and two fragments. Van Stekelenburg discovered an additional letter from the 1880s, which is also included here. My relatively literal translation of that letter, when it is compared with those in Lucas, 2:15–74, suggests that they were indeed "freely" translated.

[4] Yda Schreuder, *Dutch Catholic Settlement in Wisconsin*, pp. 44–64.

Arnold Verstegen portrait, no date.
Courtesy of Calvin College Archives,
photo collection.

paper mills, small shops, and shipping. Consequently, by 1870 Fox River's Dutch Catholics were beginning to become townsfolk and urbanites rather than farmers.[5]

Yda Schreuder's study also demonstrates that as Dutch Catholics dispersed to regional towns and cities such as Green Bay—a process the Catholic hierarchy encouraged—they joined ethnically mixed parishes. In these circumstances intermarriage with Catholics of all national origins became commonplace, though the Dutch most frequently intermarried with German Catholics. The Catholic Dutch assimilated, then, along religious rather than ethnic lines and their experience conformed to Will Herberg's theory of the triple melting pot.[6]

The Verstegen letters terminate long before these developments became obvious, but they clearly demonstrate that, unlike Michigan's Protestant settlers, the Fox River populace encountered several ethnic varieties of Catholicism in addition to the dominant Anglo-American commercial establishment. In contrast to Jacob H. Dunnink's characterization of Zeeland, Michigan, there was no talk of the Fox River valley being exclusively preserved for the Dutch, and the Catholics of Little Chute were less ethnically exclusive than their Protestant counterparts.

[5] Ibid., pp. 103–23.
[6] Ibid., pp. 127–59; Will Herberg, *Protestant, Catholic, Jew: An Essay in American Religious Sociology* (Garden City, N.Y.: Doubleday Anchor, 1960), pp. 6–41.

Arnold Verstegen to Delis Biemans Family
Little Chute, Wisconsin, to Erp, Noord Brabant
August 12, 1850

Dear Father[-in-law],

I have tried to write a letter about my journey to and arrival in America for several weeks but could not find the time because there was so much work to do for my brother, planting, looking after crops, and building my house.

After leaving Rotterdam on the 22d we sailed with the wind behind us and made good progress until we reached Terre Neuve, where we experienced a bit of a storm and had more wind against us than earlier. Our ship developed a leak, so we had to pump all the time. We had a very bad ship, but arrived in New York on the 20th of May, where we boarded a steamboat to Albany. From there I took the train to Buffalo while my fellow travelers chose the canal boat. Because of that they arrived nineteen days later in Little Chute. We started to get worried because we heard that a steamboat on the lake had burned. Luckily, however, none of us were on that boat and we thanked God for our good luck. We all went to confession and received Communion. The priest celebrated a mass for that purpose.

I met my brother in Green Bay, where he was on business. He saw my wife sitting at a distance, thought that he recognized her, and came quickly. He was astonished because he did not expect us for another two weeks, but we were happy to see each other. He found a boat to take us to Little Chute and we arrived there on June 8. There we met Rev. van den Heuvel who arrived the day before us by traveling through Milwaukee where he spoke to the bishop.

I must tell you that I did not like it here at first. My brother had predicted that, because everything is so strange. He told me that he had the same experience. Also the first crops I saw were not good because of a drought. They did not have any rain throughout the spring, and the prices had gone up so much that one had to pay $18.50 for a barrel of flour, which is 200 pounds. Shortly after our arrival we had a good rain, and now the prices are down and reasonable again. But flour is still $6.00 a barrel, and bacon is eight cents a pound. The summer crops leave nothing to be desired. The bean seed from Holland which I planted are twice as high as I, and the potatoes which I planted late are up to my knees. I like it very much here now and can see that everything my brother wrote is the truth. So it is not necessary to change your views. My wife liked it here right from the start.

I bought forty acres of the best land I could find. It is better than the best land along the Maas River because it does not depend on the water [that is, on annual silting]. It really is as fertile as any you can find over there. It cost ten dollars an acre, that is, $400 or one thousand guilders for forty acres.

We are now working on my brother's house because we want to live together. We have opened a store, but have nothing to sell yet. He is planning to stock everything. My brother knows the language somewhat already. We want to sow and plant everything on my brother's land first because then we do not have so much to fence in. Later we will do this together on my land and thus work together like brothers.

My land lies 200 steps east of my brother's, and close to the locks of the canal. It is a rectangle and takes five minutes to walk along in length and width. It is twice as wide and half as long as the land of my brother. I won't write more about the soil near Little Chute, because my brother described that earlier. But there are three things I must tell you. The first is about the death of our little son. He was sick when we finished our sea voyage. His strength diminished during the journey overland, but he weakened even more rapidly here. Our reverend priest tried as much as he could to cure him, even while he was saying that there was little hope for recovery. He died on July 28 and was buried the day after. Eight children carried him to his grave. They say that he died of consumption.

The second is the confirmation by the bishop, which I attended. None of the other immigrants were here yet. This ceremony was very beautiful, there were, besides the bishop, four priests—Van den Broek, Van den Heuvel, Ferenacci, an American priest, and Bouloick, an Italian. Father van den Heuvel and Bongers met the bishop in Green Bay. Before they arrived in Little Chute my brother went to meet them and after he found them on the road he returned to inform our priest that the bishop was no longer far off. Then a procession went out to meet him. When they met they received the blessing from the bishop. At the same time bells announced to the inhabitants that the bishop had arrived. It was around half past seven in the morning when he arrived, and after staying for a little while in the church and the parsonage he said the mass with the other priests and confirmed the children, who then received their First Communion. Then he gave all the people a heartfelt admonition, both before and after the confirmation. It was very impressive.

The third is that the priest [Father van den Broek] has bequeathed all his possessions to the church here. All that he has and ever will possess has to stay here for use by the church and its priest. His successor is not allowed to change it. It is his wish that this church, which he built and where he planted the Roman Catholic faith, will always be served by a priest. He has left enough behind so that a priest will have a good living here. The Reverend Father van den Broek is still in his customary good health, but if he should die suddenly the Father van den Heuvel will carry out everything until the bishop makes the official decisions. Father van den Broek wants to make the church twice as big and asks us to help him in this. He has decided against a brick church, as that is too expensive, and wants to finish this one in wood.

Well, Father, I think I have told you all the news and I wish you and all our friends much prosperity, health and blessing. We remain respectfully,

Your loving son and daughter,

A. Verstegen and Anna Maria Verstegen

P.S. The rye and wheat are bad this year, because of the drought, but the corn looks good.

After reading this letter please send it to my parents. I will send my next letter to them. When they have something to write, they can enclose their letter with yours. My address: Mr. A. Verstegen at Little Chute, Wisconsin, U.S.A..

This letter was first translated by by Maria de Groot.

December 26, 1851

Dear Father and Mother-in-law, brothers, and sisters-in-law,

We received your letter of February 19 in good health, and we are still healthy. You asked about agriculture—if it is good here. Everything that I sowed and planted grew well. The corn that I planted is eight to nine feet high, the oats and buckwheat, beans, peas, and potatoes are doing reasonably well, and we have enough of everything. The potatoes, however, have the same sickness that you have in Europe, but not as bad. We sowed the buckwheat on July 3, and we mowed it during the week of the fair. I sowed five acres with rye and wheat and have four more acres to plant which I tilled last year plus another four acres of meadow. I am planning to till five additional acres next spring—land already reclaimed.

I built a house this summer thirty-two feet long and twenty-four feet wide, with straight walls and fifteen sliding windows. Every window consists of twelve panes . . . and can be opened for half its length. The house has two floors; the lower floor is eight feet high and the upper only seven and a half feet. On top is an attic. The roof is made with shingles, which are cut from wood and look like slates from afar.

The main road, which runs between my house and the stable, is being made with wood planks and will be three hours long [about nine miles walking]. There is also an electric telegraph line here. We are four minutes from the Fox River and five minutes from the church.

You asked how much livestock I have. I have two horses, two cows and a calf, ten pigs, and eleven chickens. We slaughtered the two oxen; they weighed more than seven hundred pounds each.

This letter was first translated by Maria de Groot.

June 16, 1852

Dear parents,

Your letter of April 24, received here May 23, afforded us great pleasure. Not getting an answer sooner, we were afraid that perhaps our letter might have been lost. You tell us that Mother has been sick, but is now improving; we wish her a speedy and complete recovery.

While I was reading the rest of your letter, tears came to my eyes. You suggest that we take our inheritance at this time; and I read between the lines that you are under the impression that we are living here in great poverty and are too proud to ask for help. We are happy to hear that we still have a place in your heart, although undeserving of it, since we came to America against your advice. But, Father, we are not poor, we are rich! We have more and better food than we ever had in Holland; we live in a warm house and have good clothes; we have mass in our church each Sunday; and the children go to school and catechism. The little patch of land which we have cleared is sufficient to supply all of our wants. No, Father, don't give your money away; rather keep control of what is yours as long as you live, and may that be for many more years.

If, however, you have some money lying idle in the house, and wish to invest it, that is a different proposition. I need a few more horses and cows, and have no money on hand to buy them. My credit is good, and I can borrow the money here, but not for less than 12 percent; some moneylenders charge as high as 30 percent, although the legal limit is 12 percent. Two hundred dollars is all that I need, and I will promptly pay you 6 percent; in this way we both will make a profit.

The best way to send money is to buy a money order from a bank in Rotterdam which has connections with a New York bank. They will give you three drafts if you ask for them; mail them to me, one at a time, about a month apart; one out of three will always reach its destination.

Storekeepers in Appleton are glad to give me cash for them. Instead of going to Rotterdam in person, you could ask Doctor van Loo in Veghel to arrange that matter for you; his first wife was a sister-in-law of Mr. J. Wap, the banker in Rotterdam.

It has been two years now since we arrived here, and we are becoming accustomed to the country and its people; so I shall give you my impressions. The country is still in the making, and much of the improvement is of a makeshift character. The land, after clearing, is left full of tree stumps, which will be removed as soon as the roots have decayed enough so that they can be pulled out. But in the meantime we must plow between them the best way we can, and everything grows without fertilizer. The buildings are mostly constructed of logs; there is no beauty about them, but they are warm and serviceable. The roads are rough, and during a wet spell heavily loaded wagons have to keep off, lest they sink into the mud up to the hub.

This is a free country where only a few necessary and useful laws are made. Ordinances and restrictions which would benefit only a few, and would be a burden to the people generally, are wisely avoided. And with few laws and few officers to enforce them, the people have respect for the law and like to see it enforced; as a whole the people cooperate with the officers, so that transgressions are few.

There are policemen in the cities, but we never see one; still we don't have to lock the house or the stable or keep a vicious watchdog to frighten burglars away. You can leave a spade or any implement or tool in the field after using it, and it will still be there whenever you go back to use it again.

Is there a kommie [revenue collector] in Little Chute? Of course you think that no town should be without one, to watch everyone's every move, to prevent illegal butchering, brewing, or baking, etc. No, we have no kommies, and that is another reason why I like this country!

There is no compulsory military service here. Every state in Europe maintains a large standing army because each country is afraid of its neighbor. The United States has no dangerous neighbors, and the quarrelsome nations of Europe are too far away to cause any serious concern. We have only a small army of volunteers, and no compulsory service.

There are no game laws; you can go fishing or hunting whenever you please. There is plenty of game, big and small, in the woods; the rivers are full of fish.

Do we pay taxes? Certainly we pay taxes, and enjoy doing it! I am paying taxes on 160 acres of land, and I am highly assessed because my land is of the best; yet I am only paying twelve dollars a year, and that includes school tax. My brother John has been elected tax collector, the highest paid office in town; he receives 5 percent of all the money taken in, and it will bring him the neat sum of $80.00 a year, but he must go from house to house to collect it.

Now, Father, you will understand why we love our new country, and you will not be surprised when I say that we have made up our minds to make it our home for the rest of our days, bringing up our children to become American citizens. But to come over to Holland for a visit and spend a winter with you is what we are wishing and praying for. However, it will take at least two more years of hard work before the conditions of our farm will allow us that luxury.

Now for a bit of local news. The Fox River, a river as big as the Meuse, is shallow and fast-flowing, because Lake Winnebago, its origin, is seventy-five feet higher than the Green Bay, into which it empties, and the distance is only forty miles. A plan has been adopted whereby the river can be made navigable. Dams are being built at several points to retard the flow and raise the water to a higher level, and locks will be installed at each dam to help the boats from one level to another. One of the locks will come right opposite my land. Water transportation will be a great boon to towns along the river. At this moment the work has stopped on account of a dispute between the contractor, Mr. Martin, and the governor of the state. They say that will come to a lawsuit, and that it may be some time before the work will be resumed.

Another public work, now in progress, is the paving of our main road with planks. They want to straighten out the road, and run it through my land, which will necessitate the moving of my house. There is also a dispute here between a certain road boss and one Mr. Verstegen, governor of this manor! They have not come to terms yet about the cost of moving the house, and the price of the land. In the meantime they have skipped my land and are already two miles beyond it, grading the road and making a bedding for the planks. The planks have been laid for a distance of five miles, up to the house of brother John, and that part of the road is open for traffic.

The price of produce is as follows: wheat, per bushel, 75 cents; rye, 60 cents; buckwheat, 60 cents; oats, 30 cents; beans, $1.60; peas, $1.00. Flour is $4.00 a barrel (200 pounds); salt pork, per pound, 10 cents; butter, 14 cents; coffee (not roasted), 14 cents; rice, 8 cents; and eggs, 12 cents per dozen.

Father is still with us. Adriana and Anna Marie are going to school to learn English, and are beginning to read and speak it quite well. J. van Lisshout says that he will pay his share and that you can go ahead.

With best wishes, respectfully, Your children,

Arnoldus Verstegen

Anna Maria Verstegen (Biemans)

This letter is reproduced from Lucas, *Dutch Immigrant Memoirs* 2:157–59.

August 30, 1857

Dear parents,

Arnold Hurkmans, a friend and neighbor of ours, will be leaving in a few days on a visit to Holland. We would like to go with him in person, but that being impossible, he will bring you our portraits. They have been made by a new process, not painted by the slow brush of an artist, but by a clever device which does the work quick and neat, although the pictures are small. It must be a new American invention, because I never heard of it in Holland. There is a man here in Appleton who knows all about it and gets many customers because he is doing wonderful work. A few weeks ago I went there with Ma and the two youngest children, the ones who were born in America, Anna Maria and Egidius. The machine that performs the mysterious work is simple enough—just a square box that has a big glass eye in front. I was told to sit down a few feet away from the machine and hold the little girl on my knees. Next he told me to look pleasant and to try not to move. Then he removed a cover and let the magic eye look at us for a few seconds, and that is all there was to it. Ma and the baby were next. A few days later we got the pictures and they were just wonderful. When I look at mine, I seem to be looking at myself in the looking glass. It is too bad that the children's faces didn't turn out so well; they are a little foggy.

Are we not living in a wonderful world? One marvelous invention looms up after another. It took us two months and a half to come to this country, and that is only seven years ago, and now your letters reach us within a month.

The wild land we undertook to tame a few years ago has seen a great change. We have almost forty acres under cultivation, a nice herd of cattle, and can take life a little easier this year than any previous year. But Hurkmans will tell you all about that. He knows us and our circumstances. Just ask him, and he will tell you everything. In Holland they think that visitors coming from America are fond of telling tall stories, that they like to make things look twice as big as they really are.

However, Hurkmans is not that kind of a man; everything he says can be taken at its full value.

Hoping to receive an answer with Hurkmans, I am your obedient son,

Arnold Verstegen

P.S. We recommend Hurkmans to your kind hospitality.

This letter is reproduced from Lucas, *Dutch Immigrant Memoirs* 2:160.

October 28, 1858

Dear parents,

We received your letter of October 20 of last year, but did not answer because Arnold Hurkmans was on his way to Holland with a letter from us and would bring all the news personally. In the meantime there has been an increase in the family. On the 15th of September a baby boy arrived. His name is Hermanus. That brings the total again up to five, three girls and two boys. The baby is doing fine, but the mother suffers from cramps in the legs, although she is otherwise in good health.

Hurkmans tells us that you liked the pictures but that you would sooner have seen us in person. It has always been our plan to come to see you as soon as the condition of our farm would allow us, but we overlooked one thing and that is the children. For no money in the world would Anna leave them to the care of strangers. A few years from now it will be different; Adriana, who is a willing and handy worker and already does much of the housework will then be able to take the place of her mother, and then you can expect us. We left Holland, not because we disliked the country, but to give our children better opportunities. Here I will be able to put each of them on a farm, something I never would have expected to do in Holland. But if it is God's will, we hope to see Holland once more, and walk the streets of Erp and Boekel and Uden, and meet our old friends and have a happy family reunion.

Hurkmans tells us that he spent many hours with you, and that you were delighted to hear of the progress we have made on our farm. He told us, too, how he had to draw maps of Little Chute and point out the location of our house, and the house of John, and of the church. I am sure you now have a pretty good picture in your mind of the entire town.

Late in the summer an unusual sight was noticed in the sky; it was a star with a tail. As weeks passed by, the tail grew longer and the head grew brighter, and it seemed to come nearer the earth. In the month of October it began to look so threatening that people began to fear that something was amiss, and that the end of the world was coming. One

Sunday our priest talked about it in church and said that it was a comet and that similar stars had been seen in the past; that it was a friendly wanderer of the universe, not intent upon any mischief, and that it would disappear noiselessly, just as it had arrived. The papers tell us that it was seen all over the world; you must have seen it in Holland too.

Father has been very sick this summer and hasn't been in the church for three months; he was anointed, and for a few days his condition was such that any moment he was expected to pass away. To the surprise of everyone, he recovered, and is going to church again, although he is not quite as strong as he used to be. Next summer he will again be seen working in the garden and doing odd jobs around the house and taking the children for a walk.

Now a little about the weather. There was so much rain this spring that the work in the field was much delayed. The horses would sink in the mud as deep as the land had been plowed before. It was July before all the seeding was done. Then a dry hot spell came; once the thermometer registered 105 degrees; and the latter part of the summer was wet again. Wheat is only 85 cents a bushel, so that farmers in some states, considering the low price and the poor quality of grain, have set fire to the crops, not thinking it worth while to harvest them. I myself have two acres of wheat still standing in the field; it has plenty of straw but little grain, and even that is infested with smut.

The money you have sent I have put on interest. Home breeding has taken care of the increase of my stock, so that I need not buy any more. When I see a good piece of property I will buy it.

I was told two years ago that Cornelius Elsen was married. Is it true that Uncle Cornelis of Boekel is also married? Give my best regards to all relatives and friends.

Yours truly,
A. Verstegen

This letter is reproduced from Lucas, *Dutch Immigrant Memoirs* 2:161–62.

January 2, 1860

Dear parents, brothers, and sisters-in-law,

Anna has been telling me right along that the new year was coming fast, and that it was time to look for pen and ink and send our New Year's greetings to Holland; and I kept on saying that there was no hurry, for no other reason that I know of, except that I dislike the mention of pen and ink; that puts the blame on me for their coming so late.

Accept our sincere wishes for a happy New Year. So far God has been kind to you and given you a good share of the blessings of this life, and we pray that you may enjoy the same happiness for many more years.

Your welcome letter of January 8, 1859, found us all in good health, except that Anna is still suffering from cramps in the legs; it is four years now since she began to complain, and now it is so bad that she has difficulty in walking; otherwise she is in good health.

Wheat, rye, and oats were fairly good last year, but most of the winter wheat had to be seeded over in the spring. Early in the month of July a severe frost did much damage to turkish wheat, buckwheat, and potatoes and another killing frost the last days of August aggravated the damage done earlier in the season. That is the climate of Wisconsin—impetuous extreme cold and long winters, and short, hot summers; everything must grow in four months' time; and it is surprising what a wealth of grain and fruits can grow in so short a period. Buckwheat seeded the latter part of June is ready to be cut during the week of the Boekel kermis [fair]. All in all we did fairly well this year.

The prices of produce are as follows: wheat, $1.00; oats, 30 cents; potatoes, 50 cents per bushel; flour $5.00 the barrel; butter, one shilling [12.5 cents], per pound. I have two fine work horses for sale and three milk cows; that would leave me seven horses and as many cows; but although grain brings a good price, livestock is cheap and I don't like to sell at the prevailing price. I think I have told you everything worth while mentioning, and we remain as ever, with respect and love, your son and daughter,

Arnold Verstegen
Anna Maria Biemans

This letter is reproduced from Lucas, *Dutch Immigrant Memoris* 2:162–63.

August 20, 1860

Dear Mother, brothers, and sisters-in-law,

We received your May 30 letter in good health and learned that Father died. I hope to remember his soul, and have begun doing that by offering a mass every month on the day of his death. I hope to keep this up for a year, on the 23d of every month. At the moment we do not have a priest in this village, but we hope to have another one next Sunday, as was promised.

It looks now as if my wife will be able to come along at All Saints [the scheduled departure date for a trip to Holland]. When I come, I hope to see you and talk to you. For the time being, then, I think that you should keep the money there. If things change I shall write you.

My wife gave birth to a daughter late in July. Her name is Ardina and both are healthy, except that my wife still suffers from her old ailment. I waited so long to write so I could tell you about the birth.

Concerning the harvest: much has grown, the wheat is harvested . . . [and] the oats and other crops look particularly good, but we had many thunderstorms and much rain this year. Halfway through this year I bought a threshing machine, which cost me almost a hundred dollars. I can thresh a hundred bushels a day with it.

There is no more news here.

Greet all friends and acquaintances, also in Boekel. We remain, with high regards, your son and daughter,

Arnoldus Verstegen

This letter was first translated by Maria de Groot.

May 6, 1861

Dear Mother, brothers, and sisters-in-law,

I must tell you about my journey [back to Wisconsin after visiting Holland]. On Wednesday we left for Veghel, and a day later we left for 's-Hertogenbosch. On Friday we left for Rotterdam. Saturday we sailed for Hull, England, and we arrived on Sunday. We stayed till Monday and then went to Goole and from Goole to Liverpool, where, on Wednesday, we were taken by a small boat to the big one. Thank heavens we arrived there safely. After sailing for a day and a half we arrived in Queenstown, Ireland, on Friday morning. We stayed there for a half day, and about two hundred Irishmen joined us. Our ship then had four hundred passengers aboard, and we arrived in New York on the Wednesday after Easter. We stayed there for two days and went to Albany to meet an American. From there we went home, where I arrived with much joy and happiness on all sides including my Dutch and French acquaintances. Since then I've had many visitors and much to report. When I got home I found everything in good order, both in and out of the house.

Concerning the revolution [the Civil War], the fighting is heavy but it is far away from here and they ask only for volunteers. The North is losing forts, but they are saying that few men have been killed. Quite a few volunteers have joined from Little Chute. They are paid $8.00 per month and will get 160 acres of land when it is finished.

Crop prices are going up now; wheat costs from $1.00 to $1.10 a bushel. We had a lot of snow here this winter and so much rain this spring that it is too wet to sow. When we have a few days of dry weather, it rains again for hours, soaking the land. We are afraid that we shall have a bad harvest because of the great danger of smut which comes during damp seasons.

As far as my money is concerned, everything arrived in good order. . . .

Greetings from my wife and the children to Mother, brothers sisters-in-law, and all other family and acquaintances.

We remain with high regards your submissive son and daughter,

A. Verstegen and Mrs. A. M. Verstegen

This letter was first translated by Maria de Groot.

June 19, 1862 [Fragment]

Dear Mother, brothers, and sisters-in-law,

I must write to you about the loss of my eldest daughter, Adriana. Fourteen days after her wedding she needed medical treatment. She died of consumption of the liver and suffered from the beginning of Lent till May 24. She was just skin and bones; nobody had ever seen a thinner person when she died. Those who saw her did not recognize her, because she used to be heavy. Her patience was great, she trusted in God and surrendered to the Lord. Before then she was completely involved in her marriage, which, in my opinion, would have been a very good marriage.

On May 24, eighteen hours after the death of our eldest child, my wife had a healthy daughter whom we also named Adriana. I hope that she will be as virtuous as our eldest child.

Concerning the country—they are very busy building the railroad, which is only 500 steps from my door or 300 steps from my land. At first they planned the route through my land, but now it runs in between my two pieces. They are also talking about broadening the canal by 50 percent, so it can be used by the big steamboats that sail the Great Lakes. That will give lots of work.

This fragment was first translated by Maria de Groot.

December, 1863

Dear brothers and sisters-in-law,

I had hopes of sending you good news about the birth of another child, but now things have changed, and I must report the death of my wife instead of a birth. She died on December 18 and was buried on the 21st. So now I am left with five children out of the ten or eleven[1] that were born.

The disease was the same from which she has suffered over the past seven and a half years. Her last days were terribly painful and it was difficult for those who visited to see her suffering. She died from the pain.

Our war or revolution continues with little change. We have had two military conscriptions. The last group has not left yet and they are allowed to buy substitutes for $300. Many who have the money try to be exempted. The conscription goes this way—the marshal orders someone to write the names of all the men from twenty to forty-five years of age. Those of twenty to twenty-five are first class, both married and unmarried. Unmarried men up to forty-five are also first class. Married men [between twenty-six and forty-five] are in the second class and probably will not be conscripted. Men [who claim to be] under twenty must have sworn testimony about their age. . . . Fathers are allowed to select one child as a breadwinner who is then free [from conscription]. Many others have also escaped conscription, but they need to take legal action which is costly.

Our harvest was reasonably good. Although some complain, I and most others I know are doing well. But the yield from late spring crops is less [than normal]. Prices are: winter wheat, $1.20 [per bushel]; summer wheat, $1.10; butter, 18–23 cents; meat 5 cents [per pound]; and bacon, 6 cents. Our mill is doing rather well.

Wages are high. I pay $18.00 per month to J. van Haandel's son, and his brother works in the woods for $26.00 per month. The wages are high enough so that everyone can make a good living.

The railway train passes through here every day and they are going to lengthen the track to reach Lake Superior.

I think I have provided everyone with some information. If anyone wants more, let him ask and I hope I can answer him.

Greetings to all—brother, sisters-in-law, and also to uncles and aunts in Boekel.

Respectfully, I remain,
A. Verstegen

I wish a happy New Year to all of you and an afterlife in our heavenly fatherland.

Greetings to Pieter Teune from his sister.

This letter was first translated by Maria de Groot.

1. Apparently, Anna Maria died during a pregnancy that would have produced the eleventh child.

November 17, 1870

Dear brothers and sisters-in-law,

I am pleased to answer your long-awaited letter. Now that I have learned from Martinus Dirksen that you did not receive my 1869 letter, I am less worried that you no longer love me. I did not write until now because I was fearful that my letter would be disagreeable and upsetting to you [because he had remarried following his wife's death].

My wife has met a man who traveled here from the Veluwe and wanted to see me. I was not at home but I hope we can meet because I am eager to talk with him about how you are doing. I want to assure you that I like you just as much even if I have married for a second time. I have not forgotten my former wife or her family in my prayers.

I want you to know that I was remarried even before returning here from Holland. I did not want to upset you then because she is a poor person. I regard virtue more highly than money. Everything is going rather well now. I have now had two children with this wife and she had three.

Would it be possible for you to send me a portrait of my eldest daughter Adriana? The other child [named Adriana] is also pretty. I sent you a photo of my former wife but if you are not able to have a print made of it, send it back.

My cousin, Johannes Verstegen, is now the priest and pastor of Freedom [Wisconsin]. He likes it a lot, and my daughter works there as his maid. I'm afraid that if I keep her here at home she would get married too early because there are many such opportunities here and most often with [men who are] too young.

Greetings from my wife and children to my next of kin. I remain

A. Verstegen

I am looking forward to your answer.

This letter was first translated by Maria de Groot.

October 20, 1871

Dear brothers and sisters-in-law,

Because of the disastrous fires in our state I feel obliged to report on our health. The fires were everywhere in the forests, but you can hardly imagine what forests are here. You probably think that the [pine growth in your] heather is like our trees. These are not forests for kindling wood but contain all kinds of trees. Everything was on fire. Every afternoon the wind rose and spread the fire farther.

In Chicago at 10:00 P.M. on the 8th of October the fire broke loose. We heard about it on the following morning. I was in Appleton that day and the news came by telegraph every minute. By evening 2,000 acres [of buildings] were reduced to ashes and many people lost their lives. The city was very beautiful and the fire hit the very center of the city. People thought that most of the brick houses and buildings were fire-proof. The stone walls did not melt, but the iron columns under the buildings melted like water. They tell us that some of the houses cost up to a million dollars and they contained many valuable goods. The damage has not yet been calculated.

But that's not all. In Peshtigo, Wisconsin, another fire burned every-thing except a boardinghouse. On the Sunday evening of October 8 the fire came through the air like a heavy snow squall. Everything burned within four hours—all the houses and 800 people. That's as many as they know but they find more daily. It is impossible to tell you everything. I leave it in God's hands. All of us must carry our crosses.

It was not only our state which suffered, but also Michigan and other states. There was so much smoke here that we had to put oil into our eyes in order to stand it. Johannes van Rijsingen, from Uden is also reported to be dead. Others who were burned by the fire continue to die every day. Some people saved themselves by clinging to trees which drifted in the rivers. They stayed under the water up to their necks but even then the hair on their heads burned. I have talked to some of those survivors. They told me that they had to stay in the river for four hours and keep dipping their heads under to keep wet. Even the trees, lying in the water but not totally under the water, burned.

Well, I must stop or I could be writing all day. I and my family, thank God, are all healthy and well.

We had a dry year so the wheat did not grow well. The rest of the harvest is rather good. The hay was good too, but that which was kept outside, a common practice here, burned up. My own work is at the flour mill and my oldest son Johannes Egidius Verstegen works there now also.

I asked you to answer my letter. [Did you refuse] because my wife is not rich enough? She is certainly as good a mother to my children as a rich wife and she is strong. I shall not write about this anymore, but hope for an answer. If you have other things on your mind, please write and I will answer.

[Closing]

====OFFICE OF====

ZEELAND FLOURING MILLS, &.

A. VERSTEGEN, Propr.

»}} Manufacturer of and Dealer in {{«

FLOUR, FEED AND GRAIN.

*ALL MILL WORK PROMPTLY AND WELL DONE.   BEST BRAND OF FLOUR CONSTANTLY ON HAND.

Little Chute, Wis., _____ 188

Waarde Neef Johanes J. Biemans te Erp
ik kan niet nalaten om uw eenige lehren te
schijven wat mij en mijne kindere aan gaat
wij zijn alle nu weer goed gezond, maar
mijne kinderen zijn de meeste ziek geweest
wat wij vernemen door de Nieuws bladen
als dat het in Europa het zelfde ook is
geweest maar toch nagenoeg niets van gester
ven is en bij mij alles hersteld is, wat
mijne rijs aan gaat, ik was den 10 Augustus
in Antwerpen op den Boot gegaan en
den 21 in New York aan gekomen zoo
dat wij maar 11 dagen op de see geweest
waaren en 1½ dag tot mijn huis toe
dat was ook een schoon plazier rijs voor
u en ik zal u met vreeden ont vangen
dan zoude u nog wel wat van de wereld
zien het verschil tusschen hier en bij u

Arnold Verstegen's September 1882 letter (p. 1) to his cousin Johanes J. Biemans in Erp, Noord Brabant

P.S. Concerning me and my brother's wife, we are at the moment not on speaking terms because of the inheritance of my brother. In his will he gave me and my offspring the mill with its appurtenances.

This letter was first translated by Maria de Groot.

Arnold Verstegen to Johanes J. Biemans
Little Chute, Wisconsin, to Erp, Noord Brabant
[September] 188[2]

Dear cousin Johanes J. Biemans,

I would like to write a few lines to you about myself and my children. All of us are healthy again, but our children were more seriously sick than we. From what we read in the newspapers it is the same sickness that you had in Europe, but hardly anyone died from it and at my house everyone is restored.

Regarding my trip, I boarded the ship in Antwerp on August 10 and arrived in New York on the 21st. So we were at sea for eleven days and then one and a half days to my home. That would be a nice pleasure trip for you too and I would welcome you with pleasure. Then you would see something of the world and the difference between this place and your place. My absence from my family passed by quickly. They made more money [in my absence] than I spent on the trip. For many years now I have saved more than $2,000 every year. That is a large sum to save in the short time of a year. Anyone here, who has money and who watches his expenses with care, earns money. At the moment, however, it is not so good for farmers because everything is so cheap—$25 to $30 [per acre]. Horses are expensive; a good horse can cost as much as $200 each but not many are buying them. Wheat here is 65 cents to 75 cents per bushel. A bushel is equal to two containers [type and size not specified]. Hay is 20 cents [per bale]. Employment is generally very weak. But more people are at work locally because two paper mills were built here last year but they only use half of the workers that they could [at full employment].

Now, greetings from my wife and children to you and also to your wife and your father and mother.

I remain respectfully yours and willingly at your service,

Your cousin,
A. Verstegen

This letter was first translated by Herbert Brinks.

3   Harm Avink

In 1869 the Avink brothers, Arendjan, Engbert, Harm, and their families, immigrated to West Michigan from the small city of Borculo in Gelderland. Although they had been weavers in the local cottage industry, they all became farmers in Blendon, where they purchased and developed adjacent forty-acre holdings.[1] About the turn of the century, as their forty-acre farms became economically obsolete, the Avink descendants relocated in neighboring cities and villages to pursue employment as craftsmen and factory workers. In 1912 Henry, Harm Avink's nephew, took a more adventurous path when he migrated across the continent to resettle near Ripon, California. Thus, the Avink family migration, which began in 1869, stretched across the Atlantic to the Midwest and terminated near the Pacific coast, traversing about five thousand miles.[2]

Harm Avink's correspondence provides detailed descriptions of frontier farming in Blendon. Even though the Avink letter collection, 1883–1909, begins fourteen years after the family immigrated, the letters clearly disclose the cycle of initial settlement and subsequent efforts that led to moderate success.

Addressed to his in-laws, the R. W. Bouwmeester family in Lochem, Harm Avink's correspondence reveals the changing status of his family and those of his brothers. Clearing the land, draining the lowlands, and plowing up stumps kept the Blendon farmers busy through many summers and winters, for, though Harm Avink purchased his farm in 1873, he was still struggling with stubborn stumps in 1888. In a letter of October 30 he declared, "It is hard plowing here between the stumps, and even though we have worked this land for fifteen years the oak and pine stumps are still hard." Although both of his brothers owned horses, Harm considered them something of a luxury, commenting in his March 30, 1884, letter that "a person cannot do very much with horses here except ride along the roads and work in the corn with a cultivator." Furthermore, they could not be left to roam in the woods like oxen but required pasture and winter feed, which was "too expensive." So Harm

---

These letters were donated by the Bouwmeester family, 1976, and first translated by Egbert Post.

[1] Van der Aa, *Aardrijkskundig woordenboek* 2:588–90; Swierenga, *Dutch Emigrants*, p. 6; Harm Avink to Willem Bouwmeester, December 3, 1903, Immigrant Letter Collection.

[2] Henry Avink Diary, 1915–1943, Calvin College Library Archives.

Blendon Den 30 Maart 1884

Zeer Geliefde vader Broeders en zusterskind
wij hebben uwen brief in Gezondhijd ont
vangen en gezien dat gij allen wel varer
de zijt tot ons groot genoegen inde hoop
dat uw dezen in gezond hijd moogt ont
vangen maar tot mijn leet weezen moet
ich schrijten dat den brief is verdwaalt ge
weest wij hebben hem gisteren eers ontvang
hij heeft heel ront geswandelt daar waren
ag stempels op het pos kantoor het
anderen naam het is niet meer Ohio
Wills maar Soutt Blendon blendon
aan gaande dat geld sturen dat is volko
men goet maar het land kopen daar is
nog niet van ge komen eers vroeg hij
drie hondert aan een ander man bij on
en toen ich hem vroeg toen was het 500
dat was ons teveel want daar zit ook
veel werk in daar moet watter lijdin
van 400 trat en die moet men zelf be
kostigen als het water langs den weg wil
lopen dan doet het den toon of de ko
miscie die over de wegen en het water
gestelt zijn maar in het land moet
men het zelf betaalen al en dier er voor
deel van hebben want als ich een watte
lijding door mijn land krijg en het lan

Harm Avink's March 30, 1884, letter (p. 1) to R. W. Bouwmeester family in Lochem, Ge
erland

kept his oxen, Kees and Hans, to push through the root-strewn fields until 1892, when he bought his first team of horses, Bill and Jim.

That same year (August 25) Avink advised his brother-in-law and a friend named Levenkamp to come to America because it was "a land of plenty." Recounting his own experience, Harm wrote, "It is not so easy to become a farmer as it was twenty years ago. Land is much more expensive now. Today, a forty-acre farm with house and barn costs about $2,000. I place the value of my farm at about $2,000, and you know that, even with the money I borrowed from you, I had only $600 when I arrived here. Today the land, house, barn, wagon, animals and all the rest are free of debt."

Avink's friend Levenkamp did immigrate, but he settled in Iowa; and the journey was too expensive to attempt a reunion. In 1904 the Avinks and Levenkamps were reunited when Levenkamp came to Chicago along with a carload of livestock destined for the stockyards. Thus Avink wrote, "Gerrit Levenkamp visited us this spring. He had been to Chicago with a load of fattened cattle. Then he was one hundred and fifty miles from here."

Over the years Avink had written that land in West Michigan had become expensive, but land out west was still cheap. Government land was available "for almost nothing. Out there homesteads are granted. Anyone who is a citizen can get eighty acres for practically nothing. He must live on it for five years and then he becomes the owner."

At seventy-seven years of age, Avink had no intention of moving west, but he recognized the dim future that faced the small farmers. "Forty acres is not enough," he wrote in November 1906, "to support cattle. . . . Arendjan's son Hendrik has sold his land for $2,750. Now he has bought the farm of his father-in-law, Havighorst. . . . Now Hendrik has better land."

"Better" land and more of it—these were the farmers' constant objectives—and the Avinks had similar goals, but the second generation inherited too little land in Blendon to remain on the farm.

Harm Avink to R. W. Bouwmeester Family
Blendon, Michigan, to Lochem, Gelderland
March 30, 1884

Dear Father, brothers, sisters, and children,

We received your letter in good health and it gave us great satisfaction to read that you were all well. We hope you will receive this in good health. The letter you sent was lost so that we did not receive it until yesterday. It had been sent around a great deal and had several post office cancellations on it. Our post office has a new name. It is no longer Ohio Mills, but South Blendon.

We received the money we requested in good order, but nothing has been done about buying the land. At first he [a Mr. Kool] was asking three hundred but when I talked to him he asked five hundred. That was too much to suit us because the land requires lots of work. It needs four hundred feet of drainage tile which we will have to lay ourselves. The township takes care of water that runs along the roads, but private land-owners must take care of their own land. . . . The land is good low soil but it is not suitable for building a house because it is flooded at present.

[Mr. Kool] was a crooked land dealer who sold much of his land because of his debts, and now he hopes to make a profit on the land he still owns. He should be debt free in about six months. He once owned the largest sawmill in this area but now he has nothing.

I am happy now that you did not yet sign off the money because we do not need it at this time. If we buy something later, I will tell you immediately. We have fifty dollars cash on hand and can easily raise another fifty dollars.

We have eleven head of cattle with five cows. We are milking three and two will come fresh in April. We have only one calf but we plan to keep two more. We also have four hogs and I think two are with young.

The crop has been small because of all the rain. There is almost no corn—not even enough for seed. But we have some buckwheat for seed and some old beans.

The winter is almost past and we did not have much winter until the eighth of March. But then we had four days of snow which was very good because the farmers could use their sleighs to bring wood to the city for fuel for six dollars [a load]. Then they can buy food for the horses, hogs, chickens and themselves. Feed is quite cheap here. Corn-meal, or maize, is $1.25 for a hundred pounds. Potatoes are thirty to forty cents per bushel. Butter is twenty-one cents per pound and eggs are ten cents a dozen. Cattle are not cheap but few are being sold.

Our children are growing well. Hendrika is seventeen years old and taller than Geertjen [his wife]. Our daughter Geertjen is eleven years old —a fine fat girl. Hendrik is eight years old—not fat but slender and all there. They go to school where they are taught in English. I must teach them Dutch at home.

About a year and a half ago we sent you photographs of Hendrika. You never mentioned that they arrived. We sent five, one for all of the uncles and aunts. When you write again do not forget to tell us if you received them.

Now I will answer my little nephew's questions. I will enclose a sewing thread, one rod long, in this letter. Forty acres is eighty rods long and eighty rods wide. So every side is eighty times as long as this thread. Forty acres is a square eighty rods long and eighty wide. So now my little nephew can measure it once by himself. A bushel of wheat weighs sixty pounds, but ten pounds here is equal to nine pounds where you are.

Now, as to money—a dollar is one hundred cents here. Silver, gold, and paper all have the same value. If you come here with a rijksdaalder [2.50 guilders] you will get $1.00 in exchange. Paper money came here during the [Civil] war. The states could do that easier than borrowing money which costs interest and paper costs nothing. Now that was a good way to pay bills but the paper was worthless. The government guaranteed the paper but the money [gold] was not there and sometimes gold and silver were valued fifteen to twenty percent higher than paper. But now there is enough silver and gold to cover all the old worn-out paper dollars. Now you can figure out how much one cent is worth in comparison with your cent. We pay five cents for postage stamps and you pay twelve and a half cents. Our tax last year was $6.00, which gives free education to all children.

Hendrik is standing beside me here begging to fill the paper. He would like to see his cousins sometime. So if Gerritjan and Johanna ever come here that would please our children very much. They will not have to eat rye bread here but the finest of wheat. Then they can learn English with [their uncles] Arendjan and Engbert. They are all well. They each have a horse and two oxen. I do not like that very much because a person cannot do very much with horses here except ride along the roads and work in the corn with a cultivator.

Now I wish you God's richest blessings. Greetings from the entire family.

                                        Harm Avink, Geertjen J. Bouwmeester

Address: Harm Avink
          South Blendon
          Ottawa County
          State of Michigan, North America

January 10, 1888

Dear Father, brothers, and sisters,

We are all in good health and have learned that you are too—except that Janna had a sore leg. That is a difficult thing, but all things will turn out for our good, including the sufferings we must endure in this life which come from His hand and cause us to think more about Him because we have no abiding place here. We are strangers on this earth and pilgrims on the way to a never-ending eternity. As a person sows, so shall he reap. If we think only of the things of this world we are spiritually very poor. But our Savior calls us to be citizens of his kingdom. . . .

You asked me about Welmers's return trip, but I have heard nothing about it. He was well satisfied with your hospitality. He has only been here once. He was at Arendjan's place on Christmas Day but that was just on a Sunday and because the factories were so busy he could not stay longer.

Also he is more tied to his home at present because his brother Evert died after a short illness about five weeks ago. He left a wife and six children—the oldest a nineteen-year-old son and the youngest a child of fourteen days. So, you can imagine that it is a difficult situation for the wife and children, but also for the brothers and sisters and their church. He was an elder, and loved by all who, with him, feared the Lord in truth and uprightness. So, he departed in peace. After he had committed his wife and children to the Lord, the pastor asked him if he had a request to make and he answered, yes—that the pastor should warn the catechism pupils to "remember their creator in the days of their youth before the evil days come when one will say, 'I have no pleasure in them' [Ecclesiastes 12:1]." He was a catechism teacher.

Hendrika was here for a three-day vacation around New Year's Day. She is still working in Grand Rapids where she earns $2.75 each week, the same as six guilders and sixty-seven Dutch cents. I think you will believe me but others will probably say, "I don't believe it." But you have talked with Welmers recently and he probably told you all about these things. It is the absolute truth!

*   *   *

You wrote that I paid you too much interest, but I figured on the basis of five hundred guilders, so seventeen guilders is not too much. You, by coming up with fl13 interest must have been figuring on fl400. If I had borrowed fl500 (the same as $200) it would cost me $14.00 here annually or fl35. So, as you can see, it's better for me to send you fl17 than to pay $14.00 here. So when you write to us again you can decide what you want. We do not want to abuse your generosity to us by paying too little. By God's grace we have more than enough here.

Although everything is cheap here, money is also in short supply. We sold two cows for $36.50 and a fat hog weighing 392 pounds, so we made $60.00 from these. Potatoes bring high prices but they are scarce. It has been very dry here so things did not grow well. There is not much corn and feed for cattle is scarce. We have nine head. Every day we boil two pots of oats to feed them. We milk four cows and we have three hogs.

One, a boar, I offer for breeding at forty cents. They are very fine hogs, but it has not cost us much to feed them because we have so many beechnuts in the woods. They are in good condition—almost fat. We butchered two for our own use and, although we did not have as much as last year, we had plenty of lard and pork.

We have enough wheat on hand for the entire winter. We have sorted out fifteen bushels of potatoes to sell because, in general, the potatoes were small. Many farmers here must buy some for planting at eighty cents a bushel. They cost as much as wheat. Butter is nineteen cents, eggs are twenty-two cents a dozen, oats are thirty-five cents a bushel, and corn is fifty cents. Good houses sell for from $130.00 to $150.00 and the best go for $200.00. Breeding costs from five to twenty dollars. The son of H. J. Bruggink came through the neighborhood with his stallion to offer services at $8.00.

It is snowing today. We planned to bring some wheat and buckwheat to the mill in Zeeland, but it is a good thing we are at home. The snow is drifting over the land. We have not had much cold weather so far. On New Year's Day it snowed with a strong wind. I went to church, but more out of duty than desire.

I have been elected as deacon. We now have our own pastor, Gerrit de Jong. Our elders are Gerritjan Holstege (a cousin of Chris van't Over-laan), Hemkes Elzenga, Jan Shook, Piet Steegeman (from Holten), Hendrikjan Nieuwenhuis (from Rijssen), and Harm Avink from Geesteren. That is our consistory, but our elders are good leaders at reading [sermons] and praying and visiting the sick. I have not known such capable elders in the Netherlands as we have here.

Much is done here to prevent raising ignorant children. They start school when they are five years old and the law requires that all children must attend school for a certain length of time. The government always pays a portion of the cost. It amounts to a great deal and I have heard that eighty million dollars is spent for elementary and higher education in the United States. The teachers here are not the sons of the wealthy but of the laboring people. That is their background. Our local teacher was a carpenter before he became a teacher and now he is a very good one.

You wrote that our photographs were poorer than yours, but they are not as expensive here. We get twelve for f6.50 or $2.50. Last year our taxes were $10.57 and we must pay them before the New Year. That is three percent less than last year. The more land a person has the more taxes he pays and with that free education is given up to age twenty.

Everyone is well at Arendjan's house. He has two horses but I am still an oxen driver. I am leery of horses because I have not worked with them. When Hendrik is able to drive them we will have them. He often asks, "Father, when are you going to buy horses?" Then I tell him, "When you are grown up." In May he will be twelve years old.

Everyone is well at Engbert's. His daughter is married and he has built a new house.

*   *   *

Write again and tell me how father is getting along. Is he still able to carry the burden of life? Is he looking forward to eternity?

[Closing]

May 12, 1888

Dear brothers and sisters,

We received your letter in good health and learned that you were all well but that our aged father had exchanged this temporal life for the eternal. God blessed us richly by allowing us to have our parents for such a long time, especially when so many fathers and mothers are taken away even before their children can know them.

*   *   *

Hendrika was married to a young man from the Netherlands. His name is A. J. Terbeek. He works in a [Grand Rapids] factory for $1.25 per day.

*   *   *

Our Hendrik was ill this week, but now he is sitting beside me and rocking with his legs crossed.

*   *   *

Everything continues as usual by our brothers.

*   *   *

If Father has left any bequests see to it that they are carried out fully. . . . Please be so good as to tell us how much interest we owe you and we will send it. If you wish to send your son here to use it that is also fine.

[Closing]

January 6, 1892

Dear brothers and sisters,

I have put off writing because we have been very busy this fall. We had good weather to clear the new land and plow it.

* * *

It is winter at present. Until Christmas we had mild weather and then for two days it was cold with snow. The summer was not unfruitful but not as warm as usual. We had frost in May at times. The wheat was already up, and then it froze so that it was sparse and short.

* * *

We can drive to Grand Rapids ourselves with our own tram. We have horses now. We traded our oxen for horses. We paid an extra $116.00, harnesses included. One is six years old and the other eleven; both strong animals. They are called Bill and Jim.

* * *

We are already enjoying the new land this summer. Last year we burned it over and I sowed grass seed in it which grew remarkably well this summer. We had thirteen loads of hay from three acres.

* * *

After butchering we still will have six head of cattle, two horses, two hogs, fifty chickens, and four beehives. Here the bees are kept in wooden boxes with a small slot at the top. Inside is a small box into which the bees bring the honey and when it is filled it is taken out and another put in. So we always have new honey. Many bees die in the winter. Some people say that they freeze but others say that they are idle so long that they smother. No one knows exactly. Mine have died twice. But now I have made hives like those in the Netherlands. I have three and I will see how they work out. Honey costs from ten to twelve cents a pound this summer—not as much as during cold weather when it was eighteen cents.

Everyone at Arendjan's is well. His son is taller than he. Everything is about as usual at Engbert's. His daughter is married to a fine farmer, his name is Andriesjan Eversen. He has four horses and a stable full of cattle.

Geertjen and I have been to Grand Rapids to visit Hendrika. Geertje and Hendrik stayed home alone.

I hear that everything is scarce and expensive in Holland and that there is a famine in Russia. If only those people were here where there is an abundance of everything for the support of this temporal life.

I thought that one of Levenkamp's sons might come here sometime. Are they not interested? If they were not satisfied they could return easily because young people earn an average of one to three dollars per week. That's enough to be able to return. Daily wages are $1.50 with work every day. A farmer's hired man earns $12.00 to $15.00 per month. Clothing is not expensive, from $8.00 to $20.00. And at times an entire suit complete with coat, vest and trousers can cost $40.00 to $60.00.

*   *   *

[Closing]

Just after I finished this letter Lamert Wassink came for a visit. He lives fifteen miles away and is a fine farmer. He has rented a place but he also owns forty acres, which he works. He is in good health. He has three sons and one daughter. His wife is very short of breath.

August 25, 1892

Dear brothers and sisters,

*   *   *

We understand from your letter that you have almost decided to come here for various reasons. I heartily approve because this is a land of plenty. Could you and Levenkamp each send one of your sons? Then they could look around for themselves. For young able men there are good prospects in the city and everywhere. If Levenkamp came here with his sons he would not have to work. But it is not so easy to become a farmer as it was twenty years ago. Land is much more expensive now. Today a forty-acre farm with a house and barn costs about $2,000. I place the value of my farm at about $2000.00, and you know that, even with the money I borrowed from you, I had only $600.00 when I arrived here. Today the land, house, barn, wagon, animals and the rest are debt-free. I had four beehives, but now I have eighteen. . . . So if you come here and get along as well as we did you will not be sorry. But acknowledge the Lord in all your ways and He will lead you along smooth paths.

You wrote about false preachers in the Netherlands. We have them here too but we regard them like pests. Our pastor has been back to the Netherlands this summer to bring back his father, mother, brother, and two sisters. He is a Frisian named Willem Pool.

* * *

The family is still about the same but we are getting weaker [with age]. This teaches us that we have here no abiding place.

[Closing]

June 27, 1893

Dear brothers and sisters,

We received your letter in good health but ... have noted that the Lord has caused a loss in your family by taking away a wife and mother—a great loss for father and children. But keep your courage up. Our heavenly Father is still the same, for as He visits us in preparation for eternity, He also promises us His love and the hope for a better future.

* * *

You asked about the Levenkamp boys who live in Iowa. That is a long distance from here. If Levenkamp writes to you, ask him to send us the address so I can write to his boys again. As I understand it [Iowa] is a good place with large farms and fruitful soil. There is not much woodland and they call that prairie land. Here in Michigan there is a lot of woodland. Getting it cleared is costly at first but it is also worth a good deal of money. It must be nice in the winter there because, I suppose, there is not much work to do.[1]

Geertjen has been in the city this winter. She is coming home Tuesday and Hendrik is going to get her from the station [the Interurban in Zeeland] ... six miles away.

We now have thirteen beehives. They did not swarm as well as last year. Last year we had honey from one swarm that weighed ninety-seven pounds (at nine cents per pound). Many bees die in the winter. I left fourteen standing and five had died.

[Closing]

1. Land clearing was usually done during the winter in Michigan.

November 18, 1895

Dear brothers, sisters, and cousins,

I am writing this letter on a snowy day. God has blessed us with very good health and we hope to hear the same from you. The summer has passed again with all of its happiness and sorrows.

It has been especially dry and warm here with the result that, at the end of July, everything was dried out—especially the pasture. And then the heavens gave rain to man and beast. It was, however, too late for the oats, but the grain grew well. There is an abundance of potatoes which cost between fifteen and twenty-five cents per bushel. I brought two loads to the city and it was hard to sell them at twenty-five cents. I still have about sixty bushels. I'll have to see if they sell better. Wheat costs sixty cents per bushel and oats cost twenty cents. Butter is sixteen cents a pound and a fat pig is four cents a pound. Cattle are also cheap because of the hay shortage. And I cannot sell the horses. We have three—nine, five, and three years old. We have five cows and a calf after selling two. We have four pigs and sixty or seventy chickens. We sold one hundred pounds of honey at ten cents per pound. There is no market for honey and one has to go directly to the customer who eats it.

Things go on as usual here. Hendrik is big and will be twenty years old. He is a strong and vigorous boy. Hendrika and Geertje are in the city. Hendrika has four children, but, with God's blessing, they have a good living. Jan Terbeek works at a railroad company where he earns sixteen cents per hour. Sometimes, but not very often, they have weeks when they work nine-hour days. Usually it's ten hours, which makes $1.60 per day. Geertje still works in the city at $2.00 per week [no doubt as a maid].

There is a lot of complaining in the city about low wages. It is not the same as twenty-five years ago when every working person made $2.00 daily. But the price of bread is also a bit less. Some people have done well but others have no more than when they came here. We have a family of three people and we have enough work to do. Besides we are getting old, sixty-five years. So the world is leaving us. We are depending on the blessed hope of eternity where God will rule over all who love Him.

*   *   *

Geertjen is spinning wool. And Hendrik and I go to the forest to saw wood and to clear the ground for planting. Many trees in our forest were burned. In that way they disappear quickly, and we get a bit more land every year.

Much of the work gets done easily. We cut the hay with a mower and with the horses we use a rake and a self-binder. For the wheat and oats we have nothing to do but set things up and then the threshing machine comes and in only half a day everything is done.

Just this past May we built an addition to our barn—about twenty-four feet. The barn is now sixty feet long and twenty-four feet wide. It is all finished with wooden boards. The floor also has thick wooden boards.

At Arendjan and Engbert's things go along as usual. We received two letters from the Levenkamp boys. We answered the first but not the last one. When you get this letter please write and tell us if Levenkamp is here also. Iowa is about seven hundred miles from here.

* * *

I must stop writing now. . . . Hendrik is going to catechism class and this letter will go with him to be mailed.

[Closing]

January 11, 1898

Dear brothers, sisters, nephews and nieces,

I am writing to tell you about conditions in America. . . . About one year ago we received a letter from the Levenkamp boys saying that their father, mother, and brothers might well be coming here this fall. Geertje was home at that time and wrote back to them. . . . Since then we have not heard anything from them. Now, it does not surprise me that they do not come here because we are at least two hundred hours [in walking time] away from them—at least six hundred miles. At three cents per mile the railway fare is $18.00 so $36.00 both ways. The cost is almost as much as going back to the Netherlands. So we didn't gain much in the distance between us. Still, to see each other again after a twenty-eight-year separation would certainly be an event. I don't think we would recognize one another. The trip is perhaps too costly for them and it is also quite difficult for us.

There are now just three of us at home. Geertje is a maid in Grand Rapids, and Hendrika is married to a man from Neede [Gelderland]. He has always had a rather good job—nine-hour days at sixteen cents an hour. Only Hendrik is here with us and we have much to do. But we are getting older. We have three horses—twelve, seven, and three years old. By April we will be milking six cows. Each morning we bring the milk to the creamery and return with the skimmed milk. So we are up at 7:00 A.M.. Hendrik makes the trip once a week in the winter and otherwise three times a week at 7:00 A.M.[1]

* * *

It's winter here now. Arendjan, his son Hendrik, and our Hendrik are in the woods sawing wood. The wooded area is getting smaller, and what remains of it is mostly burned dead to the stumps. Arendjan and I don't have much to do in the winter besides getting wood and splitting it.

We have four pigs—two fat and two with young. There is enough feed here—corn, wheat and oats, but potatoes were not so good. We didn't dig very many either. We sold sixty bushels at forty-five cents each. It's a dry fall and the winter wheat is mostly sown. We have nine acres of wheat this fall.

Fat pigs sell at forty-two and a half cents a pound and butter is fifteen cents. Creamery butter is one or two cents higher than self-churned butter. If we deliver the milk [to the creamery] we're not required to churn it.

Soon a young girl is coming here from Zelhem [Gelderland]. She is a niece of Engbert's wife. Engbert's wife died last April and now there are three of them with no wife—Engbert, Hendrik, and Harm. Hendrik is thirty-four years old and Harm is thirty-two and no marriage in sight. The girl is also a niece of Hendrikus Wassink. I don't know if he is still living. Someone from here is going to the Netherlands and he will bring the girl back with him. The man's name is Zuidsma. He has gone to get an inheritance and will return in the middle of February.

It was not pleasant news to hear that you have suffered so much with your leg, brother Willem, but we were happy to hear that you have recovered. There is much joy in this world but also much sadness. Sin is the source of all misery. Happily we have learned to know ourselves as poor sinners and to know Jesus as the rich Savior. Therefore, with God's help, we will overcome all the difficulties of life.

All is quite well at our brothers'. Engbert has lost his wife, and we grow old while she is in her grave. We are growing old. Arendjan is seventy-two, Engbert is seventy, and I am sixty-eight. So our life is behind us. We will have our pictures taken and send them to you in about four weeks. Engbert's son Harm takes the pictures.

Now, God's best blessing to you.

[Closing]

P.S. Father is tired of writing and he says that I must write once. I have never written a Dutch letter and it does not go as easily as English. The spelling is wrong at times but I think you can easily read it. I will close now and write more another time.

1. The local farmers took turns bringing the milk to the creamery.

June 27, 1900

Dear brother, sisters, and cousins,

*   *   *

It is a very warm and dry summer here. We are busy cutting hay with the machine and raking it up with the horse rake. The pasture is really beautiful here. We sowed it with a mixture of clover and timothy. When the timothy is good it will grow as high as wheat.

The wheat is doing very poorly. It will be ready in two weeks, but there are little insects that chew through the stalks until it is ripe. The rye is doing good and it grows on poor soil. The potatoes are doing nicely. The oats need much more rain. The bees have swarmed. We have fourteen hives. The trees are full of fruit.

*   *   *

Now about the money that sister Gerritje has promised to the poor. That is a very decent thing, but you had better keep it there because nobody in our congregation is in need of bread. Because they are farmers they do need money sometimes but that's another matter. We have two elderly people here who are helped once in a while but they are almost ninety-five years old. You wrote about her [Gerritje's] belongings. I don't know anything about that, but if you want to give them to Van Oltvoord, that is fine with me. You know the man better than I do so I give you my full permission to do what is right. May that be pleasing to God who knows our hearts. I understand from your letter that we will get a message from the notary but it has not come yet.

Our next-door neighbor now has the post office and that makes things better. We get a letter now on the same day that it arrives. Before we had to get it ourselves and sometimes it sat there for three to four days before we could get it. If I have forgotten anything, write us back soon. When I get the letter from the notary I will send back the answer and I will send you the exact same words.

[Closing]

January 11, 1901

Dear brother, sister, cousins, and friends,

*   *   *

I wanted to write you for a long time but I first wrote to Levenkamp and waited for a letter from them, but it never came. It is winter now but there is not much snow and it is not very cold yet.

*   *   *

We had a fruitful summer—enough rain but not too much. We have seven hundred bushels of grain, five hundred bushels of potatoes, and there was enough hay. We have seven milk cows and three heifers, two workhorses, and a two-year-old calf, six pigs—two for reproduction and four to fatten.

Financially things are getting better for farmers here. Sugar beets are raised here and there is a sugar factory in Holland, Michigan. Zeeland has a cucumber factory and celery is also a good crop for farmers here. At the creamery we make butter from sweet milk. It is one hour away and we go there daily with from seven to ten farmers taking turns. The milk is brought there every morning in the summer and every two days in the winter. This fall we earned $71.00 in three months. We don't produce other products for market because we don't have enough people. We are here with the three of us and at almost seventy-one I cannot work so much anymore. But I can't complain about weakness. I can hear well and see good with glasses. I'm fairly healthy and have a good memory. It is because of God's mercy that we are healthy and still here today. The world is behind us and eternity is before us with joyful expectation of the blessing which is prepared for us by our Savior Jesus Christ in whom all of God's promises are forever true.

Things go on as usual at Arendjan's. His wife passed away. His twenty-six-year-old son will get married in May. They have six cows and two horses. Arendjan is not strong anymore. His son is already too busy.

There is a young woman working at Engbert's. Engbert is still strong but very deaf. He has two boys.

Our Hendrika and Geertjen are in the city. Hendrika has six very healthy children. Geertjen works in a tailor shop. She earns $6.00 every week and sometimes $7.50. She earns ten cents extra for every hour of overtime. Our Hendrik will probably marry Dina Vruggink. She was born here but her parents are from Eibergen [in Overijssel near the eastern border of Gelderland].

[Closing]

January 14, 1903

Dear brother, sister, and cousins,

*   *   *

We are all fairly healthy, although Geertjen has been ailing and is not much better. . . . She has not felt good for the last two years and we have visited the doctor throughout the summer. She now takes some medicine called Dr. Peter's Zokoro. You can get it here but it works slowly.

For the rest, it is winter now and there is already much snow. It is not all that cold yet. We had much rain in the spring which did much damage to the summer fruits. We replanted the potatoes up until June 20, and they were the best. . . . We delivered three hundred bushels to Grand Rapids at fifty cents and later forty cents per bushel. The rye suffered much from the rain but we still grew about 178 bushels and 272 bushels of oats. We did not make much on the pigs. Nine died although we did butcher three and a small cow that drank more than its share of milk. We still have six to milk. Now we have two heifers, one is surely with young, and two calves from last May, so that makes ten. Two horses—one is seven and the other four years old. We sold one which was twelve years old.

Our household is unchanged. Our children have a young boy who is six months and very healthy. His name is Harm. Hendrika is in the city with her family—seven children. They live comfortably and own their own house. Her husband earns $1.60 per day. Geertjen is still single. She works in a clothing store and earns $1.00 for ten hours of work. She has to make her own living now. She will be living with her sister Hendrika. Arendjan is very weak and cannot work. He will be seventy-seven at the end of this summer. His son is married to the oldest daughter of Hendrikus Havighorst and they also have a very healthy son. Things are not so good at brother Engbert's. He also has a young grandson—four or five months old—who is always sick or ailing. Engbert is fairly strong but very deaf. As for me, I am not sick but I am almost seventy-three years old. . . . Our lives are behind us. But we do not have to work so much any more because God has blessed us both temporally and eternally.

* * *

Are any of your children married? If so, let us know so we can send something for the household. Everything is prosperous here. The prices are good and wages are higher than the last couple of years. Much is happening in the city too. Wages are $1.25 per day around here. It's good that we do not need many people to work for us. Farmhands get $18.00 to $20.00 per month. The butter brought a good price this summer. Every morning we bring the milk to the butter factory. We do that with the ten of us so that Henry only goes once every ten days. That takes about half of a day. We get our money every month. For several months we received $29.00. Butter is now twenty-five cents but we have sold it for as little as eleven or twelve cents. Eggs also were twelve, fourteen, and sixteen cents but now are twenty-four cents.

[Closing]

June 1, 1903

Dear brother, sister, nephews, and nieces,

Circumstances make it necessary for me to write because a member of our family was snatched away after an illness of two years. . . . She suffered from a nervous condition and the doctors could do nothing for her. It continued until ten o'clock when Geertjen died on May 24. She suffered a great deal during the last two months with severe headaches. We could not understand much of what she said during the final week. At the end she was very calm and passed away peacefully in the hope that we will see each other again in the blessed heaven where there is no death, sin or misery. . . . Preparation for eternity is mankind's principal purpose here on earth. We live but once. May all of us take this to heart.

Geertjen was sixty-nine years old and I am seventy-three. We were married for forty years and together we bore both weal and woe—whatever God's hand caused us to experience.

We thank the Lord that he spared us into our old age and that we were able to live together in love and peace and that we were able to see our grandchildren.

I am old and have not much more to live for in the world. The world does not have much to offer.

Everything continues on the same at Arendjan's and Engbert's.

[Closing]

December 3, 1903

Dear brother, sister, nephews, and nieces,

[Lengthy report on harvest yields, prices, and weather.]

All three of us [the brothers] are old, so we are paying less attention to the world because we will not live much longer. We are all in our seventies and our physical energy is waning. Age brings its many infirmities. But I still have many advantages—good hearing, good sight with glasses, a good mind, and a strong faith in our heavenly Father who will not forsake us in our old age. I can't do much work anymore but that is not necessary either because the Lord has blessed us abundantly in this land of our sojourn.

Our family consists of four—our Hendrik, his wife Dena Vruggink, and our seventeen-month-old little boy. He is very lively.

Arendjan is failing. He can't do much work anymore. His son is married to a daughter of Havighorst. They have a son. Engbert is very deaf.
His son is also married and they have two children.

Hendrika is in the city. Her husband works at a garage and earns $1.75
per day. His son also works there and earned $20.00 a month this fall.
But that is no longer permitted because he is not yet sixteen years old.
He was required to go to school because they do not like ignorant people
here.

It is too bad that more people do not come here because there is plenty
of land and an abundance of work. Hired men earn $20.00 to $25.00 a
month.

*   *   *

It will soon be time to pay our taxes, which cost about $25.00 per year.
A person in each town is appointed to collect the taxes and he is paid
one cent for every dollar paid. A person who pays later must pay an extra
four cents on each dollar. Both Engbert and Hendrik have had that office
which is always for a two-year term. That pays all of our taxes including
school money for the children even for those who have six or eight
children. Education is expensive here. There are sometimes two teachers—a man who sometimes earns $50.00 a month and a woman to teach
the small children for $25.00 to $30.00 during the nine months of school.
That amounts to quite a bit each year. The state government pays $1.00
for each child per year. The upkeep of the school is extra for the district—things like stoves, fuel, carpentry, and painting. There is a school
every three miles so that no child is required to walk more than a mile
and a half.

I must close now because the mail car goes past our house every day
at twelve o'clock noon.

We still have bees but that is no longer very successful because the
woods are being cut down.

I do not know if sister Janna is still living. I wrote to her a year ago
but received no answer. Ask about her when you go to Borculo. I don't
know where she lives.

[Closing]

December 29, 1904

Dear brother, sister, nephews, and nieces,
    [Report on crops, weather, prices and livestock.]
    At Arendjan's things are much like our house—a son with a young

wife and a two-year-old grandson. Arendjan is very weak and at times cannot take care of himself.

At Engbert's everyone is well, but the young people have no children. They had two but both died. . . . I cannot complain of illness but I am becoming much weaker. I still keep busy in the fields and in the barn feeding hogs, watering the calves, taking care of bees, and other work when Hendrik is not at home. People do not keep bees as much as they did because the woods are gone.

Gerrit Levenkamp visited us this spring. He had been to Chicago with a load of fattened cattle. Then he was one hundred and fifty miles from here. Everything is done on a large scale in Chicago—dealing in cattle.

This week we had a letter from them. They were all well. They had good crops and good prices. They had over one hundred pigs, which they sell live from the pens to be shipped by the carload to Chicago. They sold for $4.40 to $4.60 per hundred pounds.

Verbeek is still in the city [Grand Rapids] with his family. They have children. The oldest son is already working in the factory. He earns $1.00 per day. He is sixteen years old and does not have to go to school. Geertjen is still at the tailor's and earns ten cents an hour working ten hours daily and sometimes twelve or thirteen hours.

Now write back and tell me about your family—whether you have work for all your children or whether they must go out to work. If they go out for work and if they are interested I think they should come here because good wages are paid here—$18.00 to $20.00 a month for anyone who can plow or handle machinery. There is work here for all who want it. People work from 7:00 A.M. to 6:00 P.M. with an hour of rest at noon.

The land is becoming more expensive every year. Two years ago a neighbor named Haan bought forty acres for $2,000 and this year he sold it again for $2,400. For anyone who wishes to go farther west there is government or state land available for almost nothing. Out there homesteads are granted. Anyone who is a citizen can get eighty acres for practically nothing. He must live on it for five years and then he becomes the owner.

[Closing]

November 1906

Dear brother, sister, nephews, and nieces,

We are reasonably well. The summer is past and the winter is at the door.

[Crop report.]

We now have a cheese factory in the neighborhood which makes butter from the cream and cheese from the milk. It is nearby and brings in some money for us. Last month, $38.00. The farmers are better off than they have been for the last ten to twenty years. But wages are also higher, $1.50 for ten hours of work. The corn is picked by machine now. That costs three and a half cents per bushel and then the stalks are also cut up.

Our young people now have two sons—one four and a half years old and the other eight months. The older is Harm and the younger is Garrit. A great deal is now done by machinery here—a hay mower, a self-binder, a sowing machine, a double cultivator, a horse fork (which is a harpoon to take the hay from the wagon). It is stuck into the wagon and then the wagon is empty after three or four times.

Becoming a farmer is not as easy as it was thirty years ago. The land is more expensive because there are no more woods. Forty acres here sells for over $1,000, which ten or twelve years ago could be bought for $200 or $300. Then you must have buildings, and forty acres is not enough to support cattle.

Arendjan's son Hendrik sold his land for $2,750. Now he has bought the farm of his father-in-law, Havighorst. He had another son-in-law who had no interest in the land and he has now moved away. Now Hendrik has better land. Havighorst is weak and he trembles so that he cannot hold a cup of coffee to his lips. Hendrik still had many pine stumps on his old land. They are bad beasts. We have had some pulled out at fifty cents apiece. These stumps do not decay. There are no stumps on Havighorst's land.

Jan Verbeek and Hendrika have eight children but they make a good living. Both he and the boys make $20.00 a week and one of the girls also works out sometimes for $2.00 a week. Geertjen is still single. She works now for a tailor earning $8.00 a week. Wages for a hired man are from $18.00 to $24.00 a month. A maid earns $2.00 to $4.00 per week. They can even afford a gold ring on their fingers, but then they don't have much gold in their hands.

Things are about the same at Engbert's. He had two grandchildren but they both died. Engbert is so deaf that it is difficult to have a conversation with him. Otherwise he is well, but he is seventy-nine years old and I am seventy-seven. So our lives are hastening to an end. It is fortunate that we are here because this is a land of plenty for old and young. In His goodness God has blessed us in this alien land. This life is but a journey to eternity, a preparation during a brief life for the coming of our souls' bridegroom.

[Closing]

Harm Avink [Jr.] to R. W. Bouwmeester Family
Blendon, Michigan, to Lochem, Gelderland
February 28, 1909

Dear Uncle, Aunt, and cousins,

I am writing to inform you that our loving father exchanged the temporal for the eternal on February 18 at the advanced age of seventy-nine years and eight days. He had been ailing for two years. On May 24 it will be six years ago that Mother died and on March 24 it will be four years ago that Uncle Arendjan died. It was two years ago last January that my Uncle Engbert Avink died.

Greetings to all of you. Write back soon to let us know that you received this letter. This is the first Holland letter that I have written. It certainly has errors enough but I am sure you can read it.

We have been married for eight years and have two sons—Harm, six, and Georgie three years of age.

[Closing]

4   Frederik Diemer Family

Frederik Diemer arrived in Vogel Center, Michigan, one year before the first letter of this series was written. His native hamlet, Hollandscheveld, stood near the edge of Hoogeveen in the province of Drenthe, an area known for its peat beds and sandy soils. Turfs, dug there for fuel, found markets along the route of an intricate canal system. The sandy soil, enriched by peat and manure until chemical fertilizers became generally available during the second half of the century, supported moderately successful agriculture. Beyond subsistence, local farms produced a surplus of potatoes, butter, and some grain.

The north-central area of Michigan where Frederik Diemer settled resembled his native village in several respects. The sandy soils of both regions were only moderately productive, and although Vogel Center lacked commercially useful peat beds, its forest, like peat, provided employment and a convenient source of fuel. Moreover, as reclaimed peat lands had once provided an agricultural frontier in the Netherlands,

These letters were donated by C. J. Diemer vander Esch, 1985, and first translated by Herbert Brinks. The original letters were transcribed in the Netherlands.

Logging near Vogel Center, Michigan, about 1900. Courtesy of Calvin College Library Archives, photo collection.

Michigan's woodlands were the primary area for the state's agricultural expansion in the 1890s.[1]

Frederik's father, the Reverend Evert Diemer, pastored a small and generally poor Hollandscheveld congregation that was affiliated with the seceded Christelijk Gereformeerde Kerk. In all likelihood he received the abundant respect with which sectarian church groups are inclined to mantle their prophets, but his economic status was little better than that of the farmhands and turf diggers who occupied his pews. His four children could expect no handsome inheritance, and without an advantage of that sort the Netherlands offered little economic opportunity, particularly if they hoped to become independent farmers.[2]

It appears that Frederik Diemer arrived in Vogel Center with enough funds to acquire a twenty-acre farmstead, and he began to clear it immediately. That purchase exhausted his funds, and he sought wage-paying work of varied kinds. He lumbered, carpentered, and dug wells or ditches while clearing the land for his first crops. By 1910 he acquired an additional eighty-acre plot of adjacent stump land. But he

---

[1] Van der Aa, *Aardrijkskundig woordenboek* 5:7771–72; Lucas, *Netherlanders in America*, pp. 302–4; Dick Scheanwald, *McBain Centennial, 1977* (Privately published, 1977), p. 56.

[2] Joh. de Haas, *Gedenkt uw voorgangers* (Haarlem, Netherlands: Vijlbrief, 1984), 1:84–85.

was never able to live entirely from farming and he continued to contract carpenter work until his death in 1928. In fact, his death resulted from a construction-site accident.

The Sikkens family had migrated to Vogel Center several years before Frederik, and Dina Sikkens became Frederik's wife in 1894, the year after he immigrated. During their thirty-three-year marriage, the Diemers had eleven children with whose help they managed a farm that had grown to 120 acres by 1923. After Frederik died in 1928 two adult children remained at home to work the farm, but older siblings had moved to other places in Michigan.[3] The agricultural depression of the 1920s had severely limited economic opportunities around Vogel Center, as Frederik Diemer noted in 1927: "At present conditions are much more favorable in the cities than in the country and on farms. . . . Earlier, many individuals came from the cities to work in the woods during the winter. That is all in the past and now the opposite is true."

Frederik Diemer to the Reverend Evert and Annigje Kerssies Diemer Family
Vogel Center, Michigan, to Schoonoord, Drenthe
September 13, 1894

Dearly beloved parents, brothers, and sister,

By God's grace I am still in good health. It is at present very difficult to earn any money. I am making wooden railroad ties. These are beams under the railroad track. I make a dollar a day, paying my own expenses. I get seven cents apiece. I leave in the morning and return at night. All day long I am all alone, chopping in the woods, and see no one. H. Schoo is not content with that kind of work and he plans to move to the state of Missouri. What will the outcome be? No one is standing in his way. He has by this time made himself odious everywhere.

I have cleared about two acres of my own land. That means cutting down and burning the trees. The stumps remain for a few years. But a person can raise crops around them. If my plans do not change and all is well next year, I will plant potatoes in all of it. If things work out favorably, about 300 bushels might be harvested. A bushel now costs thirty to fifty cents. For now these are only plans.

My purse is as thin as can be after losing $30 in camp last winter and not having had a very successful summer or fall. I have a little left here and there, but things will probably come out all right if I continue to be

[3] Anne Hoeksema and Alfred Diemer, interview by author, March 12, 1991, telephone notes in Frederik and Dina Diemer Papers, Immigrant Letter Collection.

Main Street, Vogel Center, Michigan, about 1900. Courtesy of Calvin College Library Archives, photo collection.

in good health. I must make about 1,000 wooden ties. I began a couple of days ago. I could not begin sooner because of terrible forest fires. But now it has rained for a couple of days, which was very sorely needed. And as a result the fires were put out.

I received your letter of August 6 in good health. You say I did not answer your letters of June 28 and July 7. What were they about? Was that the letter in which you asked me about sending money? I have not answered that. If you were rich I would have been pleased to accept. But I know you need it badly too. I can also use it very well but I can get along without it. I get plenty to eat, and my clothes, at least those I wear every day, are a bit shabby, but the others are still too good to be used as work clothes.

As soon as I can save $100 I am going to get married. It is possible to earn enough here for food, wheat, and pork at almost any time. To get started—a small house and necessary furniture—that is a problem. We are both completely prepared for it, even though money for the morrow has to fall out of the air, and then I will have a home of my own. If times had not been so bad, and they still are, and if I had received my money last winter, maybe we would have been married already. We will see how things turn out. We will leave it in the Lord's hands.

The crop has been very poor this summer. Hardly anyone has anything to sell. And it appears that it will be a hard winter. Wherever there is work I am sure to be there, whatever it is. I do not care what kind of

Potato harvest in northern Michigan about 1913. Courtesy of Calvin College Library Archives, photo collection.

work it is: carpentry, digging, chopping, sawing—it makes no difference. As you see, I can adjust to any type of job. I have even been a well digger for a couple of days. And in that way I get along. When I have nothing to do I work on my own land and I work three days a week for my board. At this moment I still have thirty-five cents in my purse and I do not know when I will have more. I will not receive pay for making railroad ties until the beginning of next year.

Do not worry about me for I would not want to go back to the old country if I were offered twice as much money as the trip would cost. I have enough to eat but there is a scarcity of money. But I can always whistle while I work, and sing, and be thankful that I am in America. As soon as I am married and can make the arrangements, Hendrik [his brother] can come over if he wants to. There will be something for him to eat also in America. And if Grietina [his sister] has a desire to do so, she can also come along. I think that in the long run it is better in America than in the Netherlands.

If Geert [his brother] is not at home send him my greetings, and Hendrik, too. Geert asked me for a better photograph but there is no money available. That would cost about $6 all together. He mistakenly thought I had the photographs.

Greetings from me and Dina,
Frederik

January 2, 1897

Dear parents, brothers, and sister,

First of all I wish to apologize for having forgotten Father's birthday so shamefully. I don't want you to think we have forgotten you, but I thought of it too late and then I put it off. The evenings are not as long here as you think.

I work in the woods nowadays, and then I leave the house at 6:30 and come back in the evening at about 6:30. You know, don't you, that the days are longer in the winter and shorter in the summer than where you are.

I should have written to you about Dina's birthday. I had written that letter after Dina had gone to bed and I did not want to wake her for the exact information and then it slipped my mind. But now here it is— Dina's birthday is on January 9. She will be twenty-three years old.

Jan Trijs and I have taken on a job in the woods, namely, to cut down trees, saw them up, and then bring them to the river. In the spring they are floated to Muskegon. The latter we do not do. Jan Trijs came to America with his parents as a child, but thinks he remembers hearing you preach in Nieuw Amsterdam or Nieuw Dordrecht or thereabouts.

This spring Dina got a small baby buggy, but it is not used in the winter time; then it is upstairs.

Our second hog is already in the barrel, you would call it a vat. The third one will be allowed to grow until the price of pork is higher again. Our hogs were not very heavy. I think the last one weighed about 150 pounds, but it was very fat. Here we eat as much pork and beef as we like, but then you can well imagine that not much else is eaten.

Farmers who sell hogs get only $3.75 for 100 pounds.

Meanwhile I almost forgot to wish you a blessed New Year. May the Lord cause his light to shine on your pathway, and that you may be drawn closer and closer to him, and may you have peace and quiet as you travel on toward the life everlasting. May he also provide for your material needs.

Evert has grown so much that we can hardly keep our eye on him, for he gets his nose into everything everywhere. He is a real smarty.

When we have enough money, we still plan to send you our photograph, but I think times will not be much better after the election. All products are still going down in price and we see almost no cash.

Receive greetings from all of us. We were pleased to receive Geert's letter.

[Closing]

March 7, 1897

Dear parents,

Alas! I delayed writing too long. The winters here are not as pleasant as in the Netherlands. Here it is only a time to work, and usually far from home. During the whole winter I left the house in the morning before six and returned at seven in the evening. There has been quite a bit of work this winter but the wages are low. A person cannot expect more than fifty to sixty cents daily. I think economic conditions are getting worse rather than better. I do not think it is advisable for people who are making a living in Holland to come here, especially those who are afraid of doing a little work. If I did not stick my nose in every place where some money could be made, I would not have been able to exist. Sometimes with a spade, sometimes with an axe, sometimes with a saw, and then with a plane, and I don't know what else. Our well is not drilled but dug and then lined with four-foot-long boards that are joined together. It is about twenty-five feet deep and that is surprisingly satisfactory.

Our new church is still unfinished as it was last spring, but the plan is to go on with the job again this spring. Most of the Groninger fellows [visitors from Groningen province] are already back in the Netherlands. Rev. Jan Schepers is about the same. I could tell you about him, but I prefer to say nothing.

The manure from the cattle is quite necessary for this land, just as it is in your case, but since the cows roam about along the roads and in the woods, little can be done to collect it. Here only the cream is churned [and sold].

We live about a mile and a half from church. That is a half hour trip. We're two miles from Dina's parents. It has not been a very favorable winter here. There was not enough snow, although just now we have more on the ground than we had all winter.

Jan Haveman wrote me a letter. He is in Hull, Iowa, and is still working for a farmer. He did not look around much either. I do not know where B[erend] van der Heide is. I have not heard from him for more than a year. If Dina were not so attached to this place, I would also look around to see if I could not find a better area.

Evert is very lively, and is beginning to talk, saying "papa," "mama," "bread," "more," and so on. You, Mother, will easily imagine such matters.

You will receive this letter some time before Mother's birthday, although I do not know when it will be mailed. I congratulate Mother in advance on her birthday, and I wish the very best for her, more than I can write or say.

I have no reason for complaint. The Lord is still good to us. We all send our greetings.

[Closing]

April 23, 1897

Dear parents, brothers, and sister,

It is high time for me to write again. Even though we do not write so often, we are always pleased to receive your letters.

Conditions in America are not improving as Father supposes, but such news is written from a one-sided viewpoint. Everything is dormant and almost everyone suffers from lack of money, and that is the reason nowadays, I am working for about half of the regular wage—if one receives cash. I think more homestead land will be made available here soon, and then, if I can get some good land, I will give up carpentry. A person cannot make a living at it, and my present twenty acres are not enough for farming. If I wish to be a farmer I need eighty acres.

Evert is growing nicely. Dina is quite sickly and weak. She is up and around but that is about all. People have not yet begun farm work. In the Netherlands I imagine they have already planted potatoes. You had better ask a lot of questions in your letters, otherwise I don't know how to tell what is of interest to you.

This winter things have gone quite well. We have not earned much but enough for a person to get along. At present things are beginning to grow, but we have had frost for a couple of days, as if it were still midwinter.

I think you know that Jan Haveman has written to me. He is still a hired man on a farm, but I hear nothing from Berend van der Heide. We have not been to Lucas [a nearby village], where H. Schoo now lives. A. Meijering and Betje have been here a couple of times. It is too far to walk, and to rent a horse and carriage is too expensive.

I don't know what the emigrants leaving the Netherlands for America can expect. A single person can usually get along, and also someone who is already somewhat acquainted with conditions. But for a poor newcomer with a family to come to America in these times does not seem advisable. I am not saying this lightly, but as I see it and as my conscience dictates. I see no objection in the case of a young person like Hendrik, except for a few difficulties at first.

* * *

[Closing]

June 13, 1897

Dear parents, brothers, and sister,

I have delayed writing for a long time. That is because of the busy season. My crops are in the ground—corn, potatoes, and last fall a couple of acres of wheat. Presently we are busily building the church. It was open to the public for bids, so three of us carpenters, members of the congregation, got together and accepted the job for $160, that is for labor only. The job must be finished by August 1. Before I forget, I must tell you that the other carpenters are Romke van der Heide (Wielenga's friend) and Piet de Vos (a son-in-law of Rev. J. Schepers, and a real know-it-all). I think we can make a reasonable wage.

Dina is never very strong, and it seems the doctors here can't do much about it. And in addition, Mother [i.e., Dina] guesses that we will have another child in September.

Evert is always well, has a fine ruddy complexion, has a suntan, is active, and not very large or heavy. He drinks an enormous amount of milk, and likes his egg in the morning. He already asks for breakfast before he gets up. Usually he gets up with us at five o'clock in the morning and takes a nap around noon. He is beginning to talk a little, but he is a bit slow in this. Otherwise he is sharp and very imitative. His little legs are as straight as a candle. In the summer he goes barefoot, as is the custom here. When I get home in the evening, he meets me to carry my dinner pail.

Rev. J. Schepers is at present very happy about the new church. He comes over almost every day to look things over. There will not be a raised pulpit but a platform. The windows are of stained glass.

Weather Report

It has been cold here for a long time. Now it is beginning to warm up. We are free from frost here for about three months, so the crops must ripen during that time, and they do if the weather is favorable.

We have three hogs in the pen again. We have the best cow in the neighborhood. But I had to travel twelve miles to get her.

You see we have no reason to complain, but abundant reason to be thankful to God for all that He grants us beyond our desires. May He also impart His blessings richly to our hearts, in order that we may find peace with Him through Jesus Christ.

[Closing]

August 5, 1897

Received by us August 19

Dear parents, brothers, and sister,

I shall try to write sooner in the future and not wait as long.

We are sorry we have made you wait so long; we have a guilty conscience. But you will probably begin to think that no news means everything is going well. And that is true under the circumstances. I am very busy this summer doing carpenter work. We have finished our church. After that four of us carpenters contracted to build a bridge for $100. We each earned $21 in nine days. Now I am building a new house.

Our crops look pretty good. The wheat has been harvested but not yet threshed. I think we will have about enough for my own use. Of course it is threshed by a machine, which goes from farm to farm. The cost of threshing is 3½ cents per bushel.

I bought a new sewing machine for Dina. It cost $19.50. It is a good treadle machine and she is very happy with it.

We went about that bridge job in a typical American fashion. It was 15 miles from home. We set up a canvas tent like the gypsies, and we had bread, eggs, potatoes, etc. with us. And then we simply built a little fire outside of the tent to cook our food; firewood is available everywhere. At night we each rolled up in a blanket and slept on the ground. Hendrik would think this was an adventure, but what was not so pleasant was that we often had to wade in the river. But you have to take the bitter with the sweet.

We thank Mother for her motherly best wishes. I think just as Mother does: we can be thankful if we can feed our children and bring them up in the fear of the Lord.

Dina says that I must write to say that she has a large number of blooming house plants of all kinds—(which is a pleasure in the summer and a delight in the winter).

Evert is growing steadily. He is beginning to talk well, is potty trained, and goes to bed while still wide awake in the evening. Up until now we have him quite well under control, but we have not spared the rod when necessary. He comes to meet me when I come home in the evening.

We are getting along well this summer and have no complaints.

[Closing]

Frederik Diemer to Geert and Martje Diemer
Vogel Center, Michigan, to Schoonoord, Drenthe
June 6, 1904

Dear brother and sister[-in-law],

I herewith congratulate you heartily on your marriage. We are really happy about it. We wish you a happy and blessed married life, and hope you may both labor in the Lord's vineyard with zeal and blessings.

We thank you for the picture of our new sister. Dina has saved it carefully with yours, although that is a photo from a time when you were little more than a mischievous boy.

Now, when you write again, you must tell us how things are in your country ecclesiastically. Is there as much of a controversy between the Free University and Kampen?[1] Where is the theological seminary of the Christian Reformed Church? You undoubtedly belong to the Gereformeerde Church. And Father also?

Dina says you should write and tell us whether you had a pleasant wedding, and about all who were there.

Now I would like to give you some advice, since I can speak from experience. Plan to be thrifty, for if you have five healthy children in a short time, as we did, your needs will be far greater than you can imagine.

You have probably heard from Father and Mother that a fifth child was born to us. This time it is a fine girl.

You would enjoy seeing your namesake sometime, such a heroic little chap, with a voice loud enough for two people, but a little stubborn.

I would write more if I had time. If you have time you had better write more often. I wrote three letters this evening, one to Father and Mother, to Gr[ietina, married and living in Hoogeveen], and to you. Now I should also write to H[endrik, living in Amsterdam], but I do not even know his address.

[Closing]

1. These two theological schools, one in Kampen and the other in Amsterdam, served the Gereformeerde (Reformed) denomination, which was an 1892 amalgamation of two groups that split from the national church earlier in the nineteenth century. The Christian Reformed Church in the Netherlands refused to join the 1892 fusion.

May 10, 1905

Dear brother and sister,

The financial panic of last fall has not yet been overcome. There is still a great deal of unemployment in the cities. We do not notice much of it here in the country. And this is the year for a presidential election when four or five individuals declare their candidacy. Such a year is usually a tense year with businesses and trades suffering. The contest is often bitter. Speakers of all parties travel across the country. What one declares to be good, the other in turn claims to be bad. A person who does not follow the course of events becomes completely confused. In our county and in the neighboring one we have outlawed saloons in the spring election.

We are all well.
    Greetings, and commending you to God,
                                    Your brother,
                                    Frederik

Letter Summary
October 8, 1903

We received a letter from Frederik, in America, which reports that he
and his family are doing well. There is ample employment and wages
are high. He earns two dollars a day. The summer was an exceptionally
damp and wet one. Most of the clay potatoes rotted, but the sand potatoes, his included, turned out very well.

His oldest sons go to school together. They also have their own minister, who had preached his inaugural the previous Sunday [the Reverend
John Walkotten's first pastorate, 1903–1905]. Frederik was very well
pleased with him. He was a candidate.

This is an example of the summaries of F. Diemer's letters which were passed around
among his parents and siblings.

Frederik Diemer to Evert and Annigje Kerssies Diemer Family
Vogel Center, Michigan, to Schoonoord, Drenthe
October 20, 1910

Dear parents, brothers, and sister,
    Well, congratulations to all of you on the little Grietina. Our wish is
that she may grow up in good health.
    We congratulate Father on his seventy-sixth birthday. Our wish is that
the Lord may continue to spare you, and that you may become better
prepared day by day here on earth for the Father's home above. May He
grant both of you many more happy years of life.
    The children are all well. Hendrik is a real rascal. He walks and roams
everywhere, and when he sees one of us leave the house, we have to be
careful because he follows us as fast as he can. And keeps it up.
    We are having a beautiful spring here. The fall crops turned out quite
well. Mother asked whether I was satisfied with my new land. Much
needs still to be cleared because it is lumbered woodland [that is, with
stumps still in place]. I have not rented it but bought it. I had to take
out a mortgage for $375, but it is registered in my name. Carpenter work
was a bit slow this summer.

Greetings from Father and Mother [Sikkins, Dina's parents], too. They are both still quite spry.

Father must not forget "Michigan" on our address in the future. It seems they had quite a bit of trouble finding us from New York the last time. They had filled in the address with red ink there themselves, and printed another red stamp on it, but it turned out all right.

[Closing]

Evert and Frederik Diemer to Evert and Annigje Kerssies Diemer
Family
Vogel Center, Michigan, to Schoonoord, Drenthe
[November] 1910

Dear Grandfather and Grandmother,
I wish you a happy New Year. We are still all well at present. There is much snow on the ground already, and it is cold, too.

I, Ebble, Geert, Frank, and Annigje go to catechism every week. I learn from a little book of simple Bible truths.

We have worked on the farm all the time this summer. Father and I have been sawing wood every day on the new piece of ground. We still have our horse. We have three cows. We had two hogs but we butchered them last fall. There are quite a few sheep around here but no goats. The chickens are doing well. We get about five dozen eggs a day. They are thirty-six cents a dozen here.

It is time now for me to end my letter. It is quite cold today and it is snowing quite a bit.

Your grandson Evert

Dear parents, Geert, and Martje,[1]
I shall add a short letter. We hope you have had a pleasant Christmas, and we wish you a blessed New Year. Mother wrote that Father has trouble with rheumatism. Well, I have it quite badly too, especially when the weather changes.

Mother asks whether we rent our farm. No, it is our property, but we do still have a debt of $375.

The winter has set in quite early and it is very cold. We do not hear much about poverty and a lack of daily needs but that is a problem in the cities.

The children are all very well and active as of now, Hendrik included.

It seems that he is getting to be quite a real scamp. He imitates everyone, and gets into everything, especially where he is not supposed to be.

Now I will close for this time, and wish you all the Lord's indispensable blessings.

Frederik

1. The parents have moved in with Geert and Martje.

Frederik Diemer to Evert Diemer Family
McBain, Michigan, to Hoogeveen, Drenthe
March 10, 1913

Dear father, brothers and sister, and family,

We received Father's letter in a reasonable state of health. It is true, as Father writes, there is quite often a good deal of irregularity in a large family. At the present time my wife and Evert have what I think are symptoms of influenza and they have trouble swallowing. Dina's father and mother are, as far as we know, in good health.

I thought I had previously given you the name of our minister. He is Theodorus Wilhelmus Rudolf vanhetloo—a long double name that he says is foolishness. So he has dropped the double name for all his children except one. In the Netherlands his father was a minister of the Christian Seceded Church but here he accepted a call from the Reformed Church in America. His son Theodore, our minister, preferred to study at the Christian Reformed Church seminary in Grand Rapids. So he is a minister of the CRC. He is a man without special talents and does not have an attractive character. Still, he is very serious and even somewhat melancholy in the pulpit. Father, you ask me if I have ever read a sermon for worship service here. Yes, that has happened. The first time I naturally offered a short prayer and read a short sermon so the entire service lasted only an hour. I dreaded it, and I prayed a good deal about it, but after I got started it was not too bad. Next Sunday our minister is scheduled to be gone again but then we still have a preaching turn due to us from our neighboring congregation of Lucas, and probably Rev. P. van Vliet will preach here.

I am clerk of the church council now and am also in charge of the salary fund. So I am quite busy, and besides, we elders must go to Muskegon to attend the classis.¹ That takes about three days of time. I feel that I am a bit too young to be an elder, at least when it comes to admonishing the elderly. May the Lord give me the necessary ability, and confidence.

The weather is very changeable here—cold and then warm with storms and wind. There are many misfortunes at times from storms and floods. We have been spared remarkably, but in other states many thousands have lost their lives.

[Closing]

1. A governing body of proximately located congregations—in this case the Classis of Muskegon.

September 1, 1913

Dear father, brothers and sister, and family,

I have received Father's letter, and, as you advised, I have immediately sent a letter to W. Masselink [Grietina's husband] and Grietina, and have asked Willem to represent me at Hoogeveen at the distribution of the inheritance [from Frederik's aunt Hendrickje Botter-Kerssies, his mother's sister]. It was very unexpected since I had never thought of anything like that. Can Father make an estimate how much this might amount to for each of us?

* * *

We are all still reasonably well, and hope the same for you. The summer crops, beans, corn, and potatoes, look quite promising, so we expect a good harvest. We have had a great deal of stormy weather this summer, and many buildings were struck by lightning around here. God has mercifully spared us.

I gave our minister your greetings but he did not ask me to give you his greetings. He has little tact in getting along with people. He does not seem to know how, and as a result he has few friends. His preaching is not bad but he can not associate with young people. Also a current controversy about the baptism of children whose parents are not confessing members has kept many people from making a public profession of faith.

On the whole there is a prevailing lack of life in our churches. If God does not bring about a change, I think our church will rapidly become Americanized. This emphasis upon positively not baptizing children of nonconfessing members is causing offense and is detrimental to church life.[1]

[Closing]

1. According to a traditional Netherlandic view, infant baptism was a sufficient basis for church membership, and the baptism of children born to parents who maintained only baptismal memberships was permitted. The issue bears similarities to New England's "half-way covenant" controversy.

Frederik Diemer to Geert Diemer Family
McBain, Michigan, to Roden, Drenthe
May 17, 1923

Dear brother, nieces, and nephews,

You will certainly be a bit annoyed with me, and you really have a right to be. My definite plan was to write back immediately, but I do not have a separate study where I can sit down and write or study when I get around to it. Everything has to be done in the midst of the family circle or after everyone has gone to bed. Well, this evening I once more thought about you and my own negligence. I thought to myself, now no more delay, and so I have begun.

A hearty thanks for your congratulations and also for the photograph that we have received from you recently.

I am glad that you feel at home in Roden [in Drenthe province], and that things are going along smoothly in the congregation [Geert was pastor, 1923–1926]. I have seen in the papers that there are many more church groups in the Netherlands than when I was still there—at least I did not know about them. People secede or their membership is canceled for reasons of minor importance. Is that not surprising, brother, since they all base their reasons upon the Bible. (Have you ever made a study of premillennialism[1] without prejudice? That requires as much literal interpretation of the Bible as possible, which our church interprets spiritually altogether too much.)

I have also received a letter from Grietina and have answered her. Oh, how much of our earthly lives is accompanied by trials and adversities, and when we allow our feelings to have the upper hand, we often think our situation is worse than anyone else's. Fortunately, whether living or dying, we can entrust ourselves to the care of divine providence, believing the word of our Savior: "in the world ye shall have tribulation, but be of good cheer; I have overcome the world" [John 16:33b].

Do you still have stomach trouble? Dina suffers from it also.

Three of our boys are away from home. One of them, the second, is married and a son was born to him recently. So I am now a grandfather. The oldest works in Detroit, and the third in Cadillac. The fourth is at home and helps on the farm. (This consists of 120 acres, with three horses, nine cows and calves, some hogs, and chickens.)

Now I think I have covered everything. You already know that, except for Dina, we are still all well.

Dina will read this over, and will find that I have forgotten something, but we will save that for another time.

With hearty greetings and commending you to God,

[Closing]

1. Teachings about various periods of world history with predictions about the return of Christ.

June 8, 1924

Dear brother and family,

It just occurred to me that I have neglected to answer your letter in which you congratulated me on my birthday. Now this was not a case of being unappreciative, but I am no longer accustomed to writing. Dina usually does all of the writing to the children, and now I dread doing it. Sometimes I cannot find pen and ink, and then I do not like the paper, then again there are no envelopes in the house, etc.

I thank you heartily for your best wishes, and with all my heart I wish you all the blessings of the Lord, particularly in your profession. When everything is following its normal course, we cannot write much news to one another. You are unfamiliar with things here and we there. Besides, the daily papers keep us informed about the news on both sides. Everything happens so fast. Things that happen in the most remote parts of the world we read a day or two later in the paper.

We here are in reasonable health, except for Dina, who still has a great deal of stomach trouble. You wrote that it is the same in Grietina's case. Is there a possibility of a cure in your opinion? If you at any time meet or write to them, give them our best regards, and also greet Grietina and Hendrik for us. Hendrik still owes me a long letter.

[Closing]

January 28, 1927

Dear brother,

Really, little brother, I deserve punishment for delaying so long. A person hardly knows what to write, for the newspapers bring news from the ends of the earth after a day or two. If inventions continue at the same pace as during the last fifteen years, then within ten years I think we will fly across the ocean in one day. Satan is making good use of it all, but God can also use it to hasten the coming of His kingdom.

We are all quite well here, but there are the usual exceptions. The grippe [influenza] is quite common here, as it is in Europe, and causes deaths as a result of complicating lung fevers. Dina continues to cope with stomach trouble, but is not bedridden.

Our three oldest children work in Grand Rapids. Two are married and a third plans to be married in the spring.

At present conditions are much more favorable in the cities than in the country and on farms. The farmers all have trouble getting by. Many are obliged to quit or go bankrupt. Things have changed a great deal since I came to America. Earlier, many individuals came from the cities to work in the woods during the winter. That is all in the past and now the opposite is true. And there are no more immigrants arriving. As a result the Dutch language is disappearing; for example, my younger children can no longer speak Dutch. They understand some of it, probably most of it, but the answers are always in English—and my children know more Dutch than many others. This is because school and catechism are all in English. Sermons are fifty-fifty, one in Dutch and one in English. If a Dutch immigrant were to arrive who knew absolutely no English, he would feel very lonely, for the older generation is dying off.

[Closing]

Dina Diemer to Geert and Martje Diemer
McBain, Michigan, to Hoogeveen, Drenthe
June 3, 1928

Dear brother and sister[-in-law],

You will undoubtedly be surprised to receive a letter from America, but sometimes it is very necessary, and then the thought occurs to us that something has happened, which is true in this case, namely, that I have lost my dear spouse, Frederik, by death. On May 30 he left for work hale and hearty in the morning, and at two o'clock in the afternoon we received the terrible news that he had been killed where the school building was being torn down. A part of the building had been blown inward by a gust of wind, right where he was working, and there was not enough time for him to escape, and as a result he was caught underneath. His companion had just enough time to get away from the danger, after which he went for help at once, but it was too late. The accident had happened so suddenly that he could not speak, and departed in a few minutes.

But we may firmly believe that he is with the Lord. You can well imagine, brother and sister, how terrible this is, yes, it is impossible to express it in words. But we have the great privilege of being assured that he has gone to his Fatherland, which is a great comfort for us. The funeral was conducted on Saturday, June 2. Since we are not sure about the address, we are sending the news to the address of "the Rotterdamer."

If you will be so kind, let the other relatives know, and now one more request. Will you please write back to us? With this I close the letter.

Receive the regards from the deeply grieved widow and children of F. Diemer.

Your sister, Mrs. Dina Diemer

II

Rural to Rural: Clay-Soil Emigrants

Introduction

The correspondents included in this part shared Old World agricultural experiences as hired hands serving large-scale farmers of grain, livestock, and milk products. Teunis and Dirkje van den Hoek, Ulbe and Maaike Eringa, and Onno and Klaaske Heller immigrated from clay-soil regions where large landholders form the social and economic elite of the village. Big farmers of this sort (*grote boeren*) employed a majority of the regional labor force and dominated both civil and religious affairs. They were, in some cases, the descendants of a petty noble class that maintained the glimmerings of economic feudalism well in to the nineteenth century.

Farmhands were employed under various arrangements. Some, such as Van den Hoek, occupied one-room cottages on small plots of land, just large enough to stake out a few animals and raise garden crops for family use. The customarily large number of children who crowded these cottages usually worked with their parents until they could be hired out at about twelve years of age. At that time they frequently moved into one of the large farmsteads where, in return for long days of labor, they received food, shelter, and a small wage. Despite being quartered in barns, both farmhands and housemaids with fixed terms of employment (Ulbe Eringa and his wife, Maaike Rypstra, for example) enjoyed more privileges and economic security than those without contracts. Yet, the well-being of the whole agricultural work force depended on the labor supply and the employer's general character. Some were relatively generous, and others were meanly parsimonious. In any case conventional class distinctions structured every social routine. The villagers' church pew locations, residential sites, menus, wardrobes, and social relationships—each and all announced their status.

It is hardly surprising, then, that the Eringas, Van den Hoeks, and Hellers reveled in the relatively classless social structure of the United States. Nor is it strange that they measured their success in America with repeated inventories of their landholdings, livestock, buildings, farm machinery, and household goods. Holding positions as church or school officials contributed additional evidence of success. When Eringa and others could report that they owned a farmstead and had been elected as a church elder, they were legitimately implying that their status compared favorably with that of the large farmer in the Netherlands. Even more important, the achievements of their children could be cited as the ultimate justification for their decision to emigrate.

Although being chosen as lay leaders in their local churches reflected well on the immigrants' social status, these attainments should not be ascribed to a mere hankering after social prominence. Both Van den Hoek and Eringa appear to have been sincere and devoted believers under all circumstances, whether in wealth or adversity. They, and the Hellers too, consistently expressed their dependence on and submission to God's providence.

Van den Hoek and Eringa were especially inclined to pious discourse, and their general values were almost identical, but they expressed their pieties with differing emphases and they also selected different church affiliations. It would be untenable to claim that these religious styles were the predictable components of their ecclesiastical affiliations. Nevertheless, Van den Hoek's religiosity, which lingered constantly on the uncertainty of virtually everyone's eternal destination, was compatible with his denomination's (the CRC's) focus on divine election and reprobation during that era. Both Van den Hoek and the CRC were gripped by the theological formulations of the Netherlandic Synod of Dordrecht, 1618–1619. Thus, when young Willem Vogel drowned in 1871, Van den Hoek wrote, "We can only fear that he did not die in the Lord. Oh, why are some of us allowed to live on and continue to have the possibility of salvation?"

Ulbe Eringa's reactions, by contrast, were heartily optimistic when his niece Anna died, albeit under different circumstances. "Oh, I am convinced," he wrote, "that she is at home with her Lord in heaven." Eringa's denomination, also affirmed the teachings of the 1618 synod, but the RCA, in part because of its long history of cooperation with American denominations, gave less emphasis to the doctrines of election and reprobation than did the CRC. And Eringa was likewise disinclined to focus on the gloomiest eternal prospects.

As the Heller correspondence demonstrates, acquiring church membership did not automatically spawn lengthy pious declamations. The Hellers, like the Van den Hoeks, joined the Christian Reformed Church, but they shared little of Van den Hoek's compulsion to pious exhortation. Heller, Van den Hoek, and Eringa, however, did share a compelling desire to become independent farmers even at the inconvenience and expense of repeated migrations.

The Onno Heller family, apparently the poorest of the three, first settled near Holland, Michigan, in 1891. But in 1896 they moved to Oak Harbor on a coastal island off the Washington coast. There, they purchased stump land and reported their great satisfaction with their land, climate, neighbors, and church. The Heller correspondence ends in 1909. By then, some of their children were married, and they appear to have become well acculturated in Oak Harbor's growing Dutch American subculture. By 1922 most of the Heller children had left the ethnic enclave. Unlike the Van den Hoek and Eringa children, they quickly adopted mainstream Anglo-American social and religious values.

5 Teunis and Arie van den Hoek

In 1866, when Teunis van den Hoek and his wife, Dirkje, emigrated from Noordeloos to South Holland, Illinois, they encountered a flourishing village populated by several of Dirkje's uncles and cousins. The area's rich clay soils attracted its first Dutch settlers in 1847, and over the next two decades immigrants from throughout the province of Zuid Holland, and from Noordeloos in particular, were prominently represented among the newcomers. Located behind the many dikes of Zuid Holland's Alblasserwaard, Noordeloos and its neighboring villages had prospered over the centuries by draining and cultivating the polder's clay soils with techniques that were also applicable in the Calumet River drainage basin of northern Illinois.[1]

Emigration from Noordeloos began in 1847, when forty-nine villagers joined the Reverend Hendrik P. Scholte's venture in Pella, Iowa. Scholte's adherents formed a dissident subgroup within the larger schism of 1834 (the *Afscheiding*), and virtually all of them, in Noordeloos and elsewhere, departed with him.[2] The colony in Pella maintained Scholte's controversial views for about twenty years (1847–1868). During that period other immigrants from Noordeloos were not drawn to Pella but

These letters were donated by Bertha Bajema, 1977, and first translated by Egbert Post. The original letters were transcribed in the Netherlands.

[1] M. W. Schakel, *Geschiedenis van de hoge en vrije heerlijkheden van Noordeloos en Over-slingeland* (Gorinchem, Netherlands: J. Noorduijn, 1955), pp. 11–19, 199–207; Richard Cook, *South Holland, Illinois, 1846–1966* (Privately printed, 1966), pp. 15–43.

[2] P. R. D. Stokvis, *De Nederlandse trek naar Amerika, 1846–1847* (Leiden: Universitaire Pers, 1977), pp. 44–57.

joined instead the fledgling settlements in northern Illinois and western Michigan.

In 1856 a group of thirty-four emigrants left Noordeloos with their pastor, Koenraad van den Bosch, who was destined to lead a newly organized congregation in West Michigan. Although both Willem Vogel and Leendert van der Aa traveled with their pastor, they did not join his new congregation but went instead to South Holland, Illinois, where their relative, Arie van der Aa, had settled in 1854. The Van den Hoeks, who arrived in 1866, were related to both the Vogels and the Van der Aas.[3]

Following international trends, emigration from Noordeloos diminished to a trickle from 1857 until the end of the American Civil War. Then, in 1866 a group of thirty-three persons, including the Van den Hoeks, left Noordeloos in the company of the Reverend H. R. Koopman, who had served the Noordeloos seceders from 1849 to 1851. He became the pastor of the South Holland Dutch Reformed Church, where he was highly regarded by the immigrants from Noordeloos.[4] Teunis van den Hoek wrote favorably of Koopman's leadership and probably would have attended the South Holland church if he had remained there. But Teunis was too poor to purchase land immediately and his search for employment led him to Englewood, near Chicago's boundary. He worked on the Meeter farm there until 1869 when he leased a farm from Willem van der Aa in South Holland.

By 1871 Van den Hoek had purchased the thirty-acre farm from Van der Aa and had acquired an additional fifteen acres, which together cost $4,500. In 1878 he still owed $3,750 and although the value of his farm had risen, he needed more land to keep his growing family busy. Thus in 1882, when he and a friend discovered good land in northwest Iowa for $20 per acre, Teunis sold out for $110 per acre and bought an eighty-acre farm near Orange City, Iowa. Two years later the Van den Hoeks moved again, this time to a 160-acre farm in Harrison, South Dakota. "The reason my wife and I made this important decision," he wrote, "was to keep our dear children under our own supervision and control." Two years later, with an inheritance from the Netherlands, Teunis acquired an additional 160 acres.

Throughout his correspondence Van den Hoek extolled landownership and the institutional ties of church and school as the foundation for family cohesion and by 1891 his ideals had born fruit. That year he

[3] Swierenga, *Dutch Emigrants*, pp. 269–322; Schakel, *Geschiedenis*, p. 205.
[4] Schakel, *Geschiedenis*, p. 205; C. Smits, *De Afscheiding van 1834* (Dordrecht, Netherlands: J.P. van den Tol, 1974), 2:357–364.

reported, "My son-in-law and my daughter Willempje have purchased a one-hundred-and-sixty-acre farm with a house and barn for $1,000. It is located about two miles away. Jan, my oldest son, [later a pastor in the Christian Reformed Church, 1905–1924] is a bookkeeper and clerk in a large store and earns $34 per month. My youngest daughter, Eigje, is a schoolteacher and earns $30.00 per month. . . . Willem and Eben work on the farm with me and go to school in the winter."

After repeated urgings Teunis persuaded his brother from Noordeloos to join the Harrison colony. Arie van den Hoek arrived in 1893, during a time of severe drought and high unemployment, but with Teunis's directions and with charity from public and private sources, Arie survived the lean year and by 1895 he and his two sons were cultivating a rented farm. Although others drifted away during a drought cycle that lasted until 1897, the Van den Hoek families remained in Harrison and continue to be prominent in the Harrison Christian Reformed Church.[5]

The Van den Hoek correspondence is exceptional for its intense piety and its strong infusion of Calvinist theology. Although these perspectives were common among the Dutch seceders, few applied them to daily occurrences as explicitly as Teunis van den Hoek. Religious injunctions are so heavily scattered throughout his correspondence as to make up at least 50 percent of its contents. Fifteen of his eighty-seven letters are completely given over to sermon summaries and pious reflections. These occur regularly with the passing of each year and with the news of deaths among family members in the Netherlands and America. I have included enough of these to indicate the general character of Van den Hoek's religiosity without presenting the bulk of them.

One example is particularly revealing. In his July 26, 1871, letter Teunis reported the sudden and troubling death of his nephew Willem Vogel who drowned in the Calumet River:

> At noon Willem ate a healthy dinner but one hour later he was drowned. He lived with two other farmhands who could swim well and every noon hour they were teaching Willem to swim even though neither we nor his parents knew about it. And now it is eternally too late for him [to ask their permission]. On that terrible day the other worker could not go swimming because he had some work to do for the farmer's wife. She told Willem that he should not go swimming alone because he was not yet able to swim well enough. He said that

[5] Nelson Nieuwenhuis, "A History of Dutch Settlement in South Dakota to 1900" (M.A. thesis, University of South Dakota, 1948), pp. 29–40; *100th Anniversary of the Harrison Christian Reformed Church, 1884–1984* (Harrison, S.D.: Privately printed, 1984), 37 pp.

he would only walk along the riverbank, but instead he went carelessly to his death. Fifteen minutes later the other field hand came along and found clothing on the bank but Willem was gone. It was a nasty scene when we and all the neighbors were searching for him with hooks and boats. . . . We found him in the middle of the river in eighteen feet of water.

He was faithful to his parents and a diligent worker for his boss but he was among those who said to the Lord, "Stay away from me. I have no pleasure in your word." Thus we can only fear that he did not die in the Lord. Oh, why are some of us allowed to live on and continue to have the possibility of salvation? This event clearly calls us to think about the example of Lot's wife. Why was I selected and not drowned in my original and temporal sins?

* * *

The day of Willem's funeral was for me a day of wonder, prayer, comfort, and joy because the Lord allowed me to taste the surety of my salvation. That is a precious faith which cleans the heart of the stale evil prison of dead works, idle worship, and useless duties of which the Holy Spirit says they are like incense burned to idols.

With such firmly held predestinarianism it is hardly surprising to find that Van den Hoek regarded all his decisions—to emigrate and then migrate across state lines—as part of God's benevolent design for his life.

Teunis, in fact, immigrated as an impoverished twenty-nine-year-old farmhand, and he made slow, steady progress toward achieving his objectives. His migrations enabled him to gain cash from increasing land values which funded the purchase of ever larger landholdings. Eventually, with 640 acres, his holdings were significantly larger than his neighbors'.[6] Yet, throughout his trek across the Midwest, Van den Hoek remained within the Dutch Reformed subculture, which, with its churches and private schools, bolstered the values Van den Hoek cherished for his children and grandchildren.

Teunis van den Hoek to Parents
Thornton [South Holland], Illinois, to Goudriaan, Zuid Holland
May 16, 1866

Highly esteemed parents,
   With this letter we are informing you that by God's good pleasure we have arrived at our chosen destination. God's faithfulness and goodness

[6] A 1900 Harrison-area map, Calvin College Archives, indicates that most farmers cultivated 160 acres.

to us has been more than we can express. We boarded the iron English steamer [from Liverpool] on Wednesday, April 24, and by Thursday noon we were in Ireland where four hundred more people came aboard. We sailed there between cliffs that were 200 or 300 feet high. In clear weather we sailed with the wind.

* * *

On Sunday an English child died and on Monday, April 28, the brother of the ship's doctor died. On Tuesday we buried him at sea with honors. There were 1,350 people on board, ninety-five crew including the captain, pilots, sailors, bakers, etc. . . .

We began to see sand dunes on Tuesday, May 7, and we arrived in New York on May 8. We stayed there until Friday getting our baggage and then traveled by fast train. We sat on upholstered seats covered with silk and had very good service.

Willem Paarlenberg [an original South Holland settler] was in New York to meet us [probably to assist Koopman, the new pastor of the South Holland church], and we enjoyed his help very much. We arrived in Calumet on Saturday evening at eleven o'clock in good health. The Calumet [train station] is two hours from South Holland. Willem Paarlenberg went home that evening to get his wagons and we stayed at the station.

Early the next morning they came to get us with about sixteen wagons. And then there was joy on all sides. Uncle Willem Vogel and Willem van der Aa came with a wagon and two horses. The aged Pieter Prens and Cornelis, his son, who lives near the Calumet station, discovered that we had arrived and before we left they came to greet us enthusiastically. We arrived at Willem Vogel's home with mutual happiness. Dirkje [his wife] and I, along with Jannigje [Vogel], Kobes and Cornelis [den Besten], were persuaded to stay with Willem van der Aa. All the friends and acquaintances we met were well and in fine condition. If I were to write everything I've seen here it would be almost unbelievable to you.

The poorest of those whom we met have the best of food, and not Catholic flour [rye] as you imagine in the Netherlands, but white summer wheat. Uncle Willem Vogel is one of the poorest Hollanders around here and he has four oxen for plowing, two milk cows, two calves, and a sow with a litter of pigs, plus twenty chickens and Dutch pigeons. He eats and drinks as well as the richest farmer in Goudriaan. What do you think of that?

All the children of Leendert van der Aa live near each other and Leendert lives an hour away from them. They are all farmers. Bart van den Berg and Annigje have their own farm with a house and four children.

They milk four cows and are as well off as Father and Mother in Goudriaan. We live here surrounded by Hollanders, Germans, and some English mixed in.

We had very little seasickness. We had fresh white bread every morning and evening. At noon we had rice soup, unpeeled potatoes, and a good helping of fresh meat. In addition we had rice porridge with raisins and currants on Sunday. Everyone had so much butter that each person had a pound left over when leaving the ship.

Everyone here urges us to come for a visit. We are happy and surprised by the way we have been welcomed. Yesterday and today Dirkje and Jannigje worked for Gerrit and Willem van der Aa from 7:00 A.M. to 6:00 P.M. for eighteen Dutch nickels per day [about thirty-six cents]. What do you think of that! They [Dirkje and Jannigje] live one and a half miles from Uncle Willem Vogel. J. den Besten is working for Willem van der Aa for a month and Cornelis is at Gerrit van der Aa's for a month. Hendrik Bode from Overslingeland (married to Elizabeth de Jong from Noordeloos) and I have rented a house together.

Our house has two apartments, each with a room upstairs and a cellar. It has twenty rods of garden, which has been spaded over. There is a cow barn and a board pigsty. It is a newly built wooden house and it comes with an acre of cultivated land and a boat for the river. The river flows past the house. It has very good water and lots of fish. On one side of the house our land lies next to the river. A number of oak trees have been cut down and we can chop as much wood for fuel as we wish. The woods are full of wild apple trees, gooseberry bushes, and more. The total rent is $23.00 [per year]. One dollar is 250 cents in Dutch money. The acre of cultivated land will be plowed next week and we have also rented two acres of land ten minutes from here at $3.00 per acre, and according to the agreement these will be plowed free.

People here are now busy plowing land for wheat and potatoes. We intend to plant wheat and potatoes on our land. Everything here is more expensive than in the Netherlands, but everything needed is readily available in the stores.

We moved into our home on Friday. We have a fine lathed bedstead, a table, and a stove with an oven. We have good bread and baked goods. I bought a used table as good as our large table in Noordeloos for $4.50. Sixteen pounds of suet cost twenty cents, butter six cents, coffee eight cents. The mercies of the Lord are abundant every day and also the generosity of friends and acquaintances. Saturday Hap Huisman gave me four hens and a rooster and Willem van der Aa gave us three hens. We bought six more, so now we have fourteen.

Yesterday Rev. Koopman was installed by the aged Rev. Klijn using

Isaiah 52:7 as the text of his sermon. In the afternoon Rev. Koopman preached his inaugural on Col. 4:3. He prayed that God would open the door of the Word to speak the mysteries of Christ. Our church here is larger and much more stylish than the church in Noordeloos. Koopman was welcomed with unusual joy. People bring everything to him. We live a half hour from him and an hour away from H. Huisman. We are thankful that the Lord has brought us to this country and we wish that all of our friends were here too.

There is a disease here in the pigs but not the cattle. There is no poverty here. Labor is twice as easy here as with you. We each live in our own apartment and do our own cooking but we do everything else together on our land. Because we have had a time of blessing and prosperity we must cry out in wonder and humility—let everyone praise the Lord using Psalm 118:7.

Friday Gerrit de Groot arrived here and we had a talk with him—they are staying with Willem Ravestijn. It is indescribable what trouble they had. You will certainly hear more about it. Four hundred died from cholera on their ship—forty-five in one day. They were forced to stay on an island in the open air and their beds were thrown away. Marrigje gave birth to a baby boy on the train. They did not dare to write about all their troubles. Oh Lord! How different it was in our case. Praise the Lord, my soul, and forget not all His benefits. We have heard of no one who had such a good and prosperous journey as we did and we were treated well.[1] May this lead us to a dedication of our bodies and souls to the Lord and to His blessed service.

* * *

Greetings from H. Huisman to Father and Mother [Vogel, in Noordeloos]. And Father, in Goudriaan, please copy my letter and also those that come in the future. Then you can allow all our friends to read it. . . . Write back soon. I intend to write again soon.

Fathers, Mothers, brothers and sisters, friends and acquaintances—receive our greeting.

Teunis van den Hoek

Goudriaan is a village located about one and a half miles from Noordeloos. South Holland was identified variously as Thornton Township, Low Prairie, Calumet, Calumet Creek, and North Creek. The post office designation South Holland dates from 1869.

1. In an April 23, 1866, letter written from Liverpool Van den Hoek reported, "On Sunday afternoon we spent a couple of hours in the first-class cabin with Rev. Koopman and discussed various religious and ecclesiastical matters with a man named H. de Vos . . . who was traveling with Rev. Koopman. We enjoyed talking together about the Lord's ways and dealings. Rev. Koopman is interested in all our affairs and associates with us in a friendly manner.

July 16, 1866

Highly esteemed and beloved parents,

We were delighted to receive your letter of July 9 and to learn that you were all in good health. It is also clear from your letter that the Lord is testing both man and beast in our native land. Yes, dear friends, as long as there is no return to the Lord in the Netherlands and no bowing before His high majesty, His hand of wrath will remain outstretched.

We are all well. In the Netherlands I had much stomach trouble but I have not noticed it here in America. And I can also stand the severe heat here. During my first week here I was digging a ditch for an English farmer—five feet wide and three feet deep. I earned $5.00 per week with board. But he was two hours away from here. After that job I was providentially led to a sixty-year-old widow who lost her husband two months ago. She has ten milk cows, thirty acres in crops, and one hundred acres of hay land. There I was paid $4.25 per week and we have been busy haying for another two months or twenty-six working days for $20.00 per month. Board is included. The widow has three sons, two grown up, and a daughter.

Almost all the hay is mowed by machine but sometimes I must cut high or low spots with a scythe. During the day we have a break every two hours but sometimes we don't take it. Two horses are hitched to the machine and when they walk the machine blades fly like lightning. A person sits on top of the machine in a little seat like a carriage. It is possible for a man with two horses to mow eight or ten acres in a day. It then lies spread out in rows. A person does not have to pick up the rows. That is done with another machine pulled by two horses. And again a person sits on a small seat. Last week I worked for one farmer, mowing from 2:00 to 5:00 P.M., and then I piled up eight loads of hay. A person can easily fall asleep on the machine. The hay wagons are long and the longest pitchfork is like the shortest in Holland. If it is cloudy they do not mow because after lying in the rain for one day the hay loses its color—it's that hot here. People mow at eight o'clock and stay in the house in the heat of the afternoon. The wagonloads are from 2,000 to 2,500 pounds. The days are shorter here. On the longest day the sun rises at 4:30 and sets at 7:30. The time is five and a half hours later here than Holland. We are 1,900 hours [walking speed] away from the Netherlands and 500 hours from New York. Last week sixteen people died in New York from the heat and six people also died in Chicago. It was sweltering.

The place where I work [Junction Station or Englewood] is four hours from home in South Holland. I stay in [Englewood] the entire week. I make arrangements to arrive here on Monday morning and go home on Saturday afternoon. My potatoes are doing fine and the corn is in tassel. We have a small pig which is growing well.

We think of the Netherlands a great deal and wish you were here. But not that we were with you there because we are well off materially here and very happy.

Every morning now I am milking at 4:30 A.M. At 6:30 we eat breakfast and we read the Bible and sing psalms at each meal. We eat again at one o'clock and at 7:30 in the evening. Then the day is over for me. The hay crop here is better than in the Netherlands.

I am beginning to speak a little English. I know the ABCs quite well, can count to one hundred and I can name fifty objects. The children where I work know English well and also German and Dutch.

* * *

We are very eager to hear from you again and especially about the amazing and distressing circumstances in which you find yourselves. We hope that the Lord may still grant you a gracious outcome and cause the threatening judgments to be a blessing for his own sake and that of His covenant promises. We hope to bring all your needs, of body and soul, to the throne of grace as long as we live.

[Closing]

T. van den Hoek to Parents et al.
Junction Station [Englewood], Illinois, to Goudriaan, Zuid Holland
September 25, 1866

Esteemed parents, brothers, and sisters,

With these words we inform you that by God's grace we are all well. We moved on the first of August. I wrote earlier that I was working for a Frisian farmeress. She treats me like one of her own children and was very eager to have me stay here this whole year. Her former hired man, a godly person from Oudekerk on the IJssel River, came to America with Jacob van der Aa, but because of urgings from his parents and family, he returned to the Netherlands one week before I came to work for these people. The widow for whom I work [Mrs. Meeter] is a Christian and lives a very godly life—the like of which I have not met in the Netherlands.

When B. van den Berg and I went out looking for work among the Dutch people that morning I did not know I would meet her. I was very depressed that morning; then I turned to the Lord, in whose hand the lot of everyone lies, and asked Him to reveal His condescending goodness to me, a poor worm, and to strengthen me. The precious truth of Psalm 42:9 came to my mind, "But the Lord will command His loving-kindness in the daytime and in the night His song will be with me." I must frequently cry out, Oh, what a wonderful and generous God for those that fear Him.

*   *   *

Bart van den Berg had no work either and he has to work for English people who are mostly a careless folk who do not ask for blessing or give thanks at meals. I had already experienced that in the previous week and it grieved my soul.

Just as Bart and I started our trip we were able to get a ride from a Dutch garden farmer who is very knowledgeable in the Scriptures and who lives about one mile from me. He showed me the Meeter farm and brought me there. Soon we made an arrangement which was a source of happiness on both sides. I was asked to sit at the head of the table in her deceased husband's chair and lead in devotions. It was a difficult task for me at first because I was thinking too much about myself. But now I feel enlightened and encouraged by the Lord to regard this as evidence of His grace.

At this farm I have now earned $40.00 in two months and I will get $15.00 until November. In the winter months, November through February, I will earn $36.00 in all. Mrs. Meeter promised me that if I came to live here I could keep two cows in her pasture free of charge.

Nearby there is a German who has both a large and small house, and he and his wife often ride to Chicago with produce at night. He offered free lodging to us if Dirkje would milk his five cows twice each week. So now I have settled up with our former landlord and we have moved here. I bought two cows, one for $40.00 and another for $30.00, and another on September 1 for $30.00. Hopefully two are with calves. I bought the third one on credit to be paid when I am able. They are good milk producers. Two cows give as much milk here as one in the Netherlands, but we have more cream in our milk. I have two hogs worth $5.00 each. The cream here is taken from the milk and churned into butter which is very expensive, ten cents. Rice is twelve cents, sugar sixteen cents, pork ten cents, beef fifteen cents. The best cornmeal or white wheat flour costs from $8.00 to $13.00 for a 200-pound barrel.

Both rich and poor here eat white bread. Cheese costs ten cents per pound and whole milk is sixteen cents per pound. Our three cows give about twenty pounds of milk per week and that earns $3.60 per week. I have rented hay land for $2.00 per acre which yielded 7,000-pounds and I bought another 7,000 pound stack for $9.00. I bought a half load of rye grain for $2.00 and this week I bought half of a sheep, dressed, for eight cents a pound.

I have bought another stove like new for $12.00 on which two pots and two kettles can boil at once and it has an oven which bakes eight loaves of bread at one time. Everyone bakes bread here and one does not have to burn straw or twigs because there is plenty of oak wood. Last week the daughter of the farmer where I work gave us a new kettle—a $2.00 present.

It has been a fertile year but lately there has been a great deal of rain and the potatoes are drowned. Mine are probably drowned too because they are near the river [on his rented land in South Holland]. I gave my corn crop to my former landlord. Dirkje has purchased eight tin containers for skimming milk for fifteen cents each. Good potatoes here cost about $1.00 per bushel. You can buy as much yarn here for $1.00 as you can for a guilder in the Netherlands. Rice flour costs $6.00 for 200 pounds. White and red cabbage cost ten to twelve cents [per bushel].

I live near a railroad. Every day twenty-five trains pass by. I live three hours from the big city of Chicago, which is growing rapidly. Last year 1,100 houses were built and more this year. Every day is market day. The cattle market [Union Stock Yards] was built just outside the city. Four hundred men worked on it for a whole year. Every day more than one hundred trains arrive there and they are a mile long—that is twenty minutes [walking distance per mile]. Every day 1,000 to 1,200 farmers come to the city with loads from surrounding farms. The Chicago harbor is always filled with seagoing ships [the South Water Street market on the Chicago River].

There are two Reformed churches in the city, one Dutch and one English[1]—and many other churches too. I have talked with Rev. Klijn and the elders who serve the ["English"] church and have been invited to visit them sometime and to discuss church and doctrinal matters. The city where they are is to the north. We usually go to the church in Calumet Station or High Prairie,[2] which is seven and a half hours [walking] south of the Chicago church. Rev. Lepeltak, who was born in Rotterdam, preaches there and P. Prens is an elder. Lepeltak is well educated but he has little experiential knowledge. Rev. Klijn was formerly a seceder pastor in Middelburg in the Netherlands.

Cholera has spread all through America and in Chicago too, but not as bad there. We have learned, to our sorrow, that Jacob Bos died of the cholera. We heard that D. Slop and the children of Van Wout lost their home in a fire and also that there was much talk about us in Holland. I can testify to God's honor and I hope to your joy, that I am not sorry about leaving for America. By God's grace we already have a comfortable existence here and that would not be possible in the Netherlands except under unusual circumstances. A laborer here with five children can get along better than a person with one child in the Netherlands. The work here is easier by far than in the Netherlands. The workdays are shorter and the wages are much higher. You should not discourage people who, because of poverty, need to leave for America. But they should remember that at first, nine out of ten would like to return because of the trouble one has with the language.

H. Bode and G. de Groot came with me looking for work here but they could not find work with Hollanders. They worked for a few days— one with a German and the other for an Englishman—but they could not get along so they have taken their families to Michigan, about thirty hours from here. Jacob and Cornelis den Besten have also gone there and they bought a house with twenty acres together for $600.00 with a $100.00 down payment. On Monday, August 13, Jacob den Besten married our dear sister, Jannigje Vogel, and on August 16 they left us by train to go to their home in Michigan. We have had two verbal reports and also some letters from them. They are well satisfied. Kobes wrote that he now earns $1.00 per day without board and he also intends to write Father, Jan Vogel. There is still no Dutch Reformed Church in that vicinity, but they have church in their home on Sunday. If we would board the train here at 6:15 A.M. we would be in Michigan by 9:00 A.M. The fare is $3.50 for a round trip per person. J. den Besten lives twenty minutes from the station.[3]

I have talked to many Hollanders here, and of those who have been here for a few years no one wished to go back to the Netherlands to stay there. Throughout America one must learn English, otherwise there is trouble in every way. I meet many people who came here poor and are now big farmers and rich in worldly goods. America is not a poor country as some people think but a rich country.

I have had to mow hay now for two months with the machine but only three days with the scythe. I often think of how my poor brothers must slave away in the Netherlands. No one here has to carry milk with a yoke. Everyone has a cow stabled near the house. Every farmer has a lead cow with a bell and usually the cows came home by themselves with the bell cow leading the others. They are kept in the stable at night. One does not see cows without horns—just like the goats by you.

Men and women are dressed about the same as in the Netherlands. The largest bird seen here is the sand crane, which is twice as large as a stork.

* * *

We think often of you, hoping that we may still meet on this side of the grave, but we hope especially that it may please the Lord to convert this one and that one because all that is vanity will disappear, but whoever does the will of God will live eternally. May the God of heaven and all mercy grant us and you what is good for our bodies and souls, even our prayers and requests, according to the riches of His everlasting love for sinners.

Regards from us to our dear parents, brothers and sisters, uncles and aunts, yes, to all friends, neighbors and acquaintances. And also my bosom friend, Jan Spijker.

Praise the Lord, my soul, and forget not all His mercies.

[Closing]

1. This church, located near the center of Chicago, was founded in 1853. Many of its members spoke English but its worship services were conducted in Dutch until the 1890s.

2. High Prairie was the Dutch designation for Calumet Station, later Roseland.

3. This area, Three Oaks, Michigan, is a little north of the Indiana state line and near the Lake Michigan shoreline.

December 28, 1866

Dear parents, brothers, and sisters,

With this we inform you that we are, by God's grace, still in good health and we wish the same for you. We were pleased by the letters you sent. Between October 30 and November 24 I was on a trip to Three Oaks, Michigan, to visit J. den Besten and Jannigje Vogel. I returned on Monday, a distance of twenty-five hours.

You asked about postage costs. Our first letter cost sixty-four cents, the second, thirty cents, and the third, thirty-four cents. All letters [to Europe] cost at least twenty-two cents. We were happy to receive a letter from Mother and Jannigje, and also from F. Bloom. We are sending with this letter, special greetings from B. van den Berg and Annigje van der Aa. She had seven children, four still living. Bart never writes. He is a careless man.

The Dutch Reformed Church here [later called the Reformed Church in America], to which we belong, has the marks of a true church in accord with the church rules of the Synod of Dordrecht and the Word of God. This church had its origins in the Netherlands [1628–1629], or ten years after the Synod of Dordrecht, when the first Hollanders immigrated to America. At that time the Reformed Church in the Netherlands sent ministers along with the immigrants under the supervision of the Classis of Amsterdam. They settled in New York, then called New Amsterdam. Soon they had three congregations. That church was under the authority of the Dutch kings until the French Revolution. Then England gave the conquered city the name New York.[1] At that time the church had grown to the point that it was able to establish a school of higher learning [Rutgers College and Seminary]. Soon there were ministers trained in the English language because that is the native language in America. Upon investigation I have been pleased to learn that this church is legally established and does not accept members except from the Christian Seceded Church in the Netherlands. The Reformed [Hervormde] Church[2] is regarded as a false and lawbreaking church, to which I can also testify with a clear conscience. This denomination here in America consists of more than 1,000 congregations, both Dutch and English all in one alliance. It is also the most prominent church in America. In general sincere Christians are respected here and preferred for government positions. Our president upholds the church and the state more faithfully than the king of the Netherlands. [For example], when houses of prostitution are discovered they are burned to the ground with all that they contain. The operator is then hanged and the person who discovers the house is paid $50.00. Anyone who seduces a young woman must marry her or pay $200.00 to the court plus child support or be banished from the country for good. There are also many Catholics in America, but they are excluded from all government positions.[3]

We had a beautiful autumn—I didn't bring my cow into the barn until November 23. . . . There is a plan to build a new and larger church in this place [Roseland]. A recent subscription to determine how much each member could give by July 1, 1869, gained pledges of $800.00. The membership is smaller than that of the seceded church in Noordeloos, so you can understand then that there is a surplus of money here in America. The plans are to build a church costing $2,600 but using the furnishings of the old church.

I enjoyed my visit in Three Oaks. They strongly urged me to move there. The chance to get property there is greater than here. In Three Oaks land costs $20.00 to $30.00 per acre and here it costs $50.00, $60.00, and up to $100.00. I have butchered two small hogs for my own use.

*   *   *

[Closing]

1. The historical facts here are askew, but the general outline is accurate enough.

2. By this he means the state supported Reformed church as distinguished from the Christian seceded Reformed church. Van den Hoek's impression, that only seceders were admitted to the Reformed Church in America, is false.

3. These laws, the product of propaganda and local jurisdictions, were a comfort to the likes of Van den Hoek. The exclusion of Catholics was also a conservative Protestant goal in the Netherlands.

July 22, 1867

Dearest and esteemed parents,
    [Opening remarks about health and the reception of letters.]
    On July 4 and 5 I went to Three Oaks again to see Jannigje Vogel. I have strongly urged her to come back here because of the situation there [apparently her husband, Jacob den Besten, had deserted her], which I know better than I can tell you in a letter. The devil goes about like a roaring lion seeking whom he may devour. The heart of man is evil—who can know it? I have always wished to treat her as my own child, as she knows well enough, but I could not persuade her to come. She says she does not want to sit around living in with us while she is young and strong. And besides, working here in Englewood as a maid for the English is difficult. Employment is by the month and temptations are many. America is a very rich country where the devil lays many snares, but there are also many true children of God from many countries, especially from Scotland, England, and the Netherlands. For now I know of no other option than to have her stay with Cornelis den Besten which, although contrary to your wishes, will provide her with good care.
    Just now I bought a good cow and two hogs. This spring I built a house with two rooms and a double-walled barn [attached to the house, on the Saxon model]. It cost a total of $100.00 and I still owe $85.00 for that. My cow had a calf three weeks ago and in May my three cows gave eighteen to eighteen and a half pounds of butter per week. It has now become very warm, so they give fifteen pounds, which sells for sixteen cents per pound. Today I sold my three-week-old calf for $7.00. You have to be here to understand this rapid buying and selling. It is part of the American way of thinking—very scientific. . . .
    To my sorrow and disappointment my wife gave birth to a well-formed but stillborn baby girl on April 25. It behooves us to be silent before God who is righteous in all His ways. The Lord brought her [Dirkje] back to health speedily and now we are both in good health again.
    We are eager to know if brother Jacob is in military service. And Andries, we are happy to know that you are still in fellowship with those who fear the Lord. We expect, if the Lord wills and we live, to meet you soon in America. The midwife who married Hasselman in Noordeloos arrived here a few weeks ago. They are well satisfied. The godless H. van de Leden from Hoorn is also here. Father, P. Prins sends greetings to you.
    The newspaper last week reported that we have a four-million-dollar surplus in the treasury and that our president is beginning to behave like Absalom.[1] Well-informed people are predicting hard times. Blessed are

the people who fear the Lord at all times, for all flesh is as grass. Judgment day is coming when all things will burn as in an oven. Then all those who are haughty and who work iniquity will be like stubble and they will be consumed by fire says the Lord of hosts. He will leave neither root nor branch.

We go to church twice each Sunday where Rev. Lepeltak is [in Roseland]. He preaches much like Rev. Smit in Gorkom [Gorinchem]. There is exceptional love and unity in our congregation.

[Closing]

1. Absalom, who revolted against his father, King David, probably here represents betrayal of trust. President Johnson's impeachment was in progress during this time.

December 10, 1867

Highly esteemed and beloved parents, brothers, Etc.,

[Report about good health and a lengthy discussion about God's blessing and promises.]

Father, you asked about the location of my little house—it is closer to the house of widow Meeter than your house is to the bridge. My house cost $100.00 and I still owe $50.00 with 6 percent interest. In early November I added a good stable for the cow and room for my horse for $16.00. I am now working full time for the widow. I now have four good cows worth $160.00. At present milk cows are very expensive. My cows are paid for. For next year I have rented six acres of farmland and a hay field, both for $50.00. It lies next to my house. The railroad from Chicago to Pella, Iowa, is as far from my house as the west dune at your place is from the canal.

I have a white horse which I bought with a harness for $25.00. I need it to plow and fertilize the land I have rented. I also have an old wagon for $20.00. Together they cost $45.00 with 8 percent interest.

At present butter brings a high price, forty cents or about one guilder. One of my cows is dry but should have a calf in February. The other three give ten pounds of butter per week.

It has been an exceptionally fine fall. Many places had drought but we had plenty of rain. I did not have to put on my heavy underwear until November 29 and then I put my cows and horse in the stable too. Now we are having a severe winter—rain, snow, and very cold weather.

On November 27 the president declared a Thanksgiving Day for all churches to give thanks for the crops. Our new church building was dedicated then too.

Our minister preached a stirring sermon on II Chronicles 6:18a, "But will God in every deed dwell with men on earth?" The church and tower, the consistory room and a house-barn for twenty-five horses cost $3,000, or 7,500 guilders. This congregation in High Prairie [Roseland] is exceptionally united and peace loving.[1] It is one of the youngest congregations in America. It is now twelve years old and it began with eighteen members but has grown to one hundred and fifty members. The Lord has bestowed a special blessing on it so that it has a reputation throughout America [among the Dutch] for its progress. In the last three years $5,000 has been raised for the church, the minister's house, and for the poor and all other kinds of need. You should not imagine that this is the case all over America. Many congregations twice as large do not sacrifice this much. Our members were also especially blessed with good crops, but there is little room now for those who are immigrating. The area is already as thickly populated as Goudriaan and that is the reason that you hear bad rumors about America in Europe. In some places hundreds and thousands of immigrants are arriving and because they do not know the language everything is a mess at first. Everyone should expect that when they come they must begin to learn the language like a little child. We are are also learning to stammer a little and in cases of necessity we can take care of ourselves. But a person who is slow to learn would be inclined to run away in disgust when first dealing with the English-speaking people. There are, on the other hand, many compensations. It is easier for the poor to receive a bushel of wheat from the English than a half bushel of rye from the Dutch in Holland. Everyone should beware not to turn a needy person away from coming to America because that is a grievous sin against God and man. The Lord himself testifies in His Word that He has not created the world to be a barren desert, but to be planted and cultivated for man and beast. And this testimony applies to all times and places and in all situations as a lamp to guide our feet.

I am not chopping wood for fuel. I bought a quantity of wood from the railroad and I have dug up some oak stumps of which most of the roots were rotted. That makes very good firewood, but it is hard work. I also bought a ton of coal for $6.00. A ton is 2,000 pounds. If we do not have special problems we can carry on rather normally in the winter. But it is here as it is everywhere that the sin of Adam requires the sweat of our brow to eat bread. It is also true here that the lazy will wear tattered clothes and deceitfulness results in poverty. Godliness, however, is a blessing to everything both in this and the coming life.

Potatoes now cost $1.00 or 2.50 guilders per bushel. Wheat flour is $11.00 per barrel, i.e., 200 pounds. Rye flour is $7.00 to $8.00 per barrel. Land around the city is very expensive and sells for $100.00 to as much as $1,000.00 per acre. But millions and millions of acres still lie idle farther away and are being sold by the government for from $1.00 to $20.00 per acre. But many of these places are not without danger from wild people and animals. But by driving out the wild people and animals the [government] is rapidly gaining the upper hand.

[The letter concludes with lengthy pious reflections regarding the eternal destination of his friends and relatives in the Netherlands.]

[Closing]

---

1. This peaceful unity contrasted starkly to the atmosphere of the Low Prairie (South Holland) congregation, which was divisive and schism ridden.

November 27, 1868

Dear parents, brothers, sisters, and friends,

We are pleased to report that the Lord on whom we depend for life and breath has blessed us with a well-formed son on October 23, 1868, named Jan Bos van den Hoek.... He sleeps much, cries little, and is healthier than our other children.[1] We hope that the Lord will direct his life and take him as a child of the covenant for God's honor and as an ornament in His church.

And now a word about our circumstances this year. Our crops looked good this summer but there was a scourge of grasshoppers. It was very bad in some places and it also caused a great loss to our crops. In some other places whole acres were eaten bare, but the Lord saved us from that. Then in July a cattle plague broke out and it raged so fiercely in our neighborhood that in an area six miles north of us almost all the animals died. To the south of us about half died. I was safe for a time, but then it struck here too and all of my cows became sick. The best one died but the Lord restored the others to health. Millions of animals died of this pest within two months, but the plague has ended now. At first all those that became sick died. It was a severe disease which began in the liver which was almost closed by swelling. Many of the animals also had strange lice—as large as a coffee bean and some as large as a horsefly in the Netherlands.

In general, however, the crops were good. God's mercy is far greater than His judgments. I have paid the rent on my land, $125.00 in debts, and I bought a new wagon for $60.00. Now I have butchered an 800-pound cow with the widow Meeter for which I paid half of $17.50. I have also advanced $25.00 of Father Vogel's travel expense. I was then out of debt but I have now bought a fourth cow for $26.00 which is unpaid. I have also given $20.00 to the church for our debt on the new building. My crops and milk have earned $300.00, and I have brought about $100.00 worth of cabbage to the city market. I sold three loads of hay in town but still have a stack of about ten loads worth $70.00.

To our mutual joy, our parents [the Vogels] arrived here in good health after a speedy voyage. They, both parents and children, are pleased by their circumstances. Andries bought five acres and half of the den Besten house in Three Oaks, Michigan. They live together in Three Oaks. Willem lives with us during the winter and goes out to work two or three days each week while also attending an English school. The Lord has directed all according to his will. . . . Mother, I thank you most gratefully for the little present you sent along with the Vogels.

[The following segment lists the prices of nearly every commodity used by the Van den Hoeks—potatoes, sugar, carrots, etc.]

Please tell us about the conditions of your business and especially the situation of brother Arie and his wife. Further, with the passing of the old year and the coming of the new, we wish for you the forgiveness of all the old sins washed in the precious blood of God's Son. . . .

[Closing]

1. Jan was their first child to survive. Two others died in the Netherlands.

Calumet Creek [South Holland], Illinois, to Goudriaan, Zuid Holland
August 18, 1869

Highly esteemed and beloved family,
    Under God's good favor we are all healthy and hope the same for you. Our little Jan is doing well—he is always healthy and fat, but still a small person.

In May I moved to the farm of Willem van der Aa which I have rented for two years at $125.00 per year. This forty-acre farm includes pastureland and a big house with a summerhouse [for cooking during the hot months]. We now milk eight cows. In May they produced forty-eight pounds per week but now it's thirty-eight pounds—or an average of about fifty pounds of cheese per [month]. I have a work horse and two young horses (two and a half years old), four calves, three hogs, and forty chickens. Butter is now twenty-seven cents a pound and the cheese skimmed off is eight cents a pound.

In places here there has been steady rain—more than any time in the past fifteen years—especially in Ohio, Indiana, and Illinois. In large areas potatoes, corn, wheat, etc. have been drowned out. About half of my potatoes and one-quarter of my corn was ruined, but we had an unusually good crop of grass and hay. This year I have an extra cow and horse in the pasture. Half the pasture is in clover—as good as the best in Holland.

I need more hay and will have to buy an additional sixteen loads if my animals remain healthy. I have one sick calf.

I sold my house [in Englewood] for $75.00 and have, as a consequence of purchasing livestock and other necessities, a debt of $350.00 at 6 percent. In the past week I suffered from stomach pains although this has been rare here.

[The letter ends with a lengthy pious discourse which lauds the mercy of God even though there is much sin in America and even among the Dutch folk.]

[Closing]

May 2, 1870

Esteemed and beloved parents, brothers, and sisters,

* * *

And now a word about my temporal affairs. If we live and if the Lord wills it we will milk ten cows this summer. Nine have had calves and this spring was very early so that my animals were in the pasture by April 28.

My wife's father, Jan Vogel, is also farming already. He lives only five minutes away from me. Andries has had a house built for $100.00 and he bought two cows for $92.00. They are pastured by Adam Ooms for $5.00 each for six months. Andries has rented five acres for $15.00 which is located next to his house. I plowed his potato field today.

Willem Vogel lives with an English farmer and earns $142.00 per year. Andries works by the month at $18.00 to $20.00. Willempje is a maid for an English family and earns $3.00 per week. Jannigje is married again—this time to a well-respected young man, D. de Boer, from Friesland. They live in Three Oaks by J. Speyer. My neighbors to the west are—M. van der Aa, J. van der Aa, G. van der Aa, A. A. Paarlenberg, H. Verwolf, A. Rietveld, and the farthest of these is one mile away—twenty minutes walking. To the southeast my neighbors are W. Wagenaar, C. Wasselman, J. Vogel, A. Ooms, and W. Brasler from Utrecht. Janis Bosch is one half hour to the west. To the east is a large settlement of Germans and to the north there are many English and a few Hollanders.

Mother, it was a great pleasure to receive a letter from your hand. [He concludes with wishes for his mother's spiritual enrichment.]

[Closing]

This letter also contained a seventeen-page review of the nineteenth-century German pietist F. W. Krumacher's sermon on Genesis 49:14–15.

January 9, 1871

[Begins with a review of dates when letters were sent and received.]

Although we are unworthy and deserving only of damnation, the Lord has blessed us during this past year. We had an average crop and our cows, produced well. We had no accidents of any kind. I sold a horse this fall for $65.00 because it had become stiff and crippled. I bought it one and a half years ago for $100.00. I have eleven cows, all with calves. I have two horses, one colt, two young pigs, thirty-five chickens, two fat pigs (one of 250 pounds and the other 260), excellent bacon.

Most areas of the country have had good harvest and thus the prices are low. I have sold two cows, one for $36.00 and one for $34.50. If I am fortunate with the calves I will have two more cows and a horse for sale. The reasons why I will keep only seven cows next year is because W. van der Aa sold ten acres of this farm to Michiel van der Aa, his brother. And after careful consideration I bought the remaining thirty acres for three thousand dollars at 6 percent interest, the lowest rate in America.

My first cow has just given birth to a calf. Land increases in value enormously from year to year in this area. Locally it sells for $50 to $200 per acre. Two hours nearer the city it costs usually from $200 to $250. One hour closer to the city it is $500 to $600, and on the edge of Chicago and in the city it is $1,000, $2,000 and up to $8,000 and even $10,000 per acre. That land is then cut up in small pieces for large houses—like castles—and for factories. I live seven hours from the city. If I have no setbacks, in May I will be able to pay $50 to $75 on my debts for cattle and tools. This area has become so populated that it is difficult to find land to rent or to purchase. Many are leaving this area for the unpopulated and uncultivated regions. America is a spacious land and offers many occasions for greedy people without principles. Blessed is the man who controls his desires.

You wished to know about my house, barn, and so forth..... Our house is 28 feet long and 16 feet wide. That is the forward house with the living room. The summerhouse next to it is 16 feet long and 12 feet wide. On that is attached a cooking house 10 feet long and 8 feet wide. We have this because people cannot stand the heat of a stove in the living quarters during the summer. Most of the houses are of wood, although a few in the village are of stone. Mine is all wood except for a stone fireplace. We have a cellar under the forward part of the house, 17 feet long, 14 feet wide, and 7 feet high.

The building process is as follows. First they set up 3×3-inch posts two feet from each other as high as the house is. So the forward part of our house has 42 posts 15 feet high on the sides. On the front and back sides the posts are 22 feet high. The whole house has twelve sliding windows. There are twelve glass openings in each window and the glasses are one foot long and nine inches wide.

The outside of the house is covered by twelve-inch unfinished planks nailed to the posts from the top to the bottom. Then this is covered by finished boards six inches wide which overlap so that they will not break open. That is the outside of the house. On the inside of the house they nail two-inch wide wooden laths about four feet long against the posts. Between each lath there is a two-centimeter opening. Then it is all plastered with lime caulk [plaster]. The cellar is plastered with good mortar. The opening between the laths are there to make the plaster and mortar fasten to the wall. The three-inch space between the walls is for the passage of cold and hot air. Then the walls are covered with white [lime] just as in Holland. An attic covers the whole house. The six-inch square rafters lie two feet from each other—all finished wood. The floor of the house as well as the floor of the attic is of six-inch wide planks fitted with grooves. The cellar floor is of heavy oak planks. The house is painted dark blue on the inside. This summer the whole house was painted on the outside. The total cost was $36.00.

The hay barn has three crossbeams each one fourteen feet long.... The roof is eighteen feet high. Then along the length of the south side are stables with a pump and a board trough near the cows' heads. I pump water into the trough. The stables have a wooden floor.

The house and stables are thirty feet apart but in between is a cow shed, 25×45 feet made of oak posts ... covered with boards one inch thick, 6 inches wide and 16 feet long. Wood of that sort costs $14 to $16 per 1,000 square feet. Red oak posts are eight cents, white oak twelve cents and cedar fifteen cents each. West of the barn is a corncrib 12 feet long and 8 feet wide, and a 14×14-foot hog pen. West of the house is a garden 40×40 with currants and two young pear trees. We have ten apple trees, sweet and sour.

*   *   *

My land is a square and the railroad runs diagonally across it, fenced on both sides. The railroad takes up one and a half acres but for this I have the right to stop the train by raising a small red flag either to board it myself or to load my goods for Chicago. The rates are regular.

The house, stable, barn, and all the fences around the land cost $900 for material and wages. A river runs along the east side of my land. Most of the woods by my house have fir and pine trees but also cedar and oak. I have ten acres under cultivation and ten and a half acres in pasture and hay.

Anyone in Noordeloos who is interested in my situation can read this letter. . . . You asked, brother, if I do all this farm work alone. Yes, most of the time I can do it. In the four winter months I have an easy time because I only have to take care of my livestock. The reason I can handle the summer work is because one does almost everything with horses and machines—plowing, planting, mowing, threshing. I can do more with a horse and cultivator (that is a machine with five blades) in one day than a man with a hoe can do in fourteen days. I cannot explain this to you unless you come here to see for yourself. And then you will be convinced that day laborers, hired men, and maids in the Netherlands are slaves.

You also asked about the prices of butter and so forth. [Here follows a list of items with prices such as butter, twenty-eight cents. The list concludes with the comment] One can earn a dollar in America easier than sixty-five cents in the Netherlands and you can buy much more for a dollar in America than for a guilder in Holland.

[The letter concludes with three pages of pious reflections and injunctions.]

[Closing]

Two previous letters, September 2 and November 20, 1870, primarily treat religious matters, but also note the birth of a daughter, Willempje, on July 10.

North Creek [South Holland], Illinois, to Goudriaan, Zuid Holland
November 22, 1871

Esteemed and beloved parents, brothers, sisters,
[Begins with reports of good health and a favorable year for crops and prices.]

Two-thirds of Chicago burned down involving millions of dollars of loss in all the things that the world can accomplish. It was caused by a long drought and a treacherous deed. But seen with spiritual eyes evil does not come from the east or the west but from the Lord's judgment. According to reports 1,880 people were burned to death in two days in Chicago. Two days after the fire I took the train to the city with a few friends to see the results of this tragedy.

In [Holland] Michigan and [Peshtigo] Wisconsin several villages including some people, cattle, houses and barns were also destroyed by fire [huge fires, October 8, 1871]. The loss and damage are indescribable, but there has also been a generous response to help the survivors. The state of New York sent $200,000 in cash and provisions to Chicago. Eleven Roman Catholic churches in New York sent $20,000. The U.S. army sent 4,000 blankets, 2,000 overcoats, and 100 railroad cars with provisions to Chicago and northern Wisconsin. The Commission of San Francisco sent $15,000 for needy people in Milwaukee. The U.S. government gave $100,000 to Wisconsin because eighteen villages were destroyed in that state. Dr. Chapin's congregation in New York gave $12,000 in cash and an interest-free loan of $15,000 to the Universalist Church in Chicago. In addition large collections are being taken in all cities and villages for the needy. America is a fat and rich country, but more of it is destined to perish because of the country's many evils and its selfish or false religion. The Lord is merciful to the merciful, but these events should teach the impure to read and believe I Thessalonians, chapter 5.

[Closing]

February 22, 1872

Esteemed and beloved parents, brothers, and sisters,
    [The letter opens with reports of good health, thanks for receiving photos of brothers Jacob and Jan, and a page of pious discourse.]
    Brother Jan, you asked me if I go to the local church and if it has an ordained minister. At present we have no minister but meet with a lay preacher, Jacob van der Aa. He is mighty in word and deed for the people of God. I am ashamed to admit that I cannot stand in his shadow, either in knowledge or righteousness. The Lord has used him as an instrument for my soul's awakening and upbuilding.
    You asked if we have many faithful ministers here. No, by no means. For the most part they contradict their preaching in the way they live.
    Brother Arie, I noted that you bought a small house with some land—a blessing far above the average. I hope you will receive God's favor, but I fear for you my brother, and I do not say this disdainfully but sympathetically. We must learn to bow before the Lord when making decisions. . . .
    Brother Jan, you asked about Uncle F. Bloom and Jan de Mik. He lives two hours from here and I spoke to him a few weeks ago. They were all healthy then. I believe he said that he was milking six cows and he rents land. He had a good crop of onions and potatoes. Jelle works on the railroad and earns good wages. They make a good living and go to the church pastored by Rev. H. Koopman [the Roseland Reformed Church in America, 1870–1877].
    You ask if we had a report from the widow W. de Groot concerning Uncle Gerrit and his wife. In December I went to visit our family in Three Oaks, Michigan, where Gerrit also lives. The situation for Gerrit and his wife is sad. His wife is mentally ill. A few weeks ago she was taken to an asylum by the village authorities at public expense. Every available treatment was tried in vain. Gerrit and his oldest daughter Aantje are rooming in with my sister-in-law Jannigje. The two smallest

children are living with an elderly couple from Groningen who have no children. They are well tended. At times Marrigje was bowed down under the fear of her soul's eternal damnation and she was tortured by words in the Bible which wise people use for discipline and correction.[1]

On other occasions she was entirely wild and angry and behaved unspeakably. What a terrible thing for people when God gives them over to Satan's tyranny.

[The letter ends with pious injunctions.]

[Closing]

1. Probably refers to the "unforgivable sin" texts, which were common sources for depression among pious folk with mental illnesses.

March 26, 1875

Esteemed parents, brothers, and sisters,

On March 10 Dirkje gave birth to a healthy son. Mother and child are doing well. His name is Jan. In order to keep him apart from our older son Jan, we will call him Janni. That is English for Jan.[1]

[The next two pages are pious and biblical reflections about serving the Lord—following the example of Joshua, "As for me and my house, we will serve the Lord."]

We thank you for the photos that you sent. Thirteen of my cows have had calves, with four more to go. I have sold one cow for $38.00 and a barren cow for $35.00. Butter is thirty-eight cents, eggs twenty cents a dozen, potatoes $1.00 per bushel. I harvested 700 bushels last year. I hope to milk eleven cows this year. I have not rented any land except twelve acres of pasture for $50.00 It was exceptionally cold this past winter.

Andries Vogel expects to marry Dientje Schaap. Cornelis den Besten will soon be married to Huibertje Hausema. Den Besten bought a farm to the south of mine just across the public road. So he will be my neighbor. The house and barn, with 15.5 acres, cost $2,200. Andries Vogel bought fifteen acres of land for $1,605 and he will build a new house and barn on it.

Rye is seventy-five cents per bushel, oats fifty cents, coffee beans twenty-five cents per pound, tea $1.00, currants fifteen cents, raisins eighteen cents, prunes eighteen cents, figs twenty-two cents, soap eight cents, starch fifteen cents, rice ten cents, barley seven cents, good marrowfat peas six cents, the best white cheese eight cents, smoked bacon, pork shoulder, and ribs twelve cents, smoked meat fifteen cents [all per pound]. While winter wheat is $7.00 for a 200-pound barrel, summer wheat is $6.00. Tobacco is twenty-five cents per pound, white sugar twelve cents, and brown sugar ten cents a pound.

[Closing]

1. Custom required that the first son have the name of his paternal grandfather and the second son the name of his maternal grandfather. In this case both grandfathers were named Jan.

August 10, 1875

Esteemed parents, brothers, and sisters,

Our news confirms once again that "all flesh is grass" and all human beauty is like flowers of the field. The Lord of the living and dead has taken our youngest son Janni from us suddenly. He was growing nicely but last Saturday he became terribly sick. On Sunday he vomited and had a constant fever. He died on Monday evening at 7:00 P.M., July 19, 1875. He was buried on the 21st and on that occasion our pastor E. L. Meinders[1] delivered a burial sermon in our living room using the text, Romans 8:28.

Our daughter Eigje is well but not strong. She cannot walk alone yet. Jan and Willempje go to school and are learning nicely. . . .

Concerning Jacob van der Aa—his little church group has only five families left.[2] He certainly preaches the truth but his lack of study results in confusion. When I first met and visited with him I was impressed by him and his people, but I was disappointed after further investigation. The most sincere of his people have left him—including his mother and his brothers Gerrit and Leendert van der Aa. I warned him frequently that he thought too highly of himself and his followers—and that he would bring upon himself the displeasure of the Lord and of upright people. Now this is being proven. But in spite of my not associating with his group and in spite of our serious arguments, I believe he is a staunch child of God. So I have more zeal to pray for him than to slander him or lie about him as many do. Instead, we should learn from his example that we should not be haughty but fear the Lord. [Concludes with examples of fallen biblical characters, Ahab, Pharaoh, etc.]

[Closing]

1. E. L. Meinders was the pastor of the South Holland Christian Reformed Church, 1874–1886. Evidently, Van den Hoek changed from the RCA to the CRC while living in South Holland.

2. Most of his followers, Van den Hoek included, seem to have affiliated with the South Holland CRC after 1874 when Meinders came to the village.

September 5, 1876

Dear parents, brothers, and sisters,

[Opens with reports of good health.]

Our new fourteen-week-old son Jan Willem is much troubled by an upset stomach. This spring we had heavy rains so that many crops were drowned out—corn, potatoes, etc. But this summer was exceptionally fruitful so that I was able to harvest enough for my livestock. Last fall I bought another 15 acres of hay land for $100 per acre at 8 percent interest on a ten-year agreement. I bought it from Gerrit van der Aa, a quarter-hour's distance from my house. I have been milking thirteen cows. We have had plenty to eat because everything has been so cheap for the past two years. If we live and have no setbacks we will be happy to pay back all that we owe on schedule. This spring I also bought a new mowing machine for $90. Now I can mow six acres per day from 8:00 A.M. to 6:00 P.M.—and then still nap for an hour after dinner. It can mow as short as you can with a scythe and the machine spreads the hay out neatly in rows. . . .

It was pleasant to read a few lines from Arie's son Teunis, to see one generation following the other. The flood of time streams along with all its changes and finally it is lost in the ocean of eternity.

Brother Jan, you asked if our children can learn well here. With praise to God for His blessing I can answer—yes. Jan can read the gothic print of the Bible almost as well as I can. Willempje cannot read as well as Jan but she can memorize better. A half year ago Willempje was able to recite the catechism of Borstius from beginning to end. She knows many of the readings in her schoolbook by heart. Now they are studying the catechism of A. Hellenbroek.[1]

We now have a private school for a few families. H. Swets and I are school board members. The teacher opens the school with prayer and it is also closed with devotions. On each day a chapter of the Bible is read and a psalm verse is sung at the beginning and end of the day. We use the same book that the seceder schools use in the Netherlands and also the best English books that are used here in this country. Jan is now reading his third English book and Willempje her first.

Jacob van der Aa has been disqualified as a preacher and ejected from the church. God punishes the proud and gives grace to the humble.[2]

[Closing]

1. Jacobus Borstius and A. Hellenbroek were standard Dutch Reformed catechism authors.
2. In his December 4, 1876, letter, omitted here because it is exclusively a pious dis-

course, Van den Hoek reveals that Jacob van der Aa had been ordained by the Reverend C. Wust, himself a peculiar fellow who was ejected from the RCA in 1868. Van der Aa, despite his ejection, continued to lead a group of four or five women in a spirit and manner that Van den Hoek compared to that of Jean De Labadie, a seventeenth-century Dutch theologian who organized a charismatic communitarian group in the Netherlands.

May 3, 1877

[Greetings to various persons]

I was disappointed to learn that Uncle Gerrit opposes the Christian Seceded church in the Netherlands. I disagree strongly with him as I am entirely convinced that the seceders are the purest ecclesiastical body in the Netherlands and that no one with a pure faith and good conscience can be active in the Hervormde kerk [the state-supported church].

I am delighted to report that depending on the Lord's favor, two pastors from the Christian Seceded Church of the Netherlands will be arriving here on May 12. They have left the Netherlands to serve two of our congregations. Namely, Rev. J. Kremer from Wanswerd [Friesland] who will come to Grand Rapids, Michigan, and Rev. G. Hemkes from Bunde, East Friesland [a German province bordering Groningen province], who is coming to Vriesland, Michigan.

Our denomination is known here as the True Holland Reformed Church in America [now the CRC].

You ask me if I also raise grain for my own use. No, only for horses, cows, pigs, and chickens and they eat rye grain. We plan to milk thirteen cows this summer. We put the cows to pasture on April 20. I sold a good cow for $42.00. Potatoes are $1.50 per bushel. Butter is twenty cents a pound, [etc.]. . . .

I have hired L. Perenbolt, a twenty-year-old, from April 1877 to April 1878 for $110.00. My wife's sister, Willempje Vogel, was married to Joseph Meeter. Both are twenty-two years old. Joseph is the youngest son of the widow Meeter, for whom I worked three years. They have rented a small farm and will milk six cows. My cows all had calves but three have died. My sow had ten piglets but they all died.

Father Vogel is in fairly good health but he cannot work any longer. Mother, considering her age, is strong and healthy. Brother Arie, we wish you the Lord's blessing with your new son Jan as well as with the other children.

[The letter ends with a page of pious reflections.]

[Closing]

May 31, 1882

Esteemed parents, brothers, and sisters,

[The letter opens with reports of good health and the arrival of mail.]

I would have written earlier but I have been waiting to report special news. I have sold my farm to Adam Ooms for $110 an acre. I went to the small city of Orange City, Iowa, with my neighbor, A. van Driel, to visit former neighbors and to look over that country and its potential. Reformed people have been moving there in the last few years and they have established four villages. The land there is exceptionally rich. The state [Iowa] is called the American granary and Orange City is called the Dutch garden. Five large Dutch churches have been built there and the congregations pay their pastors $500 to $800. All of this is within a fifteen-mile area of new homes and barns. Some of my former neighbors are among these people as is Pieter Verduin from Noordeloos and others who went there in straitened circumstances but have now prospered with the Lord's blessing.

In short, I have bought a farm two miles north of Orange City—eighty acres of good land. The house is three years old . . . and is much like the home in which I now live and which I previously described to you. It has eight grapevines and thirty young apple trees which are beginning to bear fruit. It is 800 paces long and 400 paces wide—five minutes from the school, forty-five minutes from the church where Rev. Jan Stadt is [First Christian Reformed Church, Orange City], forty minutes from Orange City, and twenty minutes from the railroad station. On all sides there are Dutch neighbors. It cost me altogether $2,000, or $25 per acre. If the Lord wills and we live, we will move there in November by train. It is 550 miles or 183 hours [at walking speed] from here. When I went there it took twenty-five hours by fast train and twenty-four hours back again plus seven hours in a carriage. The trip cost me $30. Before we leave we will have an auction, but we will take our best furniture with us.

It has been a cold and unfruitful spring here. So the world changes from day to day but the Lord remains the same. . . . I hope, dear ones, that you will receive this letter in good health.

[Closing]

Orange City, Iowa, to Goudriaan, Zuid Holland
October 11, 1882

Dear Mother,[1] brothers, and sisters,

With these words we inform you that we are all in good health. . . . and that we held our auction in North Creek on September 25. On the evening of the 26th Jan and I left on a freight car in which we had loaded two cows, two horses, and five wagonloads of furniture and other items. On September 30, Saturday, we arrived in Alton, Iowa, after a 550-mile trip. When we arrived P. Verduin, formerly a miller in Noordeloos, met us with a wagon. The station is one mile from my home. My wife, her mother, and the children left on September 28 at 7:00 A.M. on a passenger train. They arrived in Alton at 10 o'clock the next day. Saturday noon we were privileged to meet them with joy and thanksgiving. Praise the Lord!

When Dirkje arrived J. Brinks met them with a carriage and two horses. He had been one of our best neighbors in Illinois. When my neighbors knew that we had come they hitched their horses to wagons at once to get our belongings from the train. By Saturday evening everything was in the house and stable.

* * *

There is not much dairying here. The chief crops are wheat, rye, flax, barley, oats, and buckwheat. So, I too will be a grain farmer. The land here is much like Chicago—mostly rich black soil. Our local church is part of the Holland Christian Reformed church, joined as one body with the Christian Seceded Church in the Netherlands. Ours is a large congregation with a good minister, Rev. J. Jan Stadt.

At present I am hauling brick to build a cellar under our house. The brick kiln is a mile away and brick costs $12.00 per thousand.

We live 300 feet higher above sea level than in Illinois so there is more wind and a clear and healthy climate. People from other states in America who suffer from lung and liver diseases are sent here for cures with good results. For a large area around here there are only Hollanders—a thing that one finds in only a few other places in America.

I received your last letter in good health. But I have not yet received a letter from brother F. Rietveld this summer. I have sent my power of attorney to the lawyer Slotemaker. My current address is

T. B. van den Hoek
Orange City, Sioux County
State of Iowa
North America

[Closing]

1. Van den Hoek's father died in July 1882.

January 25, 1883

Highly esteemed and beloved Mother,
[The letter begins with reports of good health and inquiries about letters sent and received.]

We are very well pleased with our new living place. We have very good neighbors among whom many are true children of Zion. Four of our children go to school every day. They have singing school on Wednesday evening and catechism at 3:30 P.M. in the school. Our children are learning well. There are two Dutch churches in the city. The Holland Christian Reformed Church to which we belong has a godly minister, four elders, and three deacons. I was installed as an elder on January 21. Now I must go with the pastor for. house visitation one or two days each week because the congregation is large and widely spread out.

It has been very cold here this winter. For six weeks now the snow has averaged one and a half feet deep and in all that time we have had no thaw. Many here wear fur coats of buffalo skin and black bear skin which are lined with wool and are very warm. Yesterday I bought a raccoon-skin cap for $3.00. It looks like a rabbit skin but it has fine silky black hair and is quilted inside with wool and blue silk. In the winter people here wear elastic shoes and boots lined with wool and mittens of sheep or buffalo skin. People here burn coal for heat which costs $5.00 a ton.

We notice in our weekly newspapers that there is much destruction and poverty in Europe because of floods. How is it by you? I have also received, signed, and returned the papers from notary Slotemaker. . . .

Yesterday it was my duty to attend a funeral—the first casualty to death here in this new year.
[Pious reflections on death and his eternal hope.]

[Closing]

April 18, 1883

Beloved and esteemed Mother, brothers, and sisters,
[Reports about physical and spiritual well-being.]

It is nice weather here and we are busy with plowing and planting. I have already sown five acres of summer wheat and eight and a half acres of oats. I hope to sow seventy-five acres of flaxseed next week. I have bought a new mowing machine for $55.00 with which I can mow five acres in one day. Jan can already plow nicely. I was pleased to hear that Rev. Jonkman has decided to stay in Noordeloos. Brother Jacob, it is wrong for you not to join the Christian Reformed congregation of Noordeloos. Do not sadden God's spirit any longer in this matter. You should be protected in the sheepfold of your spiritual companions. Do not be doublehearted, my dear brother. The Lord of the harvest is coming. Is it not a grievous matter that so many of our friends love the world and its passing friendships more than God and his pure truth?

* * *

Much money is being collected here in America for the flood victims in Europe. Last week I sent money from our church to Professor [Anthony] Brummelkamp in Kampen [a teacher at the theological school for the Seceded Christian Reformed Church in the Netherlands]. We have also had some destructive floods in some parts of America. . . .

Orange City is growing rapidly. Almost every week our pastor announces the arrival of one or more membership papers from the Netherlands or from other states in America. Our land here is exceptionally good, and the climate is too. Since I have been here five new families have followed us here from South Holland. And so the world's stage constantly changes. But, Mother, isn't it a great blessing that I have my own land and work? And that we can keep our dear children in our own house and under our own supervision.[1] When I think of all these blessings I am humbled by thankfulness. . . .

My nephew Horber Huisman from Illinois visited us last week and will probably move here this year. His daughter Neeltje is married to J. van de Griend who bought a farm and moved here this spring.

[Closing]

1. People of Van den Hoek's status in the Netherlands were forced by economic considerations to hire out their children to farmers at about age twelve.

August 2, 1883

Dear Mother, brothers, and sisters,

[Remarks regarding health, congratulations on the birth of his sister's children.]

Brother, you asked about reports of disasters here. These are scandalous lies. Not long ago we did have some heavy damage from hailstorms in America, but in our area we were spared. Elsewhere many people and livestock drowned and crops were ruined, but in our area the grain crops are exceptionally good. I bought a new mowing machine for $165.00. If the Lord wills and if I live, I will begin mowing the oats tomorrow, and wheat the following week. Two weeks later the flaxseed.

It was good to hear that Teunis, Arie's son, is a reliable boy. I and my children have often agreed that we are greatly blessed in having our work and bread here. Many times I have wished that you were all here in this land of God's favor. Many poor people come here. Almost every week more Hollanders come to join our church. Many are from Friesland and last week two families came from Amsterdam. And now two more families are coming from Amsterdam to meet my neighbor.

* * *

I am finishing this letter on August 11. We have had much rain in the last nine days. Our wheat is in the barn and half of the oats. But we cannot mow now because of the rain. Last week a disease affected one of our milk cows. I had it slaughtered and sold half of the meat. So things change, come and go, changes on the stage of the world. But the Lord remains the same and eternal. . . .

[Closing]

December 21, 1883

Dear Mother, brothers, and sisters,

[Reports of good health and comments on letters received.]

Brother, you asked me to send you some seed, but that would be useless. Crops which are grown in the Netherlands do not do well here and those that are grown here do not do well there. But we urge you to come here and share the good things of this country. I will do all I can to make your life here happy. If you decide that it is not the Lord's will for you to come here, it would please us if you could send Arie's son, Teunis, to us. If he is willing to obey us as our own child I would be ready to treat him with affection. We are sorry that such a tender youth must work under such pressure among strangers. If you could bring this to the Lord in self-denying submission [and if all of you could come] it would be a great joy to see our aged mother and all of our dear relatives once again.

[The letter ends with a six-page homily with pious injunctions.]

Harrison, South Dakota, to Goudriaan, Zuid Holland
April 28, 1884

Dear Mother, brothers, and sisters,

[Notes that his son Jan has already written about their move from Orange City to Harrison, South Dakota.][1]

Last December I traveled through the western part of America with my neighbors and visited many good friends and acquaintances. About two years ago about 500 people from Orange City and many Hollanders from other parts of America moved to South Dakota in order to establish new settlements. Only three years ago everything was still wild and as unoccupied as on the day of creation except for a few wild people and wild animals. The government bought out the Indian tribes and by force drove them farther west. They surveyed the land and built some railroads through it.

My neighbor and I each bought 160 acres of good land. I paid $1,000 but it costs a great deal of trouble and money to build a house and barn with a fence for the livestock. I sold my place in Orange City for $2,450 [about $30.50 per acre]. I now live 175 miles farther west.

We left on April 8 with two freight cars loaded with five cows, two hogs, five young calves, twelve young pigs, forty chickens, two horses, two dogs, one cat, and two canaries—plus all kinds of grain [for seed], fruit trees, and our furniture and machinery, etc. We arrived in Plankinton on the evening of April 9. An hour later my wife, mother, and children arrived by passenger train. We were then twenty-two miles from our destination and everything had to be taken farther by horse and wagons. This was a lot of trouble and very costly. The railroad expense was $112 and the trip from Plankinton to our farm was also about $112. The fare on the passenger train was $16 for my family. All of this plus my own personal expenses and labor.

Jan has begun to plow the new land with two large oxen each weighing 1,600 pounds. The work is too hard for horses. I paid $140 for the two oxen.

Last January I traveled here to build a boarded stable with help from carpenters and we are living in it temporarily with our cattle. We hope to build a house in the fall. The barn is 26 feet wide and 40 feet long with 8-foot sides. It cost me $170. I live one and a half miles from Harrison. There is a Dutch church there with a minister and a school for our small children. Very likely a second congregation will be organized this summer and a new church will be built because a stream of people arrive here every week.

A new railroad has been laid out three miles from here. There are no trees here except for those which have been planted. Coal is used here for fuel. I have planted an acre of trees here just as one would plant seedlings in the Netherlands.

The reason my wife and I made this important and desirable move, with prayerful reliance on the Lord, was to keep our dear children under our own supervision and control and to avoid special problems [that is,

to have enough land to employ the children]. One can break even financially in the first two years because the soil is exceptionally good. Under
God's direction and merciful providence I have found a very good piece
of land in a favorable location. This spring has been cold and wet.

[A pious conclusion recites his dependence on the God who made the
heavens and the earth.]

[Closing]

Now my address is:
T. B. van den Hoek
Harrison via Plankinton
Douglas County
Dakota Territory

1. In his April 15, 1884, letter, Jan van den Hoek described the move: "When Father
came here from Orange City he bought 160 acres of land for $1,000 or $6.25 per acre.
The land here is just as it was when it was created. There has not been a plow on it or
any other work except for seven acres which was plowed last year. Two wells have been
dug—one twenty-five feet deep with five feet of water and another seventy feet deep with
fifty feet of water. Good wells are needed here because water is scarce.

"The reason we moved from Orange City was the need for more land because we can
cultivate more than eighty acres. Now, suddenly, we have so much. Father has gone twenty
miles away today to get a pair of oxen which he bought this winter for $140. So if we are
well, I will plow with the oxen and cultivate with the horses. There were no buildings on
this land so we have built a good barn in which we will live this summer. But it is very
cold here and it rained so hard last Sunday that we were almost soaking wet. But we will
take care of that with a covering of tar paper. This summer and fall we must build a house
but we have no time for that now."

July 14, 1884

Dearly beloved Mother, brothers, and sisters,
    [Greetings]
    Brother Jacob, you wrote that you were surprised that we had moved
again so quickly. I am myself amazed by it, but it is true and we are well
satisfied with this place. We have good Dutch neighbors on all sides and
our crops look rather good even though we planted later. We were able
to plow 40 acres—one of potatoes, five of wheat, ten of flaxseed, and
fifteen of oats. You asked, what do you do with five cows in that wild
country? Answer—we have good buffalo grass with few weeds and no
trees or bushes. There are hundreds of places like this in America. The
cow's milk is rich with fat so the grass and hay are good. Whatever is
not used for pasture or hay is burned in the fall. At times thousands of
acres are burning at once.
    A person can make a good living here on 80 acres, but I can easily
cultivate 100 acres with my children and with American machinery.

I have had my cellar dug 22 by 12 feet with walls of stone weighing from 1 to 200 pounds. I have bought $292 worth of lumber to build my house. The plan is to have the front part 26 by 15 feet and the back part 16 by 10 feet. It will have four bedrooms, two up and two down. The whole house will cost about $500. I have the money on hand.

I thank you, brother, for warning me about the danger of being ensnared by worldly concerns. I must seek God's grace daily to use the world without misusing it.

Now, after praying that all of you may partake in the essential blessing for your soul and body, I close, your loving son and brother.

[Closing]

October 6, 1884

Dear Mother, brothers, and sisters,

[Greetings]

We have now been living in our new house for fifteen days and our harvests were moderately good and our cows produced well.

Two months ago we organized a new congregation of our church. Now I must read a sermon every Sunday and lead everything because the other elder is a pious but aged man who cannot provide leadership because of his poor health. After reading the sermon I teach catechism to twenty or thirty children. Two weeks ago we decided to build a church and parsonage for $2,445. The congregation has pledged $2,230—a great blessing. A half year ago I would hardly have dared to imagine or pray for this.

Soon we hope to call a pastor of our own. At present we hold our services in the home of a deacon who lives in town. The church and parsonage will be in the middle of the town. The school is also near the church. The church must be completed by December 1. Currently the members of the congregation are busy hauling rock, cement, and lumber from Plankinton, twenty-two miles away.

It is rumored that next year a railroad will be built three miles from our farm. And this is not without foundation because the railroad company has been surveying and they have signs everywhere. But sometimes these plans are changed.

At the same time that our church is being built an orthodox Dutch Reformed Church in America [RCA] is also building just five minutes away from our church. The cost of the church alone is $4,500. From this you will be able to understand how the Dutch folk around here have progressed. There are nearly none but Hollanders around us. But six miles away there are many Swiss, English, Russians, and Germans plus a few Irish—that is a nasty thieving Catholic folk, but they seem to be in poor repute here. Settlement is continuing steadily here and land values are rising.

My wife's mother is still strong and goes to church every Sunday. I am sending three photos in this letter. One for Arie, one for Johannes, and one for Johanna. We hope that you will receive this letter in good health.

[Closing]

July 4, 1885

Dear brothers and sisters,

We with our children are all in good health because of God's goodness and faithfulness. We hope the same is true for you.

About two weeks ago I wrote a letter to brother Johannes which informed him that we had received two certificates for the money. Now I have the money in hand, $744. I had to pay only 75 cents for the transfer of the whole amount.

Now you are probably thinking, what has brother done with that money? I have bought 160 acres of land with the money. It is 1.5 miles northeast of Harrison—$600 down and $500 on an 8 percent contract to be paid in five years. The total price was $1,100. I have $550 debt on the place where I live so together I owe $1,050.

The crops look very good. This spring D. de Boer, married to my wife's sister Jannigje, came here from [Three Oaks,] Michigan. He has bought 160 acres here. They have seven children.

Last Sunday we were privileged to have our pastor, Rev. F. M. van den Bosch, installed by Rev. R. T. Kuiper from Graafschap, Michigan.

If you have not written lately, please write us soon.

[Closing]

In three previous letters, March 6, March 18, and June 8, each concerned primarily with religious matters, it was apparent that Van den Hoek's aged mother had died and the family estate was being settled.

August 26, 1885

Esteemed brothers and sisters,

[Reports of good health and the reception of letters.]

Brother, in your last letter you wrote that you are of the opinion that I am happy in this new place because I bought more land here. Yes. We with our children are happy here. On all sides we have Dutch neighbors.

Our church has been organized just over a year ago and its membership has doubled. We have a good pious pastor, humble and kindhearted. He is respected both inside and outside of our group. The city is growing steadily. The Dutch are building three more large stores and a new school worth at least $2,000 is being built in the city.

It has been very warm here this summer—105 degrees in the shade. This has caused the death of several small children and there is much sickness among the young and very old. In many places the crops have dried out, but things are about normal here.

You asked if the land I bought has been under cultivation. Answer: 15 acres have been plowed and the rest is just as it has been for 6,000 years when it came forth from the hand of the Creator. So, brother, if you want to come here and lend me a hand, I have just bought a riding plow for $50 to keep you busy. Jan plows with this every day now using three horses. I also bought a self-binding mowing machine for $200. This is also drawn by three horses. It cuts wheat and oats—ten acres a day. Jan cut twelve acres of oats in one day and the grain sheaves come out bound.

Thank you, sister, for the photo of nephew and niece. It was also a pleasure to receive greetings from L. Terlouw and his Maria.
[Continues with pious injunctions and reflections.]

[Closing]

August 2, 1886

Esteemed and beloved brothers and sisters,
    [Reports of good health.]
    At present we are harvesting the wheat and oats. Everything looks very promising this spring but now we have had no rain for five weeks and very warm weather. Just before the drought we had a heavy hailstorm in this area which destroyed many crops. For these reasons I have only half a crop. Now we have a gentle rain. Yet, in spite of disappointments we have everything in abundance.

Things are cheap at present. Wheat is fifty cents per bushel, oats twenty cents, butter ten cents, cheese eight cents, eggs twelve cents, beef eight to ten cents per pound. The best white sugar is eleven pounds for $1.00. Seven pounds of coffee beans for $1.00, twenty pounds of prunes for $1.00, twenty pounds of dried apples for $1.00, two pounds of tea for $1.00 and twenty pounds of soap for $1.00.

A suit of blue clothes for a man, trousers, vest, and coat, costs $15 to $20. So you can see that one can obtain the very best cheaply here.

This is a good country for all classes of people. It is too bad that many unthankful people use these good things without recognizing the God who gives them. For this reason heavy calamities threaten to break out over America soon. This is especially the case with domestic problems and developments—socialists and anarchists. The Knights of Labor are the ringleaders. But, praise God, there are still many true believers and warriors for the truth. For the sake of these the days of trouble will be shortened.

[Closing]

June 10, 1887

Dear brothers and sisters,

[Report of good health and requests to greet specific persons in Noordeloos.]

We have now planted all our seed—one hundred acres of wheat, forty of rye, twenty-five of oats and thirty of flax. We have had a bad dry spell but we have had steady rain for the past three weeks and everything looks good now. Jan, Jan Willem, and I did all the planting.

We have a very kind and pious pastor, Rev. [Cornelius] Bode, and our church is growing. During the week seventy schoolchildren come to catechism and fifty come to Sunday school. Our preacher is well liked by the other Dutch congregation, the Dutch Reformed [RCA], which is much like the Reformed church in the Netherlands [the state church]. The most orthodox members from that church drift over to ours. The other church invited our pastor to preach for them, which he did willingly. They were pleased and satisfied with his service.

Our church is packed full on Sunday. When we organized three years ago I would not have dared to expect or pray for this. Back then I read sermons as an elder for a gathering of about twenty-five people in the home of a deacon. We used an old mowing machine for a platform and some loose boards for seats. Now we have a fine church and a parsonage with one of the best preachers and many hundreds in the audience. The Lord continues to work through His Holy Spirit. Four weeks ago we accepted, by their confessions of faith, six married persons and one single person. To our great joy the single person was our son Jan, who was also the first of the congregation's children to become a confessing member.

He is exemplary in learning and behavior and enjoys the respect of the congregation. . . .

My eyes are becoming weak and my hands shake. I can hardly read without glasses. Otherwise I am in good health and no longer have stomach pain. My hair is very gray. My wife is healthy and strong. She shows few signs of aging. Her old mother is also reasonably healthy and rides to church with us every Sunday. She is seventy-seven years old—so all of us are moving toward our eternal home.

[Closing]

November 26, 1887

Dear brothers and sisters,

[Begins with reports of good health and pious reflections.]

If your son Teunis is in danger of becoming a soldier, I would prefer to have him come to us in America. There is no military draft in America. Service is voluntary unless there is a war and then there is a general lottery entirely equal for a certain age group.

Brother, you wrote that if we were not so distant from you, you would like to come and look things over. But send your son first. Then he can earn your traveling expenses for you and then, if we live and the Lord wills it, all of you can come.

This year's crops were largely disappointing. I have lost $150 to the drought this year. You are always curious about how I can work so much land with my children. The reason is that we use powerful machinery driven by steam and horse power. But now and then I do have work for hired help. If your son is inclined to come here I will teach him the American ways of working, speaking, writing, singing, and behaving. My wife and I are fifty years old and in some need of rest. If the Lord continues to bless us we can go on nicely.

We had a very nice fall until yesterday, November 25. Now we have a strong frost and snow. Jan and I have plowed eighty acres this fall. Next Monday all of our children will be going to school except our oldest daughter Willempje because she is past school age.

* * *

Our congregation has built a stable near the church for forty horses. In nice weather another twenty still have to stand outside. The Lord has visibly blessed our congregation, both young and old with the preaching of the Word and Christian service. We have a kind, godly, and sympathetic pastor who is loved by all.

Yesterday my son Jan took the stagecoach twenty-two miles away to the railroad station and he took the train another 400 miles to Minnesota where he will help organize a new congregation for our church. What a shame, brother, what an eternal misfortune to acknowledge that the preaching of the Word has not yet borne fruit in so many.

[Closing]

Teunis van den Hoek to Jacob van den Hoek
Harrison, South Dakota, to Goudriaan, Zuid Holland
August 1, 1888

Honorable and beloved brother Jacob,
　We received your June 11 letter with pleasure. . . .
　We are now busy harvesting the wheat. The crop is average and it has
been extremely hot—104 degrees in the shade.
　It would be so heartening to see you once again face to face and to
talk with you heart to heart. I wish that God would give you the freedom
to come over here. I have no one here from my side of the family.
　You could make a good living and do well both spiritually and phys-
ically. My wife and children would like that too. Ask the Lord for insight
and freedom.
　Our old mother can no longer go to church. She is too weak to climb
up into the wagon, but she is still healthy. How are sister Jannigje's eyes?
Greet all of my friends in Noordeloos and especially F. de Jong and his
wife.

[Closing]

Teunis van den Hoek to Arie van den Hoek
Harrison, South Dakota, to Goudriaan, Zuid Holland
November 10, 1890

Dear brother Arie,
　[Opening words about health and God's blessings.]
　You asked about the drought here and the oppressive heat. In many
states a severe drought and constant wind killed the crops. This was
especially true in South Dakota where whole villages have been left behind, abandoned by man and beast. They have moved to other states to
make a living. Some three or four hours northwest of us all the grain
died, so that many Hollanders were also in need and moved to other
places.
　In our area we have had about a half crop of everything. We had
enough to pay our taxes and interest and also to support the church and
pastor. We had no significant rain for half the year. The ground is as
hard as stone and unworkable. Many cattle lack water. So far we have
had enough. We have held prayer days. It is my hope and prayer that
the Father of all mercies will shorten these days for the sake of those
who call upon Him day and night. . . .
　We have had about five inches of snow over the past two days. Now
it is nice weather. Our work is finished for four to five months. The

children are in school. I have a little to do with the cows and horses. I read some and visit good friends. No doubt you will be saying, brother, that I have the privilege of not having to work for someone else from early morning until sundown. [Ends with pious declarations.]

[Closing]

December 11, 1891

Dear brother Arie,

With this letter we are informing you that we and our five children and three grandchildren enjoy through the blessings and grace of God good health and well-being. . . .

This week Tuesday, December 8, my neighbor, Pieter Verwolf, left on a trip to the Netherlands. His father lives in Ameide, and Kees Brouwer in Goudriaan is his nephew and Klaas de Groot in Noordeloos is his uncle. If the Lord brings him over the ocean safely he will visit our friends briefly. Give him a good welcome. He is an intelligent farmer who has a clear understanding of all aspects of America. He is a man of adventure and experience. Just three weeks ago I bought three milk cows from him.

This is a very blessed year, the land produced abundant crops. I have 1,851 bushels of wheat, 129 bushels of flaxseed, 325 bushels of rye, 1,225 bushels of oats. I have picked 1,600 bushels of corn. All of this grain is threshed with a $700 threshing machine using fourteen horses and ten men in just five days. Wheat is 70 cents, rye 62 cents, oats 20 cents, and corn 25 cents per bushel [total yield about $2,200]. After years of drought and disappointment the Lord has given us a year of blessing and happy thanksgiving.

My son-in-law [W. Nieuwenhuis] and my daughter Willempje have purchased a one-hundred-and-sixty-acre farm with a house and barn for $1,000. It is located about two miles away. Jan, my oldest son, is a bookkeeper and clerk in a large store and earns $34 per month. My youngest daughter, Eigje, is a schoolteacher and earns $30 per month. The school is located on the corner of P. Verwolf's land. Willem and Eben work on the farm with me and go to school in the winter.

Pieter Verwolf will explain all of this to you in detail when he enjoys a cup of hot chocolate and a slice of sugar bread with you. We have sent a few gifts along with him for the children.

The old year is running to its end and the new year approaches. We wish all of you forgiveness and reconciliation for your old sins and debts. . . .

[Closing]

Van den Hoek family portrait about 1885. Center, Teunis and Dirkje; left to right, Willem, Jan, Eigje, Willempje, Eben. Courtesy of Calvin College Library Archives, photo collection.

Teunis van den Hoek to Brothers and Sisters
Harrison, South Dakota, to Goudriaan, Zuid Holland
June 10, 1893

Dear brothers and sisters,
    Hearty greetings from all of us with the exception of brother Arie's wife. They [Arie van den Hoek family] had a very swift and uneventful

trip over land and sea. On Monday, June 5, at 3:10 I and many others were waiting for them at the train station in Armour. There we met with joy and thankfulness to God. Arie and the children were in good health, but Maggeltje felt sick. She caught a cold on the ocean. She had also complained of pain in her side before leaving Holland. On the train she was still more sickly. When we met each other everyone was very happy but Maggeltje could only have a cup of tea with a slice of cake and then she went directly to bed. During the night she suffered from a severe fever and we called the doctor the next morning. He said that she was very sick. The fever continued on Wednesday and Thursday and the doctor came each day. She died on Thursday at about 1:00 P.M. Brother, you can imagine that it was a tragic experience for her husband and children. Her mind was clear until the last three hours and she had little pain at the end. . . . We must not linger over the question of her eternal destination but ask instead, am I born again? Am I by God's grace humble before him? Am I one for whom the person and work of Jesus Christ is precious?

On Thursday evening she was placed in an expensive wooden casket just like those in the Netherlands. It was made of expensive brown wood with six large silver handles. It cost $17.00. She was buried on Friday afternoon with great solemnity. The pastor, W. Heyns, offered an earnest and appropriate funeral message after the singing of Psalm 39 v. 10–14. The church was full of concerned listeners. She was buried with dignity in the large Holland graveyard by the church—near to our mother's grave [that is, Mrs. Vogel].

Arie and the children will live with us at first. Teunis has hired out to a nearby Dutch farmer for six months at $100. Jan is working for our son-in-law W. Nieuwenhuis at $40 for five months. Brother Jacob, Arie has asked you to inform Maggeltje's family of these matters with great prudence. Arie hopes to write to you soon.

[Closing]

Arie van den Hoek to Brother and Sister
Harrison, South Dakota, to Goudriaan, Zuid Holland
January 3, 1894

Dear brother and sister,

Due to God's blessing we are healthy and well and we hope the same for you. We have been expecting a letter for some time but none came. So now I will write to you.

We live 1,700 miles from New York or about in the middle of America. It is hard to imagine that so much could happen in a year's time.

We began the year together and in good health, but it did not end that way. At the beginning of this year I had no idea that we would end it in America. We have to thank you time and again for helping us. So far America has not disappointed us.

Teunis has earned $85 in five months, Jan $40 in six months and I have done rather well too. Aartje works for C. van den Bosch in town for 50 cents per week and he goes to the English school each day. The school and books are free. Arie earns board and clothing working for W. Nieuwenhuis and they also allow him to attend the English school. There is no Dutch school here. English is the primary language of America. Arie can ride a horse like an adult. He rode five miles in half an hour. Eigje and Jannigje are growing well. Leendert has learned to walk as fast as Jannigje and he has begun to speak already.[1]

Everyone speaks Dutch here. For miles around there are only Hollanders. We have two churches in Harrison—one Dutch Reformed [RCA] and one Christian Reformed. I and the children are baptized members of the Christian Reformed Church.[2] The children also go to Sunday school. We are not sorry that we came to America, but I am sorry that we did not come earlier.

We had a letter from C. Drinkwaard who writes that many Hollanders have sent home bad reports about America, and I can believe that regarding the heavily populated areas. C. van Genderen and A. Terlouw live in [Roseland, Illinois] and say that thousands are unemployed. It is not the best year here either but we cannot complain. The summer was very dry here and we still need moisture. Many wells are dry but we still have water.

We have plenty to eat, thank the Lord. We eat white bread every day and as much pork and beef as we want. We have at least 200 pounds of pork and beef on hand plus forty pounds of lard. We raised enough potatoes for the summer and winter. I bought 300 pounds of beef at three and a half cents per pound. Pork is only four to five cents per pound. Potatoes are seventy cents a bushel. We use cornstalks for fuel when it is not too cold. They grow five to six feet tall here. I can haul as many of these as I wish. Hundreds of acres are covered with cornstalks. Cows and horses eat the leaves off of the stalks after the ears have been gathered. The animals roam in the fields for miles and in the evening they come home for feed and hay.

We have had a lot of snow and it has been cold. Colder than it has ever been in the Netherlands.

I still have no money. When we came here we had just $2 left and my wife's death cost $40. Then we had to buy everything needed for a home. They do not have beds built into the walls here. So we needed two beds, heavy clothing and shoes [boots] which are worn over regular shoes. Wooden shoes are seldom worn here and they are rarely seen. If you go outside in the winter wearing Dutch clothes it's like having no clothes on at all.

Brother Teunis and his wife were here Thursday night, December 28. They are all in good health and they send greetings. I hope you will write us soon.

I have read in the paper that there are three million people out of work in America so you can easily imagine that there is great need in some places. But, thank the Lord, not here. During the winter we eat and drink well and sleep long.

Greetings from me and my children,

Your brother,
A. van den Hoek

1. Obviously Arie was left as a single parent with six children.
2. Thus, not yet members with voting rights and access to the sacraments.

April 10, 1894

Dear brother and sister,

We received your letter this new year in good health. . . . We hope the same for you. We learned from your letter to brother Teunis that your wife has been dangerously ill. We hope and pray that the God of all goodness will restore her quickly.

You asked about our voyage. We had a good ten-day trip at sea. On the third day the waves were as high as a house. We had good food and slept well. Coffee, tea, good bread, pork, beef soup, cheese, butter, and potatoes—three meals every day. When we arrived in Armour we still had some bread and cheese and $2.00 left.

We are well impressed with the people here. They are very kind and friendly. My children have earned their board taking care of cows and horses. H. Brink hired Teunis for nine months at $53. C. Doorn hired Johannes for $108, also for nine months. They started work in the middle of March.

* * *

I noticed from your letter that you have not received good reports about America. On the whole the situation is not favorable. Thousands upon thousands are out of work, but we are about in the best place. Almost all the people here are farmers. There is plenty of food but no money. Everything is cheap. Wheat is forty cents, corn thirty cents, po-

Harrison, South Dakota, creamery, 1909. Courtesy of Calvin College Library Archives, photo collection.

tatoes ninety cents per bushel, sugar five cents, syrup five cents, coffee twenty-five cents, beef four cents, pork five cents, butter ten cents, and eggs seven cents per dozen. It is not good for laborers here. A person must be able to become a farmer.

I hope that in the future my children will be able to rent something and become farmers. Otherwise there is too little work here and the work is far away. Yet, I must say that I never had such a fine winter in the Netherlands. We received a great deal of help last year. Now it is April and I have only earned $4 but we lack nothing. One only needs some cows and chickens which do not cost much, there is enough vacant land here to get started.

We have had a hard winter for twelve weeks, an average of a foot of snow on the ground. We've had a few snowstorms. We had some nice days in February, and it was severely cold in March. It can be cold here in winter with a great deal of wind.

One of my cows had a bull calf and the other cow will soon have a calf. We skim the milk and then we churn it to make butter and cheese. The calf gets the buttermilk or we boil it to make pap from it [a dish made from buttermilk and barley].

My work has been to bury two stones and now I am busy with the third. This one is 6 feet × 7 feet and 5 feet thick. In my opinion it weighs about 20,000 pounds. I am digging a big hole for it so it will be out of the way for plowing. I'm paid $2.00 each for these stones, and it is hard work. The ground is as hard as iron when you get down about two feet. Then you have to break it up with a pickaxe. If the stones are not too large I can earn $1.00 per day. It is nothing but work here, but I can honestly say that I am still happy to be here.

We continue to live in brother Teunis's house, but he cultivates the land around it. We live here free and have two acres to raise potatoes and vegetables. I hope to be able to pay the interest on the money I owe.

Everything is well at brother Teunis's house and he sends his greetings. Receive also the greetings from my children.

Your brother, A. B. van den Hoek
Write back quickly.

Teunis van den Hoek to Brothers and Sisters
Harrison, South Dakota, to Goudriaan, Zuid Holland
November 17, 1894

Dear brothers and sisters,

By God's goodness and faithfulness we and also brother Arie and his children are still in good health.

[Declares, with customary religious comments, his pleasure and gratitude regarding the renewed health of his brother's wife.]

Conditions in America are very bad and disappointing at present, especially in the Dakotas, Nebraska, and Kansas. In large parts of these states the crops were a total failure. This spring I planted 100 bushels of wheat and harvested only 82 (18 fewer than I planted), 105 acres of corn and one-half bushel picked, 80 bushels of oats—five bushels harvested, 25 acres of millet and not a handful threshed. Not a forkful of hay from 30 acres and from six bushels of potatoes we dug three bushels of small ones. And so it was for thousands and thousands of farmers.

A kind of African heat scorched almost every living thing. Many aged people (70–80 years) have seen nothing like it either in America or in the old countries. People cut hay from the open prairies and many cattle either died from hunger and thirst or are very thin.

If America were not a land of great resourcefulness, many people and livestock would have died. Many railroad cars carried food for man and beast from favored areas and it is donated to the poorest as gifts of love.

Next Monday, along with nine other relief officers, I must distribute six railroad cars of wheat flour, clothing, and groceries to about two hundred needy families to get them through the winter. These six rail car loads (the largest holds 6,000 bushels of wheat), came primarily from

Hollanders in Iowa as gifts of love. Even those who are better off, such as myself, cannot pay interest and taxes this year. We have to borrow from the banks at high rates of interest in order to keep our farms and families in reasonable condition.

Arie has already received 2,000 pounds of coal from the poor fund and he is also on the list to receive wheat flour and clothing next Monday.

There was some work available for hired hands and laborers until last fall but now almost all the farms are deserted and the unemployed workers do not know how to make a living. Teunis and Johannes [with their father Arie] want to become farmers. They have rented 160 acres and I helped them move last month. I have no idea how this will turn out. In the Netherlands people would consider this a very risky thing, but it is very ordinary in America. They already have two cows, a calf, five hogs, a young horse, a poor nag with a colt, a wagon, etc. They ride to church every Sunday, which is more than they ever did in Holland.

Compared to our life in the Netherlands we are still rich in having our children with us. But this unfaithful and ungrateful American nation, after becoming rich and fat, forgets the source of all material blessings. So it is necessary for the Lord of all creation to wield His rod of punishment to bring the wicked to repentance, salvation, and a renewing of the covenant which He has established as such a costly price.

[The letter concludes with a page of religious reflections on God's justice and the need to prepare for eternity.]

[Closing]

Arie van den Hoek to Brothers and Sisters
Harrison, South Dakota, to Goudriaan, Zuid Holland
May 31, 1895 [Fragment]

Dear brothers and sisters:

Hearty greetings. With this letter we are informing you that God has continued to spare our lives. Jannigje and Leendert were a little sick but fortunately have recovered.

We have had a year unlike any other that people here have experienced. Everything was completely dried out. Nothing was left except some cornstalks. The wheat was also completely scorched. The oats produced nothing for man or beast. And we had no potatoes or vegetables for the winter. The pastures were also parched and there was only a little hay on the thousands of acres of still uncultivated prairie land. That had to be hauled from a distance of twelve miles and it is of poor quality. There was no food for the people and also no money. Out of one hundred families at least ninety were in need. But because of the Lord's goodness we got through the winter.

The Lord moved the hearts of Christians in other states to provide for us abundantly. Every family received 600 pounds of wheat flour—enough for plenty of bread for half of the year. We also received twenty bushels of wheat to feed horses, chickens, and hogs during the winter—all free of charge. It all came to Armour in railroad cars.

We had in addition two tons of coal. We have to pay for this next fall. And for another thirty bushels of wheat and twelve bushels of oats, we must pay sixty-four cents a bushel by December.

The pastor of the Reformed Church went out preaching all across America for eight weeks and collected donations of more than $2,500. This was used to purchase seed corn and to feed the horses. We have ninety acres of farmland which must be cultivated with horses. The wheat and oats are well above ground. Teunis is now plowing land for the corn with three horses. So, you can understand that the horses need good feed every day.

There is still a water shortage. In an area eight to nine miles from here eight wells have been drilled. They are 1,000 feet deep and cost $6,000 per well. We can get water two miles from our place. These wells are drilled with a diamond or a steel rod. Then an 8-inch pipe is put down through 300 feet of rock. The water gushes out day and night. Ordinary wells are almost all dry.

We have had a year that will be long remembered. We had to buy an additional horse for $60—on credit. Now we have four horses and a yearling colt. We still need to pay for three of these horses. We owe for a plow, $20; and wagon, $50. One of our cows had a calf that froze to death in forty degrees below zero temperature. We expect another calf in June.

6   *Onno and Klaaske Heller*

Ulrum, a *gemeente* with authority over a seven-thousand-acre agricultural district containing five hamlets, has always been rather isolated and thinly populated. Nonetheless, Ulrum is known throughout the international Dutch Reformed community as the place that spawned the 1834 *Afscheiding*, the ecclesiastical secession that altered the character of Netherlandic Calvinism at home and abroad. The Hellers, who immigrated

These letters were donated by S. Noorda, 1976, and first translated by Henry Baak.

in 1891, were raised in Ulrum's Christian Seceded Church, but they also inherited a heavily traveled path of migration leading from Ulrum to Michigan and elsewhere. In 1848 the social geographer A. J. van der Aa already noted that Ulrum's population (870 residents occupying 126 houses) had been significantly reduced by the emigration of 200 villagers between 1847 and 1848.[1]

This exceptionally large and early exodus included a number of Ulrum's disaffected seceders, but the Heller family's emigration in 1891 was clearly motivated by economic rather than religious considerations. The agricultural crisis that disrupted clay-soil farming induced the Hellers to join some fourteen thousand emigrants who left the province of Groningen between 1880 and 1899.[2] The Hellers settled first in the Holland, Michigan, area, where they received assistance from relatives (the Nienhuis family) who had already immigrated in 1854. When the Hellers migrated to Whidbey Island, Washington, in 1896, part of the Nienhuis clan joined them. There, in and around Oak Harbor, the Heller-Nienhuis group joined others to reassemble a fragment of their Old World community.[3]

The Hellers quickly became enthusiastic boosters of Oak Harbor. They were pleased with their neighbors, church, and economic prospects. Oak Harbor, they asserted, offered far better opportunities than either Ulrum or Holland, Michigan. In 1896 Onno proudly declared that he had become a citizen of the United States. He confidently predicted that with the election of a Republican president, the economic future would brighten. Both Onno and Klaaske also supported McKinley's Spanish policy in 1898.

Most Dutch immigrants cheered the engagement and defeat of the Spanish in Cuba and the Philippine Islands, but the Hellers were exceptionally supportive of U.S. policy. Their nearly jingoistic assertions illustrate a level of patriotic nationalism which is not evident in other correspondence or in Dutch American periodicals.[4] And by pairing nationalism with Christian missionary zeal, the Hellers reflected something of Josiah Strong's civil religion in *Our Nation* and *Expansion*. It is most unlikely that the Hellers were acquainted with Strong's books, but his

[1] Van der Aa, *Aardrijkskundig woordenboek* 11:386–89.

[2] Hille de Vries, "The Labor Market in Dutch Agriculture," in *The Dutch in America*, ed. Swierenga, pp. 90–91.

[3] The original Nienhuis immigrants, Marcus and Martinus, settled near Holland in 1854. Marcus's letter that year gave a glowing report of West Michigan's Dutch settlements. His letter, along with the Heller family correspondence, was donated to the Calvin College Archives by S. Noorda in 1976.

[4] Lucas, *Netherlanders in America*, p. 565.

ideas were widely popular during and after the Spanish-American War.[5] The Hellers, it seems, were exceptionally receptive to cultural influences from outside their ethnic enclave.

The last of the Heller letters, a fragment from 1909, depicts a contented family. Two children are married. Hendrik, the eldest, is expected to arrive for a visit with his three children, and his unmarried siblings are either reading around the kitchen table or rehearsing in a local music society. All the adults are gainfully employed. Klaaske's comment that the two Dutch churches, RCA and CRC, "are almost alike" but that "discipline is more strictly exercised in our church" (CRC) appears to be a nearly neutral observation, and she seems to be at peace with the church and the world.

Ultimately, however, the Heller children left both the Dutch church and its community. Unlike the Van den Hoek and Eringa families, the Hellers were not persistently stalwart devotees of the Dutch Reformed community.[6]

Klaaske Noorda and Onno Heller to Noorda Family
Holland, Michigan, to Ulrum, Groningen
May 8, 1891

Dear Mother, brothers, and sisters,

We arrived well and healthy at the home of cousin Nienhuis and I hope that you too are well. Our cousins and their children are also well. We arrived here at 9 o'clock the day before yesterday. I have been washing clothes all of yesterday and part of today because there were Arabs on the boat and they were into everything. There were many Hollanders on the boat too. They stayed together and were singing psalms and hymns all the time like a singing organization. I am happy that we are here because I was tired of travel. I could not eat well on the boat and many others could not eat either. We were happy that we took butter along because they had artificial butter on board. The coffee was not good and I longed so for good coffee. Betje's coffee here tastes good and her bread is good too. We have received a welcome here which we find very comforting in a strange land.

H. Riksen and his wife were also here yesterday evening. Martinus and Hendrik are happy here and Malenus is beginning to talk.

[5] Ralph H. Gabriel, *The Course of American Democratic Thought* (New York: Ronald Press, 1956), pp. 368–72.
[6] *Anniversary Books* 1952, 1977, of the Oak Harbor Christian Reformed Church (privately published).

RIVER STREET LOOKING NORTH, HOLLAND, MICH.

We live right near here. Pretty place to live.

Holland, Michigan, central business area, about 1900. Courtesy of Calvin College Library Archives, photo collection.

Now, Mother, I hope that the Lord will comfort and strengthen you. That is my wish and prayer. . . .

Onno is going to Holland this afternoon to look for a house where we can bring our household goods. Enni will go with us to help get the house cleaned and in order—a great blessing.

And now dear Mother, brothers, and sisters, I wish you God's blessings. Give greetings to all. Your cousins also send greetings.

Klaaske Noorda

May 8, 1891 (continued)

Dear Mother, brothers, and sisters,

With this you will know that we arrived safely. We are talking around the table with E. K. Nienhuis. We are all healthy and hope that you are too. We arrived here from New York by way of Cleveland, a different way, but a more attractive way. We had bad weather on the boat for fifteen days, but none of us were seasick. One woman died en route. She had a stillborn child of seven months, and left three children behind, ages 11, 7, and 2, one boy and two girls. The father would not go to America without her and has returned to Germany. Two other children also died. Another person, a Zeelander, was thrown against the cabin by a large wave and he had five cuts in his head, but now he is almost as good as normal. He traveled with us as far as Kalamazoo. I had a fever for two days but now I am healthy. E. K. Nienhuis, his wife and children are all healthy. I have not yet seen the rest of the family. I expect to visit Mel today but they have scarlet fever at Pieter's house so I won't go there.

Yesterday E. K. Nienhuis and I went to the city to look for a stove, but we did not find one. R. Werkman has sold out here in Holland and he has gone to Benton Harbor, eighty miles away. He is setting up another factory there which is much larger than the one he had in Holland. He does this with other people's money because he has none. The factory here in Holland is still going at full speed.

[Onno Heller—closing missing]

P.S. Send us some leek seeds, as many as you can fit in an envelope. Don't forget it.

Klaaske Noorda Heller to Noorda Family
Holland, Michigan, to Ulrum, Groningen
[1891 Fragment]

It is getting dark and I can hardly see to write, but I want to write a little. About our furniture—we have a table with turned legs. A person can pull it open and lay a board in the middle of it just like the table top. We have nine comfortable chairs made of wood with cushions—good looking chairs with curved arms. We have a dresser with a mirror and a hanging lamp. We have a large cookstove with a large tin wash boiler with copper handles. The stove has a copper water reservoir in back. The stove has four openings in the front and a large oven. Everything is made of cast iron. Two pots, one for roasting, are commonly used here. The stove came with about twenty-five pieces, all for $30. Stoves are expensive here. Lena was happy to see me. Sister Maatje, I will write you too when I can. We forgot to take our kettle along. Write to us. I wish that all of you were here. Yes, all of you.

August 28, 1894

Dear Mother, brothers, and sisters,

We received your letter in good health and we were pleased to learn that you are well. You wrote that we have not written in a long time, and that is true. I have intended to write many times but I have been too busy. I hope that this letter will be ready to mail when I go to the city, but I don't look forward to that four-mile walk. Onno is working near the city pulling out stumps with oxen, so I can get a ride home with him. He has been working there fourteen days and earns $2.00 per day. That is a good wage but it will probably not last long. But it helps a lot because we don't get much cash from farming.[1]

We had two acres of oats which gave us about fifty-eight bushels. We gave that to Nienhuis for our debt. Oats sell for thirty-two cents per bushel so that was about $18.00 and we owed him $35.00. We still have four acres of corn and about one acre of potatoes and they look rather good. We also have two and a half acres for grass and clover which gave us six small loads. . . . We really need a horse during the summer for cultivating and hauling hay, but a horse costs a lot of money and it needs food too. It has been so dry throughout the whole country that there is a shortage of oats and most farmers are now using corn for feed. A farmer in Ohio killed thirty-four of his horses because he did not want them to starve. It is not that bad here. Almost every day it looks like it will rain but it doesn't.

You asked about [working conditions in the cities]. In Holland the factories are busy and there are no strikes here such as you have [in the Netherlands]. Jan is working and Papko is also earning something. He can work for a celery farmer but that will make for a very busy summer. Still it is not heavy work. If the boys were a little older they could work in the factory.

I am writing in haste.

I enclose our pictures.

[Closing]

1. In another letter from Holland, Michigan, Klaaske wrote, "Malenus walks over to us with a small piece of wood and says 'stump.' Mother, he makes little songs about everything. He looks at his little hand and sings a song to each finger as loudly as he can. . . . Now he is sitting next to me on a chair playing with the box of blocks we took with us from Ulrum."

Onno Heller to Noorda Family
Oak Harbor, Washington, to Ulrum, Groningen
[1896]

Dear Mother, brothers, sister,

This is now the third letter I am writing to you and I hope you receive it in good health. We are all healthy at present. . . . Lately we have been hearing rumors about a war with Spain. We hope and pray that the Lord will bless us.

We lost one of our horses yesterday—the oldest one. He was a good horse and just the day before yesterday he hauled a load of hay. Up to that time he ate well, but after that he looked like he had pain in his stomach and then he became increasingly ill until he died. Our other horse is younger and very spirited with an arched neck but he is not so steady at his work. The old one worked with the stump-digging machine every day.

For days now I've had an old American working with me and eating at our table. I didn't like the idea but now the time is almost past—just three more days. We have to eat cake every afternoon—taking a break just like the Americans, for whom that is important.

We had sharp frost two nights last week. That's the extent of the winter we have here and we had little rain. The weather is nice and crisp today.

Tomorrow I am going to the fort, fourteen miles from our house. Martinus brings me there. He is fourteen years old and almost a grown man. If he continues to grow he will be a big fellow. The man from whom we bought our land helps us with his steam machine and he works with us for nothing. Now, isn't that a good man. Such a man is hard to find. He wants to help us get ahead. He's an old bachelor with plenty of money, and he works to build up a little appetite.

He was in the [Civil] war too and a bullet went through his head at an angle in front of his ear. It made him very deaf and you can put your finger right inside his head. Read this to my brothers and tell Jacob to write us once. It is his turn.

[Closing]

Klaaske Noorda Heller to Noorda Family
Oak Harbor, Washington, to Ulrum, Groningen
October 19, 1896

Dear Mother, brothers, and sisters,

We received your letter of July 7 in good health and hope that you will receive this in good health. It is a great blessing from the Lord if people are healthy and can comfort each other in times of trouble during their days on earth. I know you have experienced this over the years. May the Lord continue to give you peaceful days, Mother, and to give you enough to eat. That is my wish and prayer for all of you. It is also a great blessing to be able to write one another.

You asked me, Mother, if I no longer thought about you because we did not name our youngest son Simon [according to Dutch naming cus-

Oak Harbor, Washington, church and street scene, about 1900. Courtesy of Calvin College Library Archives, photo collection.

tom]. I have already written that I am not the only boss here. I would have been happy with that name, but Onno said that the two youngest were named after my family, and now it was his turn. I called him Simon at first but Onno wanted to name him Geert, and finally, then, he was baptized Geert. He is bigger and fatter than any of our other children. Now he is teething. Hendrik rocks the cradle and plays on his harmonica. He likes to sing "Jesus of Nazareth" in English and other nice songs. He is also in the church singing society. Martinus has a harmonica, and when one plays the others join in. Martinus says that he would like to learn some Dutch songs.

We still do not know if we can move to our land this fall. There are so many papers to get ready if you don't have cash—Workman has always promised to help us because we were the first ones to work the ground. But that also caused the problem we had with our potatoes. We had them in two plots—one on our own land and the other in a place where men were still working. We put a fence around it, but cows that were foraging in the woods broke in and either trampled or ate everything. We have a small potato crop near our house but not nearly enough to get through the winter. Today we received a whole tubful of nice flounders, for which I was thankful.

A large salmon fishery has been built on the coast here, and when they take in the nets they sometimes catch lots of flounders which they throw back into the sea. If people are around they throw them on the dockside. Today all the Groningers living here, that is, five families, got a sackful of flounders each. I have put them in salt. The Lord has taken care of us in this place. We can expect more fish later, but this is the last for this fishing season.

At present we have thirteen pigs. Two sows with nine piglets, seven weeks old. We traded some thirteen-week-old pigs for two others. We had fifteen piglets but six died. Martinus and I picked lots of turnip plants for them and now we are cooking the turnips. We also have a patch of carrots which we will use when the turnips are gone. Martinus helps a lot in the house and with the feeding of the animals.

You ask, Mother, if I have much work with my little children, and I must admit that there is much more work waiting for me than I can do—that is, with sewing and so forth.

About four days have passed since I began this letter. I will write only a little more because the paper is nearly full. In the first part of my letter I forgot to inform you that Aunt Katharina died. No one in the family received a report about it. E. K. Nienhuis read about it in the paper. He told us the news as he was leaving when he came to see us. He did not know that she was sick or how long she was sick. I think that families in America are not closely bound together.

We all have colds now. We have sold four pigs and also a sow. Butter sells for twenty cents per pound and twenty-eight cents for twelve eggs. I am sorry that we have no cow of our own. Another Dutch family just moved here with $1,600! That's the truth. They were here before to find a farm and Onno helped them. They promised to pay us enough to get a new house. You should know that it is difficult for us to build a house because we have to work every day cutting wood to pay our living expenses. And if any time is left over, we need it to clear our land and plant some crops.

I don't complain without cause and I can tell you this, that I am hardly able to keep everyone in clothes because the store where we sell wood does not stock yard goods. But the Lord always helps us and I always look to Him. Even if my faith is weak at times it is still my joy and support. If only I can surely be His, it would certainly be wonderful. We have had some pleasant talks here with some people. H. Toppen's mind has not improved.

And now I hope that you will receive this letter in good health.

[Closing]

Onno Heller to Noorda Family
Oak Harbor, Washington, to Ulrum, Groningen
December 14, 1896

Dear Mother, brothers, and sisters,

Greetings to all who know us in Ulrum. That's not too difficult there. It is raining here now. We had a little winter weather, but it doesn't freeze much here. They leave potatoes in the ground here until December or the New Year. They dig them whenever they need them because they really do not expect frost here. A frost only lasts for a day or so, but now we had such a hard frost that the potatoes near the surface were frozen in the ground. We had some in a drafty wooden shed and the wind blew right through, so those potatoes froze. Strange—right? Another strange thing is the new varieties of potatoes here. Although they are frozen, they still taste good. We had some that were as soft as horse dung and still they were not sweet [from being frozen]. And after they are frozen they dry up and still taste good.

Around here they get 120 bushels of wheat per acre and 140 bushels of oats. That is for those who work up the land properly. The crop yields are almost unbelievable except for corn and peaches because the summer is not hot enough for these.

On the west side of the island where we live a large salmon fishery has opened. It has four nets which cost $2,000 each. They begin fishing in March and we can get as much fish as we want for nothing—that is, the flounder and plaice but not the salmon, which they keep. They throw the other fish away. That is the factory policy because they only preserve the salmon. They fish with nets called "traps." The fish swim in and can't get out again. So they haul the nets up two times each day. Sometimes they have thirty to forty thousand pounds in each net.

We have bought the wood for our house and if the weather permits we will build a house on our land.

We have become American citizens. I have my citizenship papers. Now we are Americans! The papers cost me nothing. In fact, I received money and a free trip to Seattle where I got my papers. I got $4.00 for the trip and it only cost $2.00. They were eager to get my vote for president and Congress and you cannot become a citizen or vote until you have been here for five years. I voted for the winning party, the Republicans, the party of good money [the gold standard].

At present new Hollanders are coming here all the time and many others want to come here. It is getting to be a Holland settlement here. The times are getting better in America again. That comes because of the election of a new Republican president.

Oakharbor den Augustus 1897

Geliefde Moeder Broeders en Zusters Neefjes en
Nichtjes

Na alweer zoolang gewacht te hebben ben ik eens weer
aan het schrijven, het is nu Maandag avond 9 uur noodig
tijd om weer naar bed te gaan want ik was van daag zoo sla-
erig want kleine Geert heeft mij van 1 tot halfvier uur
wakker gehouden hij deed niets dan kruipen en spelen
en hij had geen slaap, en deze tijd van schrijven is voor
mij het rustigste, en ik verbeel mij dat ik
t'daags geen tijd voor heb, Want ik heb buiten mijn werk
te weinig tijd voor het naaijen, en mijn kleintjes melden
haar dan ook nog zoo vaak bij mij aan, maar het is dan
integen een groote Zegen dat men te zamen gezond
is en ik hoop dat gij u allen in dat voorrecht moogt
verheugen of deelen, Anne heeft u het kunt alzoo wat ze
de deelt alsmede dat Ed. Tienhuis Vader en Moeders port-
jes hebben laaten vergrooten dat had ik niet verwacht ik
het nog niet gezien, Anne zegt dat het zoo duidelijk was al
gij daar haast levend voor hem stond gij leek't daar zoo Jon
als Anne u haast niet heeft gekend zegt hij Betje had gez
me zoo klaaske wel gauw eens komen en dat wil ik
graag maar ik vrees dat het mij zoo aandoet en het is
nog maar papier maar het is toch al veel van ha

Klaaske Noorda Heller's August 1897 letter (p. 1) to her family in Ulrum, Groningen

The factories and sawmills are beginning to start up again. The wood for the steam engines which we cut is already thirty cents more per cord. I earn sixty cents more per day and sometimes one dollar more. Our boys cut it up and I bring it to Oak Harbor. Lately we can sell more than we cut. I hope it stays that way and that it will even get better for me. We want to save money so we can begin to work on our land again this spring. People don't need to work in the cold and snow here as they do in Michigan. I would not live in Michigan again for $1,000, and that's the truth. It suits me fine here and we are all happy that we made the trip. Money? Well, there is some around here, but I always have an empty pocket.

We have eight pigs, but not in a shed. They walk around the yard grunting away. We hear them while we eat. That way we can have bacon, but not to eat. We can look at it, but not taste it. But I hope the time will come when we can eat them in good health.

Further, I hope that the Lord will spare us all and keep us in good health.

[Closing]

Klaaske Noorda Heller to Noorda Family
Oak Harbor, Washington, to Ulrum, Groningen
August 1897

Dear Mother, brothers, sisters, nephews, and nieces,

After much delay I am finally writing a letter. It is Monday evening, nine o'clock and time to go to bed. I have been dead tired all day because little Geert kept me awake from 1:00 to 3:30 A.M. He did nothing but cough and play and could not sleep.

This time, while I'm writing, is the most restful time of the day. I assure you that I have no time to write during the day because I have time for little else beside my work and too little time for sewing—especially with my little ones needing me so often. But it is nonetheless a great blessing that we all enjoy health together and I hope that you enjoy the same privilege.

Onno has also written some news including the fact that E. K. Nienhuis has had Father's and Mother's pictures enlarged. I have not seen them yet. Onno said that the pictures were so clear that it was like having them standing live before him. You [Mother] look as young as Onno. Betje [Nienhuis] says that I should come to visit her soon, and I would like to do that but I am afraid that I would be overcome by emotion. I know it is only on paper, but it is still really from Mother.

* * *

Everyone is sleeping now. Hendrik is home again from his work. In the last nine months he has grown tall and broad. All the boys are growing. Only Malenus continues to be thin and pale. We think that he will improve during the summer when he can eat sturgeon and salmon which contains much oil and is like the cod liver oil which the Hollanders [she probably means people from the provinces of Noord and Zuid Holland] use. That may help him. I cannot eat much fish because it gives me the diarrhea. It is a great advantage here that we can get such wholesome fish for almost nothing—but not for the whole year—only in the summertime, or as long as they are netting or trapping fish. You can't get sturgeon and salmon in the Netherlands. Our letters are not as you say "bacon letters" [*spek brieven*, which exaggerate optimistically] but more like "fish letters." I like bacon better than fish. It is now 10:25 P.M. and I think I will go to bed, and wish you good night or good day—whatever it is in Groningen.

* * *

It has been a week since I said good night, and now it is 10:00 A.M. Wednesday. In just three days Malenus and Magdalena will have birthdays. Malenus is eight and the other is four. Two of the neighbor's children also have birthdays on that same day. It is the custom here on birthdays to visit each other for a party, but I don't know much about that custom, and we, at least, won't have a party. We cannot bake cakes and such things. Hendrik has seen things like that with the English when he has had meals at their tables. They cover their tables with a white cloth and everyone has a little napkin in a ring sitting next to each plate. When they eat they put the napkin on their breasts and after dinner they fold them up and use them again until they are soiled. And they eat with their hats off.

Now I must stop writing.

[Closing]

[1898, Fragment]

God has blessed us with good health. We hope that you are well and that Mother is better too. We have mentioned the great distance which separates us many times, but we are especially aware of it now while awaiting reports on Mother's health. Even as old as she is she can still recover if it is the Lord's will. Our neighbor is 81, still healthy and walks all around. He comes to visit us sometimes with his son. . . . Mother, may the Lord stand by you, be your comfort and soothe any pain you must suffer.

* * *

My family is in bed. Little Geert is talking constantly and he is growing faster than all of our other children. Malenus watches the cows every day—they may forage on the neighbor's haystack, but Malenus must make sure they do not eat their potatoes. We still have two cows. We had to butcher one cow because she choked on a potato. That was last Sunday. They tried to free the potato by reaching down her throat by hand and with a long stick. They also hit her on the outside of her neck. They tried everything until they finally decided to butcher her because she was going to die anyway. It was a big cow and also a good milker. . . . If we are well and healthy we will have plenty to eat for the winter—one cow, a sturgeon of 125 pounds, a halibut of 80 pounds, a few salmon of 12 pounds, and a half tub of flounders. And we also have a small steer. The big steer is already too fat for my taste, but Onno and the boys like it that way. In addition we eat potatoes, carrots, turnips, and other things. So we have enough.

I think Onno will write too. I will save some space for that. But I want to tell you that I got a washing machine for $2.50. It is the best thing. I can wash a load in ten minutes and then reheat the water. But you can't wash all kinds of clothes at the same time.

Onno Heller to Noorda Family
Oak Harbor, Washington, to Ulrum, Groningen
March 28, 1898

Dear Mother, brothers, and sisters,
[Opening remarks about good health.]
Hendrik is working for a farmer again—a German for $15 per month. I work at the fort for $4.00 [probably per day] with board. We have boardinghouse meals that are fit for a king, more than anyone can eat.

We are building the fort on the island so the Spaniards cannot reach us. They have cannons here forty feet long and thirteen inches wide—quite something. They will protect the Strait of Juan de Fuca. No ship can stand against such a bullet. They go through steel plates ten inches thick and they go for a distance of fifteen miles. That should take care of the Spaniards! Right? But only God knows because He rules and directs everything. I hope and wish for peace and that God Almighty will preserve our country in peace. If we must fight then I pray that He will stand with us and help us. If God is for us, nothing can harm us. He is better than the large cannons, ships, and all other weapons. But the American people are in good spirits. Already thousands, indeed hundreds of thousands, have volunteered. But if it comes to war then it will cost money and blood, and a country is not made better by war. But the needy Cubans should be free or at least liberated from their terrible situation. We aim to set them free.

, Yes, we Netherlanders know what the Spanish did to our forefathers. General Weeler [Valeriano Weyler y Nicolau] is not much better than the duke of Alva. But let me say again, the will of man is not always God's will and so we pray that our wills may be the same as God's will. Then we will have no distress because those whom God keeps are kept well.

Martinus is at work pulling out stumps from our land every day. Our pastor is doing well. He is a Groninger from Zevenhuizen. E. K. Nienhuis has bought a farm near us again—one hundred acres with thirty acres cleared. The Hollanders around here are still satisfied. We have had no winter yet. I think that our horse caught a cold while working with the stump machine—he has to stand still much of the time and it is rather cold, and so he got the colic. Normally I have two horses to work with, but now only one. We don't have very much land cleared yet, so I'll have to use the horse for that. I'll have someone else bring the wood away. Or, if necessary, I can get a young horse cheaply, but I think I can get by with one. That is also less expensive.

*   *   *

[Closing]

Klaaske Noorda Heller to Noorda Family
Oak Harbor, Washington, to Ulrum, Groningen
October 26, 1898 [Fragment]

Dear Mother, brothers, and sisters,
    I don't have much news. It is raining today, fresh and pure.
    Didn't our soldiers fight well against the Spaniards? Yes they have beaten them well. Yes, indeed! The young boys from some of the families here volunteered for the war and many more would have volunteered if they were needed. They fight better too when they go as volunteers and are not forced in and then degraded as they are in Holland. There is also a heavy penalty for officers who curse at soldiers here. The soldiers live like gentlemen here and they are regarded as honorable citizens. They are treated with respect and not like slaves that can be pushed around and abused.

*   *   *

Many Hollanders here have supported the war and many have also volunteered. The commander of the troops at Santiago de Cuba fought bravely with the so-called Rough Riders who were gentlemen's sons from New York and cowboys from Texas. Yes, a million people of all sorts were there together, but the leader of these troops was a Hollander [Theodore Roosevelt]. I think he will be chosen to lead the state of New York. So now our country is enlarged again and I hope the Lord will give that His blessing. Yes, our country sends missionaries to convert all those folk. That's what America does—it begins with God's word and freedom, not with the sword like the Spaniards and the pope. Yes the Lord has blessed us wonderfully in this strife but our people and government must first give God the glory and after that the people who were led by God's hand.

Onno and Klaaske Heller to Noorda Family
Oak Harbor, Washington, to Ulrum, Groningen
[June 1899]

Good morning. I went to bed early last night and got up late this morning—so things are upside down. Life is like that sometimes—you try to catch a pig by the ears but you get the tail instead.

We are all healthy and hope the same for you. Our crops are great. Come over and have a look once! We think we will be eating new potatoes by July 4. They are already in bloom.

I was elected as a church leader. I was nervous about that at first but it is not so bad now.

Our boys went to see the battleship Iowa. It is the largest ship in our navy and it fought furiously at Santiago de Cuba. We hope the boys will write to you about that sometime.

There have been many cyclones and hurricanes in the eastern part of our country and a great deal was destroyed. In New York, Chicago, and other places people are dying from the heat. Here we are not troubled by such conditions. Every day we have nice weather—not too hot and not too cold. Good enough to make a person lazy. But the people here are not lazy—work is almost the gospel here. We have already picked lima beans and peas. They are great.

[Segment missing.]

A person can earn good wages here. If you want more information ask me. As for me, I am staying here on Whidbey Island where we can eat salmon and sturgeon. We now have on hand 200 pounds of salmon and other kinds of fish. We have two sturgeon cleaned—one of 100 pounds and another of 60. Fishermen on the coast here gave them to us. Yes, sometimes you can get more than you want. The salmon weigh 25 to 80 pounds. The sturgeon are from 50 to 300 pounds. That is a tasty fish. We eat enough salmon to satisfy our appetites—sometimes three meals a day.

It is summer now and the days are warm. But not so in Alaska. Look that up on the map and you will discover a huge area. Alaska is a territory of the United States.

I don't have much more news. Things are getting better here and are going forward again. I hope that you will receive this letter in good health. Now I am going to give the pen to my wife, who will also write something.

[Closing]

I am in good health and hope you are too. The Spaniards took a good beating. As the saying goes, "They got what they deserved."[1]

Yes, the Lord has been with our people and country. The president has also requested people in our churches and in homes to pray for the country and its people. After the victorious battle of Santiago our admiral [William Sampson] held a thanksgiving service on the ship. We must not credit ourselves, he said, but we owe the victory to God. Santiago is the same harbor where Piet Hein was victorious. Where he captured the "silver fleet."[2]

*   *   *

The boys are going out to cut wood again, and we can pay the interest on our loan from that. We also hope to have more land cleared. Our old and kind landowner died in California. His nephew inherited our mortgage and additional land around here. He willed these things to his nephew when he knew that he was near death. The landowner often stayed with a certain neighbor here for short periods, and his $1,000 mortgage was canceled as a gift from the landowner.

Malenus and Malena [shortened from Magdalina] have been in school for three months, but now school is out. Malenus learns quickly. Malena can write words but she does not know what they mean.

On Saturday morning Hendrik and Martinus plan to take a steamship ride to the harbor where a large battleship is docked. Several neighboring children are going with them.

Any moment now I may be brought to a neighbor woman who is expecting a baby. I have to help with the birth of her little child.

As soon as possible we will have our pictures taken. Soon Onno will say, "Stop writing. It's time for bed." It is 10:30 P.M. and I hope that you will receive this letter in good health. And I wish you all of the Lord's blessings.

[Closing]

P.S. Hendrik is back home again. So he writes, "Greetings from Hendrik Heller."

1. In Dutch, "Je boontje krijgen naar zijn loontje."
2. Pieter Hein's legendary capture of the Spanish silver fleet in 1628 occurred in the Matanza Harbor, Cuba.

Klaaske Noorda Heller to Noorda Family
Oak Harbor, Washington, to Ulrum, Groningen
[1909, Fragment]

Dear brothers and sisters,
  We were happy to receive your postcard and to learn of your good health.
  Onno has written most of the news and also about our married children. It is Monday evening and Malenus has gone to the music society [band] with his clarinet. Magdalena and Geert are sitting here at home reading books. Hendrik and Dora, a daughter of G. Meijer, have sent us a card saying that they will be coming here to visit. Their children are Onno Martinus, Klaaske (named Clare here), and Jennie. Little Onno is not yet baptized.
  Our boys are doing well but they also work hard. The prospects for success for young men are better here than in the Netherlands. Many Hollanders have come here since we did. We have a good pastor here [the Reverend Abel J. Brink]. There are two churches here, one Christian Reformed and the other Dutch Reformed [RCA]. Their teachings are almost alike but discipline is more strictly exercised in our church [CRC]. Last summer [the Reverend Kornelis] van Goor was here [visiting for his health].

7   Ulbe and Maaike Eringa

When Ulbe Eringa's mother died in 1881, he and his seven siblings were orphaned. Their father, Pier Eringa, had already died in 1873 when Ulbe was six. His mother, Grietje, and her oldest son, Jan, managed the

These letters were donated by the Siegersma family, 1976, and first translated by George Kamp and Alys Eringa.

family farm until 1877 when Jan began to prepare for a career in the ministry. Then, because Ulbe's brothers had no interest in agriculture, Grietje rented the farm and moved her family to Spannum, her native village. Eventually her four oldest sons became pastors, and Ulbe worked as a hired hand on several farms from 1880 to 1890.

During that decade of informal apprenticeship Ulbe learned to respect and appreciate the advanced cattle-breeding techniques of his favorite employer Sjoerd Gerbrandy. But from three other employers he also discovered that farmhands were vulnerable to the capricious whims of their bosses and to the extreme miserliness of most wealthy farmers toward their hired help. After he immigrated in 1892 his letters frequently remarked on the respect with which farmhands were treated in America and the relative ease with which they could become independent farmers—advantages generally lacking in Friesland.

In 1892, when the Reverend Andrew Wormser[1] traveled through the Netherlands seeking immigrants for a settlement in Montana, Ulbe attended one of the lectures and decided to purchase a ticket. He probably traveled with Wormser's group, but Ulbe was not destined for Montana. Before his departure he corresponded with Herman Abma, an acquaintance who had moved to Hull, Iowa, and who guided Ulbe to his first employment in Hull.

The first letter of this collection, July 4, 1892, describes Ulbe's arrival in Hull and his life as a hired man living with the Hunts, an "American" family. An unfortunate lapse in the correspondence (August 1892–April 1894) deprives us of Ulbe's immediate narration of several crucial events during those years—courtship, marriage, and land selection. When the correspondence picks up again in 1894 Ulbe is married and sharecropping 320 acres of land in South Dakota with his brother-in-law, Hedger Rypstra. Fortunately Ulbe's autobiography, written in 1942, recounts his first years in America in considerable detail.

Hedger and Ulbe began their partnership in 1893 when they rented a farm near Hull and hired a seventy-two-year-old housekeeper. When she moved away Hedger suggested that they could employ his orphaned sister, Maaike, who was a housemaid in the Netherlands. Maaike agreed to the arrangement and arrived in May 1893. That same year the landlord sold the farm they were renting in Iowa, and by the fall of 1893 Ulbe, Hedger, and Maaike had agreed to lease another farm in Bon Homme County, South Dakota, 120 miles west of the Iowa border. By the time

---

[1] Wormser, who became an RCA pastor, founded Wormser, Montana and was active in promoting immigration and land sales.

they moved there in March 1894 Ulbe and Maaike were married (November 22, 1893).

The partnership with Hedger continued during the five-year lease of the Bon Homme County farm and for another three years after they purchased a 160-acre farm near Running Water for twenty-five dollars per acre. In 1902 Hedger sold his interest to Ulbe and moved west to Washington. Then, in 1904 Ulbe purchased an additional 160 acres which enlarged his farm to a full half section.

As the letters disclose, Ulbe managed his farm carefully and judiciously. Between 1896 and 1919 his annual correspondence details the steady increase of his acreage, livestock, and crop yields. He benefited rather obviously from his agricultural experience in Friesland. Most of his letters were sent to his sister Jikke in Oosterend, whose husband, Minne Sjaarda, returned information about his fortunes on the Oosterend farm. By 1919 Ulbe's farm was debt-free, and he continued to manage it until 1926 when his only son, Pier, took over. Ulbe and Maaike then moved to Orange City, Iowa, where they remained until they died—she in 1941 and he in 1950.

Throughout their marriage the Eringas wrote regularly about their family, church, and neighbors. Occasionally Ulbe commented about economic trends and national politics, but for the most part local matters, especially the church, dominated the family's outside interests. Although Ulbe and Maaike often highlighted differences between South Dakota and Friesland, they, along with their Dutch American neighbors, nonetheless created a Netherlandic subculture that duplicated the main characteristics of their Old World communities. Already in 1892, after attending the Sioux Center, Iowa, Reformed Church, Ulbe commented with amazed satisfaction, "I almost forgot that I was in America." The church with its bilingual pastors, Dutch-language liturgy, and wide range of social activities provided an abiding core of ethnic solidarity. Endogamous marriages issued from its doors and funeral processions terminated in nearby cemeteries. As in Friesland, successful farmers like Ulbe dominated the local church boards and tended the doctrinal instruction of the children.

The names that pepper the Eringa correspondence are virtually all Dutch, and many are those of relatives who joined the Eringas in a steady procession from Friesland. All but one of Maaike's four siblings joined her in South Dakota, and Ulbe regularly assisted young men from the environs of Oosterend by employing them as farmhands in Running Water. In 1910, when Ulbe visited his family in the Netherlands, Maaike remained contentedly in South Dakota because her Old World relatives had moved nearby. Ulbe, however, eagerly anticipated a reunion with his distant siblings.

He discovered that his family in the Netherlands was generally prosperous and successful. His four brothers were well-established clergymen, and his sisters were married to independent farmers or shopkeepers. Most of his nephews and nieces were professionals (teaching and medicine) or in business. None were poverty-stricken. In many respects their achievements paralleled those of Maaike and Ulbe's children. Three of their daughters were schoolteachers before marrying, and another died in 1936 after being a missionary in Japan. The oldest daughter, Grace, did not receive advanced education (high school, normal school, or college) but married a South Dakota farmer. Pier acquired the Running Water farmstead.

Ulbe and Maaike's youngest daughter, Alys, was still living in 1992 and from her genealogical report it is evident that the Eringa family's ethnic cohesion is beginning to break up rather rapidly. About a third of Ulbe's seventeen grandchildren have disaffiliated from typical Dutch Reformed church groups and have become Lutheran, Episcopalian, or secular. Ten of the seventeen grandchildren have married outside the Dutch ethnic community. If this pattern continues, only a small minority of Ulbe and Maaike's great-grandchildren will remain in their traditional ethnic church groups. However that may develop, it is clear that the Eringa descendants have become successfully acculturated Americans. They have lost their Old World language and joined the ranks of teachers, home builders, farmers, and pastors as well as professional scholars and musicians. They are scattered from South Carolina to California, from Massachusetts to Oregon. No doubt their experience is paradigmatic for the vast majority of Dutch American families whose progenitors immigrated in the last century.[2]

Ulbe Eringa to Sister and Brother-in-law
Hull, Iowa, to Oosterend, Friesland
July 4, 1892

Dear sister and brother-in-law [Tryntje and Willem Feitsma],
    No doubt you have been awaiting a letter from me for quite some time. Through the providence of God, I had a good trip to America. It

---

    [2] The sources for this introduction are Ulbe Eringa's unpublished autobiography, 1943, and notes provided by Alys Eringa Beltman, 1992, in the Ulbe Eringa Papers, Immigrant Letter Collection. For a related study, see Brian W. Beltman, "A Dutch Family and Its Iowa Roots," *Origins* 10 (1992): 27–35. Maaike Rypstra Eringa's correspondence in this collection is featured in Annemieke Galema and Suzanne Sinke, "Paradijs der Vrouwen?" in *Vrouwen in den Vreemde*, ed. C. van Eerd and K. Oppelland (Zutphen, Netherlands: De Walburg Pers, 1993).

took us twenty-four hours to travel from Harlingen to Hull [Great Britain], and we arrived there at two o'clock on Sunday, June 5. At seven o'clock that evening we went by train to Liverpool where we arrived at 1:00 A.M. We were met there by an agent who took us to a lodging place where we stayed until noon on Wednesday. There were eleven Frisians with me—four of whom went to Grand Rapids (one day closer to New York than Hull, Iowa, my destination) and seven had to go six hours farther than I, so with these I had good companionship.

England is a beautiful country with its many small hills. Liverpool is a very large city, full of factories so that almost all the buildings are black with smoke. It is very busy there with all the streetcars and other wagons, mostly drawn by three horses because the city is built on hills. One can hardly cross the streets because of the heavy traffic. These three days were a little boring so I was glad when we could get on the boat. We sailed on a beautiful large boat—the Ohio. Six went first class and seventy went second class, and hundreds went third class. In the second class (mine) were two Norwegians and the rest were Englishmen. Fortunately, last fall and now again for three weeks, I have studied the English language, so with my books and a few motions, I could get along quite well with my English companions. Since the other Hollanders went third class, I had no chance to associate with them on our trip. A couple of days it was very misty so the boat whistled every minute to prevent colliding with other boats. It also stormed quite badly one night so that I nearly rolled out of my bed. The rest of the days the weather was good, at times really nice. I was not seasick at all, and always slept and ate well.

On Sunday morning at seven o'clock, June 19, we again saw land— the coast of America. By 2:00 P.M. we arrived in Philadelphia. We stayed here until 11:00 P.M. and then went by train to Pittsburgh. There I rejoined the other Frisians. From there we went to Chicago where we changed trains again and finally on Wednesday, June 27, at 10:30 A.M. I arrived safe and well in Hull. What beautiful scenery I saw on the trip— I will tell you about it some time later.

Mr. Abma had been to meet the train three times for nothing because we arrived later than scheduled. So he was not there when we arrived. But there was a man on the train who was willing to bring me to Abma's for a dollar so I accepted his offer and this man brought me there with a nice buggy and two sorrel horses, with white tails and manes. Abma lives an hour's drive on the south side of Hull. I was cordially welcomed there, and two jobs were already waiting for me but first I wanted to rest a little.

On Friday morning a woman came riding into the yard with two nice horses hitched to a wagon. She had heard that a new hired man had arrived at the Abma home and she wanted me to come and work for her. She came because her husband was so very busy with his farm work. She appeared to be a nice person so I went along with her and hired myself out to them. They are Americans and speak only English but everything is neat and clean and the people are very friendly. So I started working here on Monday, June 27. On Saturday Murk Abma and I went to Orange City where I met Marcus and Johannes van der Schaaf, who once worked as a hired man for our Uncle Dirk. On Sunday, I went along to the Dutch church, a nice little building, with a good orthodox minister.

Last week I had a difficult week, because I wasn't used to hard physical labor. But I've gotten used to it again. I have hired myself out for five months for eighty-five dollars. The money exchange is one dollar for one *rijksdaalder* [2.50 guilders] in Holland. If I wish, I can earn enough money to return to Holland in December. You cannot imagine what good food I get here. It is more delicious than the first-class food at Veldwijk.[1] The American housewife bakes everything herself. You certainly don't have to pity me because this is a beautiful country, and each one progresses faster than the next one. It is just the opposite in Friesland. I am still very determined to become a farmer here. Then I can have a full and happy life. I am completely at home here and can hardly believe that I am in America. I have always had a good impression of it, but it has proved to be beyond my expectations.

To my surprise I found that Hedger Rypstra lives only about a half hour from me. He is a cousin of Dirk de Boer's wife, and is an old friend of mine. We visited together in Friesland. He works on a large farm and has his own American buggy. He may use the farmer's horses, so now I've already ridden with him three times as he comes to get me to go to church with him.

Today is the Fourth of July, which is a holiday for the entire American nation. No one works and in all the cities there are large celebrations. America fought for her freedom from England and signed her Declaration of Independence on July 4. Since America gained her freedom, she has always prospered and it is said that her treasuries are full while European lands are always in debt. Railways, roads, bridges, schools, and much more are supported by the government and the people do not pay taxes.

Hedger picked me up this morning. Together we went to Hull to celebrate. My boss and his wife and their boy also went off with their team and wagon to celebrate. First this morning there was a parade of all kinds of machines, this afternoon horse races, men's races, and games, all without liquor or swearing. We watched everything. What a lot of two-horse wagons and buggies on the roads. At six o'clock we were all home again and at eight o'clock my boss and his wife went to see the evening fireworks. I didn't go because I wanted to get this letter written. So I'm sitting at home, alone. We live an hour's drive from town.

Write to me sometime. I won't be able to write again for some time because the only time I have is on Sundays. Let Trijntje and Willem read this letter too.

With hearty greetings from your brother Ulbe.

1. A Christian psychiatric hospital where he worked for a short period before emigrating.

Ulbe Eringa to Brothers and Sisters
Hull, Iowa, to Oosterend, Friesland
August 22, 1892

Dear brother and sister,

Since in the past two weeks I have received letters from each of my four brothers, namely Jacob, Dirk, Jan, and Pier, I now wish to send a letter in return. I have very little time to write, so I would very much like it if all four of you could read this letter. If John would send it to Jacob, he could send it to Dirk and then on to Pier. This coming winter I will have more time to write to each of you and I hope to answer you more speedily then.

This morning I rode to Hull with Mrs. Hunt and her ten-year-old son, in the top-buggy and two horses. This child is from her former marriage and she is now married for the second time to a bachelor about forty years old. So I am not in a large family, just Mr. and Mrs. Hunt, Arthur, and I. They are very ambitious people. Mr. Hunt told me that he is the son of a farmer in the state of New York. When he was twenty-one years old, he started to work for himself which seems to be the custom here in America. He was a hired man for about four years to earn some money because he had left home with only two and a half dollars. Then for ten years he farmed alone and prospered so much that now he lives on his own farm. About three years ago he went back to his birthplace and married this woman and brought her here. Many are not so successful but he has done well.

This morning I spent an hour in the Dutch church and then an hour in the American church. The latter starts at eleven o'clock but from ten until eleven there is Sunday school for the children. Though I rode with Mrs. Hunt, I still had to walk over the hills for some distance to the Dutch church, and it was very warm. So I was a half hour late but got to the American church at eleven. These hills are rich pastures and the roads cross these pastures. Usually I go to church in the afternoon because after church they have Sunday school for the youth, older boys and girls, and the small children. The minister teaches us, Willem de Roos teaches the older girls, Oepke de Roos the little girls, and another man teaches the boys. Each class is in a corner of the church. They study a chapter from the Bible, which is very instructive, and I enjoy it very much. They also sing a couple of English hymns, which are beautiful, and then one of the older girls plays the church organ. The children all learn English in school; that is why they sing so well. In the American church they also sing well and I am able to read about half of the song. Our minister had a call to Le Mars [Iowa] but he declined. I believe that the Hunts are good Christian people. They have at least five Bibles but they do not read from them, which is not their style. The same way with giving thanks after the meal. Mr. Hunt says a short prayer before eating but I do not understand what he says. These things work together so that I receive much more spiritual food by attending church than I did when I worked in the hospital at Veldwijk.

At present we are busy with the harvest. Mr. Hunt has cut one hundred and fifty acres of grain with the self-binder. This large machine, drawn by four horses, cuts the grain, which it also ties into sheaves and then drops them on the ground. You should see this—it is an invention that is almost unbelievable. I have to set up all these sheaves into "shocks" which we make in to large stacks. Then sometime later a large threshing machine comes to thresh the grain and about ten farmers get together with their hired men and help each other with the threshing. That goes very fast. I will write more about this later.

On my way to Hull I traveled past a large town where two thousand of the three thousand population had drowned. This town was situated in a valley along the Mississippi River, between high hills. The conductor told us that the water almost came into the railroad cars. Later we came through a stretch of land between two broad rivers and there the tracks were so weak and sunken that sometimes I thought that our whole train would go into the water and we'd all drown!

In the middle of July we had two weeks of such warm weather that for two days I was sick. I could hardly work. My blood was thin and my heart beat so fast. Mr. and Mrs. Hunt teased me that I'd have to go back to Friesland, but I soon got better and Mr. Hunt himself spent a couple of days in bed. He told me that sometimes in the state of New York it gets so warm that people and horses fall dead on the street.

Before I sat down to write, I read all of your letters again. You do not know how I enjoy getting letters from you. How I look forward to hearing from one or the other.

One Sunday Hedger Rypstra and I were invited by old Jan de Roos for dinner. They live in Sioux Center, and we talked to Jan and Kee there too. In the afternoon we went to church there—a large church full of people and a very good minister. I almost forgot that I was in America.

Old Mr. De Roos is a pious man—I enjoyed being there. When I was a child I went with Father and Mother to Weeukes to visit Aunt Trijntje Hieminga and then they were there too. They told me it was the last time that they had talked to my parents. Mrs. De Roos and I both remembered that I had been there too. I have also visited Abma's again one Sunday. They were all well. It isn't as warm now as it was in July. I'm beginning to get used to things pretty well here. Because I can understand the family I live with better, my life is more pleasant. Perhaps during the three winter months I can board with some people and take English lessons so I can learn to read the newspapers. I can easily find a farmer where I can work for my room and board in the winter. I will close now since I have to milk the cows.

[Closing]

Ulbe and Maaike Eringa to Brother and Sister [Minne and Jikke Sjaarda]
Running Water, South Dakota, to Oosterend, Friesland
April 8, 1894

Dear brother and sister,

It has been a long time since I wrote to you, I believe more than a year. It is not because I never think of you, but I just don't get around to writing. I don't always have the desire to write because I'd rather sit down and enjoy the company of my wife instead of writing letters. Also, I have to write my other brothers once in a while so then I don't get to writing you. Today it is the eighth of April and we are having a beautiful all-day rain, so that we couldn't go to church. So now I can finally get to writing you a letter.

We have sowed eighty acres of wheat and twenty acres of oats. After this lovely all-day rain it will soon be above the ground. We want to plant one hundred and twenty acres of corn—that is, the rest of the two hundred and twenty acres of our farmland under cultivation. I think we will plant two acres of potatoes—our brother-in-law, Gerlof de Roos, took about two hundred Frisian potatoes along to plant. Our pasture for the cows is forty-five acres, and then we have fifty-five acres of hay land. Of this we want to plow up about thirty acres to put into production. Our farm is three hundred and twenty acres in size. It is a rectangular piece of land a mile long and a half mile wide. Now you can form an opinion of how large a piece of land it is. Don't picture a rough wilderness—it is a nice usable, productive piece of land. When they sell or rent a piece of land here it is done eighty acres at a time. One uses one eighty-acre plot, another two, another three, and we have four eighties. Last year we had three eighties which was two hundred and forty acres. We have rented this farm for five years and we give the owner one-third of the crop so two-thirds is for ourselves. We have to pay all expenses, but don't you think we rent very reasonably? Everyone says you can farm well here if you have favorable weather and the Lord's blessing.

Our six horses are all lively and well. Our two colts are growing nicely. They are now two nice yearlings. About three weeks ago we expected another good colt from our best mare, but it only lived an hour, which made us feel bad. If it had lived seven days we would have had to pay the stallion fee of twenty-five dollars. So we didn't have to pay. Now, any day, we expect a good colt from our black mare. These were both bred to the same stallion. We now have five cows and two calves. I want to buy three more cows.

We have six old sows and six young ones who will have pigs for the first time in August. Five of the six old ones had thirty-three pigs but we lost ten of these because of the cold weather last spring so we have twenty-three left. We will breed the old sows again. We have a two-year-old purebred Poland China sow that weighs between five hundred and six hundred pounds and will get pigs in May. I wish that you could see this beautiful animal! Four of our young sows are her offspring. Last week we bought a purebred Poland China boar. A farmer has to make his money out of raising hogs. Last year we had to sell our corn, but one does not make nearly as much that way as when one feeds it to the hogs to be sold.

Yesterday we started plowing again, each with three horses hitched to the plow. We still have to plow a large piece but we do not have to plant corn until in May. I think that in September our landowner is going to drill an Artesian well here. These wells are about six hundred feet deep and the water spurts out about fifty feet high continuously, night and day. Then we will always have a good supply of water and won't have to dip water from a well. A well like this costs about five hundred dollars.

Yesterday when I rode to town with my two horses hitched to our buggy, I was wishing that my wife and I could ride over to your place that way—she could give you a better idea of our life here in America.

Our brother-in-law, Gerlof, works for our neighbor and is earning good money and his board. These people are very happy to be here. They didn't realize how good it could be—abundance of work and food so cheap. In comparison, the poor day laborer in Holland has a pitiful poverty-stricken and sorrowful existence.

Perhaps you think that I haven't received your letters. I have received two this spring and now another one. In your last letter you mentioned that in the evenings you often thought of us. This also happens to me too when I am alone. Then I recall many of the things we did when we played together in our childhood. Who would have thought then that our lives would be separated so far. You may sometimes think when you look at your children—none of them will ever to go America—but all our ways are known to the Lord. I really feel at home in this new world and believe that it is God's will that I am here. Here we have our farm, here the Lord has given me a good wife—reasons to be very thankful and to live a life to the glory of God who gave it all. Last Sunday they elected me elder with almost a unanimous vote. Now I will have to read the sermon in the service occasionally and lead the congregation in prayer. They also want to start a young men's society here and make me the president. I cannot live heedlessly here. The conditions of the church require me to live an earnest, exemplary life.

Now I've already written you quite a letter with my wife's help. Please, both of you, write sometime and tell me all the news. Do you have any pictures of your dear children?

[Closing]

P.S. Note from Maaike Eringa

Since Ulbe has written quite a bit about our farming, I decided to write about housekeeping. Even though we are not acquainted and I do not know whether you are interested in an American household, I will tell you a little about it anyway.

We have a good roomy house, and a garden and orchard with many fruit trees, mostly plum trees, some cherry trees, apple trees, and grapevines. Then there is a small plot of ground close to the house for vegetables. It is already plowed and harrowed and ready for the seeds to be sown.

Our house has two rooms in front, one has two windows and the other three, with a porch in front. Behind the one room is the kitchen. We have the cookstove here in the winter. We live and do our work there because we cannot work outside as it gets very cold here. In the summer we move the stove into a "lean-to" off the kitchen—a small room with two windows and a cupboard for dishes, and shelves for the pots and pans. We call this the "buttrie," and behind it is a little shed for coal and wood. Upstairs we have two bedrooms where our beds are. They are different from the ones in Holland. We also have a good cellar, although not as nice as the milk cellars in Holland. On each side of the house are steps with a small roof above it. We do not have a cistern, but when it rains we catch the water in barrels. It has rained a lot today, so now I have two barrels full of rainwater again. This is very nice to wash the clothes with, otherwise I have to wash with hard water. We put something in it so that we can get good soapsuds. Lately we got a new washing machine that is so nice. I wish that you could see it. It is entirely different from a Holland machine—it has a wringer with it where we turn the clothes through it so that they are almost dry. We also have very practical cookstoves that have water reservoirs on the side so that we always have warm water. The stoves have ovens in which we bake our bread, cakes, and cookies because we have to do all of this ourselves. One learns much from other women. The Americans who were born here can bake almost anything and are far ahead of us who haven't been here so long yet. But we can easily learn all this in time.

There is lots of nice furniture here in America, and lovely sewing machines. We don't have so much furniture yet but can buy more later on—the farming operation costs so much to get started at first.

Now I've told you a few things and don't know what more to write. I almost forgot to tell you that about two weeks ago my sister Teetskje and her husband and three children came here from Holland.

From your sister-in-law,
Maaike

Ulbe Eringa to Brother and Sister [Minne and Jikke Sjaarda]
Running Water, South Dakota, to Oosterend, Friesland
January 11, 1896

Dear Brother and Sister,

We are all well. Our darling Grietje is growing nicely and runs through the house giving us much pleasure. She started walking at sixteen months. She is just like your oldest boy was when he was that age. I think a great deal of her; perhaps that is because I am so far away from all my blood relatives. We can feel so plainly that these are our own children.

I thank you, sister, for sending me the death notice of our beloved cousin, Anna. This carried me back in memory to the little town of Edens and reminded me so much of our youth that is past. How often, as a child, I played there with her. In later years I often sang with her as she played the organ so well! Oh I am convinced that she is at home with her Lord in Heaven, and is rejoicing there with all the blood-bought throng. Her earthly body lies silent in the grave in Edens where also our Christian friends lie buried who died so young. May this blossom, plucked in her youth, cause us to think on our journey to eternity and spur us on to seek our salvation with fear and trembling. We can also say here with the Psalmist: "Our life here is a vapor, and death threatens every hour." We had a neighbor lady here who was up and around on Monday, and she died at four o'clock on Tuesday morning. If you see the widow De Boer sometime, you can talk to her about Maaike as they knew each other well.

I had a letter from my [Ulbe's] sister Antje who wrote to me that she would be a mother soon. We sincerely hope that all goes well with her and that they will be happy to have a child.

There is a farmer from Hull who went to visit his father in Holland near Brother Jan. I wrote Jan to contact him if he could send my gold watch and chain and my wool clothing along to America.

It is beautiful weather here at present. I am sitting in our front room where the windows are to the south and the sun is shining warmly on my hand. This year we had a pretty good year so we have a good living. We did not make much money because the grain was so cheap. But I believe that with the Lord's blessing we will be able to get ahead with farming. Our six horses are all well and now we have two young horses that will be trained this spring to help with the work because they will be three years old. I think one is going to have a colt. Last year when pastures were bare, everybody would let his horses run loose, and our neighbor had a two year old stallion that got too intimate with our horses. We have seven milk cows who will all get calves in the spring. We have four two-year-old steers and eleven yearling calves. Our forty pigs are growing well. We will breed twelve sows again and we will fatten the rest. We now have enough corn stalks and straw for the cows, enough oats and hay for the horses, and enough corn to fatten our hogs. Our one hundred and forty hens are doing well too. In December we were getting twenty eggs a day and we still get ten a day. Cold weather is hard on the chickens. We still get quite a bit of milk so we have a good living.

Our life is quite different from yours as you must notice from my letters. Though I do believe, brother-in-law, that you could become quite a cattle farmer if you lived here. You would get a great deal of pleasure out of raising and feeding cattle as it is done here in America.

In regard to church matters here I am not too satisfied because we do not have a minister at present. But we have many good books with sermons which we read in the services. But the sad part is that the young people do not learn much. Most of the people here are Frisians. The children learn English in school, so most of them cannot understand the Holland language. I sometimes think about starting a Sunday school but that would have to be done in English and I do not feel able to do that yet.

In the last while I have had quite a few letters from the Netherlands, which are always very welcome to me. I especially appreciate your letters, my sister. I hardly have time to answer your letters; otherwise I would write oftener. While my wife and I have our teatime together, I often think, oh how I wish you could join us! How often I had tea with you folks on Sundays! But our ways have parted and that cannot be changed. You wrote in your last letter too about Tjollings—Antje. Give her my greetings when you see her again. She is a good woman, I assure you. She is a quiet, sensible Christian.

In about three months I will be thirty years old. Then we will all be in our thirties and forties. A few weeks ago I noticed in the Franeker newspaper that Sjoert Gaastra was one of the nominees for a member of the city council of Hennaard. I remember as if it were yesterday that Ymte, Hotze, and I went there on a Sunday for a sweet roll.

At present I don't know much more to write about. Our Artesian well runs continuously. If you had one like that in your cow barn you'd never have to pump a pailful of water. In one hour it shoots out ten barrels of water and that never stops. Our neighbor's well gives five times as much, so you can imagine that a lot of water comes out of the ground in one day. In Springfield there is a well that produces about three thousand barrels a day. Connected to this is a large feed mill, really a complete feed factory. The water there just "flies" out of the ground. Your father, who was always so interested in such things, should see the wonders of America! If I am fortunate enough to visit you again, I would like to spend a couple of days with him to tell him at length about all these things. This fall we also bought a sewing machine for twenty dollars. That is a great convenience for Maaike.

I think both of you knew Betje, daughter of Age Harms. She left her husband and came here, and now she is married to a capable American farmer. Minne Abma also lives in this neighborhood. This man earns much money but he is always poor because he has a large family.

The sun is sinking in the west and will soon disappear behind the hills that are along the Missouri River. We live only a half hour from the Missouri. Hedger is gone today, so I have to do the chores alone. All the cattle and horses are turned loose to forage, but will all come home at night.

I close with kindest greetings from your brother and sister,

U. Eringa

M. Eringa-Rypstra

P.S. Both of you, be sure to write us again.

May 8, 1898

Dear brother and sister,
    [Opening]
    We thank you sincerely for your present, and now I will tell you what we bought with it. For Grace and Dora [anglicized from Grietje and Dirkje] we bought a little Sunday hat and a pair of shoes. We have enough left to buy a swing next fall for the children when Jessie is a little bigger. I wish to congratulate you, sister, on your birthday and hope that the Lord will spare you for many years for your family, and bless you!

                                *   *   *

    I have told you before that we didn't have much furniture but now we have a good supply. I will describe the room where I am sitting. Three new curtains in front of the three windows, a rug on the floor, and a much nicer organ than the one brother Jacob has. This organ cost one hundred dollars but I bought it at a sale from people without children for twenty-seven dollars. We have five straight chairs and a rocking chair with caned seats and backs, and a large new table with five "swirled" legs. We also have a Belgian lamp. Maaike's sewing machine also stands in this room. There are two pictures hanging on the wall, on one is written "Victory" and the other "God Bless Our Home." Then there is a clock shelf on the wall with a clock on it, and hanger for letters. In our bedroom we have two beds and also a carpet on the floor. Hedger Rypstra and our hired man sleep upstairs in one bedroom. Then we have a large living room and a kitchen and a small room with cupboards for pots and pans and dishes. Our house has four doors to go outside and ten windows downstairs and four upstairs. This is the last year that we are renting but I think we will stay here if we can buy.
    We will be getting our own minister in our congregation now. This morning we had Communion and we had Jessie baptized. Now your name, sister Jikke, is recorded in the baptismal records of one of the Holland American churches. Now you ought to put a quarter in a box every week, then you'd have enough money in about fifteen years to visit us! Then you could see the world sometime and press my darlings to your heart! As soon as the pictures are ready, I will send one to you. I am so glad that I have an organ again and that I got one so cheap. Now I can again play and sing the Psalms and the girls can learn to play the organ when they grow up.
    The weather this spring was dry and cold but now it is favorable weather and everything wants to grow. The wheat and oat fields are

beautiful. We've had a couple of good showers. We have eighty-five acres in wheat and thirty-seven acres of oats. Now we have one hundred acres already plowed and harrowed, ready for the corn to be planted. Tomorrow we start with this. We are milking ten cows, and are getting four more when they have calves. We now have sixty-two head of cattle. For three months we had hog sickness [cholera], so we immediately sold the thirty best ones; thirty died and we only saved six head. Fortunately we could take this misfortune, as financially we are doing very well. Praise the Lord! We are gradually getting ahead, while those with six thousand guilders in Friesland must surely be getting poor trying to farm. Hedger and Maaike each inherited eighty-nine guilders from an old childless aunt. With that money we helped a young man come over from Sexbierum who is working for us now. He is a good worker, so now I have a little easier life. I've been herding the cows in the valley between the hills for about three weeks since the grass grows more quickly there than on the level and hills of our pasture. Friday morning we brought twenty-seven head to another farmer's pasture for five months. These are mostly steers and yearling calves. Our milk cows are home. Our apple, cherry, and plum trees are all blossoming and it is a beautiful sight. Our yard looks like a flower garden at present. We have twenty-five little chicks and still have eight hens setting. We have a nice three-year-old blaze-faced horse. Our hired man just rode away on him. This young man doesn't ever want to go back to be a farmer in Friesland. He says he has a much better life here.

We are having war with Spain at present. Spain will soon lose against this wealthy United States.

Greetings from your loving brother and sister,

Ulbe and Maaike

Ulbe and Maaike Eringa to Jikke and Minne Sjaarda
Running Water, South Dakota, to Oosterend, Friesland
November 30, 1899

Dear sister and brother-in-law,
[Opening]
We are finished with our summer work and harvest, so now for the next four months we will not be so busy. We only have to care for our livestock and haul manure to the fields. We had a good harvest this year. The wheat crop could have been a little better but the oats and corn yielded well. We finished picking corn this past week. We had one hundred and thirty acres of corn which yielded thirty-six bushels per

acre. Each bushel has about one hundred and twenty-five ears, and each ear has to be husked one by one and thrown on this wagon. One man can pick about sixty bushels per day which is two wagonsful. This is a big job. The last week we had six men picking corn. I do not help any more as at this time of the year there is much work with the livestock. We are fattening eighteen steers, two cows, and fifteen hogs. The steers eat the corn, then the hogs eat the manure because the steers digest only half of the kernels so the hogs get fat salvaging the corn left in the manure.

We are milking eight cows at present, eight cows are dry and will be getting calves this winter. This year we raised nineteen calves and have five little calves. Too bad that you cannot see our eighty-five head of cattle! We have one hundred and sixty hens and ten roosters. Butter sells for seventeen cents per pound and we make about twenty pounds of butter each week. We sell that in the store and it pays for most of our groceries.

Now that is enough about the farming. Our minister was here for fifteen months but has left us again. We have called another one. Steadily more Hollanders are settling here, so the land is becoming more expensive. This year we rented one hundred and sixty acres in addition to our own one hundred and sixty, but now our neighbor is going to rent seventy acres of that and we will rent ninety. In this way we will hire a day laborer once in a while instead of keeping a hired man. This summer some horses and cows were killed by lightning.

I am very pleased to hear that you visit those poor old people. I consider that a very noble deed, my dear sister. Oh, there is so much haughtiness and class distinction in Friesland. Fortunately that is much better here in America.

I suppose you read quite a bit in the papers about the war between England and the Transvaal [Africa]. All of us here in America hope that the Boers will win. We read about it every day.

I am learning to play the organ again.

You must write me how you like the butter factories.[1] There is one here too but it is a little too far away and I make more money by buying small calves and raising them on milk.

When summer comes I'll write you how much we made on our fattened steers. We sell them in March; then Hedger will go to Chicago with the train carload of steers.

We like it very well on our new place. We have a nice big house and good barns and a good harvest.

Today it was Thanksgiving Day but it snowed so hard that we could not go to church. If we had been able to go, I would have had to read a sermon. My letter is not very long but I can't think of more to write.

[Closing]

P.S. by "Maaike"

Ulbe has written so much already that there isn't much left for me to write. I would really like it if you could look in on us here in America. It is very different here than near you. But I would certainly not like to return to the Netherlands. I believe that both of us consider America now as our new fatherland and it is much better here for our children's future. I sometimes tell our children about their uncles and aunts in Holland, and then they ask if we couldn't go there sometime with the buggy! This fall they all got new clothes. They each got little blue dresses, light gray jackets, and red caps. All three go to church regularly with us.

Meie Seffinga lost his wife four weeks ago. She was Popke Terpstra. Her mother was our helper when two of our children were born—she does not live very far from here. Popke left two children behind and they are with her mother. Greet Willem and Trijntje [Feitsma] for us.

[Closing]

1. Cooperative butter factories organized during the 1890s in the Netherlands.

January 12, 1902

Dear sister and brother-in-law [Jikke and Minne Sjaarda],

[Opening]

Our children were pleased with each of the cards they received. Your children can write well. Our children go to school now too although they have been home a while because of the cold weather. Our little Jessie is a quick, slender child; she will be four years old the 27th of January. If all goes well she will be the youngest in the family for only another six months.

Hedger, my brother-in-law, left for the state of Washington for a month. This is a trip of 700 hours [walking speed] west of here. It is just as far west as New York is east. He was on the train five nights and five days in order to get there. The climate there is wonderful and it doesn't rain much, so they irrigate the land with water from the mountains. He is in a valley [in eastern Washington] which is very productive. I have bought out his share of the farm and must pay him the first of April. Until now we rented land along with my own, but I have let that go and will only be working my own one hundred and sixty acres. That has one hundred and ten acres under cultivation but I am going to plow up another thirty acres of the pasture, then I'll have one hundred and forty acres of farming land. I can rent some more pasture and hay land.

I am getting a hired man from Sneek who is being brought over here by a neighbor. He doesn't know anything about farming but will also earn a little less the first year because of it. I think I can manage the work with his help. In another month I am going to have a sale of some of my livestock, and hope to sell about forty head. I am also feeding eighteen steers, which I will ship to Chicago the first of April. With that money I hope to pay off Hedger.

Everything is quite high priced at present. The hogs are extra high and corn is fifty cents per bushel compared to twenty-five last year and twelve cents five years ago. The reason for this is that the corn crops dried up in many states. We were so fortunate that we had a good crop. We have about forty hogs of which I plan to sell twelve head. They weigh about two hundred and sixty pounds each and I'll be getting fifteen dollars each for them. I'll have twelve brood sows since I traded a nice Poland China boar for a sow. I have to do my chores now and will write more later.

A month ago we butchered a good fat cow. She had been dry all summer and then I fed her corn for about two months. If everything goes well, I'll get my farm half paid off this year—one hundred and sixty acres with a good house and barns. We improved the house and painted it last fall. It looks neat and sometime we'll try to send you a picture of the house.

We have a good minister here and the congregation is getting larger all the time. We built a new parsonage which cost thirteen hundred dollars which will be paid this year. Then we will have to build a new church. I have to pay quite a lot each year for church purposes, but fortunately I know that the soul is more than the body and so I must not think of this too lightly.

Your letter made my thoughts go back to my birthplace again, and I thought of that unfortunate neighbor T. He spent so much money on liquor that he couldn't pay the rent. He's the same drunkard that he was twelve years ago. I guess he needs even more money for liquor now. You've always treated him well—better than our uncle did with his farmers. It shocked me when you wrote that he had rented his place for forty guilders [per acre]. He must think that dry bread is good enough for a renter—he who can figure out things so well. I cannot understand that this is pleasing in the sight of God. He is seventy years old and is still as much after the money as always. O brother and sister, who honor the name of your Savior, don't ever get like him. You also have a chance to be people of means. As I write about our uncle now I think of the time in 1886 when I was without a place and wanted to live with him. His cool answer: "Go hence and be warmed!"

I hope and pray that the Lord spares us long enough to see our children grown up since my wife and I both experienced what it is [to be orphans]. I am so very thankful that I am not a renter in Friesland. The Lord has led me along a pleasant path to America!

We are having beautiful weather. In December we had a couple of weeks of colder weather than I have ever experienced. We had very hard frosts. This summer it was very hot at times. My wife is reading a book that we received [as a premium] with [the purchase of] the Neerbosch calendar.

I will close my letter now. Be sure to give my greetings to sister Trijntje and her husband Willem. I should write her too sometime but I enjoy writing less and less, and you people live close together.

[Closing]

P.S. [Note added by Maaike Eringa]
    Dear Sister,
    I shall include a little letter with Ulbe's to make a request. Since we are getting a hired man from Sneek, and he will probably arrive some time in March, I would like very much to have you contact him, if possible, in February, and see if you could send some woolen skirts with him for the three oldest girls. We will send the money to you later when you tell us how much they cost. Little Jessie is still wearing that skirt we received from Trijntje. Grace wore it first for about two years. I've never bought one here since I always sew our own. One time we got some material from our landlord for Christmas from which I made nice wool skirts for Dora and Grace. The woolen material we get here is very expensive and not nearly as good as that which you buy because here it is mostly flannel. But if this is too much bother, don't do anything about it because I don't want to cause any extra trouble for you. We have been well so far this winter. At Christmastime here it is much like St. Nick's day in Holland. We bought each of the girls a nice doll. It was my birthday the twenty-fifth of December and I am twenty-nine years old.

    I will include the name of our new hired man and include a letter telling what I'd like to have you send. His address is Th. Fylstra, Rural Cost, Sneek.

[Closing]

Ulbe Eringa to Minne and Jikke Sjaarda
Running Water, South Dakota, to Oosterend, Friesland
December 20, 1903

Dear brother and sister,

We were pleased to receive a letter from you. Maaike had often said, "It's strange that Jikke never writes." We also received the picture postcards—who sent them, you or sister Trijntje? It was nice for me to see pictures of all the familiar houses. Then I could also tell the little girls where Uncle Willem and Aunt Trijntje live. J. Sippens has a nice house and the new church is also nice. Our new brother-in-law, Thijs Bakker, told us that there was a widow in Oosterend who had given five thousand guilders for that church. Do you know who that was? When I have a little more money, I'll send you some pictures too.

First I'll tell you a little about our children. Little Pier was a very cross baby at first. Our girls were good babies and hardly ever cried but this little boy lets himself be heard. It is getting better, however. He can walk already and doesn't cry if he falls. He is alert and smart. If Maaike leaves the room, he climbs on the table or gets on the sewing machine and pretends he is riding horseback. In his own way he tries to sing along, but cannot talk yet. He has precisely the same color white hair as I had when I was little, and a fair complexion. We have a small picture of Dirk's oldest boy, and our boy looks just like him.

Jessie will be six years old next month. She goes to school every day. She looks the most like my wife and sometimes I call her "little Maaike." Dora can read real well already and can knit a little. She weighs seventy pounds. She is big and strong and can carry Pier everywhere. Grace is a head smaller and about twenty pounds lighter but she is quick and healthy and learns well too. Fortunately, we are all well. I feel much better than last fall. I almost thought at times that I'd be sickly the rest of my life. We have a very good new doctor here which is a blessing for many.

Last spring my wife's sister and husband and six children came here from Sexbierum. For eight months they lived in the front part of our house and now they have moved to a farm which they rented. Brother-in-law Thijs can play the organ very well. Old Ulbe Wynia gave organ lessons to Thijs. The Bakkers came over last spring traveling second class. This cost nearly one thousand guilders. When they got here they had just enough money left to get settled. They wanted to start farming since their two oldest children can help with quite a bit of the work. Thijs's father was a big farmer in Sexbierum. Now we have decided that his father, Phillipers, should lend him four hundred dollars, that is, one thousand guilders, and I will lend him three hundred dollars, and Hedger will lend him two hundred dollars. I had a good harvest and now I can help him get started with feed, etc. I have an extra four-year-old horse worth one hundred dollars, which he will get, as well as four brood sows, five calves, and one hundred sacks of oats. Last summer they rented a nice one-hundred-and-fifty-acre farm with one hundred and ten acres in production and the rest is pasture and hay land. It is right next to the church. It has a nice house, a good barn, and many American conveniences. They are very pleased with it since they never could rent a decent farm in Friesland for a reasonable price. The farmer from whom he rents is a Norwegian. Thirty years ago this man came here without any money, homesteaded the land, built all the buildings on it through the years, plowed up the land and today he can get forty dollars an acre for it, i.e., one hundred guilders. So one hundred times one hundred and sixty acres is sixteen thousand guilders. Now these people are sixty years old and are going to retire in a Norwegian town in Minnesota. That is the way it works here in America—just the opposite from in the Netherlands. Here the poor people can get ahead so that in their old age they can own a farm and retire on the rent they get. If I was at your place I could name many people like that. This is the truth, and yet I know for a fact that you people wouldn't think of coming here and wouldn't even like to see your children go to America. What a pitiful country our beloved fatherland is!

The Lord has blessed us again this year with a bountiful harvest and everything brings a good price. We are fattening twenty-two steers and twenty-five hogs, and I have ten brood sows, one to butcher, and four for Thijs. I have twenty-five cows, six young steers, and one three-year-old bull. We milk about ten cows and the rest are nurse cows with calves. The team that we drive in front of our two-seater buggy is a four-year-old and a three-year-old, brother and sister. I have another beautiful three-year-old that I have trained and one old horse. I am renting one hundred and ten acres to my neighbor. That is why I sold four horses last year. My wife is very good in her chicken-raising business. She raised about one hundred and sixty chicks, half are hens and half are roosters. Part of the roosters we ate and part we sold to the hotel for a quarter a piece. The girls deliver them when they go to school. My wife and I pluck the feathers at night, putting them in boiling water and they are defeathered in no time. Then we clean them and sell them. They are delicious to eat. An American farmer's wife thinks a lot of her chickens. We have about one hundred and forty hens. With the eggs and butter the farmer's wife goes to the store and buys what she needs for her housekeeping.

Last year I bought some more livestock, so I couldn't pay anything off on the farm. Sister, maybe you sometimes think: "Ulbe, you are really after the money." But I am so glad that the Lord is with me and that I feel it is my duty to help my wife's relatives somewhat. This teaches me to strive and work hard in this life. If the Lord lets me live long enough to see my children grow up, I'll be able to get my farm paid off and then in our old age we can live off the rent as well as you.

I also have work to do in the church, so I do not neglect the spiritual things. I've been an elder for ten years. We do not have a Christian school here and we are quite far from church. I have just started to have catechism classes for my children and my neighbor's children. I have bought a Kaapse Children's Bible [printed, apparently, in the former Dutch colony of South Africa] and now my wife is busy teaching the children to read Dutch. The catechism classes are held in Dutch too. We also have to do quite a bit to support the church financially. We hope to build a new church soon. We have a good minister.

[Closing]

Ulbe Eringa to Trijntje and Willem Feitsma
Running Water, South Dakota, to Oosterend, Friesland
November 10, 1904

Dear sister Trijntje and brother Willem,
    With this letter we are informing you that on Sunday, October 16, our little Trijntje [Thyrza] was born. We are naming her after you so that we can keep you in our memory as long as possible. Maaike's sisters each have four girls, so their names will stay alive in their own families. Please inform sister Jikke about this too, and tell her I'll write to her sometime this winter. I received a letter from them last week.
    I'll write to you some more and hope we'll receive a letter from you too, sometime. Maaike is up and around again and is very busy. To have five children means quite a bit of work when the oldest is only ten years old. We have a very busy life, and help is scarce and costly. It is a case of "help yourself." But there is one blessing: everything is going well with us. We had a very good crop again this year. I have twenty head of cattle to fatten with corn, and fifty-four nice pigs. If we are lucky with these, we can pay off another eight hundred dollars on our land. A person can get ahead better here than in Holland, but he also has to do his best. We now have three hundred and twenty acres of land. The farm is "twenty minutes long and ten minutes wide" and is four-sided. It is already worth two times as much as when we bought it and will probably

go higher in time. We'll get the farm paid for in the near future and then we will really be well off.

We are busy picking corn at present. The best pickers earn two dollars and fifty cents a day each day. A hired hand earns more here in one year in dollars than guilders in Holland. And you can get twice as much for a dollar as for a guilder. Since a hired man always works with machinery, he can earn more money for that too.

This year we built a new church toward which we paid one hundred and fifty dollars. We do not have a minister at present. Our congregation is getting bigger all the time since more Hollanders are coming here to live. You should come to visit us sometime. Then you could see something of the world. Then you could see us and our children. It's too bad that you don't want to spend the money on it because traveling is very easy nowadays.

The widow of Jan de Roos lives near here. She still farms with her two youngest sons, Oepke and Pier, and one daughter Akke. The three oldest sons and one daughter are married and all live here in Dakota. She often talks about you, [saying] that Boukje, Sijtske, and she would visit you. That is thirty-three years ago. Trijntje Boukes Seffinga is married for the second time now. Ulbe Wynia's wife died last year. The very old Jan de Roos died over two years ago. His wife died a little before him.

Our children Grace, Dora, and Jessie go to school every day and are able to read quite well already. Dora is a head taller than Grace. Pier is a white-haired boy just as I was in my early years. He is starting to talk a lot. He is, fortunately, a very bright boy.

Yes, yes, we are getting quite a family. An oversupply of work and responsibilities but "hitherto has the Lord helped us." And we trust that he will continue to supply our needs. My wife and I often say that we are not in this world for pleasure. But neither were our parents and we are no better than they. This life isn't everything and we both hope to live for eternity through our faith in the Lord Jesus Christ as our Savior.

[Closing]

Ulbe Eringa to Minne and Jikke Sjaarda
Running Water, South Dakota, to Oosterend, Friesland
September 3, 1905

Dear brother and sister,
   [Opening]
   The postcards you sent carried me back to Oosterend. Can't my brothers and sisters come to visit us sometime? Many friends come to visit us

these days, including a neighbor from Veenwouden this spring. This man had been in the consistory with Dirk Reitsma in Holland. So we had a busy conversation about Friesland. Here the working people are so scarce and with you folks so plentiful.

We are having a good crop again this year. I can't tell you exactly how good since we haven't threshed our wheat and oats yet and our corn isn't ready to harvest. If it doesn't freeze too early, the corn will gain weight. I had good luck with my sows this spring. We had sixteen sows that raised ninety-five pigs and we didn't lose any sows. I sold eleven pigs, one died, and we have eighty-three left. These are growing well and I don't hear anything about sickness in the hogs. We get about enough corn to fatten these hogs and then we have a good year.

Prices are good for everything. Land is getting higher-priced all the time. My nearest neighbor sold his one-hundred-and-seventy-acre farm to a son of Jan and Kee de Roos for eight thousand dollars and now bought a three-hundred-and-twenty-acre farm for twenty thousand dollars. This latter farm has better land and a nicer house and barns. If we'd sell ours, we'd get fifteen thousand dollars for it, so if we wanted to go back to the Netherlands, we'd be pretty well off. But you won't be seeing us come yet. Conditions are so much better here that we'll never want to bring our family back to a country which is so overpopulated that the people can hardly earn the necessities of life. I am referring to that large group of laboring people who hardly ever get meat or eggs to eat. Now I know I'm exaggerating a bit because a true Netherlander says, "That isn't necessary either because if a laborer works every day, he can do without meat or other necessities, just so he is content with what he has."

This spring I went to Chicago again with a carload of twenty fattened steers. A neighbor of ours also had a carload of twenty head. I went alone and took care of both carloads so I could travel free of charge both ways. This year there were a lot of farmers shipping their cattle and then there is a special railroad car where they can also sleep. By this time I can speak English just as well as Dutch so that I can help myself very well on these trips. We had a very good time, and we also did a little sight-seeing in Chicago. This year I am not going to feed cattle but will do so again next year, the Lord willing. I have thirteen young steers one and a half years old which will be big enough then and I'll buy about seven head with it. This year we paid a little off on the farm again. We also have a minister of our own again. He is a fine young man, about thirty years old. We were without a preacher for about one year. About four weeks ago I went along with our preacher to a meeting of our classis a few towns west of here. Everything is much newer there. We traveled by train through a large area where the native Americans, the Indians, still live.

I always hope and pray that I can visit you sometime. But I don't know when, because since I get sick occasionally, it is hard for me to get everything done. But if the Lord's blessing doesn't fail us, we'll get along. I do think that my life is a little harder than yours but I suppose you also have your troubles in life. And yet, the less troubles you have, the happier I am for you!

Gradually several farmers are coming to America that have lots of money. One of them is Johannes van der Schaaf, who worked for Uncle Dirk and now lives in Iowa. This man now is worth one hundred thousand dollars. His sister's son preached here lately and spent a couple of nights here—a young minister and he told me this about his uncle. Dirk van der Koor is doing well, too.

I also read a death notice about Anna Dirks. They had seven children. Those poor children! I'm sure she was a loving mother. Many of the friends of our youth leave this earth.

This winter three farmers from here went to Friesland and just now one has come back from Franeker. In the past year six families have arrived here from Friesland. This spring we also contributed a few dollars to a fund to bring a family here.

Hedger Rypstra is coming to board with us again and has rented a piece of land from me. He has been going with a widow with two children for a couple of years. Write to me again sometime and be happy with me that the Lord directed my paths to America where I have an abundance of food and clothing for my wife and family, and where I may be useful here in my church and community.

[Closing]

Ulbe Eringa to Minne and Jikke Sjaarda
Running Water, South Dakota, to Oosterend, Friesland
January 29, 1908

Dear brother-in-law and sister,
    [Opening]

*　*　*

We did not have a big crop this year since hailstorms damaged our crops two times. So we had poor corn and very little of it. Last week I had to buy three hundred dollars' worth of corn. I have sixty little pigs. They weigh one hundred and fifty pounds on the average. By June first I hope that forty-four of these will weigh three hundred pounds and I will sell them then. I will keep sixteen for sows in the future. The price of hogs is not high at present, but I hope that will improve and if it does, then we will still do quite well financially. Last year we did very well, so we can stand a little hard going this year. I had hoped to buy eight steers to add to twelve nice ones I had raised myself and then fatten them and sell a carload of twenty in Chicago, but since the corn was so poor, I didn't buy any. I sold four of my twelve for one hundred and fifty dollars apiece and will keep the other eight for fattening next fall. We are milking four fresh cows with three more to follow in March. We have one hundred and forty chickens and gather thirty eggs a day. In April they perhaps will lay eighty eggs. I work all my own land. We are getting a hired man from Ferwerd, Friesland. I have a young horse three years old and a two-year-old that will soon be able to work. We expect two new colts. Horses are selling at high prices this year.

Last year I traveled with a carload of steers to Chicago and sold them there. I went on and visited Holland and Grand Rapids, two large cities in Michigan. There is a Reformed college in Holland and Grand Rapids is a large manufacturing city.

Rienk Bergsma, Jan Thomas van Tuinen, and his uncle Tjipke all live in Grand Rapids. I met these three men there. Rienk has lived in America twenty-five years and has a capable wife and three children. We were happy to meet each other.

Three years ago he visited the Netherlands, but didn't enjoy it. He advised me not to go back and visit Holland, but I hope I may be able to go in the future. He has been successful in America.

Our church and congregation are growing. We have a good minister. For his salary and other expenses we raised two thousand dollars. Our minister comes from Grand Rapids, Michigan.

I still remember where Aunt Sjoerdtje is buried and I suppose Uncle Dirk will be buried beside her. One more uncle is living and then all Mother's brothers and sisters will be gone.

We bought a new washing machine this year which saves us a lot of work and works well.

[Closing]

December 22, 1908

Dear brother and sister,

I could not get to writing earlier, so now it is high time that I write. I thank you heartily for the letters you have sent us about the sickness and death of our sister Trijntje. Thank you also for the pictures. You have fine daughters. How much your daughter T. looks like you, Jikke, when you were young. I had to look at it quite often and think of the time when we stood on the threshold of life and shared each other's joys and sorrows. But you are still my faithful brother and sister which you show in your friendly letters which my wife also enjoys reading. I am always very interested in your farming operations and am happy that you keep me posted on all your enterprises. Your house plan was neat, and I described it fully to our girls so that they now have a good idea about it.

I was thankful that Trijntje's death was so easy. She suffered much, but happily the Lord granted her much patience in suffering. This is a great mercy, because it is naturally hard to be sick. It always causes me a great struggle.

It was good that all the brothers and sisters were present at the funeral. I also had a letter recently from my brother Pier, and in it he mentioned that all was going so well with his children. This is always a source of great joy to me because years ago I often thought it was quite a burden to have such a large family (eight children). But he who goes through life with God as his helper shall not be put to shame. That is what they have experienced also.

Now I will tell you a little about ourselves. This past year we had a very good crop. I rented a little less land and had a good hired man. His parents live in Leeuwarden and he had drawn the "free lot" [for military service], so he did not have to serve. I am again fattening twenty steers, which will be ready for market in two months. When I started feeding them, they weighed a good one thousand pounds apiece on about October 1, and I think when I ship them to Chicago the first of March, then they will weigh about one thousand three hundred and twenty-five pounds. They get a good price now and I hope I will get seven cents a pound. About one hundred dollars will go off the profit for shipping expense, so you can figure out what I'll get for them.

I still have eight milk cows, one steer, and fourteen yearling calves and five small calves. We also have fifty-two hogs. They run with the fattening steers and live partially from their manure. I will try to get fifteen bred sows. We had sixty acres of corn, which yielded forty-five bushels per acre so that made two thousand seven hundred and fifty bushels. At present corn is forty-five cents a bushel, but on the fifteen hundred bushels which my steers eat, I hope to make more.

I think that with the Lord's blessing we will be able to pay off our land this year and then we will have accomplished quite a bit. This is fortunate because our family is increasing and we'd like a little better living than we've been able to have heretofore. Also I should build a large hog shed sometime. So gradually we are acquiring a very nice farm.

Jan Miedema, a son of my wife's sister, has drawn a picture of our house and grounds for you. I myself have planted seventy-five fruit trees and have eighteen acres planted with lucerne clover [alfalfa]. This is a beautiful hay crop and good forage for the hogs. It costs a lot to sow, but it will be good for twenty years. We cut it three times a year and it is outstanding hay. You have the same in the south of the Netherlands.

How earnestly I wish that you would come here once. You always talk as if it would be impossible. I thought that you had prospered sufficiently so that you could take a trip and see something of the world. You are not going to be able to take your money with you. Many people from here make pleasure trips to the Netherlands.

In the first part of June I went to the synod near New York City as a delegate from my church. I was there a week and I had all my traveling and hotel expenses paid. It cost my church eighty-five dollars to send me. I came from the farthest distance and had to travel one thousand seven hundred miles, which equals about five hundred and sixty-six hours [walking speed]. I left home on Monday morning at eight o'clock and arrived there at eleven on Wednesday evening. We are as far from the east coast as we are from the west coast of the United States. On the return trip I also went to see the Niagara Falls, which were beautiful. The river falls one hundred and seventy feet to the bottom and then goes farther on. I also went to Ellis Island, where all the third-class immigrants come and are processed. A ship was just coming in from Europe, so I saw the meeting of family members. It was very stirring to see the happiness of people reunited. I always rejoice that I have had such fine chances to see something of the world. There in the synod we had the opportunity to hear the best professors and missionaries speak. Our Dutch Reformed denomination [RCA] has one hundred missionaries in the field and six hundred ministers in America. Think about how many ministers you have in your state-supported Netherlands Reformed Church and then how few of them are missionaries. And add to that the treasures of church property that they possess! I shall say no more, but think these things over once. Does a church with so much modernism truly point to God's glory? I have heard much at our synod which did much good to my soul. It was all in English, but I have learned so much English in the last sixteen years that I could understand everything. I rode on the Atlantic Ocean again, and if the Lord is willing, I plan to come to see you in two or three years. I am very anxious to see you again, but dread taking the trip. I think we will send you a picture of all of us next May.

The children are growing. Pier is going to school too already. Trijntje [Thyrza] is so advanced for her age that she can go to school next year;

she already knows a lot of little verses. She seems also to be an apt scholar as Jikke [Jessie] is.

I now have a hired man in the summer and in the winter months my wife's brother helps me. He has his own farm near us. He pays board and room for nine months and earns it the other three months. Thus we plug along as the children grow up. This coming year I am getting a nephew of Harmen Adema as a hired man. Harmen has farmed here a year already and is getting ahead nicely. He married a fine young woman in the neighborhood and visits us occasionally. This afternoon I am going to visit Ulbe Wynia once again.

[Closing]

November 15, 1910

Dear brother-in-law and sister,

I was very happy to receive another letter from you. It also was good to hear that you have had a good year; it was a little dry, but our corn crop was better than we expected. We finished picking corn on Friday and had about three thousand bushels. I've already used up five hundred bushels for the hogs and horses but I still have two thousand five hundred bushels in the crib. I have two hundred and fifty dollars lying ready for our trip, and by middle February I will have eighteen fattened hogs to sell so my wife can send me the money for the return trip.

At present the two hired men are picking corn for my brother-in-law Hedger. We have about forty-five hogs and thirty-six cattle. The latter are gleaning the cornfields with the horses, picking up the fallen ears of corn and eating the cornstalks. I do not have as much hay as last year, but the corn crop is better than last year and I'm not feeding any steers since I'm going away.

We are planning now, the Lord willing, to leave from here on December seven and then on Tuesday, December thirteen to embark from New York, and we expect to be in the Netherlands the twenty-first or twenty-second of December. We will spend about three days or so in Grand Rapids, Michigan, which will shorten the trip somewhat. I have dreaded the trip for a long time, but that is over now and I am looking forward to [it] and longing to see all of you again. I have been exceptionally healthy the last few months, as well as the rest of the family. My wife is staying at home to look after the children, and I can entrust the farming and care of the stock to my hired man. I also believe that God's approval rests on all of this, since he has made the way smooth and given us a prosperous year. In years past, I have often prayed that I might see all of you again sometime, although in the last few years I thought less and less about it. But now it is going to happen if nothing unexpected prevents it.

We do not talk often about our plans. We will first spend a couple of days in Rotterdam, then about three days in Amsterdam, and then a couple of days at Woerden. Then I plan to visit you first in Friesland and then spend a couple of weeks in Holland before we return. I have to visit quite a few friends in Friesland, but during that time I will leave Dora with you and I'm sure you will receive her with the same friendliness and cordiality that you've given to me, the brother of your youth, and which is so unforgettable for me. Eighteen long years! What pleasant fellowship we shall have! This is even longer than the separation between Jacob and Joseph.[1] But fortunately we often heard from each other.

My wife is a bit sorrowful to be separated from us so long, but her love for Dora and me overcomes everything and she encourages me to go. Dora has enclosed a short letter also; she's already learning some Dutch. It is fortunate that I'm used to doing some traveling. Last spring I traveled ninety hours on the train, and a couple of years ago traveled sixty hours consecutively when I went to the synod.

[Closing]

1. The biblical account of Joseph in Egypt.

November 29, 1911

Dear sister and brother-in-law,

It is high time for me to write to you since you have already written me twice. Forgive me that I have not done it before and sincere thanks for your faithfulness and goodness.

My hired man picks corn by the bushel and consequently does not help with the chores of milking and feeding the animals. So the family had to struggle because there were times during two or three weeks when two or three of us were sick but we made it. Our hired man is picking corn for the neighbors now so we still do all the chores which isn't so bad now that we are well again.

We have all our corn picked out of the field and some corn fodder in shocks standing in the fields. Now the cows and horses can glean in the cornstalks during the day, and at night they can all be inside the barn and sheds. We have ninety-two hogs of which sixty weigh about two hundred pounds, average. We are feeding for market ten steers and five cows, one of which we will butcher for our own use. A month ago we butchered a calf and a hog. I usually fatten about twenty steers but this year I didn't want to buy any besides my own, so I'll sell about twenty-five hogs with the steers to fill a carload. We put these fat cattle in the feed lot the 20th of September and hope to ship them out by January 20. In about three weeks I want to sell about thirty of the heaviest hogs, which will average about two hundred and seventy-five pounds, live weight, and hope to get about six cents per pound for them. Two hundred and seventy-five times six cents equals sixteen dollars and fifty cents a head and thirty of these would be four hundred and ninety dollars. The animals are growing well, which always makes us feel good.

We are milking five old cows and two young heifers. The price of butter is good and we sell a dollar's worth daily besides what we use ourselves. I secretly hope to get nine hundred dollars for my cattle and in June about seven hundred dollars for the rest of my hogs. Then I still have fourteen sows to farrow which I can sell in November. But naturally this is all subject to future prices, and I may have to do some refiguring.

Maybe you are saying that Ulbe's future financial status looks good, and that is true, but I also have to tell you that because of poor crops I have a debt of nine hundred dollars and had to buy three hundred dollars' worth of corn. But yet, because of the Lord's blessing we have a good living even in a year of poor crops. Last year I had three thousand bushels of corn—this year fifteen hundred. Last year we had four hundred bushels of wheat besides having my own seed, flour, and chicken feed. This year we only sold thirty-five dollars' worth of wheat. Last year I had twenty-five tons of hay and the year before forty-five tons. Now, because of the shortage of hay, I had to cut up thirty acres of corn for fodder. This is good feed, but miserable stuff to handle, although we bind it in shocks with twine.

But I still have an abundance of feed. We had seventeen acres of wheat that was too short to cut with the binder so I cut it with the grass mower and hauled in eight wagonloads, which I feed to our horses. This makes very good feed and I did not thresh my oats either. This I feed to the young horses and the milk cows. This spring I had two brood mares. I had to have the veterinarian come for the one who had a dead colt but the mare lived. The other mare had a nice colt and is bred again for the coming year. Last winter we received thirteen calves and have three new ones now, and expect eleven more this winter, if all goes well. Thus far about the farming business.

It is almost a year ago that we made our plans to visit you. We often talk about you. Maaike thought the skirt you sent was very nice, and the one that she got from T. fits her well. She is wearing it this winter. Dora is making Grace a new skirt, from the goods we brought home, to wear to the evening catechism class and the the evening church service. Dora is getting to be a fine seamstress. The dresses always fit so well because she is so particular in everything she does. She is also learning to play the organ.

It was terribly dry here in June and unbearably hot. Later it got better and this fall we had two heavy rains so there is plenty of water again in the subsoil. It is surprising that we had as good a crop as we did but our land can stand the drought quite well.

Meinte is getting along fine and is a frugal boy. Pieter Los and Laurence Cnossen are doing well too. Driebergen likes it here too and writes to us occasionally. He lives some distance from here. Mr. Miedema from Oosterlittens is here in South Dakota also, about twenty hours' distance from us. A while back I happened to hear from him. He is doing well too.

We have already had lots of winter weather but fortunately no snow. The climate here is quite severe for people and my bachelor brother-in-law is going to warmer regions. Now that I have been in the Netherlands again, we think about doing this too. But I'd first have to get a good price for our farm. "Man proposes but God disposes." Now that we had such a poor harvest, I'm glad that Iede did not come with us. For someone like Iede who is so blessed that he still has both parents and lacks nothing, it is not suitable to come to America. That is especially suited for those who have lost their parents early in life and consequently have gone through much hardship. They are better prepared to face and endure the struggles in life. Yet I must say, "hitherto hath the Lord helped us" and I sincerely hope that the Lord will spare my wife and me so that our children do not have to experience what both of us did [being orphaned].

This summer I was not so strong, healthwise, and then it is a struggle to be thankful and cheerful. But I hope this will get better in time. First, after I got back from my tiring trip to Holland and meeting so many friends and relatives, I had a hard time keeping my spirits up but I have never been homesick for the Netherlands. I had no idea that it would affect my nerves and emotions since I was not bothered with that when I visited you. I often thought "I wish I had not gone back to Holland for a visit," but now I am glad I did and it did me good to have seen all of you and your children. We have a picture [of the young people] hanging in the parlor, and also one of Willem and Trijntje. Then we also have that large family picture, and a picture of the synod, where I am included with a hundred ministers and elders. Our minister is getting along fine. He got married a few months ago.

Tomorrow it is Thanksgiving Day throughout all America. We have morning church services, and tomorrow evening the consistory members and their wives are invited to the preacher's home. The children are having a little party at school. Tomorrow the people in America will be eating a festive dinner where fowls are the chief food (chicken, turkey, etc.). My wife and Grace have butchered four roosters, two for ourselves and two for the children's party. Tomorrow thousands of turkeys, ducks, and geese, and chickens will be eaten. Almost every church has a Thanksgiving service, upon orders from the president.

Now I've written quite a long letter and will let Dora do the rest. All the family has gone to bed and I am going also.

[Closing]

P.S. In the last three weeks we have had letters from you and Antje, Pier, and Jacob.

December 30, 1912

Dear sister and brother-in-law,

The year is nearly past and we sincerely wish you a happy New Year. Life presents many necessary obligations, but if the Lord spares us from sickness and catastrophes, then life can be quite pleasant. This year we have many reasons to be thankful. All summer we had good weather, not so terribly hot, and from October 1 until now we have had exceptionally lovely weather which was a great blessing for us because during the day all of our livestock could glean in the harvested cornfields. We also had a good corn crop such as we've never had before and of good quality. We have plenty of feed since we are fattening twenty animals, of which eighteen are steers and two cows. One of these cows is thirteen years old and has raised ten steer calves and two heifers. Her steers were always the best to fatten. The cattle this year are fourteen of my own raising and six that I bought from my neighbor.

The cattle here bring a very good price, especially those from the feedlot. We are preparing seventy-two hogs for market, and have thirty sows to be bred. We have lots more corn than we need, and if livestock wasn't so high priced, I'd like to buy twenty more head because I could borrow the money for it. If I would get eighty dollars for every animal, and eighteen for each hog, we could make quite a lot of money. We have eighteen milk cows and fourteen calves, about ten months old, average. We have three brood mares and three other horses, two males and one female. Now last week we bought two more mare colts. Now you know something about my farming business. However, I forgot to mention the one hundred and thirty chickens.

In the month of December we built a new barn. It is a fine addition to our farmyard. It cost $1,700.00 all finished. It can house twelve horses and sixty hogs. The haymow can store thirty loads of hay. Now I can use the old barn for my milk cows. I can have all my livestock inside at night, and I have lots of straw for bedding. In this nice weather, everything [animals] grows well.

We are all healthy and we have a very fine young minister, which is a great blessing.

We have had a busy summer. Saturday the carpenters left for good. Now we still have to shell some corn and haul the hay home from the stalks in the field. I sowed seventeen acres with lucerne clover so that now we have forty acres of hay land.

It is already two years ago that we visited you in Holland. We have heard that Iede has a girlfriend and that she is a descendant of our great-grandmother Imkeje. Her great-grandmother Sytske was also a cousin of Iede's great-grandmother Antje and so the Sjaardas and we will be distant relatives.

There have been four farm sales around here lately. I went to one and everything was quite expensive. We have our parlor stove burning again so now it is cozy inside. Bokke, our former hired man, is in Holland at present. I don't know if he will look you up but receive him cordially—he is somewhat bashful by nature. Be sure to greet Willem for us. I also had a letter from Trijntje Lambers and I wrote back to her but we never hear from Gerrit.

[Closing]

P.S. Minne must write me again about his farming operations.

September 12, 1913

Dear brother and sister and children,

Since you will be married for twenty-five years on September 22 I decided to write you a letter this evening. Hearty congratulations from all of us on this happy occasion. If we weren't so far apart we could congratulate you in person, but this is not possible. In our thoughts we shall be celebrating with you.

Fortunately, you have not experienced great sorrow—you, as well as we, have not lost a child in death, and you have not had such a large family which often creates much difficulty. No doubt you too have had disappointments which is the case with most of us. Life is not a bed of roses without a cross to bear, but fortunately His love is constant through all of it. May the Lord continue to bless you and spare you for each other—that is my wish.

We are all well. We are sending you a picture of the three youngest children [Alice nearly 4, Thyrza nearly 9, and Pier 11] included in this letter.

We had a very good wheat crop this year. We sold far more than $670 worth, and still have about $330 worth for our own use. The corn harvest is quite a bit less than last year but still quite good. In many places the corn harvest was very poor. We have one hundred and sixty-eight head of nice hogs, sixteen calves, and one colt. The mother of this colt dropped dead last week, which is quite a loss.

Financially we have never had a better year than 1913. But we built a new barn, and I have to buy a new grain binder and a new grass mower. Also, both girls, Jessie and Dora, are going to high school [away from home] and I have to hire two expensive hired men who [together] earn about $600. We put up about sixty tons of hay this year, which is worth a great deal, and up until now we've sold $300 worth of cream. We have raised sixteen calves and have about fourteen yearlings besides. Last winter we fattened twenty animals, for which we received a very good price. But this year we are not putting any in the feedlot. I'm going to keep my young stock and then if we get more corn next year, I can fatten those for market. We will get enough corn to get my one hundred and sixty-eight hogs ready for market, and if the Lord spares us from hog cholera, 1914 should be a good year again. The hog cholera is quite bad this year in America. This year we sold eighty fat hogs and this week we are going to sell another twenty sows because the disease is already in Dakota. Now you know enough about our farming business again.

I want to thank Minne for the letter that he wrote for Pier. Day after day I thought about him. Our family of brothers and sisters has already been cut in half and one wonders whose turn will be next. God only knows. May He by His Holy Spirit prepare us for that time, so that we may die in the faith and assurance that our brother Pier had. How he must have suffered! Ruurdje [his wife] has written us a long letter. Yesterday we had a letter from brother Jan, wife Gep, and Aagie.

Last week Maaike and I went to visit the widow of Hendrik Bosma (Frietje de Gavere). At that time we talked about many people from Oosterend. They live about twenty-five miles from here, so we had to ride about four hours with a team of horses and a buggy. She is going to visit us too sometime with one of her sons.

Our church's congregation has existed twenty-five years this year, so we celebrated the occasion this summer. We have a fine young minister.

Dora and Jessie will be leaving Monday by train to Orange City, Iowa, about a hundred miles from here. There is a Christian Academy to which I'd rather have them go than to the State Normal School here, where Jessie attended two years. Jessie is a very good student but I'm sure Dora will do equally well. That the Lord will bless Dora's plans [to be a missionary] is our heartfelt prayer and wish. They have all been very busy sewing for all the five girls, dresses and other clothes. Also, Dora cut many acres of hay this summer, and the three oldest girls always helped with the milking.

My one hired man, Laurence Cnossen, whose father is a cousin of Jelle Bouma, is going back to Holland this coming winter and I told him he'd better visit you people a few days. He is a capable farmer's son and will be twenty-four years old tomorrow. He has been working for us for two years and a good hired man is a great boon.

Dora has received Tina's letter and will answer it in the near future. You folks must be sure to write us again. Perhaps my handwriting seems small but that is because in the evening I wear a pair of glasses which enlarges things so that I think my handwriting is so large. You must write me sometime about each of those young people we associated with twenty-five years ago. I suppose all are married except Wiebe Reygstra.

> Hours and days and years and ages
> Swift as moving shadows flee;
> As we scan life's fleeting pages,
> Naught enduring do we see.

Well, I'll close my letter now. Dora and Grace visited Sjaardas a couple of days this spring. He rents a fine farm in Iowa. The oil is out of my lamp!

[Closing]

August 23, 1914

Dear sister and brother-in-law,

It is almost a year ago that I have written to you. Since then I have received a letter from you and it would almost seem as if the love between us is cooling off a bit. But then, the visit of H. Adema was a living letter from you, so the above does not apply to you, my dear sister.

This year we did not have such a good crop, but it was better than the first crop that we had here in Dakota twenty years ago. We had then only seven bushels of wheat per acre, twenty-two bushels of oats, and perhaps ten bushels of corn per acre. A good crop is fifteen bushels of wheat, forty of oats, and forty bushels of corn per acre. But fortunately we have quite a lot of hay of very good quality. Also lots of straw and cornstalks. Last year we didn't feed any steers for market, so now I have twenty steers of our own to fatten and then I'll just buy some feed. At present we have sixty-three animals. We have one hundred and twenty-five nice hogs and so with the Lord's blessing we can have a good living, I hope. If we had had a good crop this year, we planned to pay off some more of our land debt, but that will have to be postponed a while. In 1913 we raised one hundred and seventy hogs, all of which, except for sixteen, we have sold, and they averaged about thirteen dollars a head. For that money I bought $400 worth of corn, so I have enough feed.

You will notice that we really have to do our best to make our life successful and to get through life honorably, respectably, and virtuously. It is fortunate too that a person gets strengthened a little in the struggle.

Unfortunately, our minister has accepted a call. Now the church work and services will be up to the elders again, and I am one of them. I will have to read sermons on Sundays and conduct the catechism classes. Sometimes I feel, to my shame, I'd like to just spend my time doing my farming business. It is such a job to always be faithful working in the Lord's vineyard doing kingdom work which we have to do so often. It takes a lot to be a diligent Christian.

Maaike and Pier and Thyrza have gone on a week's visit. Maaike's nephew lives about forty miles from here and they have gone there. His name is Jan Miedema, and he is distantly related to Klaas Miedema from Oosterend. Maaike also was gone to Orange City for a week this winter, where the girls [Dora and Jessie] go to school. She visited there with the children of Meindert Sakes Tiemersma.

That war in Europe is a terrible thing. Write me a long letter sometime soon, and have Ieda write me a long explanation about the war. I surely hope that the war news will cease!

[Closing]

P.S. It is quite dry here this year but not nearly as bad as last year.

May 29, 1915

Dear sister and brother-in-law,

We received your letter a couple of weeks ago and last Tuesday the wedding announcement of Iede. We congratulate you on having a daughter-in-law and wish Iede a happy married life. Marriage makes a great deal of difference in a person's life and this shows up daily when we examine people's lives closely. A husband and wife have so much influence on each other because they have mutual interests. If a husband and wife can't pull in the same direction, then, it seems to me, it will be a lifelong struggle.

Three weeks ago Dora and I wrote you long letters and both were returned which was disappointing. That letter probably never reached its destination—very likely due to the war situation.

In January I was quite sick so I went to a different doctor and now I've been well all spring and could work as hard as usual. Pier can also help with the fieldwork and I also have a very good hired man again. Pier [12] sometimes drives five horses in front of the harrow and he does that very well. We were rather late with our fieldwork because we had such a lot of snow, which wasn't gone yet by April 1. We still have to plant forty of the one hundred acres of corn and usually we have it all finished by May 25. Now this week we have had some bad thunderstorms. Because of the heavy rains, a twenty-one-year-old granddaughter of Jouke Boschma was drowned in a swollen creek. Three weeks ago we even had some hail on a Sunday. We have an overabundance of moisture and the elements of nature are very active.

Dora comes home on Friday afternoons and sews all day Saturday. She is making two pretty graduation dresses for Jessie. Next week Jessie has to take her final exams. The Hollanders are starting Christian schools and now Jessie may change to a different school. Dora has finished two years of higher education, and Grace is a great help on the farm. She always helps with the milking and helps me to care for the livestock. She has already hatched out one hundred and sixty chicks and still has ten hens "setting" on eggs to hatch.

Last year we had a poor crop but now we are all working with renewed effort. My wife helps with the milking too now because we are so busy with fieldwork. Since the first of May we've had an abundance of grass in the pastures. Each week we sell seven dollars' worth of eggs. That is grocery money for the family.

We have seventy-two little pigs and expect approximately another fifty. We have ten little calves and expect two more. We had a nice mare colt but it died. We are expecting a mule colt. This spring we had three young horses to train and one young mule. They are all nice animals.

Your daughter-in-law bears the name of Sade Liesbeth, I discovered. Is Iede going to live in Oosterend? That mobilization in Europe appears to me a slavery. There will be many young people slaughtered because of the desires and whims of kings and kaisers. It is fortunate that you Netherlanders are so patriotic that you can accept these miserable circumstances. Yet we hope that peace will return to Europe.

We have a very fine minister again who is as good as your ministers. His name is Tietema and he was born in Tzum, the Netherlands.

Farmers are starting to ride in cars but we want to have our farm paid for first. Then we will buy a car too. But this may be a couple of years yet and perhaps even longer.

Last week Anne Miedema and his wife visited us a couple of days—the storekeeper from Oosterlittens. He works a large farm with his four sons. He rents about four hundred acres, paying one-third of the crop as rent and everything looks prosperous. They are hardworking people and fine Christians. People like that are finding America an ideal place to live.

[Closing]

P.S. Write me a postcard when you get this letter.

July 29, 1916

Dear sister and brother-in-law,

It is Saturday afternoon, four o'clock, and since middle March I've never really had a free afternoon, so now I'll just take time off and write you a letter. Yesterday it was thirty-six years ago that you lost your mother and tomorrow it will be twenty-seven years ago that you became a mother, and now you are already a grandmother. We never heard anything about the inheritance and so we were surprised that we were getting anything. I was a bit disappointed that you never wrote exactly what you received—I don't find that very brotherly. I suppose you received at least 10,000 guilders. I am glad that you folks fared so well, and my wife is very well satisfied. I hope that you will write me about it in the future, otherwise I'll have to write to a stranger to find out about it.

Pieter Los got married recently to a daughter of the Logtermans who are some of our best friends. Mr. Logterman's father was a cousin of Bos, the baker. He is a farmer too now. His father had sent him money and it arrived safely, but if [because of wartime embargoes and uncertainty] you do not trust sending it, just use it. If you do send it, send only the capital and I will tell you who is to have the interest. . . .

Too bad that Frankena has lost almost everything. I am so thankful that I was led to go to America because fortunately I still live in my own home, furnished to suit me and where I can write letters without fear of becoming poor. It could happen, naturally, but as long as the Lord grants me, with my wife and children, the desire and strength to do our best, it is not very probable. Our home has been remodeled, painted inside and out, and refurnished. We have new curtains in three of the rooms and my wife has also bought some new furniture besides the new organ. We now have a nice downstairs bedroom, a parlor, and dining room, a front hall and a storeroom. We could entertain you very well now. You could easily make the trip, especially since you have received such a generous inheritance, but I don't dare to expect it.

Last week we cut our grain with the self-binder. We haven't had such a lovely crop for years. The wheat and oats were both especially good. Yesterday we started to stack the shocks of grain in such a way that the threshing machine can ride between the stacks to thresh the grain. We have sixty-five acres of small grain and one hundred and twenty acres of corn, which looks very good and is beginning to get ears. Now we really need a good rain shower. It is a little dry at present and very warm. We have lots of grass in our one hundred and sixty acres of pasture and hay land. Our cows give lots of milk and the young stock are all growing fast. Now if we would get a good rain in the next week, we'd have a good corn crop, otherwise it may only be a half or poorer crop. Our first cutting of hay was very good but the second was not so good, and the third cutting is entirely dependent on the rain we get.

We finished cultivating the corn a couple of weeks ago. With the building project and the crop, and so much livestock to care for, we have been very busy. But now we are through the busiest time. I am always healthy, we have a very good hired man, and Pier is already a big help. Dora also helps with the fieldwork during her vacation.

Meinte is "going steady" with a niece of my wife. He works for the carpenter who remodeled our house, who is married to a daughter of my wife's other sister. A brother-in-law of Pieter Los also works for this carpenter.

Our church is also being enlarged. As a congregation we have pledged $3,000 for this project. We are giving $100. Rev. Tietema is a very good minister. If the corn crop turns out well, we hope to buy a good car next year, D.V. [God willing].

This week we had a letter from Coen Driebergen. Things are going well with him. Dora is eagerly awaiting a letter from Tienka since she wrote to her a couple of months ago. Jessie is going to be a teacher in a town school. Grace is going away for a week's visit. Thyrza reminds me a lot of you when you were young. Alys is a little more quiet.

Hogs are nine cents a pound, live weight. I still have eighteen sows to sell from which I have just weaned the little pigs. Four of these will have pigs again soon as they had their first pigs in March. The Nanninga family is getting along well. Sietske, wife of Bouke, has gotten married again to a prosperous widower, so she has a good life during her last days.

This past year I have met Johannes Dykstra and his wife. He is about eighty years old but still very spry. Ulbe Wynia is no longer living. The family complained that in the will some had gotten more than others.

[Closing]

January 9, 1917

Dear sister, brother-in-law, and children,

I am going to start a letter to you this evening and using a pencil as that is easier than using a pen. I have to remind you that in the future you must write "South Dakota" in the address instead of just "Dakota." This is because there is also a state of North Dakota and so our letter might go there.

* * *

The state of South Dakota has voted for Prohibition, so now after July 1 no more liquor can be sold. The state of Nebraska, just south of us across the river, has done the same. There are quite a few states that have voted for Prohibition.

We had severe weather in December but not much snow. Now the snow is all gone and it barely freezes any more. This past year we had a very good grain harvest but the corn crop was poor. I am not fattening any cattle but I have one hundred and ten hogs to sell. I have enough oats to feed them. The wheat brings an exceptionally high price. We made lots of money in 1916 but had lots of expense with rebuilding the house. But we were able to pay off $900 on the farm, and now we still have $1,500 debt before the farm is completely paid for. This spring we are going to buy a car, and hope to pay off the farm in 1918. We hope we will get a good corn crop this year. I have thirty two-year-old steers to fatten, and a hundred hogs, so that will help me carry out my plans, the Lord willing.

Well, well, so two of your daughters are getting married! I believe our Grace is also planning on it. She is keeping company with a young man from Blija. He has rented a farm near us and is quite interested in her. Dora is in her fourth year at the Orange City Academy and will graduate in June. She will be able to teach then. I don't know if she wants more education or if she wants to teach a couple of years first. Jessie teaches in a public school and earns $60 a month for nine months. She enjoys teaching very much. They have both been home for Christmas vacation which has been so enjoyable because they both play so well on our new piano. We have a lovely home now since it has been remodeled. What a blessing it is when a person prospers and does not have to be so concerned about making a good living.

It is also good that Willem remembered you so well in his will. Now you can also live well. When our son grows up we can quit farming. When I am sixty, he will be twenty-four. Pier is a smart boy and very willing to work. Alys is so pleasant and healthy and can already play little tunes on the piano with both hands. She is starting to read well, too.

I am glad that you are using the interest of my money. Now I'd like to have you give twenty-five guilders of the interest to brother-in-law Passchier and the rest to sister Janke. If you send it to Passchier in March then you can send it to Janke [Teffer] in August which will even it up. Then you can use the money until you feel it is safe to send it.

Land is going up in price here. I think I could easily get $80 per acre, maybe more, but naturally we wouldn't sell because we gain a good living from farming. Cream also is a good price. We have seventeen milk cows, so the breeding is profitable business. Our two hundred chickens are starting to lay again. Grace is a good chicken farmer. She raised two hundred and fifty chickens this year and so if she gets married we'll send her off with a good supply of hens. She already has a couple of milk cows and I'll give her more when she gets married.

* * *

Old Mrs. Nanninga has told me about the end of Jeffe de Vries [a farmer whom Ulbe knew before immigrating]. She worked for them and had gotten the last bottle of whiskey for him. When he was dying he still made motions as if he was lifting the glass to his lips. What a blessing that we never were victims of that awful habit.

We received your letter Saturday evening. Tomorrow Bokke Boersma and his wife and little son are coming here for dinner. He is a good farmer.

[Closing]

December 24, 1919

Dear sister, brother-in-law, and children,

Yesterday we received your letter and read it with much joy. All of our children are home for Christmas vacation. Also Grace and her husband and our grandson. Now it is evening and Maaike and I are home together. The children and a son of Maaike's sister have all gone to church to the Christmas program, with the car. The whole congregation is present at this time, and many children take part in the program with recitations, dialogues, and singing of Christmas carols by the singing groups. We always attended too, but the car would be too full with eight people, so we stayed at home.

Dora is still attending college [Central College, founded by the Reformed Church in America,] at Pella, which is approximately three hundred miles east of here. In February she plans to go to Chicago for three months to study at Moody Bible Institute. After that she would like to study a year at [Hope College, also founded by the RCA, in] Holland, Michigan, after which she hopes to be prepared to go to the mission field in 1921. In the three summer months she helps on the farm with the grass and grain cutting for hay and harvest. The rest of the time she helps in the house with the cooking and sewing. Pier helps me greatly which is very comforting to me because I am gradually slowing down. I have worked hard for forty years and have done my share, I believe. But I do not dare to quit yet and hope that my strength will not decrease too fast.

Our daughter Grace and her husband Jan van der Wey will be moving in March to a farm they have bought about two hundred and fifty miles west of here. They have done well with farming these three years. Here in America the families are often spread out quite far apart. The United States is so large and there are so many chances to move farther away.

We are all quite healthy and hope the same for you. The influenza last year caused many deaths but I don't hear much about it anymore. Our hired man, Jan Jonkmans, who has worked for us for four years, has now returned to the Netherlands for a pleasure trip. His mother lives in Oppenhuizen. I have told him that he should visit you people sometime so that you could hear about us. I assured him that you would give him a kind reception. In case he has been there before you get this letter, I would be disappointed because we are more used to welcoming strangers here in America than the people in the Netherlands. I am sure you are the exception in this case. Jan has been in America seven years now. He has been careful to save, so that he has accumulated a nice sum of money.

We had a poor wheat harvest this year but an exceptionally good corn crop. We have one hundred and sixty-five head of hogs that are seven months old, two nice colts, and only eight calves since some of my cows calved too soon. We have about two hundred and fifty laying hens. We had such severe weather in November and December that they quit laying, but will start again when the weather improves. My wife's brother [Hedger Rypstra] lives on an island in the Pacific Ocean [Whidbey Island, Washington] and runs a big chicken farm. They get two hundred eggs a day and receive seven cents per dozen. It never freezes hard there and the days do not vary much in length.

Last week I sold some cattle for which I received $3,100 after expenses were paid. During the war farming paid very well, but clothes, labor, machinery, and everything is getting so expensive, and the hogs are cheaper. So I don't think we'll be making so much money anymore.

We have forty apple trees that I planted fifteen years ago by hand, and they are bearing much fruit. We've had apples since August 1, and are still eating them. In addition we have well over a hundred jars of apple-sauce that my wife canned with sugar in glass jars. That will be good food until the next crop ripens. Besides that she has canned several other kinds of fruit such as peaches, pears, and cherries which we buy in the store. One can buy all of these already "canned" but it is much more expensive and not nearly so good tasting. She also cans beef and pork in jars, which works very well.

Now we have a telephone too. When I was in Sioux City to sell my cattle, which is about eighty miles from here, the time for the departure of my train had been changed and I was late. So I telephoned to my wife by long distance to say that I would be a day later than planned. I could talk to her as plainly as if I was right at home with her. An hour ago she listened on the phone a moment and heard her two sisters talking to each other. The automobile and the phone have certainly shortened the distances between places here, which are much greater than in your country.

The auto is for us what the bicycle is for you. Every farmer has one. I don't know how many millions of cars there are in America. How eagerly I wish that you would come to America once so you would get some idea of how things are here. Then you would also know what the Red Cross is doing for the hungry lands of Europe today and even for Germany. You would also learn how much respect people here have for the Netherlands for all the good that they have done for the refugees. You should think better of our country. I imagine sometimes that we may see the time come when we will have to set England straight if she starts to think about ruling the whole world. Many people here think that our President Wilson is too big a friend of England and France. I'll tell you that that war has had a great influence on our land. It has turned much upside down. Our congregation contributed twenty-one young men to the war effort but fortunately all returned safely except the son of Lou Palsma. He died in France of the influenza. That was very sad since years ago his parents also lost a young son in an accident with a manure-spreading machine.

As farmers we made a lot of money during the war years but now everything is getting very expensive. People contend that many of the big companies are withholding their goods so that prices will go up. Also, the taxes are rising enormously. However, I believe that at present the farmers are not in danger of having to give out more than their income allows, just as long as the Lord protects us from crop failures. But it is much different in the big cities, and the city folks envy the farmers if they do well. The motto here is, "A farmer had better work hard long hours and not have much enjoyment while the city people work only eight hours in the day and then waste their money at the movies and theater." The situation in the large cities is not good. The foolishness and unbelief there is getting worse. When will the time come when the masses will return to serve God? The time for humbling oneself has not yet come with this war.

[Closing]

October 24, 1920

Dear sister and brother-in-law,

I decided to write you again this evening. I am not sure whether it is my turn, but that doesn't make any difference—it's getting time to write again.

We are all well and enjoying a quiet, restful Sunday evening. The children have gone to the young people's meeting with the car. On Friday evenings they go to the adult catechism classes even though Thyrza has already made confession of her faith. Jessie is attending the State Normal Training School in Springfield for another year. She comes home for the weekends from Friday evening until Monday morning. She has already taught school five years, but by spending this year in school, she will have a life certificate for teaching.

Dora is busy with her last year in college at Pella, Iowa, and then she can go to the mission field after eight years of preparation. Grace and husband John are well settled in Todd County and this past summer they had their second child, a little girl. At that time Maaike went there for three weeks while Dora and Thyrza took care of the household duties here besides helping with the milking and the hay and grain harvest.

We now have a furnace in the basement, which is a big improvement over setting up stoves in the fall. In a month or so we expect to get electricity in our home from a central plant in Springfield. Then we can wash our clothes with an electric machine and iron them with an electric iron. It will light up the cow barn and horse barn and all the rooms in the house by just pressing a button! We are also buying a new automobile again. So you see we are gradually getting a very comfortable way of life.

Monday evening we had a missionary and his wife from Japan speak in our church. They spoke to us about Japan and also showed pictures. They had worked there thirty years and have been very useful in kingdom work. I am very pleased that soon Dora will also go as a missionary to work in God's kingdom to carry on the Lord's work, because there is so much need among the heathen to hear the Gospel. Oh, that all parents would offer one of their children for that purpose and encourage them to go to the mission field. Then there wouldn't be so many heathen to be lost eternally!

Our years in the land of the living are rapidly passing by and then we can do no more work for time or eternity. Therefore we must make the most of our opportunities now.

Our farming operations are going well. We have a good corn crop, a good oat harvest, but poor wheat. We have been able to put up a lot of hay for the winter. We have thirteen horses, fifty head of cattle, one hundred and thirty-five hogs, and two hundred and thirty chickens.

R. wrote me this summer about coming here, but I did not dare to recommend it very strongly. I did not want to encourage him too much because I felt that he was too used to a nice home and not too eager to work while we are all used to hard work and put all our time to good use. Just tell him that I am sorry that he didn't go to the trouble to answer me, since I did my best to answer his letter in a kind and tactful way.

Most of our farm work is finished again for this season. We have started to harvest the corn crop. We have to pick sixty acres, and we have fenced in forty acres and let the hogs eat from that.

[Closing]

Ulbe Eringa to Minne Sjaarda
Running Water, South Dakota, to Oosterend, Friesland
June, 1923

Dear Brother-in-law,

You probably have been wondering why I did not write to you. The reason is mostly that this whole spring season I have not been feeling very well and then a person doesn't feel much like writing—I simply could not get around to writing. This past week I was sick in bed a couple of days again. Now I have recovered from that, but I am too weak to do any work. So today I'll express my sympathy to you and your children in the loss of your loved one. It is certainly a sorrowful loss, as she was such a good wife and mother. After I received your letter I thought of her and all of you constantly the first two weeks. I remembered the days, thirty-five years ago when she and I were orphaned and unmarried, and we were a great comfort to each other. And how, in the later years, we always corresponded with each other, and how we enjoyed meeting each other twelve years ago! Now that is all finished; yet you and I have to keep up correspondence as long as we are in the land of the living. I hope that the Lord will comfort and sustain you in your loss and that you may still have enough love for life left, because otherwise living would be difficult and one would almost give up.

This year we had a nice mild winter and I was always quite healthy and could carry on very well with my work. But in March I got influenza and I just can't seem to get my strength back. It is difficult to do my work and this causes me to be despondent at times which takes the joy out of life. It is hard for me to rejoice in my farm work, and although everything is growing and crops are beautiful to see, it's hard for me to appreciate all of it as I did before.

Last year it was quite dry here but now we are receiving plenty of rain, but not too much. We are cultivating our corn and bringing in our first cutting of hay which does not progress very fast because of the wet, cloudy weather. Last year there were several farmers in this vicinity who lost their crops partially or entirely to hail, but fortunately we were spared from that. Now we are very unfortunate because our one hundred and fifty hogs ate but did not grow as they should. It took much longer to get them ready for market. And the prices have gone down so much that we only get six cents per pound, live weight. As a farmer, you can understand that this has been a great loss to us.

Conditions in America are such now that the workers in the cities and the factories are getting big wages and the farmers are getting far too little for their products. The laboring class has the upper hand—for instance, the carpenters and painters in the cities earn eight dollars a day. All those who work on the freight trains earn a great deal, and everything that we buy or sell has to be moved by rail. You can imagine that the farmers in the Midwest are handicapped by the high cost of transportation. All this is the result and aftermath of the war. The farmers, as a whole, were against the war because they didn't want to offer up their sons to be killed to help France and England, but the city people were eager to carry on the war to free us from Germany's attempt to rule the whole world, not realizing that France and England had the same thing in mind. Well, the farmers are feeling the aftereffects of the war, while in the cities the people are reveling in their inflated wages. But this is not likely to continue and in the future the people in the cities may yet have to face something unpleasant hanging over their heads.

At present the family is in good health but Alys had an accident, cutting her leg on the barbed-wire fence. So she has been using crutches for a while. We take her to the doctor twice a week to prevent blood poisoning, and it is getting better.

Our minister has had a few calls and has declined each time. Piet Los, the brother of your minister, is living in California now. They were living in Todd County where Grace and Jan, our children, are living.

[Closing]

February 17, 1924

Dear brother-in-law,

It is already a few months ago that I received your last letter. I was pleased to hear from you again and from your children and grandchildren. Years ago we sat together on the same school bench and later we grew up as youths together. Now we are both grandfathers and in a short time we won't be living on this earth, but we hope and trust that we will then have our abode in heaven prepared for us by our Savior, Jesus Christ.

Today it is Sunday. Maaike and the children and the hired man have gone to church with the car for the afternoon service, but I have stayed at home all day. Pier is gone for a couple of weeks to visit our daughter Grace and husband in Todd County where he can also visit his fiancée, Lillian Walkling.

The winter days are short, and since in the last few years we do not have a hired man during the winter, I hired a young man to help me while Pier is gone. But all the responsibility of the chores rests on me and that is why I stayed home from church. I read a sermon by [Charles H.] Spurgeon, the great English preacher and translated into the Dutch by Adema van Scheltema.

At present I am feeding twenty-four head of cattle for market and next week will butcher one of them for our own use. Besides that, we have forty-three head of cattle, mostly milking stock aged two years, one-year-olds and young calves. Those in the feedlot have been fed about four months and in another month we will be selling them. We have one hundred and thirty head of hogs; twenty-six of them are brood sows and the rest will be sold when ready for market. We also have eleven horses, so you can imagine that Pier and I have plenty to do in the winter. In the summertime we don't have so much work with the livestock, but then the fieldwork keeps us busy. Then we have a regular hired man again, good machinery, and fine work horses. If everything goes according to plan, and with the Lord's blessing, we hope to farm a couple of years yet and then rent the farm to Pier. Then we hope to move to town so that the girls can continue their education. But these are our thoughts and we don't know what God's plans are for us in the future.

Jessie is a teacher in the state of Washington now. She is a long way from home but she wanted to see more of the world than the state of

South Dakota. Dora is getting along well in Japan. Her life was mercifully spared from the great earthquake. She is beginning to learn the language quite well even though it is a very difficult language to learn.

The fattened cattle are a pretty good price at present, but the hogs are very cheap. We had an especially good grain crop this past year, and the corn crop is fairly good too, but the farmers in general have had a couple of bad years. However, the businesspeople and laboring classes in the cities are doing very well. Here in America they earn excessive wages and spend it rapidly. But fortunately I am learning to be reconciled to the fact that the farmers have to bear the brunt of the costs of a war. . . .

Today we had some snow but without a storm. Usually we get our snow with strong winds and then sometimes we get snowbanks five and six feet high. We had an exceptionally nice fall—it hardly froze before January first, but then we got a month of very cold weather. This month we are having nice winter weather. The livestock does well in this kind of weather, and seven of our eleven horses are outside night and day. They feed off of the cornstalks and a large oat straw stack in the field. They remain fat without our feeding them grain.

Our pastor left us in November but another one has already accepted our call and we expect him in a couple of weeks. We have been vacant four months and two ministers declined our calls.

My wife and I visited Klaas Wynia in Platte a few days. They told us quite a bit about their visit to the Netherlands. I also had a nice letter from Jan Noordmans and will answer his letter soon.

Be sure to write again soon and greet all your children for me. Ask them to enclose some letters with yours now that my dearest sister can no longer write to me.

[Closing]

III

Rural to Urban

Introduction

Although all the correspondents whose letters appear in this part emigrated from rural villages, only half of them (Niemeijer, Zondervan, and Plaisier) were clearly farmhands in the Netherlands. The other three may have worked on the land during harvest seasons, but they were also skilled or semiskilled craftsmen prepared to perform a variety of tasks, as was commonly the case in the preindustrial era.[1] Between 1835 and 1880 about 60 percent of the Dutch immigrants were defined as either skilled and semiskilled or, simply, laborers. In general they were more inclined and better prepared to settle in cities than their cohorts who had worked exclusively on farms. According to I. J. Brugmans, village craftsmen and laborers were also healthier, better educated, and less poverty-stricken than factory hands.[2] Given their general flexibility and work habits, the village workers were well stationed to become successful immigrants. By contrast, factory workers were probably too poor to emigrate. In any case, they made up only a small fragment of the Dutch populace before 1900 and constituted only 4 percent of the immigrants before 1880.[3]

Two of the six correspondents represented in this part became farmers. Klaas Niemeijer raised vegetables for the Chicago market from 1907 to 1921, and then he became a wholesale produce dealer, traveling between West Michigan and Chicago. Most of his descendants are located within a belt of Dutch enclaves strung out along the south and southwestern

[1] G. H. Ligterink, *De landverhuizers: Emigratie naar Noord-Amerika uit het Gelders-Westfaalse grensgebied tussen de jaren, 1830–1850* (Zutphen, The Netherlands: De Walburg Pers, 1981), pp. 13–24.

[2] I. J. Brugmans, *De arbeidende klasse in Nederland in de 19e eeuw*, pp. 167–94.

[3] Swierenga, "Dutch International Labour Migration to North America in the Nineteenth Century," in *Dutch Immigration to North America*, ed. Ganzevoort and Boekelman, pp. 1–34.

shores of Lake Michigan between Muskegon, Michigan, and Chicago. Although Aart Plaisier immigrated as a skilled cabinetmaker, he and his family had been independent farmers in the Netherlands before going bankrupt around 1900. Their return to the soil in 1914, after four years of industrial employment in Grand Rapids, marked the restoration of their lost status. By the 1950s Aart Plaisier's descendants had become prominent market gardeners in Michigan, and most of the current generation of Plaisiers continues to reside in West Michigan.

Immigrants who settled in and remained in the cities were strongly inclined toward family business ventures. The three woodworkers in this chapter (Jan Wonnink, Marten Schoonbeek, and H. W. van der Bosch) were all self-employed for periods of their lives.[4] The Schoonbeek and Wonnink children continued in that pattern. Only Tjerk Zondervan appears to have continued as a daily wage earner, but after he deserted his family in 1907, precise information about his life is not available. His wife, Maartje Lautenbach, reported rumors in 1911 that Tjerk was living in Dalton, Illinois, a village on the south side of Chicago, where he was a farmhand.

In general these rural villagers adapted readily to urban industrial life in the United States and apart from Tjerk Zondervan, they and their children became self-employed tradespersons, farmers, and merchants. In that respect they reflected the general characteristics often ascribed to Dutch Americans: they were inclined to small business ventures and they invested their savings in property. Although few acquired great wealth, the vast majority eventually owned homes, farms, and businesses.[5]

8   H. W. van der Bosch and Johan Philipsen

Gendringen, H. W. van der Bosch's and Johan Philipsen's native village, stands near the German border in the southwest corner of Gelderland. The proximity of the Rhine River, the large German city of Emmerich, and the Rhineland itself, together with Gendringen's distance from major cities of the Netherlands, gave cultural currents from Germany great strength in Gendringen. That background surely contributed to the ease with which Gendringen's immigrants acculturated into the German community in Auburn, New York, where H. W. van der Bosch and his family became loyal if not leading members of Auburn's German

[4] Carpenters consistently ranked third and fourth behind laborer, farmer, and farmhand among the occupations ascribed to Dutch immigrants, 1834–1880. See Ibid., p. 20.
[5] Henry Lucas, *Netherlanders in America*, pp. 617–22.

Catholic parish. Together with work and family matters, the Saint Alphonsus Church and the Catholic faith provided major topics for comment in the correspondence.

In Gendringen, unlike Auburn, Roman Catholics constituted the overwhelming majority of the population. In 1848 they outnumbered Protestants by about five to one. Auburn, with but three Catholic churches among its thirteen congregations, was predominantly Presbyterian and Episcopal in 1868. The city's founders and leading citizens had migrated mainly from eastern New York, Massachusetts, and Connecticut. The names of its elites (in business, law, politics, religion, and education) indicate that Auburn was a white Anglo-Saxon Protestant stronghold. Its most famous citizen, William H. Seward, was a leading Republican who became Abraham Lincoln's secretary of state. Most of the area's Roman Catholics were Irish, but the much smaller German parish provided comfortable associations for the Van der Bosch–Philipsen family.

In other respects Auburn and Gendringen were more alike. Both cities provided a wide variety of employment in artisanal trades including metal, wood, textile, and stone work. H. W. van der Bosch's carpenter skills found a ready market in the Auburn area, which supported 190 carpenters and cabinetmakers in 1869. Johan Philipsen, van der Bosch's stepgrandson, though he had been schooled as a tailor, was also readily employable because Auburn featured both wool and cotton mills together with five clothing manufacturers and many retailers.

Auburn's agricultural potential was also excellent; its climate, soil, and rainfall supported such major crops as corn and wheat. The city served an agricultural marketplace with flour mills, a wagon works, a tannery, and farm implement shops. The outlet from Owasco Lake provided sufficient water power to turn millstones and the belt-driven machinery of over fifty shops. The Philipsens carved their New World livelihoods from this busy and productive community, which, though not yet a modern industrial center, provided employment to both factory hands and artisans. Over five hundred young women and boys, for example, were employed in Auburn's textile mills.[1]

Industrial mechanization of such proportions was new to the Van der Bosch clan even though their native village was more industrial than agricultural. Gendringen's economy depended on local markets for products crafted from its bog iron and charcoal-fueled blast furnaces. And furthermore, the Industrial Revolution had made little impact in backcountry villages such as Gendringen, or in the Netherlands at large, be-

[1] Van der Aa, *Aardrijkskundig woordenboek* 4:524–26; Henry Hall, *The History of Auburn* (New York: Dennis Brothers, 1869), pp. 470–506, 529–79.

fore the 1880s. Thus, Van der Bosch and Philipsen came to Auburn as traditional artisans. Yet, they were able to adapt readily to Auburn's industrial economy, and H. W. van der Bosch penned an enthusiastic description of a mechanized carpenter shop which in 1868 employed twenty-eight persons, including several family members. Only his son, Noles van der Bosch, became a farmer, while the others, stepchildren and stepgrandchildren, joined Auburn's urban work force. Among these, Johan Philipsen, his stepgrandson, who arrived in 1867, wrote eight of the letters included in this series.

The H. W. van der Bosch letters date from 1855, when he reported the death of his wife, Mechtilde, in Port Byron, New York. Apparently, Van der Bosch moved to Port Byron in 1850 after spending some time in New York City. His November 28, 1867, letter indicates that he had immigrated in 1847 and that he moved to Auburn in 1856 after Mechtilde's death. Apart from periods when his work took him elsewhere, Van der Bosch spent his remaining years in Auburn and died there in 1871.

Johan Philipsen's correspondence, 1869–1877, illustrates a common acculturation pattern among Dutch Catholics. His association with Auburn's German Catholic parish and his marriage to Anne Waldbaum in 1872 altered his resolve to return to Gendringen. Then, with the birth of two children and the purchase of a house, Johan's life began to revolve around his growing family. As his last letter indicates he was rapidly acculturating into the German Catholic subculture.

My efforts to discover Johan's descendants have been unsuccessful, and that is a special disappointment because the donor of these letters (1976), T. Philipsen in Braamt, Gelderland, hoped to correspond with the American branch of his family.

H. W. van der Bosch to Hendrikus and Hendrika Berendsen Philipsen Family
Port Byron [Auburn], New York, to Gendringen, Gelderland
June 2, 1855

Dear and esteemed children—Hendrikus Philipsen, Hendrika Berendsen, and children,

I am writing once again after a long delay to answer the pleasant and comforting letter written by your oldest son on May 25, 1855.

It would be wonderful if all my letters could, as in the past, be as joyful and pleasant as your letter to me. But the good Lord has other plans.

These letters were donated by T. Philipsen, 1976, and first translated by G. H. Ligterink.

He sends crosses and disappointments, and with these He wants us to learn to trust and depend on Him.

He also teaches us in the Lord's Prayer that His will must be done on earth as it is in heaven—and that we can always be certain that it is for our well-being—if we from our side try to do as much as possible to accomplish His will, and rest in it.

This encourages me to write freely of intimate things—even though I must inform you with tears and grief that it has pleased the Almighty, on the day of His Ascension, on the morning of May 17 at 5:15 A.M. to send His angel to call your [Hendrikus's] beloved mother from life and unto Himself. Certainly she was called to experience this festive Ascension day with Him and His saints and angels. No one can earn this distinction, but it comes only from God's goodness and grace. All of us who knew her Christian behavior, believe that her reward is eternal joy. She was always ready to care for the grandchildren and they were always in her prayers and thoughts. They had her constant attention. She did not cease praying and so we believe that her prayers will be answered. Because the Savior said to Nicodemus, "God so loved the world that He gave His only Son so that all who believe on Him will not be lost but will have eternal life." She believed on Him and followed all His commandments as well as those of the church. She was generous with love and help. She was kind to the poor, and a loving and well-meaning mother to my children and hers and also to the grandchildren. If through human weakness she fell into sin, she did not fail to make amends with the sacraments and penance.

If it may be that some small punishments may for a short time delay her entrance to perfect joy, then we must be helpful with our prayers so that through God's mercy she will speedily enjoy rest and peace.

Yes, dear children, her death was completely unexpected; for however old she was, she was still strong and vigorous, and everyone who knew her expected her to live many years longer. In the summer she always sat near an open window where the wind blew freely. I'd ask her, "Why do you do that? It's too cold for me." She answered, "I don't know."

During this whole spring your brother Evert who lives in Auburn, eight miles from Port Byron, wanted Mother to stay with him for a few days. As long as the weather stayed cold, I wouldn't permit it. But Evert's wife [Mechtilde] was sick, and then Evert insisted that Mother should come to assist with the housekeeping and caring for the children. With good weather, beginning on April 18, she went by stagecoach to Auburn with the agreement that I would follow on Thursday of the second week, in order to return home with her on Saturday, May 12.

When she arrived in Auburn she stopped to visit a dear friend who operates a lodging house. His name is Frank (he comes from Groenlo [a village near Gendringen in Gelderland] and is married to Wentia's daughter). After a few hours' visit she continued the trip to Evert's house in the company of Anton Hessing from Anholt [a German village across the border from Gendringen] and Willem Philipsen [the son of Jan Philipsen].

As planned, I arrived there on May 10 and then she was already sick. On May 3, when we had snow, she had already caught a severe cold. On the 11th of May, one day after I arrived, we called the doctor. He said, "She will be convalescing for two or three days because she has a severe cold." But then in the course of the next three days the cold worsened. Then the doctor returned and said that the cold had inflamed the lungs, and because of her age he said it was rather serious. But he told us to be calm because he could make her well. But instead the illness grew worse and especially so on the night when she died. But even then, sick as she was, we had no thoughts of her dying so suddenly. She was so strong of will that even then she wanted no one to lift a hand to help her. I was up with her the whole night and we had much conversation. A half hour before she died she had tea and a bite to eat. A quarter hour before her death she sat upright in bed, then she lay down again and shortly thereafter she died—without a movement of her hands and feet, and with almost no change in her face.

Of course nothing was too good for our good wife, mother, grandmother, and great-grandmother. We obtained the casket from the store where Willem and his partner F. Snitke stock all sorts of furniture. The casket was of the best mahogany. It was trimmed beautifully, upholstered with the finest materials, and decorated with the best handles and hardware. On the casket lid we placed a beautiful silver nameplate which was engraved as follows:

> Mechtilde Stegeman
> Wife of H. W. van der Bosch
> born 1771 died in Auburn May 17, 1855

As is usual here the burial ceremony included a beautiful hearse and four coaches for the closest family members. Thereafter friends and acquaintances follow. They drive their own carriages or travel with others. They line up in a very long train in order to accompany the casket. And thus the body is removed from the home and taken to the church. When they stop there, the body is removed from the carriage and placed in the middle of the church. The buggies waited outside during the service. Under the somber tones of the organ we expressed our loss and grief in song. After the mass and benediction, a moving eulogy was delivered in the English language.

Thereafter the body was placed in the carriage again and everyone returned to their buggies. They went from the church to the graveyard where the casket was again removed from the coach. At the cemetery we had a vault sent in from Port Byron which was constructed of the best 1½-inch fir. The mahogany casket was placed inside of this. The vault provided about 3–4 centimeters of space between the casket and the vault. Then it was placed in the grave. After a prayer for the departed, everyone returned to their own carriages and invited guests then returned to the home of the deceased.

This cemetery is new. It was dedicated by the bishop and belongs to the Catholics. Willem, Evert, and everyone else in the family has purchased a plot of ground there which is inherited by each family. We now plan, as is ordinary here, to place a decorative iron railing around the grave plot.

You are probably thinking that I have written rather lengthily of these matters. Yes, I took the trouble to do this for those who are not familiar with American customs—those who know us well and with whom we lived in the Netherlands. I assure you that I do not write out of pride or for praise but only to be certain that the proper information about her life, sickness, death, and burial will be passed on to her children.

Yes, children, even though she was old, I still miss her very much. She always cared for me. When anyone was sick, she was always there at the bedside to provide what was needed. We discussed everything together and had great comfort from each other.

God's will has been done and so we will try to follow her good example.

Even though I have written a great deal about this matter and about the cemetery it will not be superfluous to add that you would be astonished if you were to visit the cemetery here and see the marble gravestones and monuments. It is very pleasant to wander through the cemetery, to see the stonemasons' work and to read the inscriptions. Almost every grave has a stone with attractive border designs and inscriptions—and also beautiful lathe work and other decorations of many sorts. Each plot has its own plants—flowers, roses, bushes, and flowering trees. People come to walk through the grounds almost every Sunday. The cemetery is located on high ground and the white marble can be seen from a great distance.

Let me ask you, esteemed children, to inform my sister in Anholt, J. Verhey in Zwanenburg [a village near Amsterdam], and others whom we know of my dear wife's death.

Now just one more request, now that your mother is gone, let us, nonetheless, remain friends as long as we live.

Be so good as to write back speedily—tell us how you are and what you are doing. Send us the exact birthdate of Willem Philipsen. A birth certificate is not necessary.

Many greetings from Willem Philipsen and us, as well to his sister Drika.

P.S. We have heard about the high water and damage caused by the Rhine River dike breaking. And we were deeply concerned about the possibility that you might have suffered loss from it; but we persuaded ourselves that you were not affected. Fortunately Anton Hessing had just received a letter from his mother when we arrived in Auburn, and we could read that Hendrikus and Leen had suffered no damage. I hope that is the case. We urge you to write us about it.

June 2, 1855

In answer to your letter of May 25, 1855, let me begin by saying how pleasant it was to hear that all of you are in good health.

With respect to your questions about sending your oldest son[1] here to learn the carpenter's trade, I find the idea most attractive. You write that he is thirteen years old—well, it is common here to teach a trade to a youngster of that age. If he waits until he is sixteen that will also be early enough. We have recently acquired an apprentice in the carpenter shop. And we are also obligated to employ Willem Philipsen, your brother Jan's son. He is already as big as his father. Currently he is a counter clerk but we are hopeful that he will soon learn the carpenter's trade. He will continue as clerk for the summer, but in the fall or as soon as his contract expires he will come in with us. After he is with us for a year he will be advanced enough for us to take on another apprentice.

Your mother, who loved and cared so much for him, is no more, and I am pledged to assume her place in caring for him. He is a very nice young fellow. I was in Auburn just the other day and met him in the shop. I couldn't help expressing my surprise at his competence in handling money and accounts. But it is very dangerous here for young people who are not properly supervised in matters of faith and worship. There is a tide of opposition here to the Catholic faith. A huge number of people from all parts of Germany, from Italy, and from France—those who fled following the failed Revolution of 1848 in Germany and elsewhere—curse and rage against God and the commandments. For them, belief in heaven and hell is too childish and they hurl their rage especially at Catholic beliefs—at popes, bishops, and priests. Many who may be of

Catholic origins will no longer acknowledge their faith. Even ordinary Americans, people you meet at work or in stores, when they discover that you are Catholic, try to change your mind. And almost all of them are smooth talkers. And it makes them more and more bewildered when they discover that the more they storm and rage the more the Catholic faith progresses. Currently there are forty bishops in America, many monasteries, seminaries, and other religious organizations. We build the most beautiful churches throughout the country, and this can only be accomplished with liberal giving. In addition many learned and prominent Protestants have become Catholic. At the same time many immigrants from good Catholic families in Europe fall under the influence of those unchristian propagandists and lose their faith.

My paper is nearly filled and so I must close. The last two winters have been the most severe in local memory, but by contrast, this spring is beautifully green. Now we really need some rain, but it fails to arrive. Meanwhile all the crops, and especially the winter wheat, are in need of rain. People say that all of Europe has had bad weather and prices are very high. It is also bad in America. . . . Money is scarce and prices are high. More than enough was harvested, but Europe, France, and England in particular, have purchased so much that the cost of living is high here too. But it is not really too bad. Anyone who works has little to worry about. Thank God, we are all in good health.

Reumer, Christina, and their children are also well. Jan van Nus, who married Reumer's daughter Johanna, is well too. A. Hebing, married to Reumer's daughter Mientje, is also healthy and has worked with us in the shop for years.

I would pay good money to have you here to see our shop and all its machines for a day—to see the workers plane wood planks while others scrape, shape, and saw a variety of things. One machine cuts window frames of all sorts—and another drills holes. All of this is powered by a steam engine, as are also two lathes. All is done by machine. The men have only to place the wood properly and it is done in a minute.

Many hearty compliments to all your children and Grandfather Berendsen—to all our old neighbors—receive our friendly greetings and enduring regards.

We are at your service always,
Your father, H. W. van der Bosch

P.S. Yes, Hendrika Berendsen, I do not disagree with you very much in your not wanting to come to America. Not everyone is successful who comes here. On the other hand, your being here would give me great pleasure. Send my greeting to my sister in Anholt. Tell her about the death of Bullink in Breedenbroek [a crossroads village near Gendringen].

Tell her also that Anton is doing well. He is writing with me and so you will also have a letter from him.

This second letter in the series, also dated June 2, 1855, is probably an addendum to the first letter, which is primarily a death report clearly intended for circulation among friends and relatives in Gendringen.

1. Willem Philipsen was the oldest son of Hendrikus but he did not emigrate. Instead, his youngest brother, Johan, came to Auburn in 1868. The last eight letters in this series were from Johan to his parents and siblings, including Willem Philipsen.

November 20, 1867

Dear and esteemed son, H. Philipsen, and daughter, Berendsen,

I received your letter of February 10, 1867, and read its contents with much pleasure. It is very comforting in my lonely situation to read that I still have sympathetic friends. Yes, friends, this loss has been very hard on me. She[1] was very good and cared for me very well. We had the most pleasant life possible. We owned our own house and rented part of it for six dollars per month. And in addition, I worked a little to make extra money. Although I don't wish to boast, I can say that our furniture was as good as that of the best families in Gendringen. But because we lived in only part of our house, we did not have much furniture. We had things arranged so we did not have to worry about future difficulties. But in spite of all our saving and planning for the future we have been separated.

But what could I do after she died? I did not need all that furniture. I gave part of it to your brother's wife, who stood by my wife throughout her long illness and also did the necessary housework here. The balance of the furniture, apart from some of the best that I have in my sleeping room, has gone to Willem.

Yes, children, when you reflect about the course of life, some people must experience a great deal in the short span of their years. And I'm only thinking about my experience in America. The money I took with me to New York was gone before I moved to Port Byron and Auburn. And at first we could earn only enough for food and clothing. I would have liked to strike out in a new business but your mother was too old for that and she said she couldn't do it then anymore.

As you know from my letters your mother died on May 16, 1855. I stayed in Port Byron until the summer of 1856, when my fortunes changed. Willem's company constructed a large building in Geneva, about thirty miles from Auburn, and I was hired to supervise the construction. After that I supervised the enlargement of our church here in Auburn. The building project, which included the drawings, took three years. And I earned good wages during that whole time. Meanwhile I roomed in the nice hotel of our countryman, J. A. Frank van Grol.

With that work I gained a good reputation in this area, but still more fortunately, it was through this connection that I met, courted, and married the niece of Frank van Grol. And that was not all. With her I received $400.00 just at a time when houses and land were at very low prices because so many people were moving out west. I was able to buy my house and property at a third of its real value. And so, with that, I was able to set up my own household again. And then, because Willem was the boss in the carpenter shop, I always had work. And, in addition, I always had my carpenter's bench there and could do my own work. I only worked for the shop when I wished. I worked by the hour which is very common here. When you work less than a day the time is figured to the half hour. Ordinarily people work ten hours per day. Now I will return to the story of my life in America.

Over all the changes in my life, the death of my [second] wife has cast me from the highest to the lowest depths. I lost both my wife and all prospects for a pleasant future. I had to give up the house which I loved so much and in which I had lived with joy and satisfaction. The prospects are that I will never live there again and I feel like an orphan. I still don't know how to cope with her death. When your mother died it affected me very much, but I was able to cope with it. Then we were living with your brother Willem. But now I don't know what to expect and it is unwise to expect too much. Along with my adversity I should still confess that I am well off. My house and land are paid off and I collect some rent from it. I work enough to pay for my own costs. I will remain independent and be the master of my own life as long as possible.

You were so kind as to invite me to come and live with you. And I have been thinking about that for the whole summer. If I could get a good cash price for my house, I would almost resolve to come over and stay with you and Frank in Groenlo. Everything here is so bitterly expensive that I cannot survive without working part time. I could live decently here in a respectable rooming house in the city for $5.00 per week, although I don't pay that much to live in Willem's house.

Everything is very expensive here, but still things do flourish. As long as I've lived in Auburn at least seventy new houses have been built every year. Yet, when someone wishes to rent a house they are almost impossible to find. As prices rise, so do the wages. Willem still has three men working in the shop. He pays them $2.50 per day but the actual cost is $3.00. Then he has other men who earn $2.25 and $2.00 but they also cost $3.00 per day to keep.

I can no longer come to the Netherlands this winter, but meanwhile

I will try to sell my house for cash. I would have answered your letter much sooner, but with all the consequences of such a decision it is difficult simply to write and say I will do this or that. It would be a great help to have a letter from you which tells about the cost of living in the Netherlands. At present the prices here are: wheat, $2.50 per bushel; 200 lbs. of ground red wheat meal, $16.00; white flour, $17.00; potatoes, $.75 to $1.00 per bushel. Willem bought twenty bushels of buckwheat at $1.00 per bushel and then had to sell it for $.75 per bushel. Butter costs 45 cents. Pork is cheap at present. Willem bought some today for seven and three-quarters cents per pound—that is the same as nineteen and three-quarters cents in guilders. Things are not expensive here because of crop failures but because too much is shipped to other countries.

In the twenty years since I left the Netherlands I'm sure much has changed there. And as you can imagine, when I read your letters I want to know more about these changes. I should add that, because of my age, I need someone to travel with me.

*   *   *

I am tired of writing and also out of time because I'm going to send this letter along with Lucas Kosters.

*   *   *

[Greetings from many of the Philipsen clan in Auburn.]
Best wishes and blessings to both your body and soul.

1. H. W. van der Bosch's second wife, whom he identifies only as the "niece of Frank van Grol." She must have died late in 1866.

August 10, 1868

Dear son and daughter, H. Philipsen, and children,

Your son Johan and I are concerned because we have not received a letter from you in some time. Johan has written two letters and I sent a note from him along with a letter to your brother's wife Mechtilda in Gendringen. It is now four months since then and we have not received an answer from you. Jan is worried about you. I am afraid as well that you sent a letter and that it went to Auburn and is still there. Letters are not brought door to door here but must be gotten from the post office. There are more than 2,000 post boxes in the Post Office. Everyone who does business, and thus writes frequently, rents such a box. Willem has a box there and all the Van der Bosch letters are placed in it. Perhaps you did not place the address properly on the letter. There is also a department in the post office where people can ask for letters by name. Johan has not yet inquired there. We will see if your letter is there. Letters that are not picked up on time are listed in the Auburn newspaper one time. If, after a particular time, that gets no response, the letters are sent to Washington, where they are opened. When the senders of such letters are from the U.S.A. and can be identified they are returned, the rest are placed in the dead-letter file and burned. Now it is possible that that is what happened to your letter because no one in our family reads the newspaper that prints the list of unclaimed mail.

As you will notice from Johan's letter, he has been ill. He was already sick when he arrived at our house. He was coughing and spitting. He took medicine for a cold, but he became more and more sick. At times he could not work. He went to a doctor who said he had a lung infection—and that's what I suspected from his appearance. He was under doctor's care for six weeks, and now, for the past three weeks, he has been comfortable and healthy. But the doctor advised him to stop working as a tailor to avoid a return of the infection. Johan had already concluded before then that constantly sitting at work was not good for him. So he has an agreement to work in a large store beginning next month.

At present Johan and Bongers[1] work together in a large store which employs at least 200 persons—men and young girls. They sell nothing but tailored clothing. Rich people come there to be measured and then they select the material from which their clothes will be made. The most skilled and well-paid workmen make up individually ordered clothing. But newcomers who arrive here without knowing English do not get the best work. But Jan and Bongers both get a portion of the best work and can earn good wages. You have no need to worry about their progress because they are industrious and economical.

As for myself, the prospects get poorer with time. It is my custom to go to the shop every day, but this summer I was absent a great deal as I can do no heavy work anymore. Light work is not always available for me, but to do no work and not go to the shop is a miserable life. That is especially the case because I'm so used to working and also because I need to earn some money. I don't want to suffer financial losses, as long as I can earn something. I still have many expenses and spend a great deal each year on such things as I need.

I would like to come over and visit with you this September. My house is listed for sale in the newspaper this summer. But it is rather exceptional to sell houses or to move in the summer around here because almost every householder has a large garden under cultivation and they do not generally move until after harvest. Also I have some money due to me in this area and despite asking, I can't get the money back early. So I am bound on both the left and right sides, and I must wait until my money comes back before I can leave.

The city of Auburn grows yearly with the addition of about 200 houses. It is one of the most beautiful and pleasant cities in the area. Nearby cities include Syracuse to the east, Rochester to the west, and also Buffalo to the west. These are all far larger than Auburn, but Auburn is three times larger than Emmerich [Gendringen's largest neighboring city] and contains a population of 20,000. It is also a rich city with some houses like palaces because so many rich people live here. We have 28 employees in our shop.

This summer has been very dry, and the whole month of July has been exceptionally hot. The summer crops have suffered from it with potatoes an almost total failure. More important, though, most of the crops in America are good—and also the corn (what you call Turkish wheat) is doing well. Much of this is cultivated here. We've had three good rains so that much of the summer crop will survive.

We all greet you—including your brother's wife Mechtilde.

H. W. van der Bosch

1. Apparently a young man from Gendringen who immigrated to Auburn with Johan Philipsen.

November 1, 1868 [Fragment]

Esteemed children,

It is Sunday and your son is in my room writing a letter to you. So I thought I would write a few lines along with my friendly greeting to you, my old and good friends. Thank heavens I am relatively lively and healthy. I met your sister, Mrs. Romers, in church this morning. She has a daughter living here. At present she is healthy but she had been ill for a few months. She sends her greetings.

Your son Johan is still living with us here. He is healthy and works industriously. They do piece work in his place and that motivates because they can earn a good wage. A tailor here can save more money in a year than in a whole lifetime in Holland.

I still go to the carpenter shop every day to earn a little money and fill my time. It is a very interesting time here at present. On the third of November there will be a presidential election across the whole of America. There are primarily two parties. Both parties want their candidate to take the presidential seat. What they won't do to win is unbelievable, especially for those not acquainted with the process. Hundreds of thousands are spent in order to win.

February 23, 1869

Dear children, H. Philipsen, your wife, and children,

Today is Sunday, the 21st of February, we have just returned from the high mass conducted in our German church. It was very slippery this morning. We had an ice storm. So Jan is writing in my bedroom where I keep a stove burning. I keep all the furniture there that I kept from my household.

Jan's writing inspired me to pen a few words—to indicate that I am still alive. But what shall I write to you. First that, through God's goodness, I am in reasonably good health, and I wish the same to all who read this letter.

I still go to the shop daily to work, but I usually go late in the morning. I work for hourly wages—and by each Saturday I usually accumulate about thirty hours or three days of work. Sometimes I work less than thirty hours. My current work is to make a new pulpit in our German church. And now that I'm writing about the church, I'll tell you a little about the exceptional progress of our church and belief here in America.

You would find it difficult to believe how many new churches, schools, monasteries, hospitals, orphanages, and other useful public buildings and institutions are built here by the Catholics.

In 1850, the year we first came to Auburn, there was just one small Catholic church. At that time the priest served Auburn only once every other Sunday because Auburn could not support him alone.

In 1856 I made a drawing of a new building for the congregation. The foundation was 133 feet long but soon that church was too small, and today two large Irish congregations have grown out of it. In 1850 the Auburn Catholics were fortunate to purchase a Protestant church that was only four years old—and constructed of sandstone. This sect was called "Tabernacle Christians," but it gained too few followers and had to give up. The church is about 40 × 60 feet. For the present it is large enough for the Germans. This fall we built a house for the priest, and two months ago we acquired a regular priest.[1] He is an Austrian from the imperial city of Vienna. I am certain that within five years the Irish congregation will have to form a new group and build still another church. Thus, anyone who wishes to go to church as they should has plenty of opportunity to do so.

In the larger cities, hardly a year goes by without new Catholic churches being built. Some are very costly, large, and beautiful. But I must also tell you that much money must be given. But my paper is nearly full and I'll have to write another time about beliefs and the church.

Let me add that Jan is healthy and very industrious at his work. With esteem and greetings, I am

H. W. van der Bosch

1. Father C. A. Vogel was the pastor at Saint Alphonsus in 1868.

Johan Philipsen to Hendrikus and Hendrika Philipsen Family
Auburn, New York, to Gendringen, Gelderland
February 22, 1869

Dear Father, Mother, brothers, and sisters,

I am writing to let you know that, thank God, I am in good health and also that I received your letter of January 24. You can't imagine how comforting your letter was. When I read about your concern for me, I could not go on without bursting into tears.

I thank God too that you are in good health. Brothers, you wrote a great deal of news, and you can't imagine how wonderful it is for me to get some news from Europe. You wrote about those who have died—a not very pleasant topic—because it reminds us of our own mortality. We all long to see each other once again and to live together in joy. That is possible, but not just yet. I have to earn enough so I can return to you and live with little work. It would seem very strange now for me to work for such poor wages as you earn. Food and drink are unbelievably better here than in Gendringen. We eat meat and eggs in the same quantity as you eat bread at home. It does not follow, of course, that this alone makes life satisfying here.

Brother Willem, you asked me what I think about your dearest Wilhelmina Mulderman. Do your best; it sounds like a good prospect to me. I hope I'll have the opportunity to call her sister. And don't forget to give my friendly greetings to her.

Brothers and sisters, you cannot know how hard it was to part from you. We are separated for a time, but not forever.

[The letter breaks off at this point.]

Johan Philipsen to Brothers and Sisters
Auburn, New York, to Gendringen, Gelderland
July 25, 1869

Dear brothers and sisters,

Thoughts of Europe and of you and all my esteemed friends make me want to sit down and speak a few words with you. I want you to know that I've received the letter which you sent to me via Eggbert. The letter was a great comfort to me. I can see that your concern for me, and especially the concern of brother Theodorus, has not diminished.

Eggbert's wife has passed on your friendly greetings. You may rest assured that I also think of you. I think often about sending money to you, Theodorus, so you can come here, but I can't tell how you will get along during the first year without knowing a trade. After you have been here a few years and have learned English you will be able to earn a good living as a bookkeeper or a store clerk. I can't promise that I will support you until you reach that point because living expenses are high here and you can't count on help from other family members.

Fifteen years ago Father should have said, "We are going to America," and then we would be well established people. But instead, rather than behaving like a man, he allowed his wife to be the boss.

It is presently not a good time for my kind of work. I make a living but cannot save very much. But good times follow bad times. My health continues to be good, although I have a sore on my foot. Brothers and sisters, pray for me because all my fortune depends on that. Believe me it is not for nothing that I've come here to save money. Even if I should enjoy no pleasure from it, it will benefit you as an inheritance.

Eggbert has rented a house near us. He has money enough. Bongers's brother has taken my room and Bongers is renting Grandfather's old room. Grandfather and I are now boarding with Aunt Philipsen. I cannot say if Grandfather will come to you. He told me that he has not yet made up his mind where he will spend his last days. But, Father, I must tell you, he is a wealthy man and he is used to a better life than that which you live.

In all kindliness I urge that when you write to me, place my full name on the envelope—Johannes Wilhelmus Philipsen. Then I will be certain to get the letter. There are several Philipsens here.

Dear brothers and sisters, I cannot express enough my brotherly love to you. Not being with you is like a sword in my heart. I want to know immediately if any of you become seriously ill. I believe that I would return in such a case.

I have a request for you, brothers. Find a pair of good boots for me. Huisman will pay for them. Tell me in due course how much they cost. I would also like a tobacco pipe, but I have not spoken to Huisman about that. Tell him, and he will pay for it. Find me a good one. I can't send the money to you because we can't exchange such small amounts.

Brother Willem—I will certainly repay you the amount I owe. Also, brother Willem, as the oldest son you must take good care of all the family, and especially Father. Tell me also how things are going for my sister Katrina and how your courtship is going. Does Theodorus also have a girlfriend? Tell Hendrikus Geerlings that his sister will write very soon. Give him her greetings.

I am anxious to receive a letter from you.

I remain respectfully your son and brother, Jan. Pass on greetings from me and Grandfather to all our friends and acquaintances.

Johan Philipsen

Johan W. Philipsen to Hendrikus Philipsen Family
Auburn, New York, to Gendringen, Gelderland
May 29, 1870

Highly esteemed Father, brothers, and sisters,

Dear brother Theodorus. I received your letter of May 13 which proved that you have not forgotten your brother Jan in America. I can never read one of your letters without crying, and that was especially so with this last letter because it reported Father's sickness this winter. It was a joy to read that he is now better.

I urge you, dear Father, in all kindness, that at your age you are obliged to think about the welfare of your children—particularly since one of them has not learned a trade. Don't think ill of me. As his brother, I am obliged to have as much concern for him as is possible. I know, Father, that as long as you live, brother Theodorus will suffer no injustice. But, Father, you can't place all your expectations on an inheritance from Grandfather. Even if I don't receive another red cent from you (and that is your business in any case), you must think of Theodorus.

I've decided to tell you how much I have saved—five hundred dollars, equal to one thousand guilders and I collect six percent interest.

I am not very strong, but I have work enough. Grandfather and Aunt Philipsen are still healthy and we still live with each other. I am always pleased to hear news from Europe. I would like to know where my sister Katrina lives and what kind of a suitor she has. I am also pleased to hear that brother Willem has reached his goal. His experience teaches that despite the behavior of envious people, what must happen will happen.

Brother Theodorus, you must write to tell me how you celebrated Willem's wedding. I would have loved to join all of you and I've promised myself time and again that I would join you once more.

When you write my name on the envelope do it like this—in big letters, Jan W. Philipsen. Mail service here is irregular.

Dear brother and sister, be so good as to pass this letter on to brother Theodorus. Give greetings from all of us to our friends and acquaintances. Greetings once more from me, your son and brother,

Jan W. Philipsen

November 3, 1871

Very esteemed Father, Mother, brothers, and sisters,

After such a long wait, it was a great pleasure to receive a letter from you and learn that you are all well. You will have to excuse my poor writing because I did not learn it well—probably because I spent my time learning my trade.

Esteemed brother Theodorus, I am, thank God, healthy and have work enough and can save money. The money I wrote to you about is now returned to me and I have deposited it in the State Bank, where it earns 6 percent interest. I am now resolved neither to give nor to lend money to anyone again. I am surprised that I have been able to save so much money, especially since the cost of living is so high. You must promise to keep this a secret, but I will tell you about how much I am worth. If I were to come home I could take one thousand dollars in gold coin with me and be dressed like the richest person in Gendringen. I bought a gold watch that is worth one hundred dollars.

Dear Father and brother, you write that you would like to see all of us together again, and that is a precious thought for me too. I am also interested in this—especially on your account, Father. I don't know how old you are ... but my heart has been burdened with the need for you to care for my brother's future before you die. That can happen unexpectedly as it did with Grandfather van der Bosch. I can't believe that you would allow your own flesh and blood to survive you without care.

Esteemed family—you certainly want to know about Grandfather Van der Bosch. I've written all about it in two letters that seem to be lost. When I came to America he was so overjoyed that he could not do enough for me. He said then, "Jan, count on me. I will never forget what your father has done for me." Grandfather was good to me during the whole time that I've been here and I did everything for him. He said, "I have an obligation to you and I will carry it out."

On Sunday evening, the second of May, we went to the church that he had built. After the service we stopped at the inn and had a glass of liquor. He talked about putting me in his will and promised to sell me his house and lot. When I brought him home that evening he did not feel well. He was sick for a week and did not leave the house. I stayed up with him for three nights, but I could not carry on a reasonable conversation with him. After receiving the sacrament of Last Rites he died on May 11, 1871.

I received nothing from him, but I lost much. His son was named as heir. So, Father, you see what can happen. For my part I want to do my duty as a good brother. And I want you to know my good intentions. If it should be the case that you intend to leave me a portion of your estate, then Theodorus must receive my part. We can make a living, but he cannot. I am going to make up my will and will talk about it with a good friend. I want to be certain that when I die you receive my money and that brother Theodorus alone will receive as much as the whole family. Brother, read this letter to Father and ask him if I could do things better than this.

With God's help I am planning to come to you in the spring of 1873. That is the reason I have not yet married. But you can't imagine how hard it will be, after my visit, to take leave of you forever. Don't tell anyone about this. Regards to all my friends and acquaintances.

Respectfully I remain your well-intentioned son and brother.

Johan Philipsen

May 12, 1872

Dearly beloved Father, Mother, brothers, and sisters,

Brother Theodorus, the very comforting letter which you wrote on Easter has arrived. For that, I must express my admiration. If it were not for you, I don't believe I'd hear much news from Europe. The others seem rather cool toward me, and I am not embarrassed to say it. It does my heart good to know that you are all healthy and it is also good to learn of your friendship with the Wissings. It also seems proper that my sister Katrina has returned home. I hope that she can live with you in peace and unity.

Now, after answering your questions, I can't wait to tell you about the new life which began for me on January 23. I have already exposed my intimate feelings to you about this, but I was not then able to tell you that I would be married January 23, 1872. I couldn't tell you because at that time I had not the least idea that it was to happen. All this has occurred in a wonderful way.

A German family lives here in Auburn. Their name is Waldbaum. He has been in America as long as Van der Bosch. They are good Catholics. They come from Germany near Pruismunde. It is a good respectable family. He has six children. His oldest daughter is Anne and she is my wife. Her parents had a very pleasant wedding at their house. My heart was pained because you could not be with us. We were married in a high mass and I must say that we live very pleasantly. She is a good house-keeper and good for me. We live as well as the richest people in Gen-dringen—except that we must work for a living.

I have work enough all the time and can save money as easily as when I was unmarried. I was unhappy in a strange boardinghouse. At the first opportunity I will have a photograph made to send you. You have not yet told me if you received the photo I sent two years ago. Now, I must close with a few words to you, Father. If it had been possible, I would have done my proper duties in asking your advice and consent, but it is obvious that it makes no sense to do it now. But you can be assured that I have made a good marriage.

Dear brother Theodorus, be so good as to read this letter to my brother and sisters. I am anxious, too, for any news. Katrina, my wife, Anne, says she would be happy to see you and your brothers come here. Father, we know, cannot come. I send greetings from my parents-in-law and also from my wife.

Johan Philipsen and Anne Waldbaum

September 21, 1873

Highly esteemed and dearest Father, Mother, brothers, and sisters,

This Sunday I have resolved to answer your letter of June 29. I have seen from your letter that you are all healthy and can write the same for us.

When you learn the reason for the long delay in my writing, you will excuse me. It was our intention to wait until we could make a blessed and pleasant announcement—an event for which we have been waiting with fear and trembling. Now I will tell you what the Lord has given to us.

It is pleasant, I am sure, for an aged father to learn that his sons (when possible) have perpetuated a good and respectable name. Now, Father, I am your youngest son, but I believe that I am the first to have this honor.

Esteemed family, our blessing is this: We have had a young son on the 14th of August and his name is Hendrikus Johannes. I must tell you that the child is healthy. He is big and fat and beautiful, like no other that I've ever seen. My wife is very pleased by all this.

I have a wife more beautiful than any in all Gendringen. We want you to see proof of this and we will have a photo made of the three of us to send to you. My wife says constantly, "Jan, I would like to see your family." I would like that too, so I plead with you to send your portrait.

My wife is in good health. We had a doctor and also a woman who looked after my wife and our Hendrikus. That costs considerable money here.

Now a few words to my brother Willem. I've waited a long time to hear pleasant news about the enlargement of your family. I say diligence is better than abstinence [Ik geloof het is beter wachten dan vasten].

Now something else. I am in good health and continue to work for the same Griesvold firm. This April I moved to the house of Bernard Smink from Anholt. There I pay seven dollars rent per month.

We have had a hot summer, and the crops are good. Everything costs a lot, but there is money enough. We do not lack anything.

Father, I must send greeting from Uncle and Aunt Reumer in Port Byron. She is getting older and can do little but he is considerably stronger than she. Greetings from Noles van der Bosch and his wife. He has a farm. I would appreciate it if you wrote a few lines to my wife's father and mother. They are good people.

In closing, I hope that this letter finds you in good health. Greetings from all of us. We remain with respect your son and brother,

Johannes Philipsen and wife, Anne Waldbaum

February 18, 1877 [Fragment]

Dearly beloved Father, Mother, brothers, and sisters,

I hardly feel like writing because of all sorts of circumstances. I know that I've received two letters from you. I said to my wife, "I'll make a virtue of necessity."

We are all in good health and hope the same of you. My oldest son, named Hendrikus after Father, will be four years old on August 14. Our second son, Johannes, was born on April 27, 1876. This summer we will send you a photograph of all four of us.

It would have been irresponsible for me not to buy a house and lot here, but that also makes my return to Europe unthinkable. In the space of one year times have become so hard in America that I can't even give you an idea of it.

There are two political parties here in America. Every five years they elect a new president—a bit like a king. Democrats are Catholic and Republicans are Protestant.

Almost all the factories are idle, but those that are open still work. . . .

9 *Jan Wonnink Family*

Jan Wonnink's immigration to Grand Rapids in 1871 clearly exemplifies chain migration. The account of the family's arrival is punctuated with the names and services provided by friends in Grand Rapids who had

These letters were donated by the Peterkamp family, 1976, and first translated by G. H. Ligterink.

previously moved to the United States from Borculo, their native area.
E. Grooters, for example, met the Wonninks at the railroad station and
transported them to Antonie Hanink's residence, and H. Avink, their
new next-door neighbor, hosted the Wonninks for their first dinner in
Grand Rapids.[1] And most important, the new arrivals, all ten of them,
moved directly into a house that had been rented and furnished by their
friends. No doubt they also helped Jan and his son Hermanus find employment in the nearby village of Rockford, where they worked in a
sawmill.

It is highly probable that Jan and Hermanus boarded out in Rockford
during their brief employment there in 1871. As he plainly asserts, Jan
was delighted to find work in Grand Rapids and thus to have the opportunity to participate more fully in the religious and social activities of
the Dutch subculture. On Williams Street, near the city's center, the
Wonninks were within walking distance of riverside factories and Dutch
churches, and they could also enjoy associations with the many Gelderlanders who clustered there until the 1920s.[2]

Even though they had virtually no prior experience in manufacturing,
the Wonninks readily adjusted to the city's industrial economy. Their
native Geesteren was, by contrast, almost exclusively agricultural, and
because of the exceptionally high quality of its soils, the area had been
dominated successively by a petty noble class and wealthy farmers who
employed farmhands like the Wonninks.[3] It is hardly surprising, then,
that Jan imagined a better future in America for himself and his large
family. As his correspondence indicates, he was not disappointed. Other
sources disclose that the Wonninks became independent businesspeople
by 1889, when they owned and operated a wood-turning shop.

Jan's son Egbert managed the business until about 1920, and until they
married, Wonnink's daughters worked as domestics, as they would likely
have done in Geesteren, where teenaged girls usually worked for wealthy
farmers. After acquiring married names, four of the daughters dropped
from the available records, but Gertrude Wonnink served briefly (1906–
1908) in the China mission field for the Reformed Church in America.[4]

Jan must have been pleased by Gertrude's missionary service, for his
letters abound with piety and religious concerns. His explanations for

[1] Avink came from Borculo, the *gemeente* that was within walking distance of Wonnink's
birthplace, Geesteren. Neede, similarly located, was the native village of both Grooters
and Hanink. Swierenga, *Dutch Emigrants*, pp. 6, 98, 102.
[2] Edwin Kornoelje, "Breaking New Ground" (student paper, 1990), in Calvin College
Library Archives.
[3] Ibid.; van der Aa, *Aardrijkskundig woordenboek* 4:480.
[4] Kornoelje, "Breaking New Ground," p. 9.

affiliating with the Reformed Church rather than the separated Christian Reformed Church were plainly cultural rather than theological. He described his Grand Rapids congregation as a near duplicate of the Geesteren church, and that was justification enough.

Today it is obvious that Wonnink behaved in much the same way as most other Gelderlanders. Their inclination to join the Reformed Church stemmed from their loyalty to Albertus van Raalte, who had served their province (1844–1846), just prior to his momentous trek from Arnhem to Michigan. Van Raalte and the vast majority of his followers affiliated with the Old Dutch Reformed Church of New York. Historian Jacob van Hinte is generally accurate in asserting that until 1873 "most of the Frisians, Overijsselers, Hollanders, and Zeelanders joined the Reformed Church when they entered the United States, but the Gelderlanders seemingly did so as a matter of course." Van Hinte's concluding line, "Only the Groningers joined the Secessionists," the Christian Reformed Church, is inaccurate. The Groningers did influence the CRC a great deal but not until the late 1870s and 1880s when they immigrated in large numbers.[5]

There can be little doubt that Wonnink thoroughly enjoyed the familiar and comfortable routines he discovered in his Grand Rapids church. Seventeen months after arriving his testimony was entirely positive. "Our experience," he wrote, "was that we were completely at home from the first moment we set up our household."

Jan Wonnink Family to Berend Peterkamp Family
Rockford [Grand Rapids], Michigan, to Geesteren, Gelderland
July 1871

Esteemed friend B. Peterkamp and family,

Although we are widely separated, yes, too far to speak with each other . . . we can still clearly communicate our thoughts to one another and describe our circumstances with letters.[1] Yes, dear friend, we cannot continue our custom of frequent visits, but, thank God, He has allowed mankind to learn writing. May God continue to be near you and spare you for a long life.

And now, dear friend Berend, as you requested, we shall write about that which God has given us to experience on our trip and in addition, how things are here in the New World.

As you know we left Geesteren on Saturday morning, April 22. Our

[5] The quotations are from Van Hinte, *Netherlanders in America*, p. 379. See also, Herbert Brinks, "The Christian Reformed Church and the Reformed Church in America: A Study of Comparative Cultural Adaptation in America," Great Lakes History Conference paper, 1979, in Calvin College Library Archives.

first stop was Lochem and there everything began. Station Laren (2), Zutphen (3), Brummen (4), Dieren (5), De Steeg (6), Ede (7), Veenendaal (8), Maarsbergen (9), Zevenbergen (10), Utrecht (11), Woerden (12), Gouda (13), Nieuwerkerk (14), Rotterdam (15) arrival at 10 P.M. We had to transfer at Arnhem and we met brother Hermanus in Velp. In Rotterdam the men went to the office of Van Es in order to take care of the necessary business. Afterward we had free lodging in a hotel until nine o'clock in the evening. Then we went to the boat which was to bring us to Hull, England. We left Rotterdam at about 4:30 A.M. We passed Delftshaven, Schiedam, Vlaardingen, and Hellevoetsluis. Then we saw the last of the fatherland. We finally lost sight of the Dutch coast at 10:00 A.M., a truly important moment, right? It was continuously wet weather and then we came to the tempestuous North Sea. In a short time everyone was so seasick that they vomited like herons. It came from the rocking of the boat. The North Sea [lanes] have sea buckets [buoys] that are fastened to the sea bottom. Toward evening the seasickness passed and everyone attempted to rest their wet bodies—not knowing what they were about to encounter. But God knows all things and He ordains and cares for everything.

We sailed nicely until about 10:00 P.M. when we stopped suddenly. Then whistles and alarms sounded. We did not know what it was all about. We moved forward slowly until a sudden shock awakened everyone. Then the water came into the boat like streams. What wailing—what noise. Death was before everyone's eyes. Anguished screams arose from the multitude which pen cannot describe. Mothers mourned their children. Husbands their wives and wives their husbands. A most confusing spectacle. God, however, foresaw our need and saved us by weak human hands. To Him be thanks.

Everyone climbed on deck to look for help. All the sailors were busy making every means of salvation possible. A French boat, the *Frankland*, came directly alongside of ours but the thick fog made it difficult to tie up with each other. But soon the *Frankland* was ready to take on passengers from our ship. It was sinking fast, so that the passengers were standing in water up to their knees and their arms. But God kept the water below their lips. Everyone was brought over to the other ship. No one remained. But one German fell into the water between the ships. Immediately, her husband jumped into the water and because he could swim they were both returned safely to the boat.

But what a scene! Confusion and emotion reigned among the shipwrecked people. Just think about it! Husbands could not find their wives and mothers could not find their still-nursing babies. Still, God cared for us and brought everyone back together.

Then we thought, now we are safe. And for the moment that was actually true. Our belongings were lost because our first boat was sinking. When everyone was off that boat the rope was untied and we continued on in the second boat. The poor cows, twenty in number, were all lost under the water with the old boat. But then the sailors from the new boat banged the alarm and sent up fireworks in a most frightful manner. But we, in our simplicity, did not know what they signified. It's a good thing we did not understand our situation.

* * *

The second boat had sprung a leak from banging against the first boat. But fortunately, by God's goodness, another boat came from behind us and took us in tow. Then we were truly in safety and we arrived at Grimsby's in Hull at 10:00 A.M. Monday.

There we received coffee and ship's biscuits and we remained there until 1:00 P.M. when we took the express train across England to Liverpool. England is a very mountainous country. We had to travel underground twelve times through what are called tunnels. One tunnel was actually so long that it took half an hour to pass through and it was as dark as night. Elsewhere we passed through cities such as Sheffield. When we came to Liverpool we received free room and board (paid in advance at Van Es in Rotterdam). Liverpool is a nice city. Those who have money enough can buy everything there—something that many of our fellow travelers had been waiting for.

Thursday morning at eight o'clock we boarded the ship *Austria* and were on the great ocean. There we had it good. We had as much bacon and meat as we wanted along with sweetened coffee and white bread. The boat was 150 cubits [250 feet] long and 15 [25 feet] wide. A beautiful boat on the inside—as nice as the nicest house—with an astonishing number of people on board—about 1,100. At first the boat sailed very majestically. At 7:00 A.M. Friday we saw land on both sides. On one side many mountains and rocks—little under cultivation—that was Ireland. We docked there at 10:00 A.M. and after loading cargo we left again at 5:00 P.M. The sea was calm with little wind. On Saturday we saw nothing but sky and water except for sea birds that looked like [plovers]. In the afternoon we saw brown fishes that tossed in the water and were as large as horses. We sailed past two sailships and two steamships.

* * *

In the afternoon of May 5 we saw an iceberg along with a distant land on the right hand called Newfoundland. We passed an iceberg on the left side which was about twenty paces away. It was about as big as the church in Geesteren. It looks like a huge pile of snow. It snowed on

Saturday but the sea was calm. On [the following day] Monday we saw land on both sides—rocks, woodland, and also some houses and churches. But little was farmed. Now we were in the neighborhood of the New World. On Tuesday, about 3:00 A.M., the cannons were shot off and at about five o'clock we, through God's goodness, were on firm ground. It was Quebec.

Seasickness was not as bad on the ocean as on the North Sea. During the trip one Swedish woman died and five children were born. Thus our numbers increased. Now it was time to travel in another manner, but we were tired of the sea anyway. Even so, by God's goodness, we had a speedy twelve-day voyage.

We stayed in Quebec until 4:00 P.M. and then went to the train, which traveled quickly both day and night. We reached Montreal at 7:00 A.M. on Wednesday. It is a beautiful city surrounded by nice meadows. Before reaching Montreal we crossed a huge railroad bridge, which was covered just like a tunnel. American trains are exceptionally long and have as many as eight to twelve wheels. The cars are nineteen paces long, nicely constructed, and splendidly furnished inside. They have from twelve to sixteen windows and an aisle through the whole car. The railroad runs mainly through thick forests, although in some places one can see pleasant pastureland and cropland. The trees are cut off several feet above the ground and stumps can be seen standing all over. All the wood is burned here. Oh! If only you had such wood in Holland. The wood piles along the tracks are so long that one could walk alongside them for hours. Locomotives use wood for fuel here.

We finally came to Detroit on Thursday evening and stayed there until the next morning when we took a boat [across the Detroit River] to the other side. At noon we set out on our trip to Grand Rapids and at 7:00 P.M. the conductor announced our arrival, a joyful thing to hear. We stepped out and said goodbye to many fellow travelers from the Netherlands who had become our friends. E. Grooters picked us up.

Now you are probably thinking, "Boy oh boy—you with your big family! And everything lost—not even a change of clothing. In a word, almost naked." Yes, friends—but be patient a moment. Human shortsightedness might lead to such despair, and we were tempted to despair too, but God foresees everything. He knew our needs and did not allow us to be shamed. Immediately, E. Grooters brought us to our dear friend Antonie Hanink, who had been expecting us for a long time. He was the means in God's hand to take care of us.

Soon after our meeting Hanink brought us to the house he had rented for us which was next door to H. Avink. We had our first dinner with the Avinks. The [proportions] of the menu were entirely different from those in Holland, but the foods were about the same. Here meat and gravy are the main items and potatoes are only a side dish. You have enough then on just three potatoes. H. Avink has his own house and both he and his son, H. J., each earn 14 shillings per day. That is $1.75 each. Thus you don't have to ask if they have enough to support themselves.

In the evening we went to our own house where we found four beds, an American stove, chairs, a table, blankets, bacon, meat, etc.—all arranged by our friend Hanink. What a blessing from God—to be so quickly in possession of furniture. Who would have thought it possible! So, friend, I don't believe that it is so poor here as in Holland.

On Sunday we went to church where we heard the preaching of Rev. C[ornelius] van der Meulen—an old but fervent man. He preaches twice every Sunday and holds Sunday school and other classes for young people. G. J. Bannink came to visit us Saturday and he will take us to Rockford where we will work in a paper and sawmill. It is two and a half hours from Grand Rapids.

With respectful greetings from
the household of Jan Wonnink

1. Evidently these letters were composed by the adults in the Wonnink family and written by Jan's son Egbert. Personal references to the young people's organization in the Geesteren church are probably Egbert's. The writers' standard closing, "with respectful greeting from the household of Jan Wonnink" and the general use of "we" indicates joint composition.

December 28, 1872

Highly valued friend Berend Peterkamp and family,

It has now been very long, yes, too long, I must admit, since we last exchanged letters with one another. You could easily have begun to think that we have entirely forgotten you and have stopped writing letters. But, no, that is not the case. To be honest we must admit that we have not written because of simple laziness.

We can inform you that, by God's grace, we are all in good health and we wish the same for you. The old year is again past and with it all its sorrows and burdens, its prosperity and poverty, its sweet and sour. Yet, with so many evidences of God's patience, if we confess our sins before Him, He draws us to Himself with love and blessings. . . . So we stand ready to walk into a new year.

*   *   *

America is a good country for a worker who is willing to make an honorable living by the industrious work of his hands. This, I know, has been written many times, but it is true. Even so it would not be fair simply to invite everyone to come over. Some people discover later that it was not God's will for them to come here and many other people come here and find it totally undesirable. Our experience was that we were completely at home from the first moment when we set up our household. Because we lost everything [in the shipwreck], we gladly took the first work that was offered to us and stayed with it [in Rockford] until God opened up another opportunity for us here in the city. We like this better because we can now go to the church and Sunday school regularly. We (that is, Hermanus and I) could not do that when we worked in the paper mill because of its distance from the city.

Now, Berend, I will tell you a little about the church. Father and Mother came here too, and after previous investigation, have joined the Dutch Reformed Church [now the Reformed Church in America]. Both in teaching and confession this church is in agreement with the separated [Christian Seceded Church] in the Netherlands. The congregation has about 1,200 members. Our pastor here is Rev. van der Meulen an old gray-haired man of seventy-two. He was born in the province of Zeeland and was one of the early seceders [also the pastor and leader of the Zeeland, Michigan, colony in 1849]. Soon he will lay his shepherd's staff aside because he is becoming weaker with age and that does not permit him to lead such a large congregation. Catechism classes meet five times each week. Sunday school meets on Sunday afternoons and is attended by two hundred and fifty children and is taught by twenty-five teachers— both in English and Dutch as each class desires. We attend Wednesday evening meetings. They do not have a Young People's Society here but most of the young people go to Sunday school. Hermanus and I also go to the Sunday school. Last week Wednesday afternoon we voted to call a new minister—he is Rev. [Nicholas] Dosker from Zwolle in Overijssel. He received a majority of the votes, so the call will be sent to him.

Now I must respond to [rumors] that my writing exaggerated reports. I wrote only the plain truth without coloring. Perhaps you don't know what this is about. But Hermanus Broekmaat wrote to us one time that we exaggerated. That's why I'm writing this. We thought all of our let-ters contained only the most ordinary and simple truth—like well-worn wooden shoes. We have not written the slightest grain of falsehood in our letters. The simple truth is enough and fully satisfying.

Your young people's organization must be small these days.[1] I won't ask you to comment on that remark because it is not necessarily our business.

You have asked if [our church] is not very careful in allowing people to partake of the Lord's Supper. We can only say that it is the same here as with you. The church exercises discipline so that anyone who falls into open sin and does not humbly seek forgiveness is not permitted to take the Lord's Supper. Otherwise, each person must examine himself.

* * *

You have asked about G. J. ter Winkel. He sends his greetings and reports that he is doing well. He lives near us—no farther away than the distance between us when we were neighbors in Holland. He has two little girls. His wife was born in Groningen. He makes a good living. He works in the same factory where Hermanus and I work and, like us, he earns $1.50 per day. So you can imagine that he makes his way decently. Earlier he worked on his own by digging sewers and such, but that was not steady.

Don't be angry, Berend, because we did not write more quickly. The evenings are long now. It is winter and very cold. In some places the thermometer went 45 degrees below zero. In Grand Rapids the temperature was 30 degrees below. That is six degrees colder than it has been for twenty years.

With respectful greetings from the household of Jan Wonnink

1. Suggesting, perhaps, that emigration has reduced the number of members.

June 7, 1873

Dear friend and family,

[A long opening paragraph asserts Wonnink's continued regard for and loyalty to the Peterkamps.]

The reason we have not written in direct response to your last letter is this: you have probably heard that Rev. Dosker, the pastor of the seceded congregation in Zwolle, has accepted the call to become our pastor and preacher.

He and his family arrived here on May 17 and he was received by our people with open arms. Meanwhile a furnished house and full pantry stood ready to welcome him. Shortly after his arrival he addressed the congregation. On Ascension Day afternoon he was installed and commissioned by our former pastor, Rev. van der Meulen. His scripture text was Romans 10, verse 15, "How lovely are the feet of the messengers of peace." In the evening Rev. Dosker preached his inaugural sermon and he spoke to a very large assembly of people from these essential words, "Beloved, let us love each other." I John 4, verse 7a.

Grand Rapids, view of dwellings on the east bank of the Grand River, 1871. Courtesy of the Grand Rapids Public Library—Michigan and Family History Department.

The people are well impressed by him, and in fact, he is a treasure given to the congregation under God's providence. No congregation can overestimate the value of such a gifted preacher. We delayed writing to you in order to write about this. He taught his first catechism class last Wednesday and he seems to be very kind, but also very keen. Yes, God has dealt wonderfully with His Dutch folk here—even in this strange land he has sought us out by means of His ambassador. Dosker commented on that too, saying, "For many years I have seen many Hollanders going to America, and later I heard from them that they enjoyed a generous portion of daily bread. Many times I sighed to the Lord, 'May I be worthy, Lord, also to bring spiritual bread to them.' " He said that this desire was first awakened in him when Rev. Oggel[1] left for the United States. "Because," Dosker said, "Oggel was my dearest friend."

And now other matters. We work at the same place and are clearly blessed. The city keeps growing and this summer another six hundred houses will be built. If you should come to this city on Sunday, you would find it completely at rest. All the hotels and shops are closed except for the drug stores. If a hotelkeeper should dare to open his bar on Sunday, and if the police catch him, he must go to the police station and pay a $30.00 fine—unless it is the first offense. That is law and order!

The summer here is in full bloom—good! This spring we had constant rain and now we have warm sunshine. Vegetation grows more quickly here than in Holland—so much so that people are surprised by it every spring.

A plan is being formed to build a new church here. Our church, which was built two years ago, is already too small and cannot contain all the members. Sometimes the crowds number 1,600 to 1,700. We do not yet have young people's societies here ... but I think Dosker will do something about that. Yes, dear friend, we would certainly like to have you visit us.
Then you would have something new to see.

With respectful greetings, the household of Jan Wonnink

P.S. Write to us and tell us who Rev. de Bes [Wonnink's former pastor in Geesteren] has married.

1. The Reverend Pieter Oggel immigrated in 1856 and died in 1869 while teaching at Hope College in Holland, Michigan.

10   *Marten J. Schoonbeek Family*

On May 3, 1873, Marten J. Schoonbeek, his wife Frouwke Pul, and five of their six children emigrated from Nieuwolda in the northeast corner of Groningen. This agricultural village with about two thousand residents was sustained by exceptionally fruitful clay soil and dominated by a few leading farm families. The whole community, apart from about twenty Jews, were members of the state-supported Reformed (Hervormde) church.[1] Marten Schoonbeek, a carpenter and wooden-shoe carver, left the village with few obvious regrets.

The Schoonbeeks traveled successively by wagon, railroad, and sea to reach England, traversed that country by train, and set out across the Atlantic from Liverpool. After traveling for twenty-one days, they

These letters were donated by the Robertus Schoonbeek family, 1987, and first translated by Egbert Post.
[1] Van der Aa, *Aardrijkskundig woordenboek* 8:176–77.

reached Grand Rapids on Saturday morning, May 24. The whole venture cost about one thousand dollars.

The family had arranged no housing in advance and was forced to seek temporary shelter in a barn. The search for better quarters on the following day, Sunday, was fruitless because, as Marten reported with some chagrin, "A person cannot buy a cent's worth of anything here on Sunday and no one was around to talk with." Finally he located an acquaintance, Geert Stel, who offered temporary shelter in the basement of his home on Spring Street.

These initial setbacks did not dampen Marten's optimism; almost immediately he began to urge his son, a schoolteacher in Nieuwolda, to join them in Grand Rapids. During Marten's first year he and his family did make rapid progress. As a carpenter he found work readily and his two grown daughters, Tryntje and Harmanna, gained employment as housemaids. The family moved from Stel's basement to a nearby apartment, and using wages and savings brought from the Netherlands, they purchased household goods, building materials, and made the down payment on a lot at 36 Logan Street. By September they had moved into the small house Marten built there.

But the euphoria engendered by early success dimmed considerably when the 1873 financial crisis severely limited local sources of income. More crucial still, Marten began to experience chronic bouts of diarrhea and vision disorders. Nonetheless, he managed to construct his house while earning a meager income by selling homemade wooden shoes door to door. Then his health suddenly worsened, and he died on May 14, 1874.

During this whole period both Marten and especially Frouwke were buoyed by the prospective arrival of their son Jacobus, but after Marten's death Jacobus delayed his plans to immigrate and finally decided to remain in the Netherlands.

Frouwke Pul was left alone with three dependent children, one of whom, Klaas, was mentally handicapped. Sporadic support from her grown daughters, together with public aid and neighborhood generosity, kept the household from total destitution. Meanwhile their land payments were in arrears. Nonetheless, Tryntje and Harmanna wrote regularly that all was well and that their mother was grateful to be in America rather than the Netherlands. Later, on June 27, 1875, Tryntje advised her brother Jacobus to remain in the Netherlands because the teaching profession offered fewer opportunities in the United States than in Holland.

At that time the girls were already courting, and by 1876 both were married. Consequently, they were keeping most of their wages to set up independent households. As Frouwke's financial circumstances deteriorated, she became desperate enough to plead for help from Jacobus. Her daughters, she wrote, "had abandoned her."

Desperation was also the probable motive for her 1876 marriage to a man identified only as "Berend." Eight years later the couple separated. Berend had been so abusive to Klaas that the police were called in to arrest him. Following that and other difficulties, Frouwke locked Berend out of the house for the last time in 1884. Then she pleaded with Jacobus to get her back to the Netherlands. But she remained in Grand Rapids. After this troubled period and nearly until Frouwke's death in 1889, her younger children, Jetje and Harm, remained at home and worked to support her.

By 1877 both Tryntje and Harmanna had become parents. Tryntje and Anthony Stormzandt had three children, and Harmanna and Gerhardus Rosenboom had seven. Much of the correspondence in this collection came from these older siblings, who wrote to Jacobus from 1874 to 1931. Because these letters report rather broadly the whole family's experiences, they disclose a general pattern of cultural adjustment.

It is clear, for example, that upon their arrival in 1873 the Schoonbeeks were neither active church members nor particularly pious. Marten did become a member of the First Christian Reformed Church in Grand Rapids, but not before confessing that, until then, he had not practiced his faith regularly or properly. Apparently, Frouwke and the minor children joined him at worship, and during her widowhood Frouwke continued to attend the services.

The older children, Tryntje and Harmanna, married husbands who attended church regularly. Tryntje, who joined her husband Anthony Stormzandt as a member of the Third Reformed Church, even complained that Harmanna had become hyperreligious. She commented, too, that Frouwke's church attendance was far more regular in America than it had been in Holland. It also seems that the other children conformed to the prevailing religious mores of the Dutch Reformed community.

All but one of the Schoonbeek children married into and remained in the ethnic subculture; only the youngest, Harm, left the enclave after marriage. He moved successively to Detroit, Cincinnati, and Toledo. None of his seven children returned to West Michigan, and one of his daughters migrated to Texas to combat tuberculosis.

Harm Schoonbeek's exceptional migration pattern may have stemmed from his frustration with what he perceived as his siblings' religious hypocrisy. All too often and too readily, he complained, they excused themselves from their fair share of the burdens necessitated by brother Klaas's mental illness. The three sisters declared themselves too busy with their families or too short on funds either to visit Klaas in a Kent County infirmary or to help purchase clothes for him. "What do you think of that?" Harm wrote, "And from three Christian people who are so taken up by going to church. If this were for the pastor or for the church, the money would come quickly."

Of the second generation—Marten and Frouwke's twenty identified grandchildren—60 percent dispersed rather widely. Harmanna Rosenboom's daughter Theresa married George Madison and moved to Detroit in 1922 with her husband. Her sister Frouwina married a local merchant, Gerrit Broene, and later moved to California. The other five Rosenboom children married into and remained within the ethnic enclave.

Tryntje and Anthony Stormzandt's three children included Marten, who attended Hope College and then pursued an academic career at colleges in Los Angeles and Hollywood. The other boys, including a mentally retarded son, Pieter, worked in the family's house-moving business. In 1913 two of Jetje de Graaf's three children, Marten and Henry, were employed in Canada and Detroit, respectively.

Thus, in the short period of about fifty years (1874–1925) at least half of the Schoonbeek descendants joined American social structures outside the ethnic enclave. Today it is virtually impossible to reconstruct the genealogical threads connecting Marten and Frouwke Schoonbeek with their descendants.

Marten Schoonbeek to Jacobus Schoonbeek
Grand Rapids, Michigan, to Nieuwolda, Groningen
May 29, 1873

Dear son,

*   *   *

Saturday morning at eight o'clock we arrived in Grand Rapids and were able to leave the train. Then we faced the problem of where to go. It was agreed that the men would go into the city and that the women and children would stay at the station. After we had some refreshments we (R. Rosenboom, Jan Stuit, Eiso Wiegman, Geert Klooster, and I) went out to find shelter. We stopped first at the business of Steketee and Kim because I had written to them before we left. But that was a mistaken effort because these people have nothing to do with housing. They had received the letter all right but did nothing about it. These people own a drug store. They were very friendly and although they wished to help us they could not give us any information about housing. So, we just had to go on and look for ourselves.

All the places we looked up had been rented because so many immigrants are arriving here that the number exceeds all previous experience. Finally we located a small house next to the landlord's business place, but we were too late. But this businessman, a Hollander, was very gracious and he was moved by our situation. Finally he said, "I can furnish you people with some shelter. I have a vacant barn and you can use that in order to get off the street." Naturally we accepted the offer because it was Saturday and we needed shelter badly. Immediately we hired a coachman and went to the train station to pick up our wives and the baggage that was there. Rosenboom's, Stuit's, and Wiegman's baggage was there but not ours, so we had to share with the others. We could not expect our trunk to arrive until 6:00 P.M. We went to the barn, which fortunately had straw in it and we slept very well that night because it was not cold.

On Sunday, May 25, I went out walking to find a home. But I couldn't do much because a person cannot buy a cent's worth of anything here on Sunday and no one was around to talk with. That is how strictly people observe the Sabbath here. Finally I made contact with an old acquaintance, Geert Stel, who had lived near us in Nieuwolda as a hired hand. How fortunate! G. Stel has been here for three years and he had an experience similar to ours when he arrived in Grand Rapids—worse, in fact. But he is successful now and owns, along with his home, several apartments. These people were so good and obliging as to allow us the use of their basement. And we got along well there. We placed a stove there and had places to sleep. Two doors down from them a first-floor apartment was to be available in fourteen days. If only our baggage had arrived on time we would have been all right. But since nothing can be done on Sunday and no trains are running either, we had to stay in the barn until Monday.

Monday morning Ringelberg and I went back to the depot where I found three of our bags, but the fourth bag and the trunk were still missing. We searched but they were not there, so I decided to wait one more day so all the things could be moved at once. Otherwise we would have double expense.

I went back to Stel's house in the afternoon and his very fine wife went with me to buy a stove, six chairs, and a bed. These were delivered at once. Then on Tuesday morning I hired a drayman and went back to the depot. Fortunately my fourth bag and trunk were next to my other baggage. But Geert Klooster's things were still missing. So my entire family went to Spring Street in the carriage and moved into

G. Stel's cellar. We unloaded our things and the driver received seventy-five cents.

The next thing was to find work because our money had decreased remarkably. But we were more fortunate than many fellow travelers who came ashore with an empty purse. That was not true in our case and we were able to provide for our necessities.

Now I will end this account with the observation that from Harlingen to Grand Rapids we have been the victims of indecent treatment and much swindling. It is surprising how much of our property was lost due to damage and rough handling. So, shipping by Prins and Zwanenberg is definitely not to be recommended. This was also true for others who have complained even more than we.

Your father,
M. Schoonbeek

June 29, 1873

Dear son,

We are still living in Geert Stel's cellar, but we have rented a fine first-floor apartment two doors from here from a Mr. Piet Otte. Tryntje will clean the house tomorrow and we will move in on the following day. Piet Otte and his wife are Hollanders. In fact most people around here are Hollanders.

Yesterday Harmanna started working for English people, but we don't know where. They picked her up with a small carriage. The English here are partial to green Dutch girls. Tryntje has been out to do washing for one day and I have worked two days for Otte. I'll continue there for another two days and then try to find regular work. I can't comment on wages yet because I don't know much about that.

Almost all of us are a little under the weather, but we are improving without a doctor. . . . We eat as much beef as we please. It costs only five cents per pound and pork is ten cents. Twenty-five pounds of the best white flour is one dollar and twenty-five cents. A pound of coffee is thirty-two cents and butter is twenty-two. Clothing is also cheap.

So, now, after a very difficult trip and much inconvenience, we can rejoice. We don't know what the future holds but everyone encourages us and we can see that they are all getting along well as long as they are healthy. So, in short, I'm well impressed here.

As far as I know Rosenboom and the others who came here with us are all housed and at work. Geert Stel, who lived near us in 1860 as a hired hand, married a little later and lived in Winschoten for a time. He has now been in Grand Rapids for about three years. He was in debt when he came but he now has his own house and another which has two rental flats. He told me that he receives rents of four dollars and fifty cents per month for them. He said if anyone offered him 5,000 guilders to live in Winschoten again he would refuse it without hesitation. That is a common view here. So I think a person can do well here.

People go to work at 7:00 A.M. and go until noon. They begin again at 1:00 P.M. and work until 6:00 P.M. So, a ten-hour day and not hard work either. It is generally warmer here than in "the old country" as the Netherlands is referred to here. It is said that winters are more severe, but in my opinion the climate is more healthful here.

I cannot express how much we long to receive letters from you. It would be such a pleasure to have you here with us. You would be able to get along very well here—even as a teacher. And if you were a seceder [Christian Reformed] you would be well cared for because they cannot find a good teacher here. But you would have to learn the English language. That's an absolute necessity here. Those who can use it succeed the most because the English pay the best wages here—although I think there are more Hollanders than English here. So make work of mastering the English language. Then you will be able to become rich here in a few years.

People are well behaved here and drunkenness is not condoned. Everyone is willing to help others. I find that very nice. With such unanimity almost anything can be accomplished. And there is certainly no lack of money. Anyone who starts out with a little money can earn as much or even more than he pleases. A person who has a house can sell it in a year for double the money. It happens every day here.

Now I will close and write again in fourteen days. So, dear son, write to us every fourteen days.

Your father, M. Schoonbeek

August 18, 1873

Dear son,

We were pleased to receive the letter which you wrote between July 4 and 13. All is well with us, but I cannot deny that I still have the diarrhea. I am bothered by it a great deal and went to a Dutch doctor but he was not able to cure me. So I have gone to another one. He impresses me more favorably although he has only given me one kind of medicine. This doctor lives five hours from here, in Zeeland, Michigan. I'm going there again tomorrow and hope that will be the last time. I have been home working on our own house for the last fourteen days. I have finished about as much as I can for now and will go back to my job on the dock, which should be fin-

Grand Rapids city center, 1890s. Courtesy of the Grand Rapids Public Library—
Michigan and Family History Department.

ished quickly. After I have worked on our house for another fourteen days
we will be able to move in. We will have little debt and we will not have
much more to wish for except that you were here with us. Without you, I
can tell you, there is not much for us even though we have everything else
in abundance. So come as soon as you have the money and, by all means,
learn the English language.

Now, I'll answer your "dozen" questions. First, what is Grand Rapids
like? Answer: Grand Rapids is a large, widely spread-out city with beautiful buildings, pleasant places, and streets. Most of the important streets
have tracks on them for streetcars. Question two: What are the sources
of employment? Answer: The main source is factories with a great deal
of business and the trades. Question three: How about the people? There
is no one type. I will add no more about that. Question four: Describe
your home for me. Answer: We have a very decent home and must pay
two dollars a week rent. But our landlord, on his own initiative, reduced
it to one dollar and fifty cents because of my illness. Question five: What
are people paid? Answer: The wages are usually high. Question six: What
are the common prices of regular living necessities and clothing items?
Answer: Everything is very inexpensive.

As I see it our way of life here is a good one, and as I have written
repeatedly, we are happy here.

Harmanna is still with those English people and is doing well. Tryntje
still lives with us at home but she goes out to do washing and that is
going well too.

Come to us! Then you will be able to see and experience it yourself. Believe me. I am not misleading you. I would rather die than mis-
lead you.

* * *

I will tell you a little more about our new house. It is about one half hour from our present home. It is located on Logan Street where we have purchased a lot. There we are building a small neat house as shown in the enclosed drawing. We still need seventy-five dollars' worth of material. Many people start out this way because it is possible to add on to the house and eventually it can become large. Then, if you sell it, you can come out ahead.

*   *   *

[Closing]

September 7, 1873

Dear son,

Our current circumstances could be better, but they are not too bad. I have not been well, but I am a little better this week. And in any case, I have been able to work continuously. We have been living in our own house for a week now. At present Tryntje and Harmanna must help support us. Both are working for English people and they live next door to each other. They each earn two dollars and fifty cents per week. So today Harmanna gave me three dollars and Tryntje two dollars.

Our house is finished on the outside but much must still be done on the inside. But we can put that off for a time. I must first earn some money because we need some furniture before winter sets in. The way people describe winters here they must be bad.

Mother is well satisfied here and now especially so because you plan to be here with us within one year. But really now—must you wait so long? Do you think you must serve the Netherlands first? That is not necessary. You should inquire if Mr. Plensinga will pay something to Grandmother for leaving her room by May 1874, and then the old woman's property will have to be sold too. Then she can easily come with you. . . . The sooner both of you come the better. Grandmother will be very well off with us. We have a large garden where she will able to spend her time pleasantly. It has sandy soil and by next spring we will also have a cow.

We have had a difficult time for the past seven weeks because I have been under doctor's care and that costs a great deal here. Naturally our building program has also cost a lot of money and at present I am earning nothing. In short, our surplus is spent. Thank God, I am almost well again and will be able to earn a little again. We have some debts, but not many. The material for our house is all paid except for ten dollars. We have a fine house built entirely of wood. But wood is cheap here— fourteen dollars for one thousand board feet. On one side the house is

Reuben Wheeler lumber mill on east bank of Grand River, about 1870. Courtesy of the Grand Rapids Public Library—Michigan and Family History Department.

decorated with windows that have eight panes. Each window cost one dollar and eighty cents and they are well made.

Now, after writing with many details, I will close with the hope that you can manage your affairs in such a way as to make the trip with Grandmother by April or May.

[Closing]

Marten Schoonbeek to Jacobus Schoonbeek
Grand Rapids, Michigan, to Oude Pekela, Groningen[1]
November 19, 1873

Dear son:

We received two letters from you fourteen days ago with the news of your appointment in Groningen and that the Oude Pekela board members decided to raise the salary of assistant teachers to five hundred guilders. That is fine and it doubtless pleases you. But to have it effective at the beginning of the new year is a postponement which once again clearly indicates stinginess. The winter will be half over before you get it.

Now, something about our situation. People told us so much about how disagreeable winters were here that a person could become scared. And that prospect was especially bad for us because our house was not ready to withstand a hard winter. And sure enough, it began to snow fourteen days ago and it continued for a week. There was an intervening thaw, but eventually the snow was half a foot deep. But last Sunday we had another thaw and the snow was all gone. This week the cows were grazing in the pasture and we have had fine weather again. We have had no storms yet but it does get bitterly cold occasionally. But we are seldom chilled because the living room makes us as warm as summertime. Fuel is cheap here. In fact, until now we have not had to pay for firewood.

Our house is now completed to the point where we don't have to worry about the winter. It gets so warm inside that at times we have to open the door. We have postponed finishing the work because we don't wish to incur too much debt. I want to earn some money first. We receive some from Tryntje and Harmanna now and then because they are repaying their travel expenses. That is a blessing, for I have not earned much this year because of my illness. The first year is always difficult for an immigrant because a great deal of money is needed to set up housekeeping. It's like young people starting out with nothing. Without money a person cannot get along in America any better than in the Netherlands.

We have come to the point where our lot must be fenced in to enclose the garden. Everything is fenced in here because there are no ditches, canals, or hedges anywhere. Cows roam about wherever there are no fences.

* * *

Greetings to you, dear son, from your parents who long to see you.
Your father, M. Schoonbeek
Your mother, F. Pul

1. Jacobus had accepted a teaching job in the village of Oude Pekela, about ten miles south of Nieuwolda.

December 7, 1873

Dear son,

Tryntje and Harmanna visited us last Sunday and were picked up in the evening by two young men. We expect to see them again today and hope they will bring a letter with them. They live nearer to the post office than we do and we do not have mail delivery yet. We live about thirty minutes from the post office and it is difficult to make the trip in the winter. The weather varies here a great deal.

* * *

Tuesday there was no snow left and it was so warm that I was sweating all day while making wooden shoes. The cows were roaming all around looking for food. Today it is freezing again with some snow on the ground.

Last Tuesday I talked to Brink, the storekeeper, about you. He is an important Holland merchant here in the city with a large store. . . . Brink has told us that you will be able to get along very well here and that shortly after your arrival you could earn seventy dollars per month. But when you come you should go to school for a few months to learn book-keeping and to learn the English language because without that you will be considered nothing other than a Dutchman. Brink has promised to discuss your situation with an Englishman who knows more about it than he. I told him you could speak German, French, and English. There is a great demand for such people here. You would even be able to organize your own school, for which there is also a great need. In that case you could be in business within two days. Teaching is entirely unregulated here so you could begin at once without a permit from some authority.

I sent a letter to the Germains along with my last letter to you. They have plans to come here and that would be very good for those people. But there are also some strings attached to that advice. If they have no savings they will be in trouble because they will need everything im-mediately—furniture, including a stove, which costs twenty-two dollars, chairs, a table, beds, and that is only half of the housekeeping needs. A person can soon spend fifty dollars and if they do not have that they will be in trouble. You have to work a long time to save that much while also meeting the daily expenses.

[Closing]

P.S. The Germains can move in with us. We will be able to get along that way for a few days.

February 8, 1874

Dear son,

The fourteen days are past again, and I will fulfill my promise [to write every two weeks]. We are all healthy and that is a great blessing, is it not? Now we wish the same for you as you receive this letter.

It would be impossible to count the times we have wished you were here this week. Why? This week especially? Because you would have been able to become a teacher immediately in a Dutch school. The teacher there lost his life in a very sad way. Boys ride sleds here a great deal when there is snow on the hills. They ride sleds here as much as boys in the Netherlands go skating. Skating is not possible here this winter because there is no ice. So a few boys, sitting on a sled, went down a hill at the speed of a fast train and they struck this man, the teacher. Both of his legs were broken and he died the following day as a result of the accident.

Grand Rapids d 8 February 1874.

Geliefde Zoon!

De veertien dagen zyn weer om, en
ik zal myn pligt weer vervullen,
Allen gezond, dat is al een groote
rykdom, niet waar? Nu wy wenschen
dat gy in het zelfde genot dit briefje
Zult ontvangen,

Hoe menigmaal wy dezen week gewenscht
hebben, dat gy hier waart, is niet te
bepalen, Wel! Zult gy misschien Zeggen
waarom? waarom juist deze weeks Zoo veel
dat zal ik u Zeggen, Dan had gy dadelyk
onderwyzer kunnen worden, in een Holan-
sche school. Die onderwyzer is op een
jammerlyke wyze van het leven geraakt.
Hier word veel gebruik gemaakt, door jongen
van sleetje ryden, als er sneeuw ligt, even
Zoo veel als in Holland schaatsryden,
want schaatsryden kan men hier niet, om-
dat er geen ys is. Zoo hebben dan eenige
jongens, op een slee gezeten, by een berg

Marten Schoonbeek's February 8, 1874, letter (p. 1) to his son Jacobus in Oude Pekela, Groningen

He taught in a special school—but it's quite different from a special school in the Netherlands. If you were here you could have taken over his position. A brother of Schipper from Pekela has done so temporarily but I do not think he has the proper qualifications. So he has the position on a provisional basis. He told me that he had been educated to be a teacher but that he had not taken the examinations. Please write back at once to say if you are interested in this position. If so, then write a letter to that effect and I will show it to the church consistory.[1] I don't know what the position involves but it is worth a try. If you are not satisfied you can decline. I am waiting for your reply as soon as possible.

I keep busy making wooden shoes and sometimes [I go out selling them from door to door]. When I come to a door where Yankees live I often hear, "No! No! These are hard times. I have no money." Then I say, "But don't you like them—my wooden shoes?" They say, "Yes. But I have no money." Then I leave and go to another place. Actually the Yankees do not want to wear wooden shoes.

Perhaps it does not seem proper to you—that I have to go door to door to make these calls. Well, it is not pleasant, I admit, but this is America, and people here respect a person who tries to help himself in an honest manner. And then a person does not have to be ashamed.

You doubtless understand that I have no money because I earned very little during the summer. I have been ill most of the time and in addition I have built my own house. Now it is winter and there is a great deal of snow on the ground—more than a foot. It is impossible to earn anything except by sawing firewood and that does not pay much. And anyway— chopping trees in the woods an hour from home—that I do not dare to undertake. So I just make wooden shoes and go out peddling them— that's what they call it here. Actually I enjoy it rather well. I make only a little money from it, but a person can buy quite a bit with a little money. But this winter we have to buy everything that we need because we had no chance to build up supplies. We hope, if we are well and alive, that things will be better situated next winter.

Sometimes we receive money from Tryntje and Harmanna, so we will be able to manage and to take care of ourselves this winter. Then, I think, we will have won out.

I have heard little about the money crisis here lately but I experience the lack of money daily. No one tries to hide the fact that he has no money because it is a common ailment.

[Closing]

---

1. The school was owned and supervised by the Spring Street Christian Reformed Church. For a detailed account of the accident see Chapter 17.

April 12, 1874

Dear son,

Last Monday we celebrated Easter Monday, which is done here only by the Netherlanders.[1] The English pay no attention to this. So on Easter Monday we were able to receive a letter from you at the post office.

*   *   *

Conditions in Nieuwolda must be in a state of disorder—farm laborers in revolt, Van der Woude insane, a young woman having hanged herself, etc., etc. I am glad we are gone from there and so far away that we don't have to be involved in any of it.

Boer[2] was preaching in another church Sunday, so a sermon was read to us. I did not enjoy it and became quite bored. There are some modernist churches here where the sermons are preached in English but I don't understand them at all. So you can understand how desirable it is to master the language. Yes, the language is a very important matter here.

We must still pick up our letters from the post office because we live just outside of the city. I would like to have that changed.

You had better change our address as follows:

Mr. J. Dykstra
Groninger Buurt [neighborhood]
Grand Rapids, Michigan
North America
To be delivered to M. Schoonbeek

[Closing]

1. Who observed the European custom of celebrating religious holidays over a two-day span.
2. The Reverend Gerrit E. Boer, pastor of the Spring Street Christian Reformed Church of Grand Rapids, 1873–1876.

April 26, 1874

Dear son,

It is about one year now since we last saw each other. We remember it so vividly. . . . What a change in our lives. What a change in our work! It is remarkable how many privileges we have enjoyed—having suffered no losses and now also enjoying good health. All of this reminds us to show gratitude to God Almighty. May our hope, that we be together, soon be realized.

* * *

I, along with many others, still have no work. This is the result of the
money crisis. Ordinary people are quickly out of money and those who
still have some are afraid to spend it.

Next Wednesday I will be going back to a job but I don't know how
long it will last. Things are still going well for Tryntje and Harmanna.
Tryntje, however, has a new position, but Harmanna still works for Mr.
Freeman.[1] They now live several blocks from each other and cannot walk
to visit as much as formerly.

As far as I know, all our traveling companions from Nieuwolda are
doing well. Gerhard and Roseboom are getting along well. Geert Klooster's wife gave birth to a stillborn child but she has recovered completely.
Jan Stuit and his wife are also well. Marchien Bierman, the daughter-in-
law of Eiso Wiegman, is remarried to Jan Jager. He left Nieuwolda four
years ago with his wife Albertje and then he became a widower. He now
lives in Kalamazoo, where he has a house. So things turned out very well
for Marchien. There are also several other Humrikkers[2] in Kalamazoo,
such as Willem Plaat and his sister Geesien. Two sons of Oosterhuis
own a house there too but they are always traveling away from home for
work and it is said that they earn a great deal of money. I wrote above
that Marchien Bierman was married to Jan Jager. Well, marrying is very
easy here. Jan Jager wrote a letter to Marchien and she answered that
he might come over. Then one fine day Jan came and made an agreement
with Marchien. And behold, the next day they were married by the minister! That is a legal marriage here—at very low cost, with no loss of
time, and with no danger that one of them would have second thoughts.
Everything is done quickly here. Hurry up. Time is money.

[Closing]

1. Thomas Freeman, 21 Prospect Street, listed in the Grand Rapids City Directory,
1875.
2. People from the small village of Oostwolder-Humrik, near Nieuwolda. Jacobus's
wife, Frouwke Pul, was a native Humrikker.

Tryntje Schoonbeek to Jacobus Schoonbeek
Grand Rapids, Michigan, to Oude Pekela, Groningen
May 21, 1874

Dear brother,
As I wrote in my last letter, Father has been very sick. And now, dear
brother, we have been cast into deep sorrow. Father became very ill on
May 9 and he died on May 14. According to American customs and also

because it was very warm, Father was buried on May 15. Yes, dear brother, this blow strikes us very hard. But it is God's will. Mother, all of us, and you too, brother, are saddened by this but you must bear up as well as you are able. That is what we are doing as much as possible. It is only possible when there is love and sympathy as there is in our case.

Father and Mother were just beginning to get along so well. Their little house was being improved and also the garden. They had a water well near the house. So, in short, everything was beginning to look bright. Harmanna and I had almost repaid our travel expenses and we were getting a good supply of clothes. But what are we to do now?

Still, Mother says that she is not unhappy about being here. And I also thank God that we are here because Mother will not have to suffer want. She does not need to worry about that. But Mother says so often, "Oh, if only Jacobus were here with us." We all long for that. We do nothing but await that time and hope for the best.

Now, I'll tell you how we are managing. I came home to be with Mother on May 20 and now I go out to do washing and ironing. A great deal of money is earned here that way. I pay Mother one dollar [per week] and Harmanna also helps as much as she can. She gives two dollars and fifty cents. Mother also receives some help from the English people who live near us. Those English people are, in general, more generous than the Hollanders. There is no comparison.

Dear brother, do not worry about your mother, brothers, and sisters. Do not be overly concerned but keep your courage up because we are doing the same. And Mother too—she says so often, "How good it is, children, that we are no longer in the old country."

*   *   *

Be so kind, when you are in Nieuwolda, to give the news to anyone you see fit.

[Closing]

P.S. Dear son, do not forget me, do not forget me.

Frouwke Pul

Frouwke Pul Schoonbeek to Jacobus Schoonbeek
Grand Rapids, Michigan, to Oude Pekela, Groningen
July 14, 1874

Dear son,

Tryntje wrote that no one has time to write to you anymore. But now I take up the pen and write to you and tell you that we are all well.

Klaas, Jetje, and Harm are all in good spirits! Jetje went back to school on the 13th. Often she asks, "Will Father come back?" And Klaas also asks that.

Dear son, you asked what kind of illness Father had. Father was brought home sick on May 9. So sick that he told me he had never been so sick before. He was a little better for a few days and then worse until the day he died. A half hour before his death he still got up from his bed and smoked a pipe of tobacco. I sat with him then and said to him, "How cold your hands are." Then Father said, "If only Jacobus were here. He will not forget you or leave you." Then he gave me a kiss and went back to bed. Then he became very uncomfortable and he was gone in a quarter of an hour.

Now something else. This is the way I am situated. The house is ours but we borrowed thirty dollars from Rosenboom. He is not pressing us but on August 10 he must receive three dollars for the interest. I must still pay five dollars and seventy-five cents for the land. He does not exert pressure for that either but I do have to pay by July 25. The man who sells me wood must also be paid one dollar. And I must buy a new stove. Where the money for that will come I do not know. Tryntje and Harmanna each give me one dollar per week, but the way I figure it, Tryntje does not pay for her board. But when I ask her for more she becomes very angry. Well, you know her very well. And then she tells me a lot of things—and that she will get married as soon as she can. Just after Father died she told me, "We will not leave you to yourself," and then she pressed my hand.

But, dear son, when you write be careful not to offend her because then matters will become still worse. Tell her that she must help me until you arrive. And tell Harmanna that too. She will be coming home in fourteen days. But she has a boyfriend whom she thinks about all the time, and she forgets about her mother and brothers and sisters. But you, dear son, do not forget your mother.

You wrote that I must have good neighbors. There are two boys at the home of Isaac de Pagter and they help me as much as they can. Cornelis van Partsen is a boarder there and the other is a son, Leen de Pagter. Cornelis helped me a great deal when Father was sick. And, as you wrote, we must be thankful for that. They favor the seceders [the CRC], but Father was always so glad to see them.

Dear son, I so wish that you were here with me. Dear son, do not forget your mother.

Your mother,
F. Pul

Tryntje Schoonbeek to Jacobus Schoonbeek
Grand Rapids, Michigan, to Oude Pekela, Groningen
July 23, 1874

Dear brother,

*   *   *

I know you would like to know how we are getting along because you
are so far away. . . . Mother is as spry and as well as she could wish to
be and can adjust to her situation very well.

Let me tell you exactly what her situation is. As you know, dear
brother, Father bought a lot for two hundred and forty dollars before he
died. And he built a house on it himself. Now that house is Mother's
except that when it was finished he was thirty dollars short and he borrowed that from Rosenboom with the promise to pay it back in three
years with interest. The lot upon which the house is located must be
paid off at five dollars and seventy-five cents quarterly. These are all the
payments that Mother has to make. But as for Mother's living expenses
with Klaas, Jetje and little fat Harm, both Harmanna and I are working
and we each give Mother one dollar a week. So she can live on that
during the week. Harmanna earns two dollars a week and I earn two
dollars and fifty cents. So we do as much as we can for Mother. Although
the matter has not yet been settled, Mother will probably receive an
additional two dollars a week from the city. There are some good people
who also help Mother in other ways: Mrs. Stel, for example, who lives
on Spring Street where we lived when we first arrived. And there are so
many others who are very good to one another.

You would probably like to help Mother too, but you certainly cannot
do that. You will have all you can do to make preparations for your trip.
We hope you will try to come to this very large country very soon and
make plenty of money. You can do that if you are able to speak the
English language well—as well as Harmanna and I and also little sister
Jetje who goes to an English school every morning. She leaves home at
eight o'clock and returns at four o'clock and takes her dinner with her
in a little basket. You would not believe how strong and smart she is
becoming. She speaks English all the time. Our little brother, Harm, or
rather that "big" little one, is such a dear. Klaas is becoming calmer than
he was before.

*   *   *

If Mother were still in [Oostwolder-]Humrik, she would be in want.
Mother often says, "Thank the Lord I am in America." We all long very

much to see you. We hope that we have already lived through the longest time during which we have not seen each other. We cannot tell you how much we all long to see you.

[Closing]

September 21, 1874

Dear brother,

[Opening]

Well, dear brother, we are all here together on the evening of September 21 and we decided that we should write you a letter. Mother said, "Do it right now because the letter will be on its way a long time and then it will be a long time before we get one in return."

[We are all very well.]

Tomorrow Mother and I are going downtown together to see if we can get a little more than one dollar per week and free firewood. When people are in need they have to go to a city board and report about it. People who have been here for more than a year are helped. Mother hopes that she will not be refused, because there is a man on the board, Steketee, who understands Dutch very well. But I have some time tomorrow and I can go with her. That is better for her. In my next letter I will write about how this turns out.

On November 1 we will have to pay five dollars and seventy-five cents on the lot again so we are having a hard time taking care of everything. There is very little money around here and we can't explain the reason for that. Some of the English seem to know, but no one knows for sure. The common opinion is that there are too many people and so there is not enough work. But you can be sure of one thing—the Englishmen are in control. And they prefer to have nothing to do with anyone who does not understand English.

So we hope, dear brother, when you come here you will know the language. Then you will be able to get along better in America and make more money than you can in the old country. Our greatest longing, dear brother, is that you were here with us.

[Closing]

P.S.

Dear son,

Do not forget your mother. Do not forget me.

Harmanna Schoonbeek to Jacobus Schoonbeek
Grand Rapids, Michigan, to Oude Pekela, Groningen
October 6, 1874

Dear brother,

We are all in good health except Mother, who has caught a bad cold. But don't worry, she still has a good appetite. Mother cannot take the fall weather and she always catches something. But she will not protect herself against the cold and continues to work—hot or cold. On Sunday, October 4, Mother was forty-six years of age. On Saturday evening we gave her a real treat which pleased her very much. If you were here you could have joined us. We hope you can do that next time.

*   *   *

Mother has been given another fifty cents per week from the poor relief fund. Now she receives one dollar and fifty cents from that and one dollar from Tryntje and one dollar from me. I would say that three dollars and fifty cents per week is enough. She would not be able to live on that in the old country. The poor relief fund has also agreed to supply Mother with fuel for the winter. She asked for that, and it is better to ask for help than to go hungry. Don't worry about her. We will help as much as we can.

Saturday morning a wagonload of wood was delivered to Mother from her neighbors—for her birthday. The neighbors said they didn't have to pay for it. One woman's son works at a large building where a lot of wood is thrown out. He brought the winter fuel from there. A Dutch farmer would not do that—give fuel to someone.

Now something else. There is a great demand for teachers here. If only you were here, dear brother. . . . When Mother talks about Jacobus it's as if you were coming tomorrow. Those six months last forever! If only we can meet one another in good health. But the sad thing is Father is no longer in the house.

*   *   *

On Monday, October 12, our little brother Harm will be four years old and on October 24 your sister Harmanna will be twenty years old. Time goes by so fast. You become old before you realize it.

[Closing]

C. van Aarten to Jacobus Schoonbeek
Grand Rapids, Michigan, to Oude Pekela, Groningen
December 21, 1874

Dear friend,

Your mother has asked me to write this letter because she did not feel capable of acquainting you with her circumstances in writing.

You know that your mother, being a widow, is not able to provide for her needs, and was obliged to call upon the poor administration for help. But when it became known that your mother had two adult daughters to support her, this help did not continue. However, these two are proud and spend all their money on themselves.

In the beginning they helped your mother, but now they have withdrawn completely. That leaves her in a strange land deprived of all help. Now her eye is turned toward you, and she waits impatiently for an answer to her inquiring lines. She has gone around many times, trying in every way to present her needs to the officials but the charity administration seems to be looking to the young women (your sisters) who are living in wealth, and continue to neglect your mother.

And now, my friend, there is still another solution, and that is by way of an advertisement in the paper, describing the conduct of your sisters, and publicly requesting support for your mother and three needy children. This would destroy the honor of your unworthy sisters. They deserve that, however, because they have continued to live in constant contention with your mother.

Another possible solution might be for her to sell the property and to return to the old fatherland. The latter would, it seems to me, be the least desirable, because what would there be for her to do in the Netherlands? To depend upon charity is like being allowed only to smell the bacon.

And now, friend, I have acquainted you as far as possible with the state of affairs, so that you, in turn, may assist your mother with advice and support.

One more matter in connection with your sisters. They say that they have withheld support from your mother because you have not been inclined to come here, and then they think they will be left to support her by themselves. I cannot advise you in this matter because you would not find it easy to change your line of work. But you will have to decide what is best for yourself.

And, now, finally, your mother is asking for financial support, so that she can provide for herself and her children. Your mother and her children enjoy good health, a tonic amid all her circumstances.

Now, my friend, having brought your mother and her pathetic circumstance to your attention, I close this letter,

Your friend,
C. van Aarten

In the name of your mother,
F. Pul

Frouwke Pul to Jacobus Schoonbeek
Grand Rapids, Michigan, to Oude Pekela, Groningen
February 18, 1875

Dear son,
I am taking up my pen to write you a few lines and to tell you that we are all well. I was pleased to receive the twenty guilders, [eight dollars and eighty cents]. But something else. I would like to return to the fatherland and now I plan to sell all of my property because Father said so often, "If Jacobus were here and Grandmother, then it would be all right." But now there is no possibility of that. I have spoken about this to Mr. Kim.[1] He said he would come to visit me but not just now. You write, dear Son, that you hesitate to come here because then you would be unhappy and I would be unhappy too. But you must help me get away from here. Don't worry about my needing food. That is easily taken care of. But all that which Tryntje and Harmanna write is only big promises. Nothing happens because they want to play ladies.

F. Pul

P.S. Help me to get away from here for I write you honestly, dear son, please help me.

1. Of the business Steketee and Kim.

Tryntje Schoonbeek to Jacobus Schoonbeek
Grand Rapids, Michigan, to Oude Pekela, Groningen
June 27, 1875

Dear brother,
We have received your letters in good health but my sister Harmanna, Mother and I read it with regret because you wrote, dear brother, that perhaps you would not come to America. On the one hand, we long for that . . . but I would also not dare to recommend that you come to this

country. And that pertains to your teaching because in that work you would not do as well as you are doing now. Here most of the teachers are young women and in addition each school has a supervisor. If you could get such a position, which is most unlikely, things would be better. So it seems almost certain, dear brother, that there will be no opportunity for us to see each other.

But what shall we do? This is very hard on all of us, even harder than Father's death. Although that was also hard for us we know for certain that we will never see him again and we must be reconciled to that as the will of God.

* * *

Now regarding Mother's situation—if you get this letter before you receive one from her explaining her plans, please do not tell her that you already know about her plans. But I think it is my duty to inform you that Mother has another proposal to marry a thirty-eight-year-old man who is a bricklayer and a plasterer. That is a good occupation in America. He has never married and so he has no children. He boards with his sister. That is all that Mother has told us about him. I was disturbed by this news from Mother and I also believe, brother, that she will marry this man. [I can only hope he will be good for] little Harm, Jetje and Klaas.

Well, dear brother, Harmanna was angry at you for accusing her of being a "small" person. She does not deserve that because I can tell you that she has a big heart in her and she is as generous a person as you are. She is a very good and religious person and modestly goes to church every Sunday. If you saw her you would be amazed, not only because of her personality but also by her speech. She is very good and we enjoy each other too.

Now I'll end with my pen but not with my heart. Greetings to all our acquaintances and especially to our dear grandmother. When you write again please write a few lines directly to Harmanna.

[Closing]

Frouwke Pul Schoonbeek to Jacobus Schoonbeek
Grand Rapids, Michigan, to Oude Pekela, Groningen
June 18, 1877

Dear son and daughter,[1]
I am sitting down to write you a letter and to tell you that all is well and I hope the same for you. I cannot delay telling you about Tryntje.[2]

She gave birth to a son on June 15 and she is as well as can be expected. She said to me, "How happy Grandmother will be when Jacobus tells her!"

But now something regarding my own situation. I wrote you on February 12 that Harmanna gave birth to a child[3] but you probably did not answer the letter because I also told you about my unhappy marriage. But that is no reason to forget your mother or my grandchildren.

But I must tell you, son and daughter, that I must get away from here because I cannot stand it any longer. So I plan to return to Holland in the month of September because that man treats me and the children in a terrible way. He says he would like to dash open our heads with an axe and he beats me too. On the sixteenth he walked out and he came back on the eighteenth. Then I showed him the door. Money is the main problem because there is no work, and besides he doesn't care. I don't know where to find food for myself and the children. If you want to know about my situation write to Mr. De Jonge. He knows about my situation. Your father bought the land on which we live from him.

1. Jacobus had married.
2. Tryntje married Anthony Stormzandt in 1876.
3. Harmanna married Gerhardus Rosenboom, also in 1876.

[Enclosure]

Jacobus de Jonge to Jacobus Schoonbeek
Grand Rapids, Michigan, to Oude Pekela, Groningen
June 18, 1877

Dear friend J. Schoonbeek,

You see, herewith, your mother's own writing about her predicament. I have nothing to add to it. She wishes me to add a few lines but I hardly know what to say. But her situation is critical. If possible she would like your support as her son. . . . I am not in a position to give her advice. Do you have any advice? Answer her soon! Can you help her? Do not delay. She is *your* mother.

Your father purchased that little plot of ground on which she lives from me. But nothing was paid down on it and they now owe thirty dollars in interest. So you must realize that her situation is serious. In her widowhood your mother has been the most courageous and completely honest person that I have ever met. I have asked her husband if he could provide some aid, but he said he could not and now, as you see, he has left her.

Her situation is sad—sad indeed. So, dear brother Schoonbeek, consider her condition and answer soon. Address your letter to me.

Mr. Jacobus de Jonge
121 Spring Street
Grand Rapids, Michigan

Tryntje Schoonbeek Stormzandt to Jacobus Schoonbeek
Grand Rapids, Michigan, to Oude Pekela, Groningen
January 1, 1878

Dear brother and sister,
[Opening]
Our little son Anthony is growing well and he is spry and healthy. . . . On January 12 he will be seven months old. Fourteen days ago I took him to the scale and he weighed twenty-five pounds.

* * *

When you visit Grandmother please read this letter to her. We write her often and never get a letter in return. Perhaps the letters do not reach their proper destination.

Mother is becoming very impatient. She talks to one person and another and says, "I wonder if Jacobus is still alive? Yes, he must be or someone would at least write about it." We await your letter to set us at ease. So, please write. If not for my sake, then at least for Mother's sake. I cannot express in writing how much she longs for a letter.

I can tell you our brothers and sisters are in good health and also that Mother is about the same as usual. She does rather well, and at times better than normal. She has no reason to complain. She does one thing better than she ever did in the old country. She goes to church regularly and I often sit near her.

Harm and Jetje go to school regularly and they can speak English well.

The Gerard Rosenbooms are well at present but he has no work. Geert Klooster has been ill for a week with a sore throat but he has recovered, fortunately. As for Klaas—he is healthy and is growing. He is a fine lad, but his mind, as far as we can detect, has not improved. The Lord only knows what the future holds for him.

Your sister,
Mrs. Stormzandt

January 8, 1878

This is the second letter I am writing to you in a short time. . . . when I finished the first letter and mailed it I remembered that I had not wished you a happy new year.

* * *

I further wish to congratulate you on your daughter's first birthday. . . . I do not think as much is made of New Year's Day here as in the old country. Here people make much more of Christmas—especially the English. You cannot imagine how bad that is here. If you were here I could tell you so much more.

As far as I know Mother, our new father, and our brothers and sister are all well. We do not get together very often. Nor do we see Harmanna very often. They live more than an hour away from us and, since it is as cold as any winter we have had here, we don't go out so much.

It is quite cold at present, which is a good thing for poor people because there is more work then. There is still a great deal of poverty in this city. Many have no work. Fortunately, my husband has a job. He is employed in the drug store of Mr. Shephard and Mr. Hazeltine—a large store with a great deal of work.

Last week we bought a new clock and it cost seven dollars. I don't believe a single farmer in the old country has ever seen a clock as nice as this one.[1]

[Closing]

1. Larger wall clocks were and are a major ornamental feature in the living rooms of wealthy Netherlanders.

Gerhardus Rosenboom to Jacobus Schoonbeek
Grand Rapids, Michigan, to Oude Pekela, Groningen
February 21, 1888

Dear brother-in-law,

We received your letter in reasonably good health and learned from it that you are well too.

* * *

You asked how Mother is, what her husband's name is and her address. In the first place, Mother has been ill, but thank God she has recovered. It is difficult to write about the other matters, but since you are her son I will not hesitate.

You know that after Father died she remarried—and to a man who can neither read nor write. But that is not important. They lived together in a good relationship for eight years and then he began to leave her. Between times he would be at home and then he would be with someone else. It was a bad life for the old woman. They struggled along that way for a couple of years until Harm, your brother, and your sister Jetje said that if she was going to put up with that man any longer they were going to leave. After that, when he left again, she would not take him back. So, you understand, they no longer live together. Jetje and Harm are at home and they earn a living for Mother. Jetje works at a basket factory and earns about three dollars a week. Harm is a baker's assistant and earns six dollars a week. That is what they live on.

Now you may ask, what was the reason for all this unhappiness. Well, brother-in-law, I can only give you my opinion. You know that your brother Klaas is not normal and he is troublesome besides. And then to have a stepfather—well you can probably imagine that that would not be a source of happiness for Klaas. Now it happened that Klaas was causing some trouble and Berend (as we call him), who is short-tempered, became so angry that he went so far as to beat Klaas. Mother did not like that and the neighbors didn't either. So the neighbors reported Barend and he then spent a day in jail. That was the root of the problem as I see it.

Continued February 24, 1888

With this letter I am sending you pictures of the two houses we rent at present. The large house is where we lived previously. But the small one, with the windows showing, we have always rented out. We now live inside the city. The other houses are about five miles outside. Last winter I built the new house where we now live. It is somewhat larger than our other house but it is not yet completed. We plan to finish it this spring and then we will be able to say that we have a good house—conveniently located too. It makes life much easier for me now that we live in the city because I have to go out frequently in the evenings for my business. I always have plenty of work. At present I have four houses under construction and last night I signed a contract with an Englishman. His house will cost $1,145. I prefer to work for the English. They pay more for labor and they are not as tight as the Dutchmen. That's what they call Hollanders here.

Brother-in-law, you asked what I know about Rev. Hugenholtz.[1] Truthfully, I don't know much about him. His people have built a church on Bridge Street and I heard him once but he is too liberal for me. He has what is called an independent congregation here. Your sister Tryntje was angry that you asked about Hugenholtz because she thought that you might be leaning in that liberal direction too. There is no end of Dutch churches here—thirteen, I think. Anyway you can see from that that there are many Hollanders here.

As for our family—we now have four children, three girls and one boy. Two of the girls are in school and about the other two—we have no complaints. They have good appetites.

Your brother-in-law Anthony Stormzandt has three children—three little boys. At this time Stormzandt is busy moving houses. You probably don't understand that kind of work. They move houses from one plot of ground to another. You must understand that when a person first settles here in America he usually begins by building a small house to keep his family in. Gradually it is enlarged until it is a complete house. But if they cannot add to it decently that is no problem. They sell the old house and move it. Then they build a completely new house on the lot where the old one stood. That is what Stormzandt does—he moves such houses from one place to another. That work pays well but the worst part is that there is little to do in the winter and thus little to earn at that time of the year.

Now some more news about Mother. My wife went to see her today and found that she was quite a bit better than last time and that she can do her work fairly well. Jetje has been with her for about three weeks, but she went back to her factory job last Monday. You will understand that she had to go back to work because if all the expenses must be covered by what those two earn, there is little left over for a sickbed. The doctor's bill has to be paid. Klaas is a grown man and, even if his mind is not right, he needs food and clothing.

*   *   *

You wrote, brother-in-law, that we would be welcome any time we could come to pay you a visit. I don't think that will happen for some time. It's more easily said than done. It would not be so difficult for me to come by myself, but to cross the ocean with a household of children would be no fun. So we will just have to wait awhile.

[Closing]

1. The Reverend F. W. N. Hugenholtz pastored a modernist congregation in Grand Rapids which denied the major tenets of orthodox Calvinism.

Tryntje Schoonbeek Stormzandt to Jacobus Schoonbeek
Grand Rapids, Michigan, to Oude Pekela, Groningen
September 29, 1888

Dear brother and sister,

* * *

In response to your letters I am sitting down to reply immediately—
and on my husband's birthday at that. He is thirty-five years old and
next June our oldest son, Anthony, will be eleven. Our second son, Martin, is eight and our third son [Peter] became six on November 2. If our
fourth son had lived he would have been two on March 2. Next March
12 it will be a year since he died. That is all the children that we have.
On May 26 I will have been married to Anthony Stormzandt for twelve
years. My husband is from the province of Zeeland. He came to America
three years before we did.

We were very happy to hear from you and our sister and your dear
children. It is difficult to realize that your oldest is already able to write—
and your little son also. My oldest would like to write a letter to you but
he cannot write in Dutch. He could write it in English and maybe Jacobus could read it. I think he could, so Jacobus, soon you will receive
a letter in English.

* * *

I do wish you could visit us sometime—and our mother. Harm is a
big fellow now and Jetje is a big girl. She would not take a back seat to
any rich farmer's daughter in the Netherlands in the way she dresses.
She is eighteen now and takes good care of Mother and Harm. And how
big he has grown to be.

Mother was so happy when Harmanna came with your letter that she
cried. She put on her glasses to read it immediately and then sent Klaas
over to get me. We live only twenty minutes away and I came over
immediately too.

* * *

We have two houses of our own and rent one of them for $5.50 per
month. When my husband works he moves houses and barns and puts
new foundations under them. He makes two dollars and fifty cents a day
or fifteen dollars a week. Gerard Rosenboom always has work—winter
and summer—and he seldom makes less than three dollars a day. They
have three houses and rent two of them besides the one they built last
year. It is a regular castle. We also have a large house—two rooms up-

stairs and three rooms downstairs. My husband has just bought two hundred dollars' worth of equipment to move houses. This spring he will begin his own business. He has not done any other kind of work during the eighteen years he has been in America.

[Closing]

P.S. Brother, you asked us to obtain information for you about Rev. Hugenholtz. We appreciate that man but don't ask G. Rosenboom to tell you about him because they are strict seceders. That is an independent congregation and oh so pious. We go to the Reformed Church of Rev. Kriekard.

There are five Reformed [RCA] congregations here in Grand Rapids—

1. Rev. Moerdyk
2. Rev. Winter
3. Rev. de Pree
4. Rev. Kriekard
5. Rev. Joldersma

The congregation of Rev. Hugenholtz is independent. And that Rev. Hulst[1] is also independent. That Rev. Hulst—oh, he is so profound [ponderous].

Our address is Mr. A. Stormzandt
No. 13 Packard Street
Grand Rapids, Michigian
North America

1. The Reverend L. J. Hulst left the Reformed Church in America in 1881 because he opposed that denomination's tolerance of Masonic lodge affiliation by some of its members. Hulst and his congregation remained independent until 1883, when he brought his followers into the Christian Reformed Church, that is, the "seceders."

Harm Schoonbeek to Jacobus Schoonbeek
Grand Rapids, Michigan, to Oude Pekela, Groningen
November 4, 1890

Dear brother and sister,

It seems very strange to me that I have not received a letter in answer to the one I wrote after Mother's death. It may be that you did not receive that letter.

* * *

Until that last day of her life she felt so well that Ike [Americanized Jetje] and I helped her out of bed just as she asked us to do. Soon after we brought her back she died. I went to get the doctor but she died before I returned. It was a terrible experience for me. As you can easily understand, she was terribly worried about Klaas. He is so big and strong, but to become mentally ill at such an early age in life and never to be able to take his place in society—well you can imagine how difficult that is.

The main reason for Mother's fear was that her new husband had always been very mean to us and to her. I will give you an example. After Mother died Klaas did not dare to stay in the house. After the funeral I brought him to people who are good to him. And even now he is afraid to go into the house where we lived. And then Mother's husband gave away her things to strangers and he even sold some of it. That is enough about this man. I have never known a person like that.

* * *

Herewith I am sending a picture of sister Ike and her baby, who was five months old at that time. He will be two years old this spring. I will have a copy of Mother's photograph sent to you and I will also have a picture of Klaas taken for you. Brother-in-law De Graaf will also send one as soon as possible. I am pleased to have a picture of you and your wife. I can see that you are both looking good.

* * *

Your wrote that you would like to have me come to the old country sometime. I think about that often and if it is possible I will come to visit you next fall.

* * *

Sister Ike has been married for three years and they are doing exceptionally well. Brother-in-law De Graaf is in business with his father. They have a pleasant life. He is a little older than Ike. He is thirty-four years old, but that is all right.

* * *

My address is:

> 334 North College Avenue
> Grand Rapids, Michigan

March 27, 1894

Dear brother, sister, and children,

It seems strange to my wife and me that we never received a letter from you even after we sent our photographs. Did you receive them or not? What is the situation?

*   *   *

Both of us are healthy—my wife is fat and heavy. I think she is heavier than your wife. I am still doing the same work in the bakery, but at present the economic situation is sad. Thousands of people are out of work and many are without food. The circumstances of our country are terrible at present, but I have no difficulties. We live with my wife's father and mother, both elderly people. They had their own home and now they rent that house.[1] As you can imagine, I'm not sorry about that.

*   *   *

Now, as you requested, I will write something about Mother. Her second husband was a very bad person—to be honest, a scoundrel. I can tell you that we and Mother have gone through a lot—and especially Klaas. Klaas is now in a good place with good food, drink, and clothing. Twice each year he comes to visit relatives for eight to fourteen days. And I go to visit him occasionally.

*   *   *

[Closing]

1. Harm is probably tending the needs of his in-laws and receiving their rent income as compensation.

[Ca. 1894, Fragment]

*   *   *

I can see that you have a genuinely deep brotherly feeling for our unfortunate brother. And I also do all that I can for Klaas . . . but I do have some angry discussions about this with Ike, Reet, and Manna.[1] To-gether we pay for Klaas's board, room, and clothing. However, whenever he needs something special it always goes the same way. They always say, "We have our own children and Harm is single." I do everything I can to see that he has it good. And I give just as much as the others so you must judge for yourself if what I do is not enough.

A few months ago I spoke to Ike about giving brother Klaas a new suit for Christmas—that is the least we can do for such an unfortunate young man. Her answer? "We cannot do that. Klaas can get along well enough with what he has for the winter." And other complaints, "My husband is earning nothing now and I have to live on house rents." What do you think of that? And from three Christian people who are so taken up by going to church. If this were for the pastor or for the church, the money would come quickly. I think it would be better to give the money to our unfortunate brother. And so it always goes.

* * *

1. Nicknames for Jetje, Tryntje, and Harmanna.

Harmanna Rosenboom to Jacobus Schoonbeek
Grand Rapids, Michigan, to Oude Pekela, Groningen
December 25, 1900

Dearly beloved relatives,

* * *

We are all in good health and the trip [to see Jacobus in the Netherlands] has been good for my husband. He often says we must do it again if his health permits. In any case we now have a happy memory of one another again. Now that I have seen all of you I have a much stronger tie with you, your wife, and children. Everything has become new.

As far as I know all is well with the relatives.

* * *

Tryntje lives in Grand Rapids again. Their son Marten is no longer in school. He is a reporter for the newspaper here. . . . We expect your daughter Marktje, to come here in the spring—if her mother is feeling better then. Take good care of your mother, Marktje, and give her a big hug for me now and then.

* * *

Things are back to normal. The children go to school. My husband is building houses. Frouwina [Harmanna's daughter] is back at her old job as a bookkeeper. So I am home alone during the day and my thoughts often turn to you in the Netherlands.

[Closing]

[A pious postscript or inclusion follows:]

What is the time here on earth as compared to what we will enjoy in the hereafter, which will never end. We know that our days are uncertain and that we may be called home at any time. For it is written, "Prepare thy house for thou shalt die." There is no use resisting. We must all die and then the question is, "Are you prepared?" My hope is, dear family, that our eyes may always be directed to that time and that we will feel the need to cry out with the publican, "Lord be merciful to me, a sinner."

Gerhardus Rosenboom to Jacobus Schoonbeek
Grand Rapids, Michigan, to Oude Pekela, Groningen
February 25, 1908

Dear friend,

[Lengthy inquiry about a rumor suggesting that Jacobus had died—obviously false.]

Two years ago Rev. Broerstra also heard that you had died. We met him at a park and he said he would inquire further but he was ill while he was in the Netherlands and had no chance to follow up.

Now you will probably be wondering what this "park" is and where it is. It is a place about thirty miles from here by the lake, where it is cool in the summer.[1] Persons who have the means buy small lots and cottages there to spend the warm season near the lake. During that time they enjoy fishing and swimming. As you can imagine, that is enjoyable. We usually go there for two months—July and August. In September our little girl must return to school. Schoolchildren usually have a ten-week vacation.

Lately I have had some free time because I am not very busy. There are many people without work and that is bad in the wintertime. It is not so bad for Americans, who can usually take care of themselves. But there are many immigrants who arrived here just last fall with empty hands and they were not able to earn anything. That is bad. I do not think there are many Hollanders who came here last fall. Most of them, I think, are Russians, Poles, and Italians. But that makes no difference. They are human beings. Now, you may ask, what is to be done about such people. You can't just allow them to starve. And they do not. As you can imagine, there is much discussion about this situation. People who have lived in this city for six months are entitled to public charity and when they knock on the door they are supplied with what they need to survive. But this winter there have been many here who have only been here for two months. The charity office does not know what to do for them. Such people have no right to ask for help and the office has no authority to help them. They are supposed to be covered by a law which states that the transportation company is responsible for them during the first six months. So the government says that the companies must make provision for them. That causes a great deal of difficulty in the legislative chambers. But there is also a good side to this and that is the establishment of private charity organizations which frequently step in to keep the needy from starvation.

Yes it is a serious matter when you see that in our land of plenty, these people must live in poverty. But the Lord has said, "The poor you will have with you always." You can help them if you so desire.

G. Rosenboom
728 North Lafayette
Grand Rapids, Michigan

1. Probably the Holland, Michigan, lakeside park and resort area. "The lake" usually means Lake Michigan rather than one of many smaller lakes in the area.

Harmanna Schoonbeek Rosenboom to Jacobus Schoonbeek
Grand Rapids, Michigan, to Oude Pekela, Groningen
November 27, 1919

Dear brother and children,
    [Opening]
As you probably know, we have experienced much as a result of the war. From the daily papers . . . we have heard that the Netherlands is also experiencing hard times. Here in America we have a surplus of everything but it is expensive. Prices rose and are still going up. But fortunately, the war is over and our boys have returned—apart from those who lost their lives in France. There are so many sad parents who will not see their sons again—sons who were killed on the battlefields and have given their lives for the freedom of our country.

My son [Ropko] also served in France for nine months. He was wounded and in the hospital for four months. Brother, I cannot describe the worry and trouble I have gone through, but he has returned after many experiences. But his wife's brother was killed.

Now, we may think we are at peace, but that is not so. The war has ruined the country and there is no peace or unity among the people. There is one labor strike after another. The minority insists on having

Grand Rapids vegetable market, the Ludwick brothers, about 1916. Courtesy of the Calvin College Library Archives, photo collection.

the upper hand and the working class also wants the upper hand. If this continues we will have a revolution in this country because there are so many nationalities here. It is not like the Netherlands.

* * *

[During the war] my daughter Hermina lived with us because her husband [Gillis van den Berg] had to leave but he did not leave the United States. He went no farther than Hoboken and came back when the war was over. I now live with my youngest daughter [Hermina] and we are getting along well. Theresa works as a bookkeeper at the Grand Rapids Show Case Company and earns twenty-five dollars a week. She works seven hours a day. My son [Joseph] has worked for the same company for nine years. He is an engraver.

All is well at sister Tryntje's but she is getting old—sixty-nine this summer. As far as I know all is well at your brother Harm's. He lives in Toledo, Ohio, but I have not seen him for six years. His wife writes to me now and then. Brother Klaas is also well. He lives in the county home.

Herewith I am sending you cards and photos.

[Closing]

Tryntje Schoonbeek Stormzandt to Jacobus Schoonbeek
Grand Rapids, Michigan, to Oude Pekela, Groningen
May 12, 1926

Dear brother and children,
    [Opening]
    On May 26 we will have been in America for fifty-three years and on

that same date we will have been married for fifty years. We will celebrate our Golden Anniversary with our children and four grandchildren.

We do not hear much from brother Harm. Brother Klaas comes to our house now and then, but never to Harmanna's. I don't know why that is—she is good to him—but that is how it is. We feel sorry for him.

We have had a long winter. . . . soon I will be doing my housecleaning. The work takes me a long time because I cannot keep at it all day. On June 5 I will be seventy-six, and my husband, Tony, will be seventy-three in February. He works half days. He is more worn out than I. He can no longer raise and move houses. That is heavy work. We are not so rich as sister Harmanna. She lives on her money and lives expensively. But not so expensively as formerly. She is very tight with her money.

* * *

Our son Marten will be coming home this fall when his school year ends.

[Closing]

Harmanna Schoonbeek Rosenboom to Jacobus Schoonbeek
Grand Rapids, Michigan, to Oude Pekela, Groningen
September 27, 1931

Dear brother, Martha, and family,

I spoke to Marten Stormzandt [Tryntje's son] this month and he told me about the relatives in the Netherlands [where he had visited]. I feel bad [Martha] that your father is in bed all the time and cannot see. I'm sure you will take good care of your father, Martha. You will be rewarded in the hereafter.

Marten also told me that your son had an operation and that things do not look very good. I hope everything turns out all right. His family can hardly do without him—and he is in the prime of his life. I hope the Lord will spare him and return him to good health. But your father is old and there cannot be much hope for him.

Next month I will be seventy-six and I am beginning to feel weaker—especially when I walk. But the children often come to get me with the auto and I can take the streetcars in Grand Rapids. I have been to see my daughter in Detroit twice this summer. I take the train in the morning and arrive by noon. Then a taxi cab takes me to her home. They have an eleven-month-old baby. They had been married for ten years when she was born. She is a most lovable child named Shirley Ann Madison. I'm enclosing a photo of her on my lap. We are seated on the porch of their home. Kind of cute—right?

All is well at my sister Tryntje's but she is also old and worn out. Her son Marten does a great deal for them because they have little to live on.

I still live alone in an upstairs apartment and can get along quite well.

*   *   *

I know there are many errors in this letter but you had better overlook them.

[Closing]

11   Tjerk and Maartje (Lautenbach) Zondervan

In 1889, the eleventh year of their marriage, Tjerk and Maartje Zondervan immigrated to Paterson, New Jersey, where Tjerk found employment in factories, the building trades, and general cartage. Like his father, Tjerk had been a farmhand with little formal education, and following local practices, he had probably hired out at about twelve years of age to labor on one of Friesland's large farmsteads. Thirty-six when he arrived in New Jersey, Tjerk had already worked for over twenty years on several dairy farms. Following his marriage in 1878, he and Maartje (née Lautenbach), lived in Minnertsga (1878–1886) and Firdgum (1887–1889), Maartje's home village, a tiny hamlet linked for religious and educational services with Tzummarum. Nearby cities included the port of Harlingen, five miles to the south, and Leeuwarden, the provincial capital, ten miles eastward.[1]

These cities and villages, including Tjerk's native Marrum, were located in Friesland's fertile northwest quarter, which had provided farmhands with agricultural employment on dairy farms over many centuries. Both the Zondervans and Lautenbachs originated from this productive clay-soil region, which contributed heavily to the general emigration peaking in the last decades of the nineteenth century.

Three years before emigrating, in a letter to her brother Sijds Maartje had reported their expected move to Firdgum, where Tjerk and his father would be employed by a farmer named A. Wierda. Of their general circumstances Maartje declared, "You asked how many children we have, and I answer herewith, two. Thus we live with five of us [including her

These letters were donated by Jacob Lautenbach, 1990, and first translated by Maria de Groot.
[1] Van der Aa, *Aardrijkskundig woordenboek* 3:33, 7:379–82, 11:272–74.

father-in-law]. We have, considering the general condition of working people, a goodly supply of life's needs because there are also those, although not too many, who have no work at all and thus no food either. When they do find work, they earn only a little, and so their poverty persists. For ourselves—we have it good and cannot, at present, complain about very many disappointments. We are always healthy and have ample food. It is true that our path is not always strewn with roses—thorns are also evident. But people can endure these easily enough. When we look at people who have much less but are just as worthy as we, it is a blessing that we do not know the future. Otherwise our burdens would be greater still. The paths to the future are hidden; only parts are known, and the rest will be revealed soon enough. Only one thing is certain—the end is death. Then whatever concerns this life will be gone."[2]

When the Zondervans immigrated to Paterson in 1889, they settled among other Frisians, and together they noted many differences between their new and ancestral surroundings. Already in 1881 Pieter Westerhuis had reported, "People who live in Holland cannot imagine what it looks like here because instead of canals and ditches we have high mountains from which water runs down into a river. Otherwise one does not see water here. Owners of land put posts around it—not ditches as in Holland. Land that is being cultivated has big rocks around it. In Holland they would say that nothing could grow on it, but here they grow everything on it. But some places are not usable, as you can easily imagine with all those rocks. . . . One can look out across the fields here, but not as far as in Friesland because here there are mountains in the way. . . . We do not have peat here. We have to make do with wood and coal. I only wish that that was the worst problem; we also have to pay awfully high rent here—even for a room. One does not find brick houses here. They are all made of wood, but they are just as beautiful as in Friesland. We have to pay eleven dollars a month for rent. That's quite a lot in a year's time, and you have to pay before you move in."[3]

Similarly, J. G. Boekhout wrote, "Friends, the soil here is not very good because there are lots of forests here and mountains of rock. Here they have fences around the land because there are no ditches. Thus, friends, agriculture is not much here."[4]

The observations of Boekhout, Westerhuis, and the Zondervans clearly reflect their rural Frisian backgrounds, which, however different from the industrial urbanism of Paterson, did not greatly hinder their eco-

[2] Maartje Lautenbach to Sijds Lautenbach, March 18, 1886, Immigrant Letter Collection.

[3] Pieter Westerhuis to Dear Friends, June 6, 1881, Immigrant Letter Collection.

[4] J. G. Boekhout to Dear Friends, December 1, 1881, Immigrant Letter Collection.

Workers at the Paterson, New Jersey, silk mill, about 1910. Courtesy of the Calvin College Library Archives, photo collection.

nomic adaptation. They found work in the silk mills, road construction, and other blue-collar pursuits, and as in Friesland, their preteen children obtained full-time employment.

J. G. Boekhout reported, "We all work together in the same factory now, and we all come home to eat. That is at twelve o'clock in the afternoon. We like that a lot better than last year."[5] Tjerk Zondervan's young daughters, Antje (13) and Jeltje (11), also worked in a silk mill, about which their father reported on November 13, 1893, "There are about five hundred people working there, and I have an easy job. Sometimes we have nothing to do. We have more work here in silk than you in Holland have in flax. I earn four dollars for fifty-five hours. Antje and Jeltje also work in the silk factory, and they work through the whole summer, too."

Walking home for noontime meals was a benefit that may have influenced residential patterns in the community. At any rate, as they grew accustomed to the city, the immigrants moved frequently, for more convenient quarters or more economically suitable ones. The Zondervan family changed addresses four times between 1893 and 1911. The last of

⁵ Ibid.

these, 52 Shady Street, housed Maartje and her married daughter, Antje, and her family from 1902 through 1926. It probably represents the setting the family identified as "the old home place."

When the Zondervans entered Paterson in 1889, the city had already achieved its reputation as the "silk city," but its identity as a manufacturing center had long predated the construction of the silk mills. The city was organized in 1792 following Governor William Paterson's approval of legislation that created the Society for Establishing Useful Manufactures, which had been inspired by Alexander Hamilton's nationally distributed "Report on Manufactures." Under Hamilton's personal direction, Paterson became a model manufacturing center. Water power, provided by the Great Falls of the Passaic River, drove the mills, which produced cotton textiles between 1794 and 1880. From about 1824 until the Civil War, Paterson was known as "Cotton City," but the war disrupted both the supply of raw material and markets.

Silk production replaced cotton after the war, and by the 1870s a flourishing handloom silk industry had created a foundation for industrial modernization, which was fully established by 1890. The common features of industrialization—crowded ethnic neighborhoods, labor strife, and at least one "great fire"—also marked Paterson's history. The famous six-month strike of 1913 was reported to have cost $26 million in lost business revenues and $5.5 million in wages. By then silk production and the production of textile-machine tools dominated the urban economy. In 1927, the year in which the Zondervan correspondence terminates, Paterson had 823 factories, which produced 75 percent of the nation's silk products.

The city also attracted thousands of blue-collar immigrants. But although Dutch families had acquired the area's first land patents in 1684, they were a small minority of Paterson's 145,000 residents in 1927. Rhine Valley Germans, northern and southern Italians, and Jews from Poland, Russia, and Lithuania far outstripped Paterson's Dutch immigrant populace in the early twentieth century.[6]

Following typical acculturation patterns, the Dutch clustered around their churches and schools, which were located on the north side of the Passaic River near the intersection of Haledon Avenue and East Main Street. By the middle of the twentieth century the Dutch had organized eight urban churches and three private schools, which in 1946 served about four thousand parishioners and eight hundred students. The orig-

[6] David Goldberg, *A Tale of Three Cities: Labor Organization and Protest in Paterson, Passaic, and Lawrence, 1916–1921* (New Brunswick: Rutgers University Press, 1989), pp. 19–82; D. Stanton Hammond, in *Paterson News*, 175th Anniversary Edition, June 29, 1967, pp. 47–69.

inal enclave dispersed after World War II as the entire community drifted northward into Haledon and Prospect Park or eastward into Hawthorne and Fairlawn.[7]

Tjerk Zondervan to Sijds Lautenbach
Paterson, New Jersey, to Tzummarum, Friesland
November 13, 1893

Dear brother[-in-law],

I let you know that we are healthy and wish the same for you. If I could write easily, I would write sooner, but I am just now learning to write, brother, and have in fact begun. I no longer work outside. I work now in a factory. It is very busy there this summer. There are about five hundred people working there, and I have an easy job. Sometimes we have nothing to do. We have more work here in silk than you in Holland have in flax. I earn four dollars for fifty-five hours. Antje [thirteen years old] and Jeltje [eleven] also work in the silk factory, and they work through the whole summer, too. Dear brother, we had a good summer here, and we are doing well.

I also talked to Epke Enga. He lives here with a farmer. We had quite a number of warm days here. We had a heavy storm. Big trees were torn out of the soil and houses from their foundations and also a [Christian Reformed] church [on River Bridge Street], and wagons were thrown aside.

One could see hundreds of people [standing] in the water there. Pieter Feddema visited us too when he picked up his mother from the boat [the Holland-American Steamship Terminal in Hoboken]. But I did not talk to him. I was at work. Lammert visited us once too and said that they were all healthy. But after that we had a letter telling us that Pieter's mother was quite sick.

Well, brother, if you need money, just tell us, and we will send some. But if I had a hundred thousand guilders, there would not be a penny for [that] shoemaker. Now, brother, write back soon, 114 East Main Street.

Greetings from all of us. And we will send you the pictures and please send one to K. Jelgerhuis and one to Baaj and Jaabik and Jerr de Vries. Also write once how it is with Auntie.

[Closing]

---

[7] *Yearbook* of the Christian Reformed Church (Grand Rapids, Mich.: CRC Publications, 1946; 1990). *Christian School Statistics* (Chicago: National Union of Christian Schools, 1946), pp. 1–9.

Maartje Lautenbach Zondervan to Sijds Lautenbach Family
Paterson, New Jersey, to Tzummarum, Friesland
February 25, 1894

Dear brother, aunt, niece, and nephew,

With this I am letting you know that we are still healthy, and we hope
the same for you. We read the name of my brother in the newspaper
here that he died. But we are not certain that it was actually so. The
paper said it was Sijds Lautenbach, thirty-six years old. We want to know
if that was my brother. We are very anxious to have you write about
that. And also we would like the address of my brother Jan [an immigrant
living in Michigan], so we can write to him. Our address is Tjerk Zondervan, 114 East Main Street, Paterson, New Jersey, America.

There is much unemployment here. Thousands of people are walking
the streets because they have nothing to do. And this has gone on for
ten months already. Our daughter Antje works in the silk factory; Jeltje
has had a throat infection but now feels better. My husband does not
have anything to do either.

It is a bad winter here. A lot of snow has fallen, and for a few days
now it has been colder than any time this winter. It is a double winter
for a lot of people—winter inside and outside. There is quite a bit of
charity here, and if that was not the case, thousands would perish from
hunger and poverty. Those who are still working have low wages, so
almost every day there are strikes.[1] So now you can understand how
things are here these days. We hope that it will change soon. Otherwise
it will be the same here as in the Netherlands.

Lambert Hoogenhuis visited with us and sends greetings. Greetings
also from all of us.

Write back soon.

[Closing]

---

1. Doubtless, she is referring to the major silk industry strike of 1893–1894.

Tjerk Zondervan to Sijds Lautenbach
Paterson, New Jersey, to Tzummarum, Friesland
February 27, [1894]

Dear brother,

We are letting you know that we are healthy and wish the same for
you. It is a long winter here. A lot of snow has fallen, and it is freezing
hard, so it is a real winter here. I have not earned a cent for eight weeks,

but Antje is working and earns five dollars a week. She works in a silk factory. We have been waiting a long time for a letter from you, brother.

I sent a pipe to you with Dirk Kasma with my address, and I thought that you would write me. I sent the new address because I was going to move. Well, that has happened. Now we are living at No. 114 East Main Street. When you write back, tell us if Aunt Grietje is still living and also your mother and Aunt Trien in Franeker.

Poverty we do not see here because Dutchmen go to church with cigars in their mouths. Girls should be happy to be here because it is not such a poor land as yours. That makes a big difference. I bought a quarter of a cow, and, if we are healthy, we will eat well. We are thankful that we are in this country. I think we will never come back—only if land would be as cheap there as here. Maybe you should come over here, brother. Not so many people are coming as last year. Maybe they will stop altogether. But there is still room enough here. Please write us the address of brother Jan and [his wife] Ans.

The potatoes are not so good here, and now most of them are frozen too because of the hard winter. Brother, you would be very surprised if you saw Jeltje and Antje. They look very good. If we stay healthy, we will send you a photograph of them. Then you will see for yourself.

It has been quite busy for the girls in the factory because the silk factories are full of silk, and that means work for the girls. I do not know when I will be working again.

Hessel Bakker died. One day he was healthy, and the next dead. He was a farmer not too far from here.

Greetings from us—from me and my wife and children.

[Closing]

June 9, [1895]

Dear brother,

We let you know that we are in good health and wish the same for you.

We sent the money to you, but it came back. We will send it again if we are in good health, but we will send you this letter first.

We have moved again, and I have rented this place for a year at four and a half dollars [per month]. We have had warm weather here for two days—and then a heavy thunderstorm. But now the weather is beautiful. We already have lots of fresh vegetables, and in May we had some new potatoes. We ate them, and they were great. We also got a new cabinet with mahogany veneer and copper handles, and also a few new rugs.

Now I am riding on the wagon with Krelis Mijers and earn $8.00 a week—steady. That is pretty good. People working in the steel factory earn $1.10 a day. My father works at a racetrack for $1.25 a day. I never get a reply to the letters I write. I begin to think that the letters do not get to you at all.

How are you people doing concerning work in the Netherlands? I think it must be hard work for hard poverty. I am always happy to be in America. Bricklayers earn $4.00 per day here. I received a letter from Jan Dovers. He gets my letters; they do not come back.

Please put [brother] Jan's address in your letters to us. The children learn English very well—better than we. We are too old. Soon it will be crowded here. Lots of people are arriving. Please send us a reply. Greetings from us all.

Tjerk Zondervan
Maartje Lautenbach and children
63 Montgomery Street

[1896]

Dear brother,

* * *

The work is slack here these days, even in the factories, but I cannot complain. I have not had one day that I did not work. We had a terrible thing happen here in Paterson. Seven children went out into the country to look for wild berries, and when they came back in the evening and crossed a railroad bridge, a train caught them. One boy jumped into the river, and another hung to the bridge. Three were dead, and two seriously injured. Four of the children were from one family, and two of them died instantly. One was badly injured, and one escaped injury. The only daughter of a family died instantly too. Last week a train from far away in America came into Paterson and smashed into some empty cars. You can imagine that everything was smashed. The train was on its side, and the stoker [coal shoveler] broke his leg—that was all. Not too bad. Lots of accidents happen here in this land—someone loses a hand, another a foot. Someone is killed or burned. That's how it goes here.

My father does not like it here. He said that he regrets coming to this land. I am glad that I did not recommend it to him. I would never recommend it to anyone. Some like it here, and others don't. But I would never go back.

Last Saturday night a big factory burned down. It was a lumber company. Lots of wood burned there at a great loss of money. People said,

"Just let it burn. That gives more work in construction. There is plenty of money in this country."

My wife and I bought a new lamp last night for $4.25. . . . We had a beautiful summer here. Not much rain and not many thunderstorms but very hot. On many days it was over 100 degrees.

Last night we were at Krelis Mijers's when there was another fire—in a silk mill this time.

Greetings. . . .

Tjerk Zondervan
63 Montgomery Street

October 12, [1897]

Dear brother,

I am able to announce that my wife gave birth to a baby girl and all is well. She is not very strong yet, but that will come soon.

*   *   *

I earned good money this summer, and if I stay healthy and the weather is good, I can work with the bricklayers until the new year. Antje just started working in the factory too, but I don't know what she earns yet. The name of the baby is Ulkje.

Employment is good here this year. This summer there was lots of work. Some time ago they were looking for laborers, as there was much work in bricklaying and much digging for sewers and pipes to get water and gas into houses, also much work on streets and roads.

If a household has grown-up children, they can earn good money if they are careful. Then they can have a good life. But we do have many bad people here who do not live right. It is the same here as with you people—everybody is different.

I wrote this letter on October 12—my birthday. Greetings from all of us.

[Closing]
63 Montgomery Street

December 16, 1898

Dear brother,

I have to write you again, brother, but the news is not so good this time. We have lost Ulkje; she was eight months and eight days old when she died. We are very sad about that, but we have to go on living and hoping. A working man always has to do that.

Tjerk [Charlie, born 1896] is good and healthy—fat and heavy.

We have had a bad year. There was nothing to do, and there still isn't much. I do not know when it will get better. Many people are walking around without a job, but I have always had a little bit of work, and the girls also. This year America is almost as bad as Holland.

Ulkje was sick for fifteen weeks—first stomach trouble and then a sickness of the intestines and consumption of the lymphs, the kidneys, and the lungs. That was too much for her.

We have rented another house—a house all to ourselves—for which we pay $9.00 per month.

Greetings,

Tjerk Zondervan
45 Hilman Street

Maartje Zondervan to Sijds Lautenbach
Paterson, New Jersey, to Tzummarum, Friesland
March 25, 1902

Dear brother and sister[-in-law],

* * *

I will tell you something about our circumstances. We had a great fire here in town—farther in the city one hundred houses burned down, churches, and more. But on March 1 we had so much rain that a dam burst and the cellar, barn, and chicken coop were all flooded. Twenty of our chickens drowned. Bridges were washed out, and streets flooded. The water has gone down now.

My daughter Jeltje is twenty now, good and healthy, and works in a silk mill. There is lots of work in Paterson. My little Charlie was six years old on March 17. He is a nice boy and goes to the Christian school, which costs twenty cents a week.

Please send us the address of our brother who is out west [Grand Rapids, Michigan]. We would like to write him. Tell us how old Aunt Trijntje in Franeker is doing. Is she still alive?

Our address is 52 Shady Street, and our oldest daughter, Antje, lives downstairs from us. They have two children, both healthy and well.

[Closing]

April 27, 1903

Dear brother,

I want to remind you about our wedding anniversary. On May 17 it will be twenty-five years since we were married. Three children are left us from our marriage. One, Antje, is married. She has three children, and they are doing well—making a good living, the same as we.

I think a lot about Holland and would like to visit you sometime. But the long journey has stopped me so far. Maybe the time will come some-day when I will come to visit you.

[Closing]

March 16, 1906

Dear brother,

This letter is to inform you that we are all very healthy—me, Tjerk, and Charlie. He is very tall and will be ten years old on March 17. I cannot understand why you never write me. I would love to hear from you, your wife, and family. Can you write me anything about brother Jan? I never hear from him.

*   *   *

As far as employment goes, it is very good.

*   *   *

Jeltje got married last year and is doing well. So is Antje who has four children, all in good health.

[Closing]

October 22, 1907

Dear brother and sister,

May grace and peace be multiplied to you and yours by Him from whom and to whom all things are. By God's goodness all is well here so far. But I have a growing sadness because my husband has left me.

Where to? Only the God of all grace who sees everything knows. From Him nothing is covered—even our tiniest thoughts.

*   *   *

Now I am alone with my youngest, so I am lonely. May it be that I feel God's nearness in this loneliness. Tjerk did not want to hear any-thing about God or religion.

Ellie [Antje] is married and has been blessed with five children. One of her children, Maartje, was severely burned, but is getting better. If ever it is possible for you to come here that would do me a lot of good.

*   *   *

I hope that the Lord will take care of me now that my husband has left and I hope that my sadness will turn into submission to God. The sadness of the world works toward death, but Christian sadness works toward conversion and salvation.

Receive greetings from all of us. May the Lord bless your coming and your going. May we meet again in joyful Jerusalem.

Your sad sister,
Maartje Lautenbach and son

December 19, 1909

Dear brother and sister,

As to your questions? Well, my husband left because he had hit a boy. People are saying that he is in California. I do not think he will ever come back. Whenever I wanted to go to church he would act up like the devil himself, but I went anyway.

*   *   *

If Tjerk does not come back I am planning to come to Friesland this summer—just for fun. What do you think of that?

*   *   *

At the moment I have a boarder and take in washing. As they say around here, "I don't care," which means I do not worry about it.

I enclose a small letter from Charlie.

[Closing]

[1909]

Dear brother and sister,

This is to let you know that I am in good health and hope the same for you. I have been expecting a letter from you for a long time, but I wait in vain. So, brother, write back as soon as possible.

Now I know where my husband is—near South Holland [Illinois] near my brother [in Michigan].

There is not much work in America these days. How is it in Holland? Tell me about those things.

I heard from others out west that my husband got married again.

Hoping that you will receive this in good health, I am

Your friend and sister

May 27, 1911

Dear brother,

I would like very much to know how you and the family are doing. We, Charlie and I, are in good health. Charlie is now fifteen years old and works in a factory. I take in washing and also work as a midwife.

I also know where Tjerk is—Dalton, Illinois. He works there for a farmer.

Antje, my oldest daughter, lives downstairs. They have had seven children. They lost one but are also expecting another child.

Wietse Ferwerda brought me the presents you sent with him from the old country. I wear the brooch all the time.

*   *   *

Brother Jan wrote me once a couple of years ago. There is not much work here—especially in the factories.

I have no more news at present but remain, hoping for a speedy reply, your loving sister,

Maartje
52 Shady Street

Jan Lautenbach to Sijds Lautenbach
Grand Rapids, Michigan, to Tzummarum, Friesland
1926

Dear brother, your wife, and son,

*   *   *

You asked about Maartje. Her address is 52 Shady Street, Paterson, New Jersey. I visited her last fall and was there for three weeks.[1] I send with this a greeting from her and her three children. They are all doing well.

The two daughters are married. Her son lives with her. Maartje lives upstairs and one of her daughters lives downstairs in the house. She is already seventy years old but she can still do housework, for which she is thankful to the Lord.

We had a good time there.

*   *   *

[Closing]

1. Jan, a widower, lived with his married daughter, Anna Bouwkamp, at 1248 Adrianna Street in Grand Rapids.

12   *Klaas Niemeijer*

By the time Klaas and Anna Niemeijer immigrated to Chicago in 1904 they had already moved several times in pursuit of economic security. Their first efforts as farmhands near Klaas's native village, Middelstum, Groningen (1891–1889), convinced Klaas that "in Holland you can work yourself to death but it is impossible to save anything if you have a family" (June 4, 1905). To escape that fate the Niemeijers migrated to Germany, where they joined others from Middelstum in the coal mines of Essen. Within four years (1899–1903) the family was able to return to Middelstum with the venture capital required to raise young hogs for market. But that effort foundered when disease decimated the herd. Desperate, but not yet penniless, Klaas then led his wife and four children across the Atlantic.

Their destination near the center of Chicago was no fluke. Many other Groningers had preceded them to that area, and a large number of them had come from Middelstum. Like him, they had immigrated to escape the agricultural depression, which was especially severe on the rich clay-soil farms of north-central Groningen. Although Middelstum was (and is) an exceptionally attractive village with ancient origins, the vast majority of its residents (about two thousand in 1900) labored for subsistence wages for the wealthy farmers who dominated the regional economy. Between 1880 and 1900 thousands of the local farmhands immigrated to the United States. Thus, when the Niemeijers arrived in Chicago they encountered many former neighbors and several relatives. Almost immediately a cycle of visiting reestablished a social fabric that had been disrupted by previous immigrations.

Links with friends and familiar institutions (the church and school),

These letters were donated by Jan Niemeijer, 1976, and first translated by Herbert Brinks.

Chicago, West Side Dutch area, about 1910. Courtesy of the Calvin College Library Archives, photo collection.

assured newcomers of a warm welcome, employment, and living quarters. Klaas's first letter indicates that his family was already settled into a comfortable routine within a month of his arrival. He worked as a teamster hauling trash from 1904 to 1907, and then he moved to an urban fringe where he rented land for market gardening. He and Anna raised their eight children on that farm and moved back into the city in 1921. Thereafter and until he retired in 1946, Klaas bought vegetables in Michigan for resale on the Chicago market.[1]

During his second residence in the city, at 1421 West Fourteenth Place, Klaas hosted his nephew Pieter, who immigrated in 1923. Describing that near West Side Dutch neighborhood, Pieter wrote,

"There was neither a tree nor a flower. Not even a blade of grass (at least in the area where we lived). Some houses were of wood and often they were painted white. They were well built and warm. But wooden houses do not make a good impression on immigrants from Holland. They remind them of a poor worker's hut, but that is the wrong impression. On the inside these houses are as nice as the brick houses which also exist in the area. The Burlington Railroad ran directly in back of Uncle Klaas's house. We lived at 14th Place and the next street was 15th

[1] Jan A. Niemeijer, *Kroniek van het geslacht Niemeijer* (Groningen, The Netherlands: Niemeijer Press, 1971), pp. 52–62.

Street. But there was no 15th Place and no 16th or 17th Street either. The whole distance between 14th Place and 18th Street, about 400 meters, was taken up by railroad tracks. The tracks were elevated and the streets were lowered so people could walk under the tracks. It was dark under the tracks and they were supported by rows of concrete pillars which made a mournful impression on me. The Burlington had many switchyards, places where railroad cars were coupled and uncoupled. When the cars banged together and the brake squeaked, you lost your hearing. The smoke of the locomotives often blew up against the windows of the houses."[2]

However grimy and unappealing, the area provided residents such as Klaas with the essentials of daily life and a firm hope for the future. Klaas, at least, never regretted his decision to immigrate. Repeatedly he assured his parents, siblings, and other relatives that he and his family were entirely satisfied with America, Chicago, and the neighborhood which he and other Groningers had created.

During his retirement, from 1946 until his death in 1955, Klaas wrote frequently about his children and the course his life had taken. In 1951 he reflected, "My wife, Anna, has already been dead for sixteen years . . . and I will not be here so long anymore. I have traveled over the roads with an automobile for twenty-five years bringing vegetables to market . . . mostly I went to Michigan. I left on Mondays and was home again on Fridays. In the winter I spent much time at home. I was very busy when I was young."

Although always a pious man, Klaas's last letters contained little besides rehearsals of his most cherished religious beliefs. And he died happy in the assurance that death would reunite him with Anna and unite them both with their Lord.

Klaas Niemeijer to the Pieter and Jantje Niemeijer Family
Chicago, Illinois, to Middelstum, Groningen
April 19, 1904

Dearly loved parents, brothers, and sisters,
Our promise to write you within four days of our arrival, if the Lord in His goodness kept us healthy and safe, is herewith fulfilled. Thus we can report that we are in good health and we hope that you will receive this letter from the far west in similarly good circumstances. The Lord has blessed us wonderfully until now. May He continue to be near and

2 Ibid., p. 54.

good to us. Let Him be before us and behind us because only then can we walk in the good way.... Therefore, beloved, let your sorrowing hearts be comforted by the Comforter Himself.

As we promised, we are writing about one thing and another such as our ocean trip. We will begin with the morning we left Middelstum. When we got up from bed our hearts were beating fast and hard because saying goodbye is always hard.... we were deeply moved ... and we will long remember having to say goodbye to you, our parents.

It is bad to take comfort from strong drink, but our hearts were so sad that we bought a half liter of brandy wine from Van Lakens and took it along on our train trip to Stedum. When we arrived there we met H. Rose and his wife and M. de Vries. Together we emptied the bottle. We repeat, it is bad to take comfort from strong drink, but it did us good this time. We traveled from Stedum to Groningen and then to Utrecht, where we stopped for a few minutes. We arrived in Rotterdam at 4:30 P.M. and then we went to the Hotel "de Zon." The service there was good but expensive. In the two days we spent there we saw much of Rotterdam. It was well worth the time.

We had to visit the doctor twice in Rotterdam and we boarded the ship at 1:30 P.M. on April 2. I said ship, but it was more like a sea castle. It was five hundred feet long and sixty feet wide.... When we left the dock hundreds of people were present and a band was playing music. So we left with six hundred passengers. We passed alongside the French coast at 2:00 A.M. and took on about fifty passengers from a small boat. We reached the English Channel on April 3 but it is so wide that it took a whole day before we saw land again.

*   *   *

Pieterke, Jacob, Hendrika, and I were all seasick. This sickness is far from nice. People bring up everything and when everything is out you think that your insides must also come out....

Many ships were sailing on the English Channel and on the evening of April 4 we saw the English coast for the last time. Everyone was sick and had nothing to eat, but by April 5 everyone except Pieterke was healthy. Anna was frightened but Pieterke was better on the sixth. The weather was pleasant and we saw three ships. On the seventh the sea was rolling. Pieterke and Anna were both sick. The waves came up over the ship and the boat was going up and down from twenty to twenty-five feet. The wind calmed in the evening. The eighth Pieterke was better and Anna too. The weather turned cold. The afternoon weather was nice. We saw many flying fish.... The weather was nice on the tenth but we were all bored from traveling. We slept poorly and many became sick again. . . . We arrived in New York on the thirteenth with beautiful weather. New York is very beautiful.

Here we saw the doctor two times again and took the evening train at 10:00 P.M. They have beautiful train cars here and I slept rather well on the fourteenth. Saw many forests and stony mountains on the way. The train went through long tunnels at a flying pace. On the fifteenth I slept poorly but the land was better. Many small farmers live here. Arrived in Chicago at 10:00 P.M. J. Krijgsheld's wife picked us up. The weather was nice and we lived with J. Krijgsheld for four days. Now we have everything in order. We have an apartment with four rooms for seven dollars per month.

I found work for ten dollars per week and we are happy that we are here. We will write later about the cost of food and other things. I have already seen Uncle Benes Klok and H[enry] van der Laan. Uncle was with Van der Laan and they were very surprised to see me. I could easily recognize Uncle Benes and others too. I will send his address later. They are doing well and send their greetings. . . . I will write later about Chicago and other things.

Write back as quickly as possible and tell us how things are.

Hearty Greetings,
K. Niemeijer and wife A. Brondsema

This is our address:
K. Niemeijer
South Center Avenue #497
Corner of 15th Street
Chicago, Illinois

[May 1904]

Dear parents, brothers, and sisters,

[Greetings from a long list of acquaintances in the Chicago area with reports about their health and other circumstances.]

When people say that they live in Chicago it can easily be that they live three or four hours distance from us. Chicago can grow still larger. The middle of the city is a half hour away. There are many nice streets but also some very poor ones. They have many wooden streets and they are poorly maintained. The sidewalks are also wood and also many houses but new houses must all be made of stone. Some streets are so full of people, wagons, and streetcars that you can't go through at times.

straaten van hout, palen en die worden
hier slecht onder houden. en daar door
worden die straaten slecht, de rijpen
zijn meest van hout, huizen zijn ook
veel van hout. maar de nieuwen moeten
nu alle van steen zijn. er zijn straaten
daar men bij kans niet kan gaan, zoo
veel mensen wagens en tram waais
(street kar) voor ons huis vaart ook
er zijn niet veel straaten daar zij
niet varen. en al tijd bij kans vol
daar aan kan men zien dat hier geld
word verdient, pronk en pracht is
hier kolosaal, Pietje leert cigaren
maken. zij hebben ons gezegt dat zij
met 5 a 6 week 6 a 7 Dollar per week
kan verdienen, het bevalt haar goed,
ik ben nog bij het verhuizen en
krijg nu 12 Dollar per week, er zijn
eet waren die hier eeg duur zijn,
maar het neemt niet weg, als men
spreekt van kost goed. dan kan
men zich het hier ... hebben

Klaas Niemeijer's [May 1904] letter (p. 2) to his parents, brothers, and sisters
in Middelstum, Groningen

But there are some streets that are not so crowded and there you can see that much money can be earned here. The display of wealth is colossal here.

Pieterke [his fourteen-year-old daughter] is learning to make cigars. They told us that she will make six to seven dollars per week after five or six weeks. She is happy there.

I still work with the teamsters and earn twelve dollars per week. There are foods here which are very expensive, but these are not necessary. If you look for good prices you can live well here. Every Hollander that is careful gets ahead here, but, naturally, it takes time. We eat mostly what we wish, but meat is not the least expensive food. We will write more of this later—if we live and are well.

* * *

Hendrika, Jacob, and Jan, [ten, nine, and seven years old] go to the Holland school. That costs $1.50 per month. They are already learning a few English words. But the language is hard for us at first. It's good that we understand German.

[Closing]

June 12, 1904

Dear parents,

Once again we take up the pen to inform you of one thing and another. Thanks to the Lord's blessing and good pleasure we can write that we are in good health and further that yesterday morning a son was born to us and all went well. We called a doctor but when he arrived the child was already born. The wife of Boersema from the village of Onderdendam helped us until Anna was back on her feet. Both Anna and little Jan are healthy and strong. We hope that things will continue to go well. May the Lord bless you and our little son who is named Jan Tienes.

* * *

[Reports on the status of many mutual acquaintances.]

The streets here run at regular right angles and it is possible to take electric trains if you wish. Then you have to take one and transfer to another and so on until you reach your destination. You have to know the system. We have to take four or five trains. If you don't know the connections, you need to take someone along who knows, otherwise you will get lost.

Frans Smid visited with us one evening last week. His business is well established here. He wishes that he had come here twenty years earlier than he did. One of his daughters was just married. One of his sons is a typesetter for the Holland newspaper, *Onze Toekomst* [Our future]. We read it too. It contains much about Holland and also about the province of Groningen. We learn about all those who die in the province of Groningen.

I continue to work for the same boss. You cannot say that there is no work, but it is not very busy either. Yet, I continue to earn $12.00 per week. As you know Pieterke is making cigars and she is satisfied with that work.

To tell you about the cost of things here I will begin with potatoes. At present a sack of the size you buy in Holland costs twelve to thirteen guilders, but people say they will become more expensive in the summer. They are both more expensive and of poorer quality at the end of the year. To have a doctor attend the birth of a child costs fifteen dollars. We had to pay eight dollars because the child was born before he came. If you call a doctor for ordinary sickness it costs one dollar and fifty cents for each visit. People have told us that a coffin for an adult costs forty dollars and with the funeral you have to figure on eighty dollars. So those who suffer from sickness must pay much. In addition fuel costs a lot here. People burn coal and wood. If you buy it by the wagonload it is not expensive, but otherwise you pay more. Now you must not think that we are not telling the truth when we say that we have hardly any sorrows about coming here. In fact the opposite is true. We are happy to be here. We say it time and again. Clothing material is also cheap here. But those who are sick must pay and pay again. Meat and bacon are not expensive here. Fat costs six cents per pound, meat six to twelve cents, coffee beans twelve to twenty cents, brown beans seven cents, white beans five-cents, flour three cents, sugar five cents, rice eight cents, rye two cents, oats seven cents, butter twenty to twenty-four cents, no margarine, petroleum eleven cents for a five-liter can, tobacco forty cents, milk seven cents a liter, and a cigar five cents. If you buy bread from a baker, it is expensive, but most people bake their own bread. Anna does too. An American pound is not as heavy as a Dutch pound. Nine pounds in Holland are equal to ten pounds here. Clothes here are no more expensive than by you. A stove here costs thirty dollars and that is not a very attractive one. Now, I have written almost everything about costs and you can see for yourself that it is a little better here than in Holland. You must remember that people earn about five guilders per day here. Anyone who comes to America thinking that you can quickly pile up money will be disappointed. There are those who earn colossal heaps of money but not by working with their hands. Those who have foresight and are not afraid can be very fortunate. They can make as much as ten thousand dollars in ten years, but that is not normal. But the chances for this are a hundred times greater than near you. In Holland this sort of thing is impossible.

With this I will close, hoping you will receive our letter in good health. Write back quickly.

Heartfelt greetings,
K. Niemeijer and A. Brondsema

September 25, 1904 [Fragment]

As we wrote yesterday evening, we planned to visit Janna and her husband. Now we are home again. They asked us to send you heartfelt greetings. It is a long ride to visit them. We had to take the streetcar and transfer four times. The streetcar was overfull every time.

G. Mulder said that T. Misker and G. Wierenga were not very happy back in Middelstum and that does not surprise us. We remember well that Mother said to us, "You are too footloose." But as we wrote yesterday and now again, anyone who has made a good wage will find it difficult to be happy in Middelstum. However beautiful Middelstum may be, a laborer cannot earn his bread there. For our part we will not advise anyone who is happy there to come here. Because those who are contented have a great blessing. But we find it better here because we earn our own bread. And thank God that He brought us here. In Englewood [the Dutch community in Chicago which Niemeijer had visited] Lamert and Janna can save money. They have at least two houses and they rent the land which they have [probably used for a truck garden].

Now we will close. Once again—our best greetings.

K. Niemeijer and A. Brondsema

November 20, 1904

Dear parents, brothers, and sisters,
  [Introductory wishes for good health, etc.]
  Brother, you wrote saying that you heard that we were unhappy here and that as soon as we had enough money we would return to Germany. It is amazing how people talk about each other in Middelstum.

* * *

When J. Karsen was here we met with her a few times, and we did talk then about Germany. And we also said that we still have high regard for Germany. It is possible that she made something of these comments. Perhaps she took from that the idea that we did not like it here. Then you should make it clear to her that she did not understand our meaning.

* * *

It is true, we told her that we have respect for Germany because we did well there, and also because two of our most beloved family members died and are buried there. Let me say once again, we have a high regard for Germany. But if you are talking about our leaving this place, we cannot say it more clearly than that we have no thought or desire other than to be here where we can earn our daily bread. In addition we are here in a land where, when we go to the house of the Lord on Sunday, we can hear the Word of the Lord in our own language and our children can go to the Holland school.

* * *

For our part we believe that America is a land exactly suited for the working man. We, at least, find it far above our expectations.

* * *

As you must know, President Roosevelt has been reelected with a large majority of votes. We believe that is a great advantage for America.

As far as we know all the relations here are well.

[Closing]

December 4, 1904

Dear parents,

As we promised in our letter of two weeks ago, we have had your portrait enlarged here. We sent it yesterday and would have sent a frame too, but we have enclosed a dollar for that as you can get a nice frame there just as well. You look good on the picture. It is painted, not traced. We had two made for six dollars, ours has a frame. Accept this as a small remembrance from your children in the far west.

We are all healthy and we are happy. You must tell those who said we are not happy here that we are exceptionally happy. We believe that America is the right country for us.

* * *

Translated into guilders, Pieterke and I earn sixteen guilders per week. You can easily figure then that we can do well here and we don't have to be so miserly, yes miserly. . . .

* * *

Our children are already learning English and they go to the Holland school. But they make them learn English there.

[Closing]

April 30, 1905

Dear parents, brothers, and sisters,
    [Opening remarks and reports.]
    The workers here are also dissatisfied at times because work strikes come one after the other. And that is nothing but dissatisfaction. At present there is a huge strike here and sometimes people use revolvers and knives. If you were here to see it you would be shocked.
    At present many people are coming into America. Twelve thousand came into New York in one day. Nothing like it had happened before, but the newspaper said that people had no need to fear because there was space for a thousand million people in America with space still left over.

* * *

I still work at the same place as a teamster. Pieterke also continues to work for her boss making cigars. She now earns $4.50 per week. You asked us to tell you what Pieterke did, and now we discover that it is said among you (probably by way of J. Karsen, because we think she has stirred up other false rumors in Middelstum) that cigar making is very bad work and that Pieterke's life would be shortened by it. We value our children highly enough, so if that were true we would not keep her there. Pieterke is very healthy and she enjoys the work.

* * *

Occasionally, it has been very cold here this winter. When it is so cold, teamstering is not pleasant. I even stayed home for one week because I caught a cold. But the weather is nice again. [Anthony] has his own wagon and two horses. Geertje [daughter] goes out to do washing. Siewert Bus, nephew of Jan Bus, is bankrupt. People say he is thirty-five thousand dollars in debt. He himself is penniless. We have not yet seen Jan Bus here. I haul loads up to two hours away but never in the area where he lives.
    If you want to write H. van der Laan or G. Wierenga the addresses are here. Mr. Henry van der Laan, 81 Hayne Avenue, Chicago, Illinois. Mr. G. Wierenga, 62d and Wipple Street, Chicago, Illinois.

Our little Jan Tienes was not well during the winter, but now that it is warmer he is doing better.

We would like to speak English better but that is a hard job. We gain a little all the time but it takes a long time to learn enough for a conversation. Our children who go to school speak English like the people on the street.

I'm enclosing an article from the newspaper here. It is unbelievably busy here in this city because Chicago is a center of great trade.

[Closing]

June 4, 1905

[Greetings]

If you think carefully about it you will have to agree that the day laborer has much to worry about in Holland (the old country). The only thing that binds us to Holland is our dear family; otherwise we have no regard for Holland. We thank the God of providence that He has brought us here. We did like it in Germany, but Germany borders the Netherlands. So it cannot be good all over Germany. If you find good work and wages in Germany you can save money, but that's not possible in Holland—not for the working man. You have to work hard in America too, and at first, when you come here, you must not think that you can eat well and not work. No indeed.

But at present in America it is so that if you work and are careful, you can save. And if you have a little money here, there is an opportunity to begin something on your own. In Holland you can work yourself to death, but it is impossible to save anything if you have a family. And for that reason we wish that our family was all here. I have no doubts that you would be satisfied here.

Old Mr. Boersema from Onderdendam has left for home again. He said that he still was not contented here. But he cannot say anything other than that he has it good here. If he says otherwise, then he is lying. But it is bad if you can't adjust here, and we won't say anything about that.

* * *

At present it is very warm here. One day last May it was 84 degrees. It can go up to 100 and over. But to reach 84 in May is quite exceptional.

[Closing]

February 7, 1906

[Greetings]

We are happy to inform you that we have gained a new son. Anna and our little Derk are in good health. So now we have four sons and two daughters. And now we hope that God who has given them to us will also bless them with good health—yes, that He will keep all of us under His wings of grace.

*   *   *

We have had a mild winter; according to the newspaper, winter has not been this mild since 1878. The coldest night of the winter was six degrees above zero. Last winter we had a night when it was twenty-four degrees below zero.

*   *   *

Last night's newspaper reported that Chicago was 189 square miles in size and that the longest street was twenty-two miles long—that is seven hours and twenty-two minutes' walking. So that is quite something.

I am still working for the same boss but Pieterke has another place and earns seven dollars per week. We think that many more people will be coming here from Europe.

There was a huge fire here last week, a huge factory. It burned to the ground, even though they had thirty-five fire hoses. There were many barrels with paint in the factory and that's why the fire was so enormous. Six fire fighters were injured.

We think that Derk and his family will be astonished if they come here.

[Closing]

May 5, 1906

Dear parents, brothers, and sisters,

You have no doubt been waiting for a letter from us or, better yet, from J. Brondsema and his wife. But dear ones, the ways of the Lord are mysterious—yes, very mysterious. But I must get to the point. Our dear brother, husband, and father, J. Brondsema, died in New York. These are hard words to write but nothing else can be said.

As you well knew, Jacob [the Brondsemas' son], had very poor eyes and therefore they had to stay in New York while Jacob was in the hospital. They were not alone there. Many had to stay there because of sickness and others stayed because they did not have enough money. Hundreds were waiting there.

Brondsema's family had to stay there until Jacob was ready, and after he was in the hospital for two days the rest of the family stayed in a building near Castle Garden in New York. But then Brondsema himself became sick. They were vaccinated aboard ship and Brondsema as well as others thought that his fever was caused by the vaccination. But the doctors said that he had pneumonia. After just four days of sickness Brondsema died at Castle Garden. Yes, beloved, the ways of the Lord are hard and mysterious. Mysterious in our eyes and difficult for our spirits. But fortunately—and tell this to all friends and acquaintances— he said, "I am going to my Jesus." With a clear mind and spirit to the last second, he said that with a smile on his face. Beloved, it is hard, yes very hard, for all of us here to wrestle through this, but we must be silent. On the ship he said, "If we only have it so good in America as we have on board ship then I will be glad that we have gone to America." And then later while in his sickbed he said to his dear wife and children (who stood around his bed), "Don't cry for me. Don't cry because I will have it much better than I could ever have had it in America." Precious words! Also for us who remain behind.

*　*　*

Brondsema was buried in New York and by then Jacob was healthy again. And so they have come to us in Chicago. But what a sorrowful meeting. We had a telegram from New York that her Jacob was dead. And then at the train station we saw it. Little Jacob was there but [his father], our dear brother was not.

[Closing]

October 26, 1906

Dear parents, brothers, and sisters,
    [Greetings]
    I can report further that I am still a teamster at $13.50 per week. And Pieterke continues to make cigars for $7.50 per week. Hendrika goes to school. When there is a celebration here she must sing a solo, the first two lines of every stanza and then the whole class sings the other verses. She can sing surprisingly well. She has sung solos in church seven times. If we live and are well she will sing again for the Christmas celebration.
    Jan Tienes has begun to talk a little. He is a fat boy. And our little Dirk also grows well but he is little. Hendrika, Jacob, and Jan all speak English well. Pieterke is far enough along to take care of herself with

English, and that goes for me too. Anna can't use much English because she is home every day and when she goes out she goes to other Hollanders.

The Brondsema family had a hard time here at first, but it is already getting a little better.

[Closing]

Klaas Niemeijer to Niemeijer Family
Hinsdale, Illinois, to Middelstum, Groningen
February 17, 1907

Dear parents, brothers, and sisters,
[Greetings]
We are informing you with this letter that we have moved. Your last letter came exactly on time. We already had our furniture on the wagon when the letter came. Now we have been here for about one month. We no longer live in Chicago, although close by—about three hours [walking] from the middle of the city but about twenty minutes from the city line. We have rented forty acres of land for one hundred and thirty dollars per year, twenty acres under cultivation and twenty acres in pasture. A house comes with it at no extra rent. The streetcar is about five minutes away. Our children go to the English school now, which is located about ten rods (one hundred meters) from our house. About ten to eleven other Hollanders live here too. They all rent land here just as we.

Before us a German Jew lived here and from him we bought two horses, a cow, a wagon, about eighty dollars' worth of hay, and corn for fifteen dollars. Also three plows, a harrow, a scythe, a shovel, two cultivators, and as they call it here, a mowing machine (but that is not worth much), a hay fork (also not much good), ten hens, and then a lot of other stuff. That's what we bought from the Jew and he also lived in this house. He had to get out of the house so we could get in. For all of this we had to pay five hundred and fifty dollars. Now we are farmers! Yes, farmers!

If we live and we are healthy we will raise vegetables and take them to the Chicago market. You ought to see how many vegetables they have at the market there in the summer. You would say, where does it all come from. And there are all kinds of Hollanders who come there with vegetables. Now we must hope for a good year. That makes a big difference for us—as much as four or five hundred dollars.

[This letter breaks off without a closing and the correspondence itself does not pick up again until 1925.]

Klaas Niemeijer to Niemeijer Family
Chicago, Illinois, to Middelstum, Groningen
February 18, 1925

Dear brothers and sisters,

It has been so long since we last wrote that I thought it was high time to write again. Things are going rather well here. As you know, our son Jan has suffered from tuberculosis for many years but at the moment he is better than in the past. He is in bed most of the time or otherwise he feels very sick. Only the Lord knows how it will go in the future.

*   *   *

Our father is no more, and brother Stoffer is also gone. According to brother Frans's letter, Mother has not improved either. So it goes on earth—the result of sin, and of our own sin, because we have forgotten the Lord who alone offers life in the fullest sense of the word. But fortunately He gives new life in Christ to all those who expect salvation and help from Him alone.

*   *   *

Our oldest daughter, Pieterke, and her husband have seven children. They are still farming on land near where we lived earlier [Hinsdale]. It goes rather well for them. Hendrika and her husband have four children. They live near Pieterke. They also raise vegetables.

Jacob has been married for several years but has no children, but they have adopted a boy. He is just over one year old. Jan is sick and lives with us. Jan Tienes, who was born here, is also married and lives in Muskegon, Michigan. They were here in Chicago around the New Year. Then we have three more at home—all born here. Derk is nineteen, Jantje is seventeen, and Arije is fifteen. And I don't think we will have any more children because my wife has all grey hair and no teeth in her mouth.

I travel alone to Michigan both to buy and to sell. I go with my car. There are thousands of them here. . . . I don't earn all that much, but I can't do everything anymore because of my bad back.

So now I have written about this and that.

[Closing]
Nick Niemeijer and A. Brondsema
1421 West 14th Place
Chicago, Illinois

Klaas Niemeijer to Niemeijer Family
Hinsdale, Illinois, to Middelstum, Groningen
May 31, 1954

Dear sister and children,

It must be a few months ago that I received the letter from your daughter with the three pictures—one with you and one of your daughters by your parents' house in Huizinge. I can remember that house very well. And one in front of the Christian school in Middelstum with two of your children and stepchildren. And one of my brother in front of the fence by the Reformed Church. Thank you. I will send my picture with this letter. It is a year old—and also one of my son Jan, who is dead.

* * *

We have so much need of the Lord's presence in our old age. May the Lord give us grace to call on Him at all times and with heart and soul to receive grace from our King Jesus Christ.

* * *

It is my hope that you will receive this letter with the blessing of the Lord. It is warm here today, eighty-four degrees. Sometimes it can get near to one hundred. But then it is really hot.

Well, Jantje, hearty greetings from,

Nick Niemeijer

The Niemeijer correspondence breaks off again between 1925 and the 1950s. This letter provides a good example of several repetitious letters written during the 1950s when he lived in a mobile home on his daughter's farm.

13 *Aart Plaisier*

Near the village of Ridderkerk, Willem Plaisier's family tilled land in the Riederwaard, a region that had been empoldered by 1442. Earthen barriers protected five thousand productive acres from the Rhine River, which had enriched the polder's productive clay soils in prehistoric times. During the nineteenth century the region was well known for flax production, a venture that also engaged the Plaisier family, but around the turn of that century Willem Plaisier encountered hard times when the

These letters were donated by the Van der Waal Family, 1986, and first translated by Herbert Brinks market for flax fiber fell victim to the growing preference for cotton. These market disruptions led to his bankruptcy, and he turned then to market gardening on leased land. But with diminished work and scant economic prospects, Willem's grown children were forced to find employment off the farm. One of his sons, Aart, became a skilled cabinet-maker, working twelve-hour days in Rotterdam.[1]

Reports of favorable employment opportunities in Grand Rapids, Michigan, induced Aart to emigrate in 1910. Soon his optimistic reports kindled a case of "America fever" in the Ridderkerk segment of the family, and by 1911 Aart's parents and six of his eight siblings had joined him in Grand Rapids. Aart's letters were addressed to Cornelius "Core" van der Waal, a cousin who remained on his family's Ridderkerk farm.[2]

Although most of Aart's correspondence over the subsequent years was posted from Grand Rapids, he and his family probably had no fixed plan to remain there. Good wages in the furniture industry enabled Aart to pay for the family's travel expenses and furnish a rented home for them in 1911. Thereafter the family prospered on the income of three adults. Willem found work in a greenhouse, Aart continued to ply his cabinet-making craft, and his brother Gerrit toiled in a gravel mine. During this prosperous era, 1911–1914, the Plaisier family enjoyed an income of about thirty dollars per week. That enabled them to begin farming near Grant, Michigan, in 1914. Most of Aart's letters, however, disclose his impressions of Grand Rapids and its Dutch American enclave.

The letters discuss employment, social adjustments, and the difficulties of learning English. And although Aart observed his "American" neighbors with much curiosity, the routines of his new life were largely circumscribed by the Dutch subculture. Courtship, church attendance, and even travel beyond the city were all linked by ethnic networks.

Although Aart recounted revealing episodes of urban life, including comments about the 1911 strike in the furniture industry, he was more enthusiastic and perceptive about American agriculture. He noted, for example, that Grand Rapids provided a larger market for agricultural products than did Sheboygan, Wisconsin, the area to which his uncle had immigrated. The relationship between Ridderkerk and its markets in Rotterdam and Dordrecht informed Aart's judgments about marketing farm products.

[1] Van der Aa, *Aardrijkskundig woordenboek* 9:404–5, 467–69; Audrey M. Lambert, *The Making of the Dutch Landscape: An Historical Geography of the Netherlands* (London: Academic Press, 1985), pp. 262–63; *Grant Area Today* (Grant, Mich.: Taylor, 1979), pp. 220–21; Plaisier family, interview by author, July 9, 1992, notes in Aart Plaisier Papers, Immigrant Letter Collection.
[2] Plaisier family interview, July 9, 1992.

On their farm near Grant the Plaisiers were less than an hour away from Grand Rapids by the rail link that served the Grant area agricultural businesses. In 1914 the Plaisiers were general farmers with a typical combination of livestock and pasture linked to hay and grain crops. Aart's letters blossom with enthusiasm when he describes his new village, farm, and church. The Plaisiers were obviously at home in their new setting. Their neighbors were Dutch, they were back on the land, and their church provided familiar amenities of worship and general sociability.

In 1919 Aart Plaisier married Christina Brink (his last letter describes their courtship) and moved to Fremont, where he cultivated the Brink family farm until his retirement in 1967. Fremont, like Grant, was an agricultural village with a large Dutch American subculture. After retiring, Aart returned to Grant Township, where his sons Willem and Peter had taken up residence in the 1940s. Both of them worked on vegetable farms for part of their careers, but Willem was primarily a grocer. Peter, still living in 1992, continued to manage a small farm after a career in garden farming. But none of his children nor those of his brother Willem have become farmers.[3]

Gerrit Plaisier [Aart's brother], who was mentioned frequently in the letters, married Martha Brummel in 1919 and joined his father, Willem, on the family farmstead. Willem retired in 1923, and shortly thereafter Gerrit redirected his agricultural assets to garden farming on recently drained swampland near Grant. With that, Gerrit's agricultural routines reverted to patterns of soil management and cropping which were reminiscent of Ridderkerk and the Riederwaard polder. The drainage of the Rice Lake wetlands in 1917 exposed about three thousand acres of rich muck soil, and by 1960 Gerrit's sons Wilbur and Jerry were actively expanding the size of their holdings.[4]

When Wilbur and Jerry were named master farmers by the Michigan Vegetable Council in 1984, they were cultivating seven hundred acres. By then, they had also entered into a partnership with the Van Singel[5] family, and together they expanded their packaging and warehousing of carrots, onions, and celery for direct interstate marketing. That, together with the operation of a mint still, created an agricultural network with features similar to the family's Old World flax business in Ridderkerk. In both instances the Plaisiers not only raised but also processed and

---

[3] Ibid.

[4] *Grant Area Today*, pp. 220–21; Plaisier family interview, July 9, 1992; "Draining Rice Lake," in Grant Public Library Staff, *The Beginnings of Grant, Michigan* (Privately printed, [1954]), pp. 8–9.

[5] The partnership was later dissolved, and the Van Singels continue to operate as the V & P Produce Company.

marketed their crops. But like Aart's descendants, Gerrit's grandchildren have also abandoned agriculture.[6]

Available data on the Aart and Gerrit Plaisier families illustrates that their thirty-one descendants (seven children and twenty-four grandchildren) have begun to adopt mainstream American social and economic patterns. Aart and Gerrit, both immigrants, found spouses within the ethnic and religious subculture, and their children followed their example. But the third generation, born after World War II, has significantly altered that pattern. Of the twenty-four grandchildren, about 50 percent have married outside the ethnic group, and although all of them were baptized into the Christian Reformed Church, only eight have retained that membership. Only eleven of the grandchildren have moved away from West Michigan (that is, Kent, Muskegon, and Ottawa counties), only three who remain in the area have retained farm-related occupations. In general the migrants—to Utah, Colorado, Wisconsin, California, Illinois, and Florida—have been or are being educated for professions that foster geographic mobility.[7] Probably the rapid erosion of ethnic cohesion which is evident in the third generation of Gerrit's and Aart's families will persist and accelerate in the fourth generation.

The letters Aart Plaisier wrote between 1910 and 1914 provide an exceptionally vivid portrayal of the cultural matrix from which the Plaisier family has acculturated over the past eighty-two years. In addition, the letters are inherently interesting and charmingly naive.

Aart Plaisier to Cornelius van der Waal
Grand Rapids, Michigan, to Ridderkerk, Zuid Holland
April 6, 1910 [Fragment]

Dear cousin,

...I want to tell you that I am pleased to be here, and that is a good thing because it could also be the other way. The difference between America and the Netherlands is very great. Everything here is different.... I liked the train trip better than the ocean travel. You don't have eyes enough to see because you can only see out one side of the train. Either side was equally nice, although they were also different. I cannot find the words to describe it for you—mountains and valleys. At times I felt like yelling "Stop!" I didn't have time enough to see. Every-

---

[6] Kurt Beckstrom, "Plaisiers Are Master Farmers," *Michigan Farmer*, May 19, 1984, p. 19; Keith van Singel, telephone interview by author, August 21, 1992, notes in Aart Plaisier Papers, Immigrant Letter Collection.

[7] Greta Plaisier, telephone interview by author, August 19, 1992, notes in Aart Plaisier Papers, Immigrant Letter Collection.

thing went by in a blur. Once in a while in a valley or on a hill I could
see little houses built of wood. They had little barns about the size of
the houses. It looked like poverty—a few cows the size of goats with no
more fat on them than a coat rack. It was difficult to imagine how anyone
could survive. But as we rode farther, the farms became better. And they
are very different from Holland's farms. In a word, it was a pleasant trip.
I cannot say more, but if you want to know more, you will have to look
me up here. You know my address. Grand Rapids is also a pleasant city,
arranged according to the newest plans. I had only one week's vacation.
We arrived on a Friday, and by the next Friday I was at work. That suits
me very well, but at first it is very difficult. You can't understand anyone,
even though there are forty or fifty thousand Hollanders in the city.

May 1, 1910

Dear cousin,

Having received your letter just this Wednesday, I will sit down to
write back to you. Usually I go to church on Sunday mornings, but
because it is raining, I will go this evening instead. . . . It is a great pleasure to hear everything about the fatherland from you. I will try to answer all your questions in full.

During our first four weeks here we had beautiful growing weather,
but in the last two weeks it was different—and at times rather cold. But
we are getting closer to summer.

At work things are going well too. We work from 7:00 A.M. to 5:00
P.M., with an hour's rest. That is, then, ten hours per day, just as in
Holland. But the work here in the factory is very different. You have to
learn a great deal at first. There are many Hollanders here in the factory,
which makes it very easy for me, but it does not help in learning English.
But I will not stay with this job for very long. As soon as I have acquired
enough English usage, I will go to another factory where everyone is
English, and I will learn much more.

* * *

You asked about autos. They ride along by the hundreds, and they
frequently have serious accidents. The other day one had to go up a high
hill, and when it was near the top, a chain broke, and it came rolling
crazily down again. Then it ran against a lamppost. There was hardly
anything left of the auto worth saving. Often you can see children, that
is boys or girls of sixteen or seventeen years, fly through the city in large
autos. It is shocking sometimes, but people here are not surprised by
this. Also, women are often seen driving horses and wagons. And women

also ride with the horse between their legs—and galloping too. It is a treat to the eyes. But it is very ordinary here.

There are also many lovely girls here, but you must be careful. If you try to stop and say hello to such a girl, she calls a police agent, and then you go to jail or pay $18.00. Yes, the stinkers do, in fact, have such a law here. Sometimes the girls walk along the streets and show off like peacocks. But then, when I am inclined to get involved, I remind myself, there are plenty of Holland girls equally attractive. And they know it too. Furthermore, there are those among them who will not run off to call the police agent. For example, when you sit in church on Sunday, some are pleased to come and sit next to you. The seats are all free.[1] Now, enough of that. . . .

You were certainly fortunate with your colts and mares. And to hear that Adrian is doing well is no surprise to me. If any person, and especially the lovely girls of Ridderkerk, are curious about me, just tell them to send a letter or postcard, and I will answer them quickly.

*   *   *

The food here is very good—you could get fat here quickly. Meat in abundance all the time, and eggs and fruit. More than you can eat at every meal. But people here say that you need more food than in Holland—that it has something to do with the climate. But we eat three times daily—six in the morning, at noon, and 6:30 in the evening. The style of clothing here is about the same as in Holland. For example, no one here notices that I wear a Dutch coat.

I don't know much about flowers and birds because it's not yet summer, but I have heard that the summer brings a delightful display of flowers. Everyone plants flowers around their houses, and the parks are beautiful at that time. You have seen the postcard of John Ball Park; well, I have been there once, and, although it was cloudy and cold out, I could still see the nice arrangement of things. The place is all hills and valleys, and some are high above the city. When you stand at the top you can see the whole city.

*   *   *

Bonjour

1. Pew rental, common in the Netherlands, was not practiced in the immigrant churches.

August 31, 1910

Dear cousin,

I received your letter on Thursday. . . . I would have enjoyed going with you on your nice bike trip. . . .

Perhaps you already know that I have changed my boardinghouse. I did not like my former place. All they ever did was argue there, and I had had enough of that. Now I live with English people, and they don't understand one word of Dutch. That is good for me, but not pleasant. English is not easily learned in a short time. But I learn more here in a week than in a month at the other place. With speaking I can take care of myself a little, but that's not the same as writing. School [evening language school] is now over, and it begins again in September.

Greet Cory and Job Huisen for me. I sent them both a picture postcard. You should have a look at them.

We are having a celebration here this week. The sixtieth anniversary of Grand Rapids' founding. But you should not imagine that it is like a Dutch celebration. From my viewpoint, they don't know how to celebrate here.

A few weeks ago I went to Holland, Michigan, on the [interurban] streetcar. That was a pleasant little trip. I don't remember much about the farmer there, but I do remember how much sweat my work produced. In succession I had to hoe corn, haul hay, and milk twenty-three cows. Fortunately, I was not very good at milking. Now you should not assume that they haul hay with a beautiful wagon. No sir. They work with one or two wagons for manure, hay, corn, and everything else. I sometimes laughed out loud from the wonder of how things worked out. They haul a whole load of hay on wagons, without brakes, going up and down high hills. Here they use only a long hitch and reins. But the horses know what to do as well as the workers.

You wrote that you didn't harvest much fruit, but we have more than enough here—apples, pears, prunes, peaches, grapes, and still more. Everything is cheap, and everyone uses as much as they can.

You write nothing about T. Huisen and his courtship. Is it still going on? You must write about that. They have an uncle in Grand Rapids. Send me his address and I will look him up.

I do not have a girlfriend. And I don't want to be tied down. I have no further news.

Greetings from your cousin,
Aart Plaisier

Aart Plaisier to Cornelius van der Waal
Grand Rapids, Michigan, to Ridderkerk, Zuid Holland
579 North Ionia Street
November 24, 1910

Dear cousin,

* * *

Most of the Dutch girls here were born in America. And they blunder
through the Dutch language. But I have met a few who speak Dutch as
well as I do. That depends directly on their parents. If the parents don't
speak Dutch with their children, they will never speak the language,
because English is much easier for them. I am now going to the English
language school three evenings each week. I'm learning English very well
now. When I learn more about writing, I will write you an English letter.
Now I would make too many errors.

* * *

I will be happy when my parents come here. You asked what my plans
are. If my parents were not coming, then I would go out west in the
spring. But now I am going to stay here. Och! Who knows what is best?
We will have to wait and see.

[Closing]

113 Courtney Street
March 1911

Dear cousin,
[He has been intending to write but has been very busy.]
By now I think my family must be aboard the *Isabella* and sailing along
the English coast. I have already rented a house for them with some
open land attached so they can do a little gardening in their free time. I
have also taken care of providing the most essential furniture. They will
be surprised by everything just as I was, but you soon get used to it.
Fortunately the winter is hastening by, but it is rather cold today. I'll
tell you more about this later.
If they all arrive here in good health, I will be satisfied. They will be
met by someone in New York and brought to the proper train, and then
they will come to Grand Rapids automatically. I would like to make that
trip again.
Are you still unmarried, or are you now hitched? I read in the paper
that Barendrecht will be the site of another great competition this sum-

mer and that the queen will attend. That is a great honor for Barendrecht. I would like to be there. Then we could have a good time
once again. I receive the newspaper every week, but I don't know who
sends it.

I have no more news.

Hearty greeting,
Aart Plaisier

[July 1, 1911, Fragment]

It is now four weeks since the strike broke out, and it is not yet settled.
It's too bad that I have to go about empty-handed, and I'm beginning
to feel the loss of money. But it will certainly come to an end. . . . I am
working a little in the garden, and there is a considerable amount of
work with that. But when it gets too hot, I take refuge under a bush or
in the shade of a nearby oak tree to cool off a little.

Last week there was a bit of a fight at the furniture factory. The boss,
who was driving from the factory in his auto, was attacked by a group
of strikers—naturally all Polanders. They stopped the auto and then the
boss, Mr. Wittekom [Widdecomb], pulled out his revolver to frighten
the crowd, and that made things worse. They hit the auto with stones.
The police arrived on the scene quickly, but they could do nothing.
Women, children (all Polish), and men, all armed with large stones, went
off to the factory with intentions of wrecking the place. A great number
of windows were knocked out.

August 11, 1911

Dear cousin,

We are all healthy despite the terribly hot weather we had here a few
weeks ago. . . . This was an exceptional year. People who have been here
fifteen to twenty years can't remember anything like it. On just two days,
July 4 and 5, three hundred horses died from the heat in New York—
and also many people throughout all of America. The sun shone as if
through a magnifying glass. I was working for a farmer during that hot
time. Because the labor strike continued, I had to find something to do,
so I spent eight to nine weeks on the farm.

If you saw how farming is done here, you would be shocked. Not
because of the beautiful farmyards but because of the operations.
Consider, for example, that in one day the three of us hauled fourteen
loads of hay into the barn, and then there were milking and other jobs
to do.

We take two wagons to the field. One is left standing. Then we hook the hay loader behind a wagon. One person drives the horses, and two stand up on the wagon. We go on then in that way until we have a good load. Then we hook up the other wagon, and when both are filled, we go home. It takes a little more than a half hour to load two wagons. Then we drive into the barn. High up in the peak of the barn hangs a large hook, something like a harpoon. This [runs down] from a reel, and the hook is thrown down into the hay. Then one or two horses on the outside pull on a rope that is tied to the fork, and about one-fourth of the wagonload is lifted up and thrown into the hayloft. We straighten it out a little, and then the process goes on and on. It is nice work, but you really sweat from it on such warm days. I could write six pages about the farm here, but there's not enough space on the page.

It is a shame that you had to lose your best milk cow. But fortunately the danger of disease is past.

*   *   *

And now Cor, I have no more news.

*   *   *

Greetings, and now I go to bed. Good night/good morning, whatever it is.

[Closing]

September 11, 1911

Dear cousin,

[He begins with news of the changing season and reports that the fruit harvest was large.]

Last week Monday I went to the city of Holland near Lake Michigan. It is just like Scheveningen. A nice beach spreads out in front of a sea that stretches beyond your sight. The lake is so large that if you board a ship in the evening, you won't reach the other side until morning. Wisconsin is on the other side. That is where Uncle Arie lives.

Last week a man came to our door to bring greetings to Mother from her brothers in Wisconsin. That was a great surprise. The man was on business in Grand Rapids. He reported that they were doing well in Wisconsin.

*   *   *

I am now back working in the factory at my old job. Now I earn $13.00 per week. So all is well. I had my picture taken, and I will send some to you. I hope that you will send me one of you, too.

*   *   *

Greetings from your cousin,
Aart

R.R. 5 West Leonard Street
October 22, [1912]

Dear cousin,
Perhaps you already know that we have moved. We have a nice big house about one-half mile outside the city. A fine place with an acre of ground—a good opportunity to raise vegetables and chickens. The big electric train goes in front of our lot and goes between Grand Rapids, Muskegon, and Grand Haven. You have never seen such a car. It is two times longer and also higher and wider than normal. It does not travel from an electric rod but by a third rail. That is a rail which is next to the other but about one foot above the ground. The trains glide over it at an indescribable speed.

*   *   *

According to our mail you had fearful weather in Holland. Gerhardus sent us a newspaper which told of all the disasters and accidents. We hope that such things did not touch you.
I am planning to buy a photo camera, and then I will send you some pictures.

*   *   *

[Closing]

906 Pine Avenue
December 19, 1912

Dear cousin,
The year 1912 is almost over, and we await the coming of a new year. Boy, how fast time flies. When I look back, it is hard to believe that it is almost three years since I left the Netherlands.

*   *   *

We are ashamed that we forgot your mother's birthday, but for this time we will say, "Better late than never."

*   *   *

Tonight I will be having the Young People's Society at our house—it is a meeting of the officers. We have important business to discuss. A few weeks ago we had our annual banquet, and that was great fun. And best of all, *I took home a dandy girl. And I am still going with her.*[1] How did you hear that I had a girlfriend? I have dated many girls but always for only a few times, then on to another one. They are available here by the bushel, but you have to keep yourself informed about these things. You once told me that the daughter of J. Huiser from Barendrecht had an uncle in Grand Rapids. I know him well. His name is Maart Huiser, and he says that he has a relative in Barendrecht who is an oil manufacturer. That seems to be the same person.

*   *   *

I was planning to continue this letter on Sunday, but instead I went out with a few friends in the afternoon and then on to church. They have church services here three times on Sunday, but I never go in the afternoon. I usually go in the morning but always in the evening, because most of the young girls go then too. In other service times they sit with their families and go home directly. We live about twenty minutes from the church.

A short time ago a pastor from Holland came to preach at the Alpine Avenue Christian Reformed Church. Our former pastor, [Samuel] Volbeda, has gone to Amsterdam to study. If you ever hear of him, then you will know from where he comes.

Our work continues as usual, but the factories are not very busy. Overtime work is about done. Father is still busy on the farm,[2] but he only has to pluck the corn from the plants. Gerrit and I work in the shop. We really have a nice house and for very little money.

You know that I was in Wisconsin to visit Uncle Arie last summer. I was not attracted to that area. I would rather farm here than near Uncle Arie in Wisconsin. That is a good place if you wish to go west, but they do not have a good market in Sheboygan, and that is essential if a farmer is to get ahead.

[Closing]

1. Italicized sentences are written in English.
2. The family had purchased a farm in Grant, Michigan.

Grant, Michigan, to Ridderkerk, Zuid Holland
July 19, 1914

Dear cousin,

*   *   *

I would like to thank you especially for your detailed description of
Grandmother's sickness and death. . . . Yes, cousin, that is now the third
grandparent that I have lost since leaving my fatherland. . . . We were
well aware that Grandmother was very ill, and we had news regularly to
keep us informed. And then one afternoon, while I was cultivating the
corn, I could see [my sister] Ing coming with something in her hand. I
knew that if it was only a letter she would wait with it until we came
home. I thought immediately of Grandmother. Ing came running faster
and faster, and I stopped the horses. I could see immediately that she
had a telegram. Then I called Father, who was also in the field. He had
the same thought that I had—"Grandmother is dead."

It must be difficult for you to be forced off the farmstead, just as it
was for us a few years ago when we had to leave our farm after living
there for twenty-five years. I can easily understand how hard that is. The
place where I and all of us were born continues to draw us. Many times
I dream of that old barn and of the orchard where we played as children.
I dream all the time of that old place. If it gets to the point that you will
be forced to move, it will be the same with you. After leaving the old
farm, we have moved so often that it has become ordinary. I hope we
will now stay here. We are sitting here very comfortably.

I wish you could come here sometime and have a look. I think your
eyes would pop if you could see how busy we are. There is so much land
behind our house, and we have to work all of it with the three of us.
Most of the work with haying is now over. We had wonderful weather
last week, and we were able to haul in as much hay as we could mow.
Last Thursday we hauled in fifteen big loads. [There follows here a
description of the process which repeats the general contents of the August 11, 1911, letter.] We now have fifty-four loads in the barn, and if
we get another twenty to twenty-five, that will be enough.

Our crops suffered a little in June from the rain, but everything is
growing rapidly now. In a little over a week we will be cutting oats, and
then we will begin to pick cucumbers. That is also a job and a half. So
you can see that we have enough to do. We won't have any free time
until frost, and then we will be ready to start over in a few months.

*   *   *

You certainly earn enough money to come here for a few months of vacation. You won't have to work, and you can eat at cost. If you want to use a horse, just help yourself. *I know you would enjoy a trip like that, and it wouldn't cost so much. We will see what the time will bring. If you don't get married too quickly, you could afford a trip like this. Now I will close because it is getting time to go to church.*[1]

> Greeting from your friend,
> Art Plaisier
> RFD 3
> Grant, Michigan

1. Italicized sentences were written in English.

January 6, 1915

Dear cousin,

*   *   *

The longer people are here, the less they think about their former homes. Perhaps you think that is not proper, but if you were here for five years, you would say the same thing. . . . But still there are times when I miss all the former things, and then they appear clearly in my mind. And that is the case this evening. My thoughts are entirely occupied with Ridderkerk. I really should be in catechism class, but it has rained all day since noon, and so I have stayed home. It is a considerable distance—one and a half miles in the dark, although the darkness is not the worst part.

We have had a pleasant winter, with storms off and on. The snow is three feet deep in many places. Thus, you can easily understand that we use sleighs. Wagons will not work. But if this rain continues, the sleighs will be done too. Yesterday I was trying to drag a few trees out of the woods, but I gave up on that. I worked until noon, but I was soaked through and through from the wet snow. So we will have to wait until the snow melts a little. At present we are doing almost nothing but hunting—I think we have eaten more than fifty wild rabbits this fall and winter. There were a lot of them this year. . . . We find most of them in flat land that is not yet under cultivation. I could tell you a great deal more about hunting, but perhaps you are not curious about that.

Every day we hear news about the war being fought. The newspapers are full of it, but I don't believe the half of what I read. . . . One time we counted the number of Germans who were reported dead, and I don't remember the number just now, but it appeared to be more than the total population of Germany. But that the war is terrible cannot be disputed. And that the whole world is involved is also true. I can imagine what a mess it must be with all the refugees from Belgium storming into the Netherlands. I think that Belgium must be totally destroyed—at least if what we hear is true. And the end is not yet in sight! How long will the sword of war reap misery? May almighty God speedily cause it to be put back in the sheath. He alone has His purpose with this war. But we must also say that those who are not involved are privileged. People talk easily about feeling the consequences of this war—that it causes damage. But I say there is a great difference between feeling and fighting.

* * *

I hope that the Netherlands will be spared and that the war will end quickly.

* * *

Why have you not yet married? Have you not had the chance yet? *That's the trouble with me. I can't get nothing which suits me. I had several different* [girlfriends], *but I don't know enough to stick to it. Brother Gerrit isn't going with that girl anymore—the one he's on the picture with. She was an American girl, and my folks didn't like that at all. But of course he got another girl again. But she is from Holland parents.*[1] Ingetje also has a boyfriend. Also a Dutchman born here. His parents came from Oud-Beijerland. I think I will go to the Netherlands and look around before I get married. Perhaps there I can tap an attractive girl on the shoulder. It is a sad situation with females here. I think they make boys here more easily than girls.

* * *

I must close now.

Your cousin,
A. Plaisier

1. Italicized sentences were written in English.

December 22, 1916

Dear cousin,

A Merry Christmas and a Happy New Year.

It has been a considerable time since I wrote my last letter to you, so I was much pleased by your answer. I thought that you had forgotten about it entirely. But as you wrote, you were exceedingly busy and then

Grant, Michigan, main intersection, about 1930. Courtesy of Calvin College Library Archives, photo collection.

it is easily possible to forget. But it was certainly worth the effort because you had much to report. And because it was written in such small letters it took much time to read. It is a pleasure to inform you that we are all healthy which we hope is true for you also.

It is solid winter here. We have a foot of snow here, and it is packed well, so we can make good use of the sleigh. I hope to make use of the cutter tomorrow and look up a girl I know. She lives sixteen miles (thirty-two km) away. I will use two horses, and then it will go easily. I have a great deal to tell you, but it would take too long to write all of it.

We live here in Grant, about twenty-eight miles northwest of Grand Rapids. A large group of Hollanders live in this area. We have an energetic church of about forty families. And our pastor, Oostendorp, is a pleasant man. Worship services are in the morning and afternoon with Young People's Society in the evening. We live about four and a half miles from Grant, through which the train runs and where we sell our produce. The prices are especially high, almost double, because of the war. Tomorrow we hope to thresh white princess beans [dry beans]. You should see that sometime. They come with a large self-driving steam machine which pulls the threshing mill. They set up the whole thing where the beans are, and when the machine goes "Toet! Toet!" everyone gets ready. Three men throw the plants in, and a few others hold the sacks. A person with a team of horses is busy hauling the sacks away. If all goes well, they are done in four to five hours, and they move on to another farm. They do the same with grain, clover seed, beans, and all. Everything, quick, quick! If it doesn't go quickly, it's no good. And so everything here flies along. Autos here are as common as bikes in the Netherlands. Anyone here who does not have an auto is not highly regarded. Thus we also are not much because we don't have a car. And it will be a while before we have one. Still, they are so ridiculously cheap here that almost everyone can afford one. For $350 you can have a dandy car for five persons. You can also pay from $600 to $2,000, but that is exceptional.

We have nothing to complain of regarding our dairy herd. We have eight milk cows. We had ten this summer, but we sold two of them last Saturday. In all, including the young cattle, we have seventeen head. We have no colts. We had the mares with a stud, but he didn't get them with young.

I can imagine to some extent how strange things must be in Holland. We received a letter today from Uncle Wouter, and he wrote lengthily about the situation. It is really something when you are not any longer in charge of your own affairs [because of wartime blockades]. I think they are pulling the rope too tightly. Time and again I am happy that I'm not involved. Not that it could not happen here—but God preserves us from it. But I think America will get its turn too.

* * *

I[1] will also enclose a picture of me wich is taking last year. I cannot send you one of my girl because I only got one of her wich I would like to keep for myself. But you'll get one some other time when we have some taking again. It would be kind of nice if you see her once. Her name is Christina Brink. She is born in this country but from Holland parents. Well my dear, I'll have to qeuit, my paper is almost filled. Greet your girl from me, if she knows me.

Now I remain with my best wish to all, from us all, but from me a handshake. Your Cusent and Friend,

Arthur Plaisier

P.S. You come over some time for a vacation trip. Your board is free.

1. The remainder of the letter was written in English.

IV

Urban to Urban

Introduction

This part's correspondents represent less than 10 percent of the Dutch migration from 1830 to 1880. Only 20 percent emigrated from cities, and not all of these resettled in urban America. Furthermore, 10 percent of the urban-to-urban migrants were Jewish, and their correspondence has not been discovered and preserved. The letters in this section, thus, can describe, at most, only half of the interurban population movement.[1] Nonetheless, these four correspondents effectively illustrate a spectrum of small business activity and urban culture.

All the urban correspondents were spirited businesspeople with imaginative plans for enlarging the scope of their careers and the profits of their ventures. But only the Lankester family's fortunes can be traced over several generations. Pieter and his son, David, settled in as gentlemen farmers near Milwaukee in 1850, but they were quickly drawn into the more enticing bustle of commerce in Milwaukee. Ultimately, the family resettled in Grand Rapids, where its descendants managed small business ventures until the 1960s. The tobacco dealer Jan George Zahn died or at least disappeared during the Civil War, leaving no traceable descendants. Cornelis Mannee's family was left in, at best, moderate economic circumstances when he died in midlife. Similarly, Willem de Lange's wife and children became destitute following his untimely death in 1874. Nonetheless, each family's struggles, hopes, and achievements are plainly recorded in their correspondence.

These urbanites were clearly more cosmopolitan than their country cousins. Rather broadly informed and gifted with ample writing skills, all of them, but especially De Lange and Zahn, plunged into cross-

---

[1] Swierenga, "Jews First, Dutch Second, Americans Third: Dutch Jewish Settlement and Life in the United States in the Nineteenth Century," in *The Dutch in North America*, ed. Kroes and Neuschafer, pp. 391–409.

cultural comparisons and judgments. Both Lankester and Mannee consistently affirmed the virtues of American business and social behavior, and although both Zahn and De Lange castigated the morals and manners of their neighbors, Zahn ultimately became an enthusiastic booster of Muscatine, Iowa, and the United States. De Lange's cultural perceptions, already beginning to change in his second letter, had no chance to develop.

Neither Mannee in New York City nor Zahn settled in Dutch enclaves—a situation that certainly contributed to their engagement with America's core culture. The Lankesters, even though they were identified with the Dutch subculture in and around Milwaukee, acquired a lively interest in the city which transcended the enclave's boundaries. These factors enabled all the urbanites to comment tellingly on topics such as American religion, the Civil War, and business prospects. Zahn was especially critical of some religious manifestations; Lankester, and especially his son, David, wrote perceptively about the Civil War. De Lange, an office clerk who became a schoolteacher in Grand Rapids, found little to admire in America and much to malign. Mannee's letters were more narrowly focused on his shoemaking business and its potential for growth in New York. All these correspondents reflected a broader exposure to American culture than that of their ethnic cohorts on farms or in ethnic enclaves of every sort. The contrast between them is both obvious and revealing.

14 *Pieter and David Lankester*

In 1850 Pieter Lankester (1799–1870) emigrated from Middelburg, the provincial capital of Zeeland, where he helped organize a company of about 150 families who sailed with him from Rotterdam. The group split up in America with the largest segment going to Michigan with H. G. Klijn, a pastor among the religious seceders. Pieter Lankester and a cluster of about twenty-five families settled in and around Milwaukee, Wisconsin, where several hundred immigrants had preceded them. But Pieter, who wished to be a farmer, selected land in Franklin Township located about fifteen miles southwest of Milwaukee. Although this Dutch settlement survived for at least fifty years, it did not flourish, for its residents were drawn into Milwaukee and to other places. By 1897

These letters were donated by the Provincial Archives of Zeeland, 1976, and first translated by Zwanet Janssens.

Franklin retained only twenty Dutch families, and by then, the Lankesters had also moved away.[1]

A wealthy immigrant, Lankester functioned as a "gentleman" farmer while also operating a small bakery on his farmstead. He had owned a bakery in Middelburg and its sale contributed to the assets that enabled him to establish two farms in Franklin.

Lankester's letters disclose an obvious inclination toward business. His native place, Middelburg, was the largest city in Zeeland with a charter dating from the early thirteenth century. Middelburg's commercial "golden age" coincided with that of the Netherlands, and, like Amsterdam, Middelburg was a principal entrepot for the Dutch East India Trading Company. Trade was the city's lifeblood, and as the Netherlands lost commercial prominence in the eighteenth century Middelburg's prosperity also waned. By 1849, when Pieter Lankester emigrated, the city's port traffic had been severely reduced (only forty-one ships left the harbor in 1844). The population in 1842 stood at 14,198, sufficient to support businesses producing soap, beer, salt, leather, and linen—that is, a largely local and agriculturally focused economy.[2] Lankester's bakery served a fragment of this economy.

Although they identified themselves as farmers in Wisconsin the Lankesters were drawn to Milwaukee's commercial life from the moment of their arrival. And it is obvious too that although both Pieter and his son, David, were listed as farmers in the census records, they spent little time behind plows. During the Civil War when farmhands became scarce and expensive the Lankester clan moved from Franklin to Milwaukee, where they seem to have lived very comfortably on income from investments and land leases. In 1860 Pieter's estate was worth about ten thousand dollars. Ten years later, after the family moved to Grand Rapids, Pieter's home at 59 La Grave Street was valued at three thousand dollars. With David he established a potash factory on Ottawa Street, and David continued in that business until his death in 1903. During that era David lived successively on Hilton, Spring, North, and Logan Streets—all fringing the downtown commercial district where his children worked in various retail shops.[3]

Prior to his immigration Pieter Lankester had gained prominence in the Dutch religious movement known as the *Afscheiding*; he was among those who were persecuted for leading illegal worship services in Mid-

[1] Henry Lucas, *Dutch Immigrant Memoirs and Related Writings* (Assen, Netherlands: Van Gorcum, 1955), 2:129–139; Jacob van Hinte, *Netherlanders in America*, p.153.
[2] Van der Aa, *Aardrijkskundig woordenboek* 7:875–914.
[3] Swierenga, *Dutch Households in U.S. Censuses*, 2:599; *Grand Rapids City Directory*, 1869, 1872, 1875, 1885.

delburg. Nonetheless, he did not cite religious persecution as the motivation for his emigration. His intent, the record indicates, was "to join friends or family" in the United States. Nonetheless, his piety and commitment to the perspectives of the *Afscheiding* leap from the pages of his correspondence. He led worship services in Franklin and Milwaukee, and he served constantly as a church elder. In 1868, just two years before his death, he was still prominent in the activities of the Milwaukee Reformed Church. Then, following the family's migration to Grand Rapids in 1869, Pieter, his children and grandchildren attended the Central Reformed Church. His great-grandchildren, however, moved into mainline Protestant denominations, and the last to survive in Grand Rapids, Stephen D. Lankester, affiliated with the Grace Episcopal congregation. Mary Lankester, Stephen's wife, attended the Fountain Street Church.[4]

Peter (1857–1928), the namesake and grandson of the original immigrant, acquired some local prominence as a businessman in Grand Rapids. Detailing his career as a sales representative and the manager of several wholesale grocery firms, the *Michigan Tradesman* indicated that Peter was active in political, civic, and religious matters. His two sons, Paul and Stephen, were also managers and owners of small business firms. One of these, the Coffee Ranch, had been passed on to Paul Lankester from his father. Stephen (1893–1969) first managed and later owned the F. S. Torrey Veneer Company of Grand Rapids. Citing his membership in the locally prestigious Peninsular Club and his burial in the Graceland Mausoleum, Stephen's 1969 obituary disclosed potent symbols of the area's social elite.[5]

The evidence of inherited wealth is also detectable in the Lankester family's migrations within Grand Rapids. From the time of their arrival (1869) until the 1940s, their homes were located among the well-off residents who clustered near the central business district. (Part of this area, Heritage Hill, gained admission to the national register for historic preservation in 1970.) In the 1940s, when the Ottawa Hills area became an elite neighborhood, both Paul and Stephen Lankester relocated in that southeastern segment of the city.[6] Thus, until these last surviving Lankesters died in the 1960s the benefits of their paternal great grandfather, Pieter Lankester, continued to structure their lives.

[4] Lucas, *Memoirs and Related Writing*, p. 133; Swierenga, *Dutch Emigrants*, p. 156; Milwaukee Reformed Church Minutes, December 1869, microfilm in Calvin College Library Archives; *Grand Rapids Herald*, September 25, 1969; *Grand Rapids Press*, April 19, 1966.
[5] *Michigan Tradesman*, April 11, 1928, p. 42; *Grand Rapids Herald*, September 25, 1966.
[6] *Grand Rapids City Directory* 1903, 1916, 1923, 1931, 1940, 1949.

The eight letters published here (1850–1867) disclose the impressions and thoughts of an agile mind. Pieter Lankester was always eager to promote his latest business venture, and in the process, he gave a lively portrayal of the Milwaukee area, which heightens the historical significance of his correspondence.

Pieter Lankester to J. M. Kuiler
Milwaukee County, Wisconsin, to Veere, Zeeland
January 31, 1850

Dear brother and sister,

I hope that you will receive these words in good health. . . .

Some time ago I wrote a letter to Mr. Minderhout which recounted our experiences, and I asked him to show that letter to you and other people. Just now I sent a letter to Rev. Snijder with the same request. I hope you have read both of them so I need not repeat myself. I requested your reply in both letters. Please do me that favor as early as possible because I need some information from you.

You certainly know from my letters that Milwaukee is a big and busy city. But because they have no starch factory, starch is very expensive there costing thirty Dutch cents for an American pound, which is only four and a half Dutch ounces. The best flour costs five Dutch cents. So according to my thinking one could make a good profit out of the starch business. Now, I have been requested to establish such a factory, which is easily done in this free country.

It is my plan to start this business on David's behalf—to give him a start. But because my knowledge of starch making is not satisfactory, I am kindly requesting that you send me the exact processing rules as quickly as possible.

This would be an excellent business for David, and even if I were to remain here in the country [Franklin], I, using my horse cart, could visit him daily and teach him the process.

One sees no coarsely ground flour here. Wheat is brought to the mill where it is husked and ground. The flour is put in barrels and the waste stays at the mill. But when you have your wheat ground you can keep the waste yourself. A barrel of flour weighs 196 American pounds (88 kilos), and costs at this time 9.5 to 10 guilders for the very best quality. That should allow you to calculate the possibility of big profits.

In Buffalo [New York] a person who had been a starch maker in Zeeland was hired to prevent him from making starch. His employers gave him a job as a foreman at fifty dollars monthly just for looking around.

I must finish now. You can get my address from Rev. Snijder or Minderhout.

> Your ever-affectionate brother,
> P. Lankester

October 10, 1850

Dear brother, sister, and children,

I hope that you will receive these words in good health, a privilege which we have also enjoyed, so that we are as healthy as we ever were in the Netherlands. We enjoy here the great benefits of being released from earthly difficulties and tyranny. We live without the burdens of suffering and we are neither tormented nor oppressed by anyone. These are great privileges in life. Thus we live as freely and restfully here as the richest people in the Netherlands. Anyone here who has a little money can live so pleasantly that he lacks nothing.

Apart from my farm, which I have rented, I have four or five cows that give so much milk and butter that my family can hardly use it all. We have more garden produce than we can use, including the same kinds of spices that you use. We have potatoes and winter vegetables from the cabbage family in oversupply. People here eat bacon and meat three times daily and as much as a person wishes. Bread is made from the purest wheat flour; the finest kind can be bought at 10 guilders ($4.00) for 196 pounds. I bake my own bread from this flour and anything else I desire such as biscuits and sweet breads. I have set up a brick oven for that purpose with two doors. I have also learned to make a good yeast, which I make every week. It is as good as that which you have in the Netherlands. So my biscuits are as good as those you buy in Middelburg. For the rest, I have nothing to do with the farm.

This summer I had a nice house built for the farmer next to my own farmyard. And a man from Velp has also built next to my farm. This man is a painter married to a daughter of Karl Remeens, who lives at the end of the city hall street in Velp. He has been here two years longer than I, and lived eighty miles north of here. After I wrote to him he came here for a visit and liked this area so well that he sold his farm and moved next door to me. We enjoy each other's company, and that is true of all the Zeelanders who live here.

I have one of the finest houses and two small wagons for traveling. With these we drive anywhere we please. In good weather I drive to Milwaukee two times each week. Milwaukee is fifteen miles away. Some of the distance is on plank roads and on these I can cover ten miles in an hour. Most people, especially in the city, have horses and buggies.

Nearly every shopkeeper has a horse and wagon because the distances are so great. You don't have to pay to use the streets except for the plank road which costs one cent per mile to cover the cost of maintenance. There is so much more that I could write, but I don't know what influence it might have, and I certainly don't want to entice anyone to come here. Everyone must decide that for himself. I only want to give you my impressions. We, at least, have no remorse about our decision to come here. From all the matters above, which pertain to material things, you can see that we find ourselves in good circumstances.

But more important than material matters, we have the privilege of worshiping Him without obstruction according to His Word. No one here is ridiculed because of his confession or religious convictions. In fact, the people are so free to worship here that the city contains signs with invitations encouraging people to worship the Lord on Sunday. We, along with our people in Milwaukee, have invited Rev. Hendrik G. Klijn to serve us as our pastor and preacher. We trust he will come here to serve our church. The Americans have offered us everything, including a parcel of land in order to build a parsonage.

*   *   *

Now I will write a little . . . concerning my will, which was drawn up by a lawyer named Van Steenwijk who lives in Milwaukee. This deals specifically with the money that David has coming to him from his grandmother—that matter about which you were troubled because of my impending emigration. From the enclosed quotation you will be able to see that I have taken care of him and that he is protected by the law. You will also see that I have asked my neighbor and friend to serve as the executor and I have selected an upright and wise man as the guardian for our children.

Our children are doing very well, and David especially. He is as tall as I am and takes great pleasure in his work here. When he is finished with his apprenticeship he will be a very capable [baker]. He is doing well with the language, both in speaking and understanding. He also handles horses well—just like the Americans. The farmers here all behave like gentlemen—dressed in wool with pleated white shirts. And they live like gentlemen too.

I must close. If you can, greet our friends and acquaintances. Some time ago I sent a drawing of my farmyard to J. Poppe. I would like to have Poppe and Adamse come here. There are still many opportunities in my neighborhood. Thousands of acres are still uncultivated. The whole of the Netherlands could be transported to this single state, Wisconsin.

The Lord reigns and He does what is good in His own eyes. You are heartily greeted by all of us.

My address is
   T. T. van der Plasche
   attention of Mr. P. Lankester
   Milwaukee, Wisconsin

[Closing]

February 15, 1855

Dear brother, sister, and children,

It was a privilege to receive your valued letter in good health. Westveer and Remeens brought it to us. We hope that you and your family are also blessed with health.

This summer I had an attack of the cholera which was quickly quelled by the Lord's intervention. Our children all look very healthy. David is taller than I. We hope that the Lord will make things pleasant for you and your family and that above all He will give you the grace to be properly prepared for eternity. Death beckons every hour, and wouldn't it be tragic to enter eternity without a portion from Christ.

* * *

Very likely you already know that because of peculiar circumstances Westveer did not get here but stayed in Buffalo. That is more than 900 miles from here. But Remeens did get here with his family. His brother-in-law is my neighbor. I picked up Remeens in Milwaukee and brought him here for a few days of rest after traveling. After fourteen days he left for the city and got a job immediately. He did his first work in America here with me. You cannot imagine how much work there is here and especially for carpenters and bricklayers. If masons are skillful they can sometimes earn about two dollars per day. It's the same with blacksmiths—and, yes, with almost all the skilled trades. Conditions for farmhands are also good here. If they work well here in this country they can earn up to two hundred dollars per year—including room, board, and laundry. If they work by the month in the busiest part of the summer they can earn twenty or thirty dollars per month. That is only for a few months.

Now, brother, your question about leavening, as you call it. This should not be used in baking bread as much as in other things as, for example, sponge cake or first-rate pigs in the blanket such as I baked in Middelburg. Doughnuts or pancakes baked with it are usually good but it can also be used for bread. I think, though, that it would be too expensive in bread.

I make my own yeast because there is no yeast here except in places where Europeans live. In those places there are many beer breweries and thus yeast also. But it is always a liquid. I have not yet seen a dry yeast. So everyone here makes his own yeast and I do too. The bread I bake here is much nicer than that which I made in Middelburg.

The wheat that I grow on my farm is of the same quality as the Polish wheat that I used in Middelburg. And of this wheat we use only the best quality. I have baked bread as good as the best with this flour—very light when divided into loaves. . . . If I could have baked with my own yeast in the Netherlands I would have made a lot of money.

The flour here is usually ground fine. You would be astonished if you could see how the flour milling process goes here. All the mills here are driven by steam or water power. When we bring a load of unsorted wheat to the mill it is dumped into a bin and seems to fall into a cellar. From there it is conveyed upward by machinery where it is separated and all the bad wheat falls out through an iron [grate]. Then it runs through iron drums which crush hard lumps, and to get rid of dust and chaff. Within a few minutes the wheat runs out pure and clean into a bin that stands above the millstones. There it is ground and then the meal is conveyed upward again where it is cooled before being dumped into a sifter. All is done by machine.

Then the miller attaches bags to three different openings—one for flour, another for "fine middling" as it is called here, and a third for bran. All this goes so fast that if we come to the mill with a load of wheat and no one is ahead of us, we can be served in from two to three hours. The flour is so choice and the bran and middling so clean, it is unbelievable.

The millers are not paid in cash, but depending on the market price of grain, they take up to one eighth of the ground wheat. When market prices are high the miller's portion decreases. The more expensive the less he takes.

Millers have almost nothing to do. Sometimes the mill is operated by one man. Whole wheat bread is hardly used here because everyone from our president to the day laborer eats the same kind of bread. It is a great shock for needy people to discover how cheap things are here. (Presently the prices are higher because of the [Crimean] war.) But pork remains cheap. Since autumn I have butchered twenty-four hogs and brought five to the city. Two were for T. Remeens who could not believe it was possible to buy a hog for so little money. Thousands of hogs come to the city daily. They are all butchered by the farmers and brought to the city by the wagonloads. They are sold with the heads on. Presently the best are sold at four dollars per hundredweight. Hogs are salted down and sold by the barrel.

This country places a great emphasis on trade. From the least to the greatest, all are intent only on making money. The western states are developing with incredible speed which is caused by the railroads being laid out to connect farmers to their markets. Farmers who live two and three hundred miles from Milwaukee and who in the past could not get their products to market can do so now. And in the future they will be able to reach the market of their choice with all that they have to sell—vegetables or cattle or crops of any sort. It is already possible to get from here to New York by train except for one small crossing by steamboat.

I must close—the paper is nearly full. If I have time I will prepare another letter to go with this one. Then you will have to pay only one postal fee. From here I can pay only as far as New York.

[Closing]

December 26, 1855

Esteemed brother, sister, and children,

Your letter of June 1855 found us in good health. Kooman sent it to us by mail, and he has also written for some advice. He lives about sixty miles from us. I advised him that if he wants to live here among us, he should let me know and then I can pick him up in Milwaukee with my horses and wagon. I have not yet heard from him. He is probably busy at work.

That is usual here because people in all the trades are so busy that I can't describe it. In a word, all the tradesmen here in the west are so busy that good carpenters earn two dollars per day. Masons easily make the same and that's the way it is with everyone who can work.

I have delayed writing in order to tell you that our son David was married on Tuesday the 18th of December, 1855. He married a Dutch girl from Zeist, near Utrecht. She is Margrieta Smit, twenty-one years of age. They live near us, in fact, in a house I had built two or three rods from my own house. David and his wife speak English as well as their native language. The other children are also beginning to speak the language pretty well for their ages. This is an absolute necessity here in America. Whoever knows the language well can succeed in all the trades.

This past summer we received many blessings from the Lord. We had a moderate summer—not so hot as others—and a very good harvest.

There were no setbacks except, perhaps, the potatoes, in which there was some spoilage.

Because of the European [Crimean] war all grain is very expensive. Grain has never been so high. Hay is also very expensive. At this time it goes for from fourteen to twenty dollars per ton depending on the quality. A ton weighs 2,000 pounds here and a pound is equal to the old Netherlandic pound. All foodstuffs are almost double the price of the time when we came here. And all other necessities are also much more expensive. But earnings and profits have also doubled.

When we first arrived here a bushel of wheat was 50 cents and at the moment it is between $1.50 and $2.00 depending on the quality. The same is true for hay but there are no complaints about that because earnings and profits are so great.

You folks cannot really understand the rapid progress going on in this country. It goes with giant strides. When we came [1850] the first railroad was being built and now, so far as I can tell, there are more than six. Goods can be sent from all sections of the country. Railroads are the key to progress in this country. The price of farms is also rising—in our area some land has doubled in price over six years.

Our children are all very happy to be here. When we speak of Holland they all say that they would not like to go back. But this is not because there is so much so-called "fun" for young people to enjoy here—the kind that young and undisciplined people seek. No. There is nothing of the kind here—no celebrations and so-called holidays. We hold religious services on all holidays and all who are able come to church. The others are busy at their jobs.

Brother, you wrote that you used the baking powder but that it didn't satisfy you. That is your fault. Thousands of people use it here and it is a main product in all the best stores, sold in half-pound packages. I never bought any that was not as good as that which I make myself. I bake all kinds of tasty little pastries with it whenever I want something delicious and fresh to eat. And it can be done quickly. As far as the yeast goes, I bake everything with it just as successfully as I ever did in Holland. If I had known about it when I still had my bakery, it would have saved me hundreds of guilders. All bakers in America use that kind of yeast and they make it themselves. Even though there are many breweries here, they don't bother to make dry yeast. I haven't seen it here yet. They consider it too unimportant a commodity. Sometimes they sell liquid yeast to private people, but not to bakers. The bakers make it themselves and they would laugh at those who would consider that an important matter.

Brother, you can't imagine the unusually large scale on which things are done here. In Buffalo I was in a hardware store that was three stories high and each floor was at least one hundred feet long. And on each floor there were more goods than in three stores in Middelburg. Each floor had an office with three or four clerks. Those store employees easily earn as much as twenty to forty dollars per month. It's the same in all the trades. This is an enterprising people who do gigantic things. It's the same with farming. The invention of all kinds of machinery is a great thing. Our crops are even harvested by machinery—fourteen acres [of wheat] per day and much more neatly than when mowed by hand. Hay is mowed in the same way.

I could close now, but I noticed that I made a mistake. (My marginal comments on the enclosed newspaper clipping were in error.) The article is actually about a plan for an unusually large steamboat. The keel will be 700 feet long and the deck 500 feet. It is 80 feet wide and 60 feet high. The first cabin will be about 200 feet long with facilities for 3,000 passengers. It will have 16 steam engines with a 14,000 horsepower capacity. They are building such vessels in Ohio that are run by steam.

They also have an invention here known as central heating for the new houses of the rich and for new churches. The furnace is in the basement and it heats the entire house or church. You see nothing of the pipes or that sort of thing, but ventilating outlets can be seen in the floors or walls. The same is true of the newly developed vessels. When I have a chance to send Weems a drawing of a fine steamship I will do so. They are nice for framing. These vessels are unbelievably gigantic and equally beautiful. If our niece Betje comes over to us she will undoubtedly come on such a ship. Have Betje write us a note sometime, or Kornelis too. That would please us very much. And I expect a letter from you too, brother, when you have time. Just put it in the mail and it will get here without problems. I have written you a rather long letter which I probably will not do again. I have been sick and could not leave my room. When I am healthy I don't have the patience to write so much and I have work to do.

I cannot now change the item you wrote about F.F.M. because Mr. van Steenwijk is presently in New York. The Honorable Mr. van Steenwijk has been appointed commissioner of immigration for the state of Wisconsin with an annual salary of $3,800. When he returns I will speak to him about this matter. Don't worry about it. He has exactly the same standing and character as that of Mr. Snijder in Veere. Greet him heartily for me.

Now I must really close because I'm constantly thinking of new things to write. I would much prefer to tell you these things by word of mouth because I would then be able to relate many unusual things, as for ex-

Veere, Zeeland, harbor scene, no date. Courtesy of the Calvin College Library Archives, photo collection.

ample, how the large cities here are supplied with a constant source of fresh water. They are also busy here in Milwaukee with the installation of such a system. They are building a large reservoir, four or five acres in size, just outside the city by the lake. Water from the lake, which is especially good, is brought into the reservoir by pumping machines. There it is filtered and purified. The same pumps force the water through pipes into the city. On all the street corners there are hydrants, which are merely turned open to get the most delicious water without any trouble. If you don't hold your glass or other container tightly you will lose it because of the great force behind the water. I was frightened by that kind of hydrant one time in New York.

We also have springs in this country, which produce water in winter and summer. They never freeze over and in the summer they are always cold and healthful. Even though you are in a sweat when you drink it, it does no harm. And no matter how dry it is, they always run over. In the same way there are other springs such as sulfur and silver which are very healthful.

Not long ago I spoke to a reliable gentleman from the Netherlands who told me that he had come from the state of Virginia where he had seen a fountain or spring of oil. The oil was scooped up in barrels and sent all over. From that all other kinds of oil was made for pharmacists. It was green in color and had to be purified.

While I was writing this letter a neighbor of mine dropped in and said that he had received a letter from the Netherlands. The letter claimed that we suffered a great deal from Indians and wild animals. How do people get hold of such lies? It is true that there are bears in our state, but certainly not where we live. We would, in fact, be willing to walk a long distance just to see one. There are a few wolves. Once by chance, when I was observing our cattle in the pasture with my binoculars, I saw one walking among the cows. That wolf killed a number of my and my neighbor's sheep. But a few days later he was killed too. I saw him fall. And as for those Indians, we see them very seldom, and those unlucky people do no harm to anyone—except, perhaps, in wild country. But here among us it is just as peaceful as in the Netherlands.

We are having very cold weather at present. So cold that one must be careful that his ears and nose don't freeze. During the winter we have two or perhaps three months when everything moves on sleighs, which are very useful here.

Dear brother, in accordance with the promise I made when I left, namely, that when my son David arrived at his majority or became married, his grandmother's inheritance would be given to him, the enclosed receipt will serve as evidence. I hope with all my heart that this will be satisfactory to you. You can rest assured that you will never be asked about this again.

We heartily hope that you will receive this letter in good health and that the Lord's blessing may rest on you and your children. And above all we hope that you may all belong to the Lord and be bound to Him soul and body for time and eternity.

*   *   *

Cordial greetings from all of us to your wife and children. . . . Greet everyone who asks about us.

[Closing]

David Lankester to J. M. Kuiler Family
Franklin, Wisconsin, to Veere, Zeeland
March 10, 1863

Dear Uncle and Aunt,
[Introduction: Apologies for delay in writing which was caused by plans to include a family portrait. The expected trip of a friend in Grand Rapids gave him an opportunity to send the photos and letter to Zeeland.]

My friend Frans van Driel is going on a pleasure trip to Holland and has promised to take them [the photos and letter] along and handle them carefully. I believe he is going to Goes, and while there, he [will repack the picture and mail it to Veere].

[David asks for a complete update on the family's history—births, deaths, marriages, and health.]

As you can see from the picture we have a family of four children. We are highly favored and blessed in that all our children have survived. . . . My oldest son is six. Then follows my daughter Johanna four, our second son, Cornelius, is two, and our youngest daughter, Anna Sebilla, will be one year old on March 28.

*   *   *

And now, loved ones, it would be such a pleasure to be with you once again in Holland. I would like to join my friend Van Driel and am a little jealous of him, but it is best that I do not think of that. There is no possibility of my going with him, not only because of my family obligations but also because of the war being waged, which makes travel by ocean more dangerous every day.

Yes, dear ones, I can easily understand that you are curious to know something about this war, and I intend to tell you about it to the best of my ability. Still, it is hard to know where to begin because the war is so huge, bloody, and destructive that pen and ink cannot describe it.

Unless God intervenes with a solution, I fear that the war will lead to total destruction on both sides because each side is determined to hold out until the last man falls—so they fight on without hope of victory. When reports of each new battle arrive, the question is not how many hundreds, but how many thousands have been killed. I don't know if you have heard how this war began, so I will provide you with a brief account of its origin. In November 1860 a new president was elected, and it is normal for such an event to create great excitement here because the contest usually involves two or more contenders for the office. In the last election the contest was between the Democrats and Republicans, and the Republicans were victorious. As soon as the largely Democratic southern region of the country knew that they lost, they also knew that the future of southern slavery was in jeopardy. Thus they instigated a rebellion and seceded from the Union with six or seven states. If the old president [James Buchanan], who remained in office from November until March, had acted immediately to quell the rebellion, it could have been contained, but [Buchanan] raised no army against the seceders, and thus Lincoln had to begin from the ground up with military preparations in March. Meanwhile, the armies of rebellion had become strong. Lincoln began his preparation by calling for a volunteer army, and people responded by the thousands. An army of 600,000 was assembled. I and other people thought that the rebellion would quickly be snuffed out, but we were mistaken, because we soon lost a major battle. We consoled ourselves by thinking that our army was not yet well enough organized and that things would go better in the future when the army was better trained. That turned out to be true, but our troops were so severely depleted from sickness, death, and casualties that the president had to call for another 600,000 troops, thus assembling an army of more than a million.

The second enlistment, last summer in July, did not go so easily as the first call. At first they got many volunteers by offering large bonuses, which were offered by the government and by leading citizens. Every city and town knew how many troops had to be delivered. But no matter how they tried the total number could not be acquired in the state. So the governor finally had to resort to the lottery because Wisconsin was still 4,000 short. Our town [Franklin] was required to provide fifty-three out of a total of 330 eligible men. I was in Milwaukee that day and it was for me and thousands of other men the most fearful day that I can describe. I will never forget to praise the Lord for allowing me to escape. Perhaps you are thinking that I was more frightened than I should have been. But you must reflect a bit and realize that at present it is quite different to be a soldier in time of war.

The lottery, though, was not carried on without difficulty, for on the day it was to be held, the people of Milwaukee chased the lottery committee and all its assistants out of town. Then the lottery was postponed for ten days, with the warning that force would be used to punish any future troublemakers. The lottery then proceeded without difficulty because the governor of Wisconsin promised that the first person who dared to interfere with the lottery would be drafted in to the army to serve for the duration of the war.

In another place, though, the people did chase the lottery committee out of town, throwing some of them into the mud and setting their homes afire. The governor then sent out a regiment of soldiers to enforce the law, but some people stationed cannons along the harbor where they expected the troops to arrive. The soldiers were too crafty for that tactic. They arrived overland from the opposite direction, and the ringleaders were imprisoned.

The lottery is conducted quite differently here than it is in Holland. . . . Here, when a person's name is drawn, he is given notice to appear before the lottery committee within five days, and he is then transported to camp immediately. You can easily imagine how depressing it must be for a man with a wife and children who must leave everything behind while giving himself over to be armed and sent off to battle— and with little hope of returning.

I can't write with too much authority about this last matter, but I know of several regiments that left in September with over one thousand men and are now less than three hundred strong. One Dutch farmhand who lived with us for a few years before volunteering with the 20th Wisconsin Regiment wrote to his father that only forty of his company of one hundred remained—and that without fighting a battle. The loss of so many folk results from fatigue and privation, for conditions are so severe that they are hard to believe. Many times the soldiers must march for days and weeks through the woods and wilderness. Then they must sleep under the sky without half enough to eat. Mostly the food consists of a biscuit with coffee unless they are in a regular camp, where the food is somewhat better. In general, though, the troops are treated like animals. Thus it is no surprise that people resist the draft.

In addition, of the 4,000 who were conscripted by lottery in this state only three to four hundred remain in service. Most did not appear at the required place and many deserted from the camp. Then those that remained were unexpectedly sent southward without an opportunity to say goodbye to their families.

We have a neighbor here, a poor man and the father of six children, who was caught in the lottery. A short time ago he had a few days leave to be home with his wife. Then he became ill and was too weak to travel back to camp. That, in retrospect, was a blessing because if he had gone back he would have been sent away without saying goodbye to his wife and children.

Now I will tell you something about the financial effect of this war. In short, there is no gold or silver coin in circulation—not even a copper cent—only paper money. At first people used postage stamps for small change and then the government came out with the plan to put paper money in circulation for small change too. So presently all of our money consists of paper money and bank notes—just as it was earlier in the Netherlands. Whenever you wish to change this money for hard currency you must pay a premium of forty to sixty percent to the banks. This, you will rightly imagine, increases the cost of all foreign goods enormously. Because in foreign trade the purchasers must pay in hard currency. Then in return for domestic sales he receives only paper money, with an entirely different value. Many items at present are, I believe, two hundred times more expensive, as, for example, cotton cloth.

Yes, Uncle, only the Lord knows what will happen to this land. From our viewpoint the future looks very dark. Recently the Congress passed another law under which almost no one will be free from military service. The president has the authority to call up another 800,000 men. The general feeling is that he will act quickly on this unless the war ends, but there is not the least hope of that. In America they conduct war as they do most other things, they like things in giant sizes.

If I should begin to write about the growth of trade and other matters here, many people in the Netherlands would not believe it. But I will not expand on that here because I would quickly fill my paper. I prefer to conclude with some information about the family.

The most important news concerns our intentions, if the Lord wills and we live, to give up our farm here and move to Milwaukee. We already have property there and we intend to build a house on it this summer before moving. From this you will understand that I have totally changed the operation of my business. But that is rather common here in America. People who are farmers one day become shopkeepers the next and then still something else. If one thing doesn't work people quickly turn to something else. There is not the least bit of difference here between farmers, city dwellers, and gentlemen. People from the poorest day laborer to the president are addressed "Mister." It is the same with respect to clothing. Even housemaids, if they can afford it, wear clothes as good as their employers. Thus, on the street, you can't distinguish one from the other. And that is also true of most of the Hollanders. Because most people are inclined to consume according to the prevailing custom. That is why most of the laboring class does not progress very much. There is much more that I could write about America, but this is enough for this time.

[The letter concludes with urgings to have photos sent to the United States with Frans van Driel, the friend who will be visiting.]

Your ever-affectionate nephew,
D. Lankester

Pieter Lankester to J. M. Kuiler
Franklin, Milwaukee County, Wisconsin, to Veere, Zeeland
April 2, 1863

Our leaving this place [moving from Franklin to Milwaukee] causes much sorrow.
Dear brother,
I was very happy to receive your letter of March 6 in good health . . . but it also told us of the loss of your son of which we had not yet heard. Yes, brother, the Lord constantly knocks at our door and wishes to make us aware of His words, "It is appointed unto man once to die, and after that the judgment." It is the great purpose of God to place us under the Gospel here on earth so we may be prepared for eternity. Oh, what a happy privilege if . . . we can say with Paul, "For me to live is Christ, to die is gain."

* * *

Oh brother, I can tell you that my soul is touched at times, when on Sundays I preach the beloved Gospel of salvation and see so many who by their deeds declare, "Depart from us for we have no desire to know your ways." . . . Presently, God's judgment has come to rest on this nation. But there is much religion here and many pious and godly people as well as godly ministers. The result is that prayer times are held daily in many places where private persons are invited to pray.

* * *

Some years ago I was appointed as a delegate from our classis to attend the annual synod [of the Reformed Church in America]. It was in the beautiful city of Newark, New Jersey, 500 hours or 1,600 miles from my home. A pleasant trip. We traveled through New York and I was away for four weeks. All at the synod's expense. . . . In New York there were daily prayer meetings at noon.

New York is a place where great events often occur. It is an exceptional commercial city and on one of its streets 700 omnibuses pass regularly every hour to transport passengers.

No doubt you are aware from the newspapers of the sad circumstances related to our totally destructive war. It is a war that has no equal in world history. Two of my hired men have volunteered and they are both fighting the rebels in the South. I get letters from them regularly. There are another three men from our congregation who have been drafted and they are also in the South. There is much talk of another conscription and that may include David because married men are not exempt. It is a dreadful judgment on this nation.

A few years ago we talked as if no war was possible in the United States, but the Lord knows how to visit a people when the measure of their iniquity is full. In this war too the Lord has a definite purpose.

This is an astonishing country and people. And however wicked they may be, they always carry indications of religion, even if they are largely misguided.

Almost every regiment has a chaplain, and the soldiers are supplied with religious, newspapers and tracts which are very good with a special emphasis on preparation for eternity. We have seen some of them. In some regiments no work is done on Sunday apart from that which is absolutely necessary. Other regiments are entirely irreligious. It all depends on the regimental commander.

There are many English newspapers in this country which are entirely religious, and they often contain reports of unusual deaths in hospitals and how the Lord converts many sinners there. Even the U.S. president's wife visits these hospitals. No one is too important to offer services of that kind. People send crates of assorted refreshments from the North to hospitals in the South, and these gifts are distributed by the women.

We have also read in these newspapers about the depraved condition of the Reformed Church in the Netherlands. A certain pastor in Leyden expressed astonishment while serving communion, saying that he could not understand how after 1,800 years such a ceremony could continue. It was merely a memorial for the death of a friend. We read that on another occasion he expressed astonishment at the mystical idea that the people in the church held regarding the sacrament of communion. Our attention was also drawn to a certain minister at Tiel who compared the Lord Jesus to Santa Claus, saying that the good deeds of both will be remembered long after their deaths. Brother, who would not shudder and shake in the face of such wickedness. And the fact that this is tolerated causes us to shake with fear for the time when the Lord's long-suffering patience will come to an end and He will visit such a country with His fearful judgments. Is that defending the faith for which our forefathers sacrificed their blood and property?

On the other hand, we have heard of many others in that same church who have been converted and also of several pastors who have turned to the right path. May the Lord continue to save many and either to cast out those who are wolves in sheep's clothing or turn them to Himself. Brother, it appears that in all times and places when a people mocks God and tramples on His truth and follows the desires of the heart—that such a country, when the measure of iniquity is full, will be visited by the Lord in a most fearful way. There are too many examples of this to enumerate which are given for our admonition.

Brother, because of the war and the resulting scarcity of workmen and farmhands, I have decided, the Lord willing, to move from our farm to the city of Milwaukee after the harvest is in. David and his family are moving too. We have bought property in the city for that purpose—two lots next to each other. On one of these there is a house for David. I will have a house built on the other lot this summer. So you can see that we are facing a great change.

I and my wife desire a little more leisure at this time of our life. David and his wife would not be happy apart from us. So we decided to stick by each other in the city. I have no greater pleasure than to be near my family. We will lease out the farm on which we lived because that is easy to do here. It is a little sad to move because both David and I have nice and convenient houses. Financially, leasing makes the best sense because the war makes it impossible to get laborers or farmhands. A farmhand is paid two hundred dollars per year here and twenty or more [per month] in the summer months. I have recently sold our 70-acre farm, and if times improve, I will also sell the large 180-acre farm. David is inclined toward trade or business, which can earn a great deal here.

You remember Elias Braam, the brother of my first wife, who lived near us in Veere and Middelburg. He now lives near us here and owns a store with all kinds of goods. He is doing surprisingly well. He has more than thirty acres of land, a good house and barn—all free and clear. Besides that he has a lot of money out at interest.

The differences between shopkeeping here and in Holland are like day and night. It is incredible how much shopkeepers here make on everything, for example, more than two Dutch cents on a pound of butter and everything else in proportion. But I must stop.

I have hastened to write you because David has written you a letter telling about the portraits which he is sending to you with a friend of

ours. His name is Frans van Driele, the son of C. van Driele and Pieternella Sonius.

*   *   *

[Closing]

Pieter Lankester to J. M. Kuiler
Milwaukee, Wisconsin, to Veere, Zeeland
May 27, 1865

Dearly beloved,

We are, through God's unending goodness, enjoying good health. On May 13 our oldest daughter was married to a widower from Madison, where he is the foreman of a printing shop that publishes the state's books. Madison is the capital of the state and the seat of the government. This man's name is Johannes W. Corscot, and he earns seventy-five to eighty dollars per month. He was born in Winterswijk, Gelderland. They moved to Madison on May 22—a busy day for us. Madison is one hundred miles away and can be reached by train in four hours.

We have had exceptional events here in America. First, the Civil War, which, as everyone expected, ended with the defeat of the southerners. Richmond, the southern capital, was overrun by thousands of soldiers, and because it was the capital, the South lost everything. A few of the southern generals resisted and had to flee but they were caught by the cavalry. The southern president, Jefferson Davis, was dressed in women's clothing to escape identification, but he was caught and also many of his cabinet. I think they will hang all of them, but you probably read all about this in the newspapers.

The murder of our brave president, Abraham Lincoln, was a second dreadful event. Everyone was so surprised by it that the murderer was able to flee, but they hunted him down and finally found him in another state hiding in a barn. There he resisted wholeheartedly. After breaking his leg in flight he continued shooting from the barn. Then, in order to save lives the authorities set the barn afire and shot at him until they got him. There was a $100,000 reward placed on his head, and I've heard that the murderer was supported by three hundred people. There are a lot of such people in Washington and they will all be hanged.

Our new president, although a southerner, will not be so long-suffering as Lincoln. Our murdered president was buried in Springfield, Illinois, but the body was also on view in Washington. Following his wishes it was transported the following day and stopped in Chicago.

People streamed there by the thousands and the train did not move for a whole day. They passed by his casket all night long. Our pastor, who happened to be there, saw him that night too. The casket cost $2,000. I have never seen such a procession. They had burial ceremonies all over just as if his body was present—including a burial coach and a funeral procession. The procession was so long in our city that it took one hour for official mourners to walk by. All the shops were closed, everything stood still and all the houses were decked in black.

All the churches were in deep mourning, and all the ministers were asked to give a suitable address and to offer prayers on the day of the funeral, which was Easter Sunday. I will send you a picture of his funeral and of the processions held in Washington, Chicago, and here in Milwaukee. I don't know if you will appreciate them.

We hear that all the drafted soldiers will be coming home. A half year ago we bought a substitute for David for $600. American military power has become so great in these last years that almost all nations should stand in fear. England's sea power is no longer equal to ours.

In all matters wonderful and awesome things occur here. They have put up a trade building here which people say is the largest of its kind in the world. It stands alongside the train station, and cars ride through the building in order to load grain. The top part of the building is for grain and the lower part for all other trading goods. It can handle 1.5 million bushels of wheat.

There are similar things in church affairs. A few weeks ago a preacher arrived here who was chosen by the synod to be a means in God's hand for the conversion and quickening of the people—to enlarge the Lord's kingdom and to give witness to the Christian life. There are an enormous number of churches here and each church has its own minister. But all of them have joined hands to help the visiting pastor in his work. He is Mr. Potter and has been with us for about fourteen days. He preaches three times each day. Other persons do most of the prayers. I have never heard such gifts. In the largest church, which seats about 3,000 people, he preaches in the morning and afternoon. Every evening at 7:30 they use a rented hall that holds about 6,000. I have never seen so many people in one place. A prayer service is held every evening before the worship service. Mr. Potter invites everyone to submit all their concerns for prayer—problems concerning themselves and their relatives. I have never heard or seen so many different kinds of persons—men, women, sons, and daughters stand in line to make their prayer concerns known to him. I have been there with our pastor several times. It is very moving to have husbands or sons on the battlefield, and their families sought prayers for these people. It brought tears to my eyes. The minister [Potter] would accept no money and no collection was taken up. This is almost never done in American churches. This is a wonderland in everything.

Just today I had another surprising experience. You know that much oil has been found in this land and that some people have earned thousands and millions from it. The oil comes out of the ground and people bore into the ground in places where they expect it to be located—sometimes 50, 100, and up to 600 feet down. Then the oil rushes out of the ground in amounts of from 20 to 300 barrels per day. After that it is refined. As you know I have some property here and on that land are eight or nine springs. These are the places which people here call living water springs. You can't run out of this water. They run day and night and when you dig a hole around the spring it never freezes over. This is also mineral water and good for your health. A few days ago I read in the newspaper that people can almost predict where they will find oil—when certain conditions are present. And that is in locations where there are springs. So we thought about our land and wondered if there might be oil there because we have there the conditions needed for finding oil.

I didn't mention this to anyone, and I didn't know that there was a group organized here to look for oil. Someone told them about my land, and without my knowledge three men rode out to my land and took samples of the water to study. The next day they came to me and asked if I would come to their office on the following day. They wished to draw up an agreement allowing them to bore for oil and also an agreement for buying the oil if they find some. We don't know the outcome because this just happened today. In a few days we will go to my property with a chemist to make a further study. But you see, brother, wonderful things occur here. Just as I was writing, David left with some people from the company and a chemist from the city to do further research on our land. The refined oil is called kerosene here. It gives an excellent light and is used to make some kinds of paint.

Now I will close. Please answer my letter and give my greetings to all who know us.

[Closing]

February 20, 1867

Dear brother,

We received your letter on January 8 . . . and were dreadfully shocked by the death of your son Hendrik. . . . Yes, brother, our life is like a vapor and everyone must experience the trouble and adversity that comes from sin in the world. We have a blessed privilege if we have the firm foundation of expecting a better life in eternity. By God's goodness we are all still living under His present grace.

Our daughter, the widow Putz, successfully delivered a healthy daughter on December 10, 1866. She is living with us again. Our youngest daughter, Pieternella also lives with us. Maria is still in Madison. They are very prosperous there. Her husband earns about $30.00 per week. Everything is also well with David. Any day now his wife expects to be delivered of her sixth child. All the others are alive, healthy, and excellently handsome.

I am writing you at David's request because he has no time at this moment. He has heard from his housemaid, who just came from the Netherlands, that a machine for peeling potatoes has been invented and it is for sale in Amsterdam. This would be very useful here. Although one can get a great many machines of all descriptions here we have not noticed this sort to be available here yet.

People pay large patent rights for that sort of thing here and David would like very much to have this machine here because it might produce unusual results. So, David's request is that you write immediately to your son in Amsterdam and have him investigate thoroughly if such a thing is to be found and whether it is successful and efficient. If so, it should cost between 20 and 40 guilders and it should be well packed in a small crate and sent over. That can be done very easily by steamship. I will enclose an address and then everything should go right. There is a company in New York which looks after property of this sort. Among them is Rev. Uiterwijk, a good friend of mine. I will write to him and he will see to it that the package gets on the express train and then it will get to me.

There are people here who have made large fortunes on such things. Recently a man invented a machine that makes curved metal spouts. They can be made by the thousands and shipped by the millions. That man sold his patent rights just in New York alone for $20,000. And he still retains his rights in the other states. It is a very simple device. I saw them being made because a friend of mine works with them.

David would like to investigate [the potato-peeling machine] not to manufacture it but to get the patent rights. It is likely that he will be able to do this because Maria's husband, who lives in Madison, is well acquainted with important people and can speak with them about this matter.

Now, brother, if you can, do this quickly. We will send the money as soon as possible. You don't have to worry about that. . . .

[Closing]

February 21, 1867

Dear brother,

I forgot one thing and another in the letter I sent to you yesterday. In my earlier letter I asked you for a machine for peeling potatoes ... and after I sent the letter it occurred to me that I would like to have some other things sent over too. I would like very much to have some pure Haarlem [castor] oil for me and my family because we are not sure that what we get here is pure. We also want some artist's brushes which are very expensive here. All kinds of brushes are expensive here because they are imported from other countries. The hair is not pulled from the hogs here although they are butchered by the thousands. The hair is mostly thrown out or hauled away in wagons for other purposes. So it would please me a great deal if you would include in my box with the machine fifty bottles of Haarlem oil and two dozen artist's brushes in three sizes, each one somewhat larger than the next.

The box must be addressed to: Rev. H. Uiterwijk

No. 41 Hamman Street, New York

P.S. The reason why a potato-peeling machine would be such a good thing here is that handwork is very expensive here and as people are generally too lazy to peel potatoes, they are served unpeeled. Also, there are very large hotels here, one, for example, has 365 rooms [where the machine would be attractive because] maids earn $3.00 per week. Anyway, people here like whatever is new.

[Closing]

15   *Cornelis and Jacoba (van der Veeke) Mannee*

Coinciding with the Dutch republic's "golden age" in the sixteenth century, Zierikzee prospered as a commercial center linked to a merchant marine and fishing fleet. Products including textiles, herring, cod liver oil, and leather, as well as ships themselves, were marketed along both inland and oceanic trade routes. By the nineteenth century, however, little remained of this prosperous activity. The inland fleet had dimin-

These letters were donated by J. C. A. Ribbens, 1990, and first translated by Maria de Groot.

Swierenga, *Dutch Emigrants*, p. 167, lists Cornelis Mannee as "Mannen," and Swierenga, *Dutch Households in U.S. Censuses*, 2:698, cites the name as Monnce, but these are unquestionably the same Mannees who wrote the letters reproduced here.

Zierikzee harbor scene, no date. Courtesy of Calvin College Library Archives, photo collection.

ished from 150 vessels in 1644 to 26 in 1851, and textile production had ceased. Instead, the area's seven thousand inhabitants gained employment primarily from the cultivation of rapeseed plants which they processed to make oil used for lubrication and in paint products.

Dingenes van der Veeke, to whom the letters in this collection were addressed, captained one of the small ships still sailing from Zierikzee. His residence on the main port street locates him at the center of this diminished commercial metropolis, whose robust past nonetheless endowed it with a more cosmopolitan cultural infrastructure than most other Dutch towns. Zierikzee, for example, supported a full spectrum of churches. The national Reformed (Hervormde) church claimed the loyalties of about five thousand, and the Roman Catholic Church attracted nearly two thousand adherents. Lutheran membership stood at 160, and there were 70 Jews and 90 Reformed seceders. The Van der Veeke family belonged to the Lutheran Church, which had gained a foothold in the Netherlands before 1580 when Reformed Calvinism became the nationally favored religion.[1]

Zierikzee's religious pluralism probably prepared the migrating Mannee family for a relatively comfortable cultural adjustment to New York City in 1847. At any rate the family's correspondence between 1847 and 1856 reveals no evidence of culture shock or discontent with New York's ethnic and linguistic variety. Both Cornelis Mannee and his wife, Jacoba

[1] Van der Aa, *Aardrijkskundig woordenboek* 13:180, 226; Lambert, *The Making of the Dutch Landscape*, pp. 138–142.

van der Veeke, reported satisfaction with their location, and Cornelis was particularly optimistic about business prospects in the city.

After a fifty-day voyage and thirty-four days in New York, Mannee wrote, "We are astounded," and added, "We like it better here than in Zierikzee." Although the Mannees arrived in New York with plans to migrate west to Evansville, Indiana, they changed their minds almost immediately, having met "a Dutchman . . . who wants to help us with everything."

Mannee found ready employment as a shoemaker and was able to establish his own shop with two employees by 1848. He also used his connections in Zierikzee to acquire leather and capital. In 1851, while managing his business in the ninth ward, he was investigating the possibility of employing low-cost labor in Zierikzee to manufacture boots for import to New York. And in 1853 he reported that his six employees, were too few to meet the demands of his business. Mannee's annual expenses for rent, wages, maid service, and lighting exceeded nine hundred dollars, a considerable cash outlay in 1853.[2]

Available sources do not disclose the outcome of Mannee's business ventures, but he was able to sell his shoe business in 1856. Thereafter, he purchased an oil-distillation facility in Suffolk County, New York, for five hundred dollars. With that, he processed some sort of wild berries or seeds, probably bayberries, into an oil-based wax that sold for four dollars per pound. By 1860, however, the census identified him as a shoemaker again and valued his house at eight hundred dollars and his chattels at two hundred dollars.

The family correspondence breaks off from 1856 to 1872, and then the concluding letters of the collection, one in 1872 and another in 1873, review the major events of the intervening years. The widowed Jacoba, residing in Newark, reported Cornelis's death and attributed it to his grief over the death of their son, Dingenes, during his Civil War service.

No doubt Jacoba moved to Newark because relatives, the Luyk family, had settled there. The Mannees and Luyks had immigrated together in 1846 and had shared living quarters during their first months in New York City. Early in 1851 the Luyks moved out of New York, probably to Newark, and Jacoba joined them there sometime in the mid-1860s.

It seems obvious that Cornelis did not accumulate a large fortune. In 1872 Jacoba wrote that she had to work very hard to survive and that she had received much help from the Luyk family. Her address, 186 Walnut Street, was in a modest neighborhood. Her prospects at age fifty-

[2] Robert Ernst, *Immigrant Life in New York City, 1825–1863* (Port Washington, N.Y.: Ira Friedman, 1965), pp. 25–98.

five were encapsulated in her last surviving letter. "As far as I am concerned," she wrote, "I shall probably never return to Zierikzee. We have bought a plot here in the cemetery where my dear husband and children are buried. And there I want to be buried too."

Cornelis Mannee to Dingenes van der Veeke Family
New York City to Zierikzee, Zeeland
February 7, 1847

Esteemed parents[-in-law],

I am writing this letter to let you know that we departed from Antwerp on November 15 and we were at sea by the evening of the 16th. We had good weather for 14 days but with a wind that carried us northward and not through the English Channel. After that we had bad weather with much wind. It was so bad that the ship's carpenter was ready to cut down the masts, but fortunately the wind calmed a little and that was not needed. But we still had rough weather, so that the voyage lasted 50 days. By God's goodness, however, we arrived safely in New York on January 4, 1847.

We were astounded when we arrived in the city because of all the remarkable things one can see here. It is impossible to describe. We rented a room immediately for $2.50[1] per week and started work right away which pays good money. If God spares us from sickness we will be able to pay all our debts within a few years. It is a good thing that we left, because life was no longer worth living in Zierikzee. My wife has a good job too and earns good money. We and the Luyk family earn together about 20 to 30 guilders [about twelve dollars per week]. So we live happily and comfortably—free from taxes and bureaucrats such as bailiffs.

Esteemed parents, you would make me very happy if you would send Neeltje [the Mannees' nine-year-old daughter] along in the spring if there are good people coming this way. Here, she can learn everything that is required to earn a good living. Dear parents, I hope that you will not stand in the way of her happiness because she will soon be able to earn a good living here. We have met many Dutchmen here who have given us well-paid work. I'm sure, dear parents, that you can easily imagine how sad we are about leaving our child behind.

We are also sad about having left without saying good-bye to you. I hope that you can forgive me because I could not have left otherwise. I hope that we shall see each other once again before God takes us from this world.

We hope that you will enjoy good health and prosperity in the coming

New York City, Mulberry Street, about 1870. Collection of the New-York Historical Society.

year. Until now, we have all been healthy, and the children too except for a bit of the cold. They are growing!

Well, dear parents, this is all we have to report, but we want to thank you again for all the goodness and privileges we have always received from you in Zierikzee. We also want to thank sister Jasje for the constant help she gave to us. If things keep going well, we hope to repay you in a few years—if God spares us and gives us health.

We have remained in New York until now to wait for the birth of our child. After that we are planning to go 600 hours farther inland [to Evansville, Indiana]. There, it is even better than here in New York. There are 800 churches here, and one street is 4.5 hours long [walking]. There are thousands of warehouses, beautiful stores, and thousands of ships with no lack of carriages. In short, we are astounded!

One loaf of bread, whiter and as big as those in Zierikzee, costs six cents. Good beef is six to seven cents. Bacon is eight cents. Coffee and sugar are about the same as yours, so groceries are not expensive. In short, we like it better here than in Zierikzee and when we have our child back we will have nothing more to desire, except that all will go well with you. We urge you to send a letter along with some reliable people at the first opportunity. They should hand the letters over to Mr. Alberts, for then it will come to us. He is a good man.

I hope that you will send the bills of what I still owe you along with Neeltje. I will be able to pay you for the boots and shoes pretty soon. I have no further news because I know too little about America, and we do not know the language yet. If we did, we would do better still. Just now, while writing this letter, a Dutchman came to us who wants to help us with everything so we can do better. So we have decided to stay in New York and not go farther west.

Now, after having hugged all of you in spirit, I must close. We remain your loving son and daughter, C. Mannee and Jacoba van der Veeke.

Cornelis Mannee

P.S. Dear parents, give our regards to the whole family and our acquaintances. Tell them that we really like it here. Send a letter of introduction along with people you know so that when they come here we can help them as much as possible. There are lots of bad people here in America who cheat others.

1. Tenement lodging rates ranged between $3.00 and $13.00 per month during this time. Thus the Mannees were paying higher than average rates. See Ernst, *Immigrant Life in New York*, pp. 49–50.

July 22, 1847

Most esteemed Father and Mother,

Oh, dear parents, we sigh from week to week, from day to day, and from hour to hour for only a single word from you. But no. You do not write. I know how hard it must be when a child whom you raised with much concern leaves without saying goodbye. But that was my fault and I beg your forgiveness.

I have a lot of work. Some days I earn seven guilders [$2.80] but on other days I make only four shillings. But that is not the important matter. If Neeltje could be with me and we could learn English, we would move to the country. Please write and tell me if you will allow her to go because if I had her here she could be earning six guilders a week within three or four years. You would have nothing to do. But I want her to come over here with good people.

Please tell me how everybody is doing. Mother [Cornelis's mother, who immigrated earlier,] broke her leg and that was quite a blow for us. Our sister Tanie [living elsewhere in the United States] had a son. We read that in a letter from Anje, and I also talked with him when he was with us for three days. We are all healthy. Dingenes [the Mannees' son] goes to the English school and can already speak many English words. Antje [a daughter] is a nice girl but Kors [a sister] was near death. We could not get one word out of her but now she is healthy. She is four months pregnant. We live right in the middle of English people and pay three guilders[1] for a small room in which I live and work. But as I have already said, as soon as I know English I am going to move to the country.

Answer this letter as soon as you receive it and hand your letter to the captain of the *Kroonprins*. His ship will be coming straight back to here from Antwerp. So write back immediately and then we will have your letter soon. Do not worry about the money. Father Maas [unknown relation] will get it but not yet. If God spares us, we hope to send all of the money.

I cannot write you about this city because it would take me three days. Every day there is something new to see. I shall write about that one of these days—after I have received a letter from you.

It is so hot here I cannot keep the children in bed during the night. They wear thin clothes. Koos [Jacoba] starts washing at 4 A.M. and by 2 P.M. it is all washed and ironed and even whiter than yours.

I have Gejanzien with me all day and the doctor who is posting this letter for me treats us like his own children. He has been living here for eight years, but now he goes with his wife to the mountains for the summer. I hope that we can do that too some time.

Greetings . . . from C. Mannee and Jacoba Cornelia van der Veeke, your son and daughter

---

1. This must be a weekly rate, which comes to about five dollars monthly, at the low end of tenement rates. In the 1850s New York contained a large surplus of shoemakers, and most of them scrambled to survive. If Mannee's shop was like that of most other immigrants, he and his family were situated in a damp, poorly lit cellar with little ventilation. This picture is partly confirmed in Mannee's comment about the heat interrupting the sleep of his children. See Ernst, *Immigrant Life in New York*, p. 45.

January 28, 1848

Esteemed and dearly loved Father and Mother,

With great joy we learned from your letter that you and our child are all well and healthy. It is a comfort to know that Mother feels better.

It is a great joy to report that Koos gave birth to a little girl this month. It was an easy delivery and we had help from a Dutch midwife and a Dutch maternity nurse. The child is not big, but it is fat.

Our health and our work are both fine, but we miss our daughter and you. Still, if we were offered a shop in Zierikzee as big as the one we had there along with 6,100[1] guilders, we would not accept it because we live here very restfully.

Dingenes speaks English as well as Dutch. Antje is a sweet girl. Dingenes is taller and fatter than he was in Zierikzee. When he stands among twenty English boys he is the tallest. Antje speaks English too, so that in a few years both children will speak English better than Dutch.

Our youngest child will be named after Mother. She will be baptized in the English church, but not before Easter because children are only baptized four times each year here.

Dear parents, we wrote earlier requesting that our child Neeltje be sent here, but if she does not wish to come you better keep her there. Let her stay there until one of us can come over to get her. That will not be possible before three or four years. But if she does come here she will be able to learn everything at no cost. I would prefer to have her here, but she must also like the idea.

Dear parents, I have an important request to make. There is a Dutch gentleman here who is willing to help me. [A largely illegible segment indicates that a local Dutchman is willing to finance the purchase of leather goods from Zierikzee and Mannee would like a sample of the goods sent to New York.]

Father, what do you think of this plan. The payment will be sent to you in Zierikzee. The cost to you will only be three to four hundred guilders. Hooger can bring the [leather goods] along with him. So think it over carefully and write us. It will mean much work for me and you will have your money back within a year. Material is very expensive here.

I don't know what else to write except that Dijkman arrived and he has given me your letter. He said that he wanted to talk with me but then he did not return. They found work on the day they arrived but Dijkman went inland.

I cannot write any longer. It is night here and our clock strikes two. I shall write more another time. Let me know what you think about the material. Put a sample in a letter and write back as soon as you can.

C. Mannee

1. This odd number may indicate the amount of Mannee's debt. In that case, he owed about $2,500, a considerable sum in 1848.

November 2, 1848

Esteemed and much loved parents,

The reason we waited so long [since May 14, 1847] to write you is that we wanted to send something along for Mother and for our child. We kept looking for someone who could take it along until now. The man who is taking it is a preacher and we hope you will be able to hear him preach because if you hear him, it will be like hearing us. The friendship you show to him will be the same as showing it to us.

We and our children are all healthy and well. Our youngest child looks like Neeltje. She has blue eyes and is growing fast.

Dear parents, you wrote that you wanted to be paid, but we cannot do that yet. It will take some time. I am working now with two men, so if we stay healthy, you will get your money soon.

I received a letter from Van der Beek who asked if it would be all right for him to come here with us. He lives forty hours away from here. But I cannot do that for a man who has always been so troublesome to us.

You wrote that I should not send a letter to Van der Kreken because he cannot pay one penny. We are sorry to hear that. Tell Van der Kreken that if he wants information he should write to us. Tell Booges that I will write soon. My sister and brother [immigrants living elsewhere] are doing well.

Kiss our child for us. You are in our thoughts all the time.

C. Mannee

November 13, 1849

Dear parents,

We received your last letter as well as the little nightcap that Neeltje knitted. We were very thankful and her mother loved it as a gift from her daughter. But children do not wear nightcaps here.

We waited to write until we had an opportunity to send this letter free, and now that Miss Van de Ven is going home she can take it along with her.

It really hurts, dear parents, that I do not receive a single letter from you which does not ask for the money I owe. I would like very much to send it. I cannot but hope to be able to do so in the near future.

For now I have lots of work and my business is doing well again. Last winter, though, I had two men working for me who worked so poorly that it cost me 150 guilders [$60.00]. That is past now and I am planning to expand my business by starting a wholesale business. So you can easily understand that I cannot pay you now.

You should keep in mind the possibility of my having an accident, as in the case of Mr. van de Ven. What would happen to my wife and children if I would not have provided for them. But don't worry. If I have no adversity, you will have everything back shortly.

I am enclosing a dress for Neeltje and some American candy. I hope she will like the dress and I hope the candy tastes good. Our only wish is that we could have our child with us. She could be a great help to us. When you are willing to let her go, tell us and then I will make arrangements with the captain of a ship who can give her a good cabin and good treatment.

I must inform you of the painful loss we experienced this summer. It pleased the Lord to take our dear Juliana from us on August 12. The cause was cholera. She is still much in our thoughts. We cannot forget the loss of such a dear child who gave us so much joy.

I hope you will forgive my writing so little this time. My work does not allow me to busy myself with writing. When you talk to Van Oppen's daughter she will tell you all about us. She lived in our house for five weeks and knows everything about our conduct. She can tell you more than I can write.

Your loving children,
C. Mannee and J. van der Veeke

June 6, 1850

Dear parents,

My business, though not terrific, is still getting better all the time. I have more work than I can manage, which is a good fortune and privilege by comparison with some other cobblers who had to let their help go.

We are living comfortably together but would be even more comfortable if we could have our dear child here. She would come in handy to help my wife around the house—especially now because in a short time our family will increase with another member. So you can understand that life would be easier for us if we had Neeltje here with us. When my wife has given birth, I will inform you by postal mail.[1]

I also learned from your letter that your business is not doing so well. I hope that God will give you a turning point and that your business will flourish like mine. Then you will make a good living.

Please congratulate Neeltje on her birthday. I pray that God's blessings will follow her always and that she will grow up in all decency so that when I meet her she won't have to blush in front of her parents. But she will be able to say, "Parents, here is your child, as innocent as when you left her." Then we shall be happy to have such a daughter.

Dear Mother, we also congratulate you on your birthday and we pray that God will give you and Father long years together and that you will enjoy much happiness together. [We pray] that we will have our parents for a long time to come even though we are far from each other. As long

as you are living we can hope to see you once again to receive your
parental blessings.

* * *

We embrace you in the spirit and commend you to God. Your always
loving children,

C. Mannee and J. van der Veeke

1. Most of Mannee's letters were hand delivered by ship's personnel sailing to Zierikzee.

July 7, 1850

Dear parents,

I wish to inform you that all of us are doing well and that my wife
gave birth to a shapely son on the 5th of July. It happened in the afternoon just as we were about to have lunch. The food was on the table,
but we had to leave it standing and by 2 P.M. the boy was in the world
already. He is a fat American, healthy and good looking. You should
have seen how happy Dingenes and Antje were to have a new brother.
They jumped around with joy. But the first thing Dingenes said was "I
am not going to rock him." He said that because he had to rock little
Juliana so much. But then Antje said, "I'll rock him, Mom." We had a
Dutch doctor for the delivery and a woman from Hamburg as the nurse.

This is all the news for now, but I ask your forgiveness, Father, for
not congratulating you on your last birthday. We thought of that after
we had taken our last letters on board the ship. With this letter we wish
you luck, blessings, and prosperity in your old age—and thereafter everlasting bliss.

Heartfelt Greetings.

November 11, 1850

Dear parents,

[We were disappointed when we picked up our mail from Captain
Smith and discovered no mail from you.]

I hope that you received the last letter. I sent it with the ship *Edwine*.
I wrote then about the July 5 birth of a good-looking son. However, it
pleased God to take him back to himself.

The little mite lived for only a short time, but he suffered terribly. He
was good and healthy at birth and I was so happy that it was a boy but

a few days after his birth he became terribly sick with *koperzuur* and a terrible rash on his body. The doctor gave him medicine to take and powder to get rid of the rash but day and night he did nothing but scream. The child was always swathed in dressing on his naked body. One day when my wife wanted to wash him she discovered that he had nothing but pus and blood on his body. I went to the doctor who told us to wash the child carefully and then we saw that he had two infected breasts from which all the pus and blood came. Only one breast was open at the time but more than a teacupful came out of each breast. When the breasts were open we thought that the child would soon be better; but there was probably more wrong with the child because it always stayed the same, screaming day and night. It broke your heart to see the poor mite suffer like that. At last it pleased God to take the child after a miserable life of ten weeks.

* * *

May it please God to end the calamities that have hit our fatherland so badly. [We hope] the new year will be a year of prosperity so that all those who still suffer in poverty may say, "We do not have to go to America to earn a living."

Neeltje, we congratulate you on your birthday. You will be twelve years old now and probably so big that we would not know you. We wish that you, while growing bigger and bigger, will also grow in goodness, obedience, and love for your grandparents. I hope to meet you once again and to embrace you. My heart is longing for you and I shall not rest until that happens.

Your ever-loving children.

May 19, 1851

Dear parents,

See above [on the letterhead] a small part of New York. It is the city hall, but it is not the only splendid building. I thought it would be nice for you to see something of this kind even on a small scale. It is nothing remarkable for us anymore because we see so many splendid buildings every day. But it is a beautiful sight for a stranger. In front of the city hall is a large park with trees and a spouting fountain. On Sundays it is a beautiful sight because then you can see thousands of people in the park all dressed up richly.

I am also enclosing a New Year's poem published by a big printing company that prints 360,000 newspapers every evening. [The newspaper]

CITY HALL—NEW YORK.　　Eiton, 18 Division St. N.Y.

Cornelis Mannee's May 19, 1851, letter (p. 1) to his parents [in-law] Dingenes van der Veeke

is four times larger than the one in Zierikzee. I thought it would be nice to see this even if you cannot read it. Maybe you know someone who knows English and can explain it to you.

Dear parents, it was a pleasure to receive a few words from you and to learn that you are still safe and sound. By God's goodness we also enjoy constant good health and work. Thank you for your birthday greetings. You are mistaken about my birthday. I did not celebrate it at sea, but in Zierikzee on September 2. My dear wife did celebrate her birthday on the raging waves, but the Lord was with us and set us safely ashore in America. He also saved us from the clutches of a number of leeches here [dockside swindlers in New York harbor].

I cannot understand how people in Holland can allow themselves to be oppressed by extortion until they have sacrificed their last penny to the government's treasury and then they have to go on welfare. One can earn a living here in freedom without having to pay heavy taxes. If people ask for your advice sometime, tell them that if they are not too lazy to work and if they are willing to behave well, they can earn a good living here without having to fear that they will become slaves. One is free here and if one does not like to work one place, one can always find work elsewhere.

* * *

Dear Mother, I hope that your [sixty-fifth] birthday will be a day of contentment and that it will please the good Lord to give you many more years. . . . I am always hoping to see and embrace you once before we leave this earthly vale and to receive your parental blessing.

We heard with great joy that our dear child is growing up and that she is a joy to her grandparents. It makes us happy to hear that she is not a burden to you but is growing in virtue and obedience. Oh what a joy it would be to have her here with us. We received a letter from Hofsma which reports that Neeltje is a good example in her way of living.

You wanted to hear about the Zeenaartsen family. Well, I can tell you that they are all making a good living. My brother-in-law Luyk lives about six hours from New York, so I have little contact with him. Concerning Giljans—he walks the streets as freely as I, even though he has been accused of having two wives—one in Holland and one in America. People think that he will win his legal case. I lent him a sum of money before I knew about this lawsuit and I cannot get the money back until his is finished.

Your loving children.

December 19, 1851

Dear parents,

I am sending you a letter by way of Bartels [a ship's first mate] who is here. . . . I inform you, herewith, that my wife gave birth to a healthy daughter on September 25. We have named her Juliana. She is small and delicate and does not grow much. She cries almost day and night because of her sour stomach. Otherwise, she is reasonably well.

We almost lost Dingenes, but luckily he was saved. I'll tell you about that. He had gone to school, where about 2,000 children go. In the afternoon at about 2 P.M. a rumor about a fire spread through the school and the children started to flee from all the rooms. It caused such a terrible crush on the steps that the staircase broke and caused almost all the children to fall down sixty feet to the stone floor. Dingenes, however, was still in the school, and not knowing what to do, he jumped from a second-floor window and was caught by a fireman.

The cause of the accident is as follows: to understand this you must know that the children are taught almost exclusively by ladies. One of them fainted and that scared the children in her room so badly that they all started screaming. That made the other children think that the school was on fire. This small matter was the whole cause of this terrible accident. There were about fifty deaths and about an equal number of injuries.[1]

You asked about the Wernaars—they are doing extremely well. They earn a good living and they are happy. You probably know that Huurling's wife died. Last week he remarried a Dutch girl. . . . You asked about the religious education of our children. Every Sunday they get educated in religion twice—but, regrettably, not in Lutheran religion. All the Lutheran churches are German.

* * *

We also congratulate our daughter Neeltje on her birthday with the hope that she will always be obedient to her grandparents and always grow in goodness and virtue.

* * *

For your birthday, dear Father, I am sending a pair of boots, a kind that you have probably never seen in Zierikzee. Not a stitch has been sewn on the bottom, but it has been made entirely with wooden pins. And for you, dear Mother, we send an American clock.

Dear parents, our only wish is to have our dear child here and in the coming year there will be a good chance to realize this. You should know that Hein Koevoets is coming to Zierikzee to marry a daughter of Mr.

Vreemans. They are most willing to take Neeltje back with them. Please write to tell us what you think about this. If you agree, I will give him the money for Neeltje's voyage. This is as good as if I came myself to take her back. We will not be happy until we have our child in our midst.

I have a little parcel that I would like you to send on for me. I am planning [with the man who will receive it] to make an agreement to have him make a number of boots. It would be a big advantage if he could make them for a good price. If this works out I hope to pay you back soon.

With this I close, and if I have forgotten anything first mate Bartels will be able to tell you more.

Your loving children.

1. See *New York Times*, November 21, 26, 1851, for a detailed corroboration of this event.

November 23, 1852

Greetings,

Concerning the children—Dingenes is beginning to read well; he goes to school every day, and on Sundays he receives religious lessons in a school. He speaks Dutch very poorly. And what is more, I think that he would lose the language entirely if he lived among the Americans for three months. He would like to write a few lines to you but you could not read the English. If he were to come to Zierikzee you would find it difficult to understand his Dutch.

Antje was with her aunt for the whole summer in Newark and is there again. She is growing well and is a nice young lady. Her aunt is well pleased with her. Our little Jantje is now fourteen months old and a dear little mite. Always sweet, and sometimes she can play for two hours at a time on the floor of our shop.

*   *   *

I had plans to come and get Neeltje from Zierikzee myself and I had set some money aside for that purpose in a bank here. In April, however, the bank went bankrupt and I lost all of the money. If I had not had boots and shoes in my shop and lots of work this summer I would not have made it. But now I am optimistic that I will soon be back to normal.

*   *   *

I shall do my best to pay you 50 guilders each year until my debt has been paid. I shall send it on about June so that it will be there in July. I shall let you know at which office you can receive it. I cannot write more at this time but Koevoets will tell you everything else.

* * *

I end this letter calling ourselves C. Mannee and J. C. van der Veeke

November 3, 1853

[Greetings]

On two occasions now I have had a lawyer at my door trying to collect 200 guilders for Mr. LeSage ten Broek. If you are paying him off on a yearly basis, they should not be bothering me here. Please send me proof that you have paid him off and then I will send repayment to you directly. I cannot understand why they have to bother me here when you have paid them off. If Mr. ten Broek thinks that he can force me to do something here, he is totally wrong. The first time I received his lawyer kindly, but the second time I showed him the door. I do not think that he will come back if I have proof from you that you have paid.

My business grows from day to day. At the moment I have six men working for me and it is so busy these days that I could use four more. These people are all boarding with me, so you can imagine how busy it is in my household if one wants to keep everything going. We have a maid now who has to earn 12.50 guilders per month [$5.00] plus board. And she will not do just any work either. When I say, "You have to clean the house," I still have to whitewash the walls and my wife has to clean the windows because the maid will not do these things.

You should not imagine that what we earn here is all profit. When you consider that I pay 50 guilders [$20.00] monthly in house rent and 120 guilders [$48.00] for six men [$8.00 each per month], 12.50 guilders [$5.00] for the maid, and 6 guilders [$2.40] for light. So we have to earn quite a bit every month [$75.40] to pay for all of that. And with that, we have twelve persons at our table every day who must be served good food. Don't imagine that they are contented with potatoes and meat. There must be more than that; otherwise you lose your help immediately because there is work in abundance to be done in the city.

If we could have our child here, she would be a great help to her mother. She has to work hard every day, and sometimes she sews for me in the shoe shop half the night. I cannot understand how you can keep our child away from her happiness. You have let so many good opportunities for her travel go by. It's almost as if you want to force me to come over for her. To do so could jeopardize my whole living and I can't believe you would ask me to risk my whole fortune. You see, my business grows from year to year and by the time I would be able to pay for my travel the business would probably be so large that I could not leave it. So, dear parents, do not pass up any further opportunities to let her come to America.

She can still find happiness here, and what will become of her if it pleases God to take you to Himself? Perhaps she will then be left to roam around like an abandoned child. Parents, please let her come and we will be thankful forever. The children ask their mother, "Whenever is Neeltje coming?"

When Visser arrived in New York, Dingenes went there [to the docks] and looked in a boardinghouse expecting to meet Neeltje. Antje was also sure that Neeltje would be with Visser. But their hopes were deceived when they did not see their sister among all the people.

Dingenes and Antje still go to school and behave well. Dingenes would like to write a few sentences but he says, "Grandfather cannot read it anyway." As for little Jantje, she is growing well and is a very sweet little girl. In proportion to size she is as fat as Grandmother. When she falls down she has trouble standing again.

You wrote that you would like to hear something about America, but my business does not allow the time. I am already working before daylight and that goes on until 10 or 11 in the evening. I can hardly take time to go out on business. But, whenever I have time I will write you a whole letter about America.

I would have liked to send a pair of boots and a pair of shoes for Neeltje, but I do not know her size. Please send me the length of her foot and I'll send them next time.

Please write me immediately by mail and enclose the proof that you have paid and then I shall send the money right away.

Your faithful and always loving children,
C. Mannee and J. van der Veeke

Cornelis Mannee to Dingenes van der Veeke
[Suffolk, New York,] to Zierikzee, Zeeland
[1856]

Dear parents,

The reason why we waited so long in writing is that you wrote us again about our duty to pay you back, but as God is our witness, we were not in a position to meet our obligations. We have had years of grief over this matter and not a day has gone by when we did not talk about it.

My shoemaker's business had a good yield, but the costs were about equal to the income. And because New York City was not a good place for our children, we sold the business and bought an oil-distilling business for 1,200 guilders [about $500.00]. We now live twenty hours from New York City and closer to the sea. This oil product is not known in Holland. It is a fruit growing wild in the forests here. Black people, called Negroes here, pick them for us. The oil I sell in New York for 10 guilders [$4.00] per pound, and that gives me a better yield than repairing shoes.[1] . . . I am also thinking about starting a distillery here this winter. One cannot buy gin here and we are hoping for success in this.

We always hope to come back to Zierikzee once. Our children would love to see you. Dingenes is a big shot here and he keeps our books. He goes hunting and fishing. He talks often about you and would like to go boating with Grandfather sometime. Liedje, our youngest, is three years old. It is difficult for me to write about this, but as you know, we lost two children in New York.

With this letter we also congratulate our child on her birthday and hope that God will give her many more years. Love your grandparents and do what is right, but love God above all. Also, love your parents. Weep no more when we ask that you be brought to us. But know that she who brought you into the world with so much pain cries—the one whose blood you drank and whose flesh you ate.

I do not know what else to write. Farewell, dear parents and child, live happily.

We are your loving children,
C. Mannee

---

1. Mannee was probably processing bayberries for oil to scent candles. That process required about two bushels of berries to gain a pound of oil.

Jacoba van der Veeke Manee to Neeltje and her husband
Newark, New Jersey, to Zierikzee, Zeeland
May 15, 1872

Dear son and daughter,

It was a great joy to receive your letter and learn that you are married and doing well.

For my part, I am making my own living, but I have to work very hard. I have experienced a lot during my time in America. Your brother Dingenes died during the war, and that was a terrible time for us. Your father was so badly hit by it that he died two years later. Also two other children died in America and so I was left with four children. Of these

Antje is the oldest [twenty-seven]. She was married for fifteen months when her husband died and left her with a child of three months. Then she came to live with me, but she married again and now she has two children. Three of your sisters are not yet married. Two live at home with me, and one is a housemaid.

I learned with deep sadness that my sister Tannetje died and that her husband remarried. I hope that the Lord gave Tannetje's children a good mother. Please give my kind regards to my sister Jasje and her husband. Ask her, when you write me, to enclose a small letter to me along with yours.

Yes, children, I have experienced many hardships in America and if your Uncle and Aunt Luyk had not helped me I would not have known what to do. They helped us so much and they were always ready to help. Receive heartfelt greetings from Uncle and Aunt Luyk. They are doing very well.

Also receive greetings from all your sisters who would all love to see you. But that is not possible. Dear children, as far as I am concerned, I do not think that I will ever see my father and mother again, and as for your sisters—I have to leave that in God's hands. What He has in mind for your sisters we cannot know.

Dear children, please write us as soon as possible because we are very anxious to receive another letter from you. After embracing you in spirit we remain,

Your loving mother and sisters,
J. van der Veeke

My address is
  Mrs. C. Mannee
  186 Walnut Street
  Newark, New Jersey
  North America

Jacoba van der Veeke Mannee, to Son-in-law
Newark, New Jersey, to Zierikzee, Zeeland
April 13, 1873

Dear son,

It is with the greatest sadness that I received both of your letters and learned from them that Neeltje [thirty-five in 1873] has died. It made me so ill that I could not write until now. Don't think that I have forgotten my child. The reason I left her behind was that I did not want to sadden my mother even more by taking Neeltje away in 1847 because

Neeltje had been raised by my mother and lived with her. The good Lord only knows how many tears I have shed over this matter.

Dear son, I hope that the Lord will help you in the circumstances in which you find yourself. From your letter I can see that Neeltje suffered much. I hope that the good Lord has her dear soul. We have to resign ourselves to His good will.

*   *   *

Dear son, you wrote asking if I did not have more daughters like your lovely Neeltje. You wished that one of them could come to Zierikzee. That will probably never occur because, in the first place, my oldest [Jantje] is married and has two children. And I think that my other daughters [Julia, 22; Elizabeth, 20; and Cornelia, 15][1] will not be staying with me much longer. The youngest, picture enclosed, is only fifteen years old. The other picture is of myself. In the future I shall send pictures of the other children. As far as I am concerned, I shall probably never return to Zierikzee. We have bought a plot here in the cemetery where my dear husband and children are buried. And there I want to be buried too.

Dear son, I am happy that you had such a good wife in my daughter and I hope that the dear Lord will soon give you a wife who will be as good for you as my daughter Neeltje was. There is no further news, but I send you my heartfelt thanks for sending the photographs and the lock of my dear daughter Neeltje's hair.

[Closing]

P.S. Many greetings for friends and acquaintances and especially to your brother Cornelis, who worked so long for brother Luyk.

   1. Julia = Juliana; Elizabeth-Liedje; Cornelia, born 1858.

16   *Jan George Zahn*

In 1856 the twenty-four-year-old Jan George Zahn traveled from Amsterdam as a rather wealthy first-class-cabin passenger. He wrote vibrantly of his ocean voyage and about his encounters with New York's dockside swindlers. But Zahn's inland destination, the Mississippi River

These letters were donated by F. P. Jantzen, 1985, and first translated by Egbert Post. The original letters were transcribed in the Netherlands.

city, Muscatine, Iowa, also provided a wide range of sights and social activities to engage his reportorial skills. Muscatine had been settled in 1833 and incorporated in 1851, but it was still a rough frontier community when Zahn arrived there.[1] His fresh and naive commentary, though frequently acerbic, provides engaging snapshots of Muscatine's people and customs. Despite his many misgivings, three months after his arrival, Zahn declared, "Yes, I live a royal life, and the brightness of the prospects adds more and more to my happiness."

Jan's letters were intended for circulation among his seven siblings who lived in or near Amsterdam. His oldest sister, "Cateau" or Catharina, married Ferdinand Jantzen and most of the correspondence was directed to their Amsterdam residence. Loneliness and hunger for news fueled much of Zahn's writing and he complained eloquently about the lack of mail from his family in Holland. His parents died before his immigration and it is apparent that Jan was closely associated with the Jantzen family, including the parents of his brother-in-law, Ferdinand Jantzen. But after Jan married Wilhelmina de Heus, in [March] 1857, and their daughter, Eliza, was born, August 6, 1858, his correspondence quickly diminished and then stopped altogether. Consequently, after 1858 only a combination of scattered evidence and informed speculation is available to trace his activities. Zahn's wife "Mina" died in 1861, and he enlisted in the Union army that same year. Because his name does not appear on the Civil War casualty lists, a genealogist speculates that Zahn joined the vast number of veterans who migrated westward. That choice seems to be consistent with his character, but the abrupt termination of his voluble correspondence, even though wartime experiences must have given him much to report, suggests that he probably died shortly after enlisting.[2]

Though spanning only three years the correspondence contains clear indications of cultural adaptation. Early on, Jan tried hard to entice his brothers away from Holland with highly optimistic views of life in Muscatine. By 1857 he was offering a more cautious assessment of their prospects for success. His own tobacco business had suffered losses, and a corroborating report from the wife of his partner, T. H. Stemerdink, indicates that heavy indebtedness caused the dissolution of the partnership. Jan may have continued the business independently for a short time, but it was certainly sold or disbanded by the time of his military enlistment. His efforts to import cigars from Holland were thwarted early in

[1] Nathan H. Parker, *Iowa as It Is in 1855* (Chicago: Keen and Lee, 1855), pp. 161–63.
[2] F. P. Jantzen to H. J. Brinks, June 2, 1992, Immigrant Letter Collection. Jantzen, the donor of these letters and the Zahn family historian, has provided the details of J. G. Zahn's family history.

Amsterdam city canal, De Lindengracht, filled in by 1900. Courtesy of the Calvin College Library Archives, photo collection.

1857, and by the fall of that year he complained that tobacco prices in St. Louis had doubled. And of course, after 1861 the Civil War interrupted the production and marketing of tobacco.

Zahn's relationship with his business partner suggests what is readily evident in his letters—Jan had a way with words. Or as Stemerdink's wife wrote, "That Zahn, who is a real sweet-talker, deceived my husband very much." Writing in 1865 and amid difficulties that she attributed to the failure of the tobacco shop, Johanna Stemerdink's assessment may be inaccurate. But her *ex parte* account of events from 1856 to 1858 provides solid proof of Zahn's presence in Muscatine. Some of his writing is so stereotypical of European views of crass American behavior that the veracity of the correspondence could, without corroborating evidence, be questioned.

Coming from Amsterdam, the cultural showpiece of the Netherlands, to Muscatine, which depended on forest products for most of its wealth in the 1850s, certainly provided Zahn with easy opportunities for stark comparisons. He exploited them almost greedily.

Jan George Zahn to [Ferdinand Jantzen] Brothers and Sisters
Muscatine, Iowa, to Amsterdam
August 26, 1856

Dear brothers and sisters,

Finally I have the leisure to tell you about the place of my destination, which, by God's grace, I reached on the ninth of August in good health. I am now located, as all Hollanders think of it, in the promised land. I also thought of it that way when I was in your midst, but it is not to be considered that way. Be that as it may, I am now here, and on this little boat, I must ride along.

I will tell you all about the conditions here in America, but I will start at the beginning—when on June 9, at 4:00 A.M., I left Hellevoetsluis on the steamboat which brought us to the North Sea. When the ship began to rock and roll terribly I became quickly aware that we were at sea.

The island of Walcheren was the last bit of the Netherlands that we could see. And when I finally lost sight of it, I can tell you that it broke my heart. If possible I would have flown back to Amsterdam. You cannot imagine what an impression leaving the fatherland made on me—to leave the place where I had experienced weal and woe, to leave it forever and probably never to see my relatives again. But I told myself to stop thinking about that because a wonderful future awaited me.

An hour after we were at sea many people became seasick—so sick that it was awful to witness. I was fortunate in that respect and did not become sick until we were four days at sea and then I did not throw up. I had no appetite for two days and could not smoke, but that was all. The captain said to me, "Zahn, you are a tough one."

By noon we were on the open sea and we were on it so long that I thought we would never leave it. We had contrary winds day and night. But if you were to ask me how I liked being at sea, I would admit that sea life agreed with me very well. Yes, it would be no punishment if I were forced to spend my whole life at sea. That is the reason why the captain, though a tough man, was friendly and courteous to me. I tell you that I became so attached to him that I was sorry to bid him farewell in New York. He frequently said to me, "Zahn, speak up if you want something. You can get anything you want from me." Three times he urged and almost insisted that I go with him to his home when we arrived in New York. He lived near Boston where he said he had a large farm. And since this was to be his last voyage he said I could go with him. He helped me make enough progress in English so that I could understand what was said to me and make myself understood.

We had one bad storm and then there was real trouble. All the sails were taken down and the distress sail was raised. The waves were as high as houses and often three or four waves dashed across the deck at once. Anyone unfortunate enough to be caught by such a wave would have a hard time. Luckily I was struck by such a wave only once and then I was knocked to the deck, dizzy and soaked, of course. An experience like that puts you on your guard. In good weather it was wonderful at sea, especially in the evening. We had a lot of mist and it was so heavy that at times it was impossible to tell if anyone was walking on the other side of the ship. We also had two bad thunderstorms.

The food was good and plentiful. At first everything seemed so strange. I heard only English. During the first days I could not carry on a conversation, but later I could talk as much as I wished. In short, I got along on the ship very well and I will never forget the captain—a fine man.

Finally the day approached when we first sighted land, on the evening of July the 27th. But it was not a pleasant experience for me. I thought why, oh why did I go so far away from home. If I could fly I would certainly have flown home.

*   *   *

The sea became smaller and smaller until at midnight we reached the East River and then we cast out the anchor. But it was hoisted the next morning . . . and at 9:30 we neared the city. People never find anything more pleasant, delightful, beautiful, and glorious (I can think of no more words to express it accurately) than entering New York. The setting of the city as one views it from the river is beyond human comprehension. At 10:30 we docked at the city.

Another boat came alongside to take on the passengers and bring them to the immigration house. Cabin [first-class] passengers [like Zahn] could not go there. They had to take care of themselves. (The immigration house is an institution established three years ago by right-minded Americans who could no longer condone the swindling and atrocities that were inflicted upon strangers.)[1] People are brought there by boat and then the organization sees to it that the stranger reaches his destination without the danger of being swindled. Passengers may remain in that building [Castle Garden] as long as they please, and they can eat, drink, and stay there for no more than twenty-five cents [per day]. That is all that they need to pay! Cabin passengers may not apply to stay there because they are told that they are able to take care of their own expenses.

By three o'clock P.M. the ship was unloaded—passengers, crew, stewards, and all others received their discharge. The captain, the pilots, and I were the only ones still on board. The captain asked me if I would remain on board because he had to go into the city and he did not trust the pilots to be the only ones on board. [He feared] thieves and cheats as many Americans are—something never heard of in Holland.

When the captain returned in the evening I asked him if I could have my trunk the next morning. He answered, "My good friend, it will be about nine days before I can help you. In Rotterdam the trunks were placed in the category of merchandise and so it is all sealed. I'm sorry," he said, "but that is the way it is. When they loaded the ship I did not pay attention to where your trunks were placed." So I thought, now what must I do. If I go to a hotel that will be expensive. Then I thought, I will ask the captain if I can sleep on board at night. He agreed. But then I became restless and the next morning I said impatiently, I must and will have my trunks. Then he said, "If you can get an official to break the seal it will be all right with me." I wondered how to go about that and went from ship to ship until I finally persuaded someone who agreed to do what I requested. The trunks were recovered and placed on the deck.

Then I ran into real trouble. They had to be opened and inspected to see if they contained anything subject to duty. It was of no avail to say that the things were gifts. The trunks had to be taken to the import duty office and everything was removed from the trunks piece by piece. Then everything was neatly repacked. Then I asked how much of value I had with me. Now, listen! I had tobacco and cigars valued at more than two hundred guilders (I reported ninety-five guilders), some fancy articles plus the items I carried from the De Heus family. I also had to pay for the clothing (eighty-five guilders). My shirts alone were more than forty-five guilders. After that they made out a paper and I had to take it to another office on the following morning. There another paper was made out and in the end I had to pay fifty dollars. With all of this they delayed me for eight days and when it was completed I was allowed to have my trunks. Immediately I found someone to take them to the baggage room of the railroad. For that I hired a Negro who was the best person I have thus far met in all of New York. The Americans are real swindlers and rascals.

At twelve o'clock the next day I left by train with my trunk from the ship and went right through from New York City to Troy. I spent one night there and left again the next morning at 10:45 A.M. taking the train to Muscatine, where I arrived in three and one-quarter days.

But, hold on! I don't want to leap too far ahead. . . . On the morning that I left, after purchasing a first-class train ticket for twenty-six dollars,

I also had my trunk taken from the ship to the train by horse and wagon. I was jostled through the city in a terrifying manner. I was trembling and shuddering when I finally arrived—not at the train but at a boat. "No! No!" I shouted, "I told you to go to the railroad, not to the ship. Ride on or I will not pay you." With a violent curse the man answered, "I will throw you from the wagon and ride off with your trunk if you do not pay me." Do you think I would allow myself to be cheated? Not by any American. But in a short time I was surrounded by about thirty men, and also the chef from the ship who told me I was in the right place but that I had to go on the boat before I could board the train. I was persuaded and had my trunk unloaded. I gave the driver his money and he drove off.

Now listen to the dirty tricks—things you can't guard against. My trunk was placed on the ship and I was waiting for the ship to leave . . . and fifteen minutes before leaving the chef said to me, "Friend, don't you know that you are in the wrong place?" Then he laughed heartily. I would have choked him if I had been there alone with him. But there were so many rascals and pickpockets around that I had to watch myself and also keep one eye on my trunk. Then I dashed onto the ship and dragged my trunk back to shore. Fortunately I found another wagon, but then the chef followed me and interrupted me when I was bargaining with the driver. The chef called out to him, "John! You know the charge from here to the railroad is two dollars." "Go to hell," I answered, "I can get there for fifty cents." Then the chef took my trunk and threw it into the middle of the street. By that time it was 11:45 A.M. and the train was to leave at noon. I wondered what I should do. I had already been in New York for nine days and now I had to leave. I had the trunk reloaded and said, "Don't worry, you will get your money, but if the train has left you will not be paid."

Then he whipped his horses and again I sat trembling as badly as you can imagine. (Now you must not think of New York streets as being paved.) There are only three paved streets in New York and in some places the bricks are laid two and three high [curbs?]. Finally I reached the railroad but could not see or hear because of all the commotion. You can't imagine what difficulty I had taking care of my trunk. Finally the train began to move—passing through the city for about half an hour. And once outside of the city I could not imagine what was happening to me. At unprecedented and unbelievable speed I sat shuddering as we passed through tunnels, woods, and alongside mountains. I could not see their tops and I became dizzy at times from looking at the scenery. At one time we were in utter darkness for a half hour. We passed cliffs of sheer rock and sometimes rocks bounced against the train due to all the noise and vibration.

When we came to Niagara Falls the train was fourteen hundred feet above sea level which was a scary sight. Now and then, as in the Netherlands, the train stopped to load and unload. But I remained seated and thought, the next time the train stops I will get out for a change and ask if it is true that we do not have to transfer before Chicago. Then I received the answer, "You should have changed at the last station. Now you have traveled south and you should have gone west." It was 4:45 P.M. when this happened so I had to spend the night there. I lodged in a German hotel called the Tray. I remained there until 10:45 the next morning and then took the train again. I firmly resolved that this would not happen to me again. After that I had to transfer four times and I was on a boat two times. My route was from New York to Buffalo, from Buffalo to Suspension Bridge, from there to Detroit, from there to Chicago, from there to Rock Island, and from there to Muscatine. It was a load off of my heart when I surrendered my last ticket. Although many people do not even think of sleeping on a train, I spent my nights quite comfortably. The warning was clear, "Watch out for the numerous pickpockets." I had a bad experience with a pickpocket in Chicago. There are no people in Chicago but only the dregs from hell. I was cheated out of 12.5 cents in Chicago, two dollars in New York, and 12.5 cents out here. I have to admit that I came out well. Not only I, but others also say that. When you hear how the De Heus family was cheated, you know how terrible it can be.

I finally arrived in Muscatine and found my boardinghouse after a long search. But I was received in a hearty and friendly manner which left nothing to be desired. But I also noticed—and the people corroborated this—that the situation here is not always as it is described to us in the Netherlands. These people admitted that they were better off in Holland. Some succeed very well, but others do not.

As you can see I have roamed about a good deal since coming here. Next week I will have a steady job—at the cigar store of Wynand de Heus, where I will earn five dollars per week. I will be boarding with English people.

And now, dear brothers and sisters, I will close, not knowing how well I have succeeded in writing this to you. But if I were to write all about how things are here you would say, "Just come back soon." Do not blame me for not writing until four weeks after coming here.

[Closing]

P.S. Do answer soon. Please. I am waiting eagerly. Believe me, I have not yet had a happy moment here in America. If it must always be like this for me I will certainly return. My trunks all arrived in good condition. Heaven only knows how I am to get over this. Oh, it would be

Muscatine, Iowa, river and skyline. Courtesy of the State Historical Society of Iowa—Des Moines.

worth anything if I could just talk to one or all of you sometime. My advice to everyone is, "Be satisfied to remain in Holland."

* * *

Cateau [his sister Catharina], I wish you could be in my place for just one moment. In the midst of all this I have not lost courage, and I will make the best of it.

My address is:
Mr. J. G. Zahn
Muscatine, Iowa

1. The Castle Garden terminal for immigrants opened in 1855.

November 13, 1856

Dear brothers and sisters,

I have been waiting a long time for an answer to my first letter. And now I am worried that not only my first but also my second letter did not reach you.

* * *

[As in my second letter] I am asking if you will be so kind as to send me the money still banked in my name as soon as possible. It amounts to at

least one hundred and twenty guilders, which I need because I and another person have taken over the tobacco business of friend De Heus. It
should be a profitable affair as we can expect to take in about thirty
guilders each day with half of that [i.e., six dollars] profit.

This is how you should go about it: go to the bank and tell them that
I wish to draw out all the money, and that they should send me a check.
They will send the money to New York, and when I receive the check,
I will take it to one of the banks in Muscatine. . . . Don't let the grass
grow under this, because the sooner I am paid off the better.

*　　*　　*

I don't have the time to tell you a great deal of news. You cannot
imagine how Americans think about time. They want an hour's work in
one minute. You hear all the time, "get going, get going." But still, I
want to add a short letter with this. I have been well and healthy all the
time. I have a good life and lack nothing at present. I have never had a
life like this. Yes, every fear that once appeared so dark has vanished.
My joy increases daily.

If you could see me now you would say, "He is no longer the same
person he was five months ago." I have become so heavyset . . . that I
have sold almost all my clothes. . . . But I earn *good money* and, fortunately
can buy new clothes.

I have become a real American in every way. The language is beginning to improve quite well. But I never had much trouble with
that.

I have become very friendly with the De Heus family and come and
go there as I please. I feel entirely at home with them and they treat
me like a brother, doing all that they can for me. I'm there every Sunday from 2:00 until 9:00 P.M. and I frequently walk over there in the
evening. They live some distance outside of town between hills, because Muscatine is very hilly. I walk over there with a large lantern in
my hand.

I have purchased a fine American hunting dog and I go hunting with
a double-barreled gun. I'm going out hunting again tomorrow to a place
about fourteen miles away. Yes, it's too far to walk so we will use a horse
and buggy. Yes, I live a royal life, and the brightness of the prospects
adds more and more to my happiness. Those prospects involve a very
fine well-educated dark young woman—dark, that is, with black hair and
a dark complexion. And there is every chance that I will persuade her to
marry me. But do not say anything about this to the De Heus family in
Amsterdam.

My partner and I get along well. He is married and lives about one-
half mile from the store. I live above the store in a neat room that I have

furnished in a completely American style—the furniture and everything is completely different from the things in Holland. I have lived in five boardinghouses here already. At present I am boarding temporarily with a Hollander. I will be leaving that place tomorrow and then will board with the most prominent family in Muscatine. They are Americans. I will pay three dollars for meals.

I am well rid of my milliner's wares. I placed some of them on display and all six of them were sold. The money is in my pocket. Those large gloves also sold and I made seventy-five cents on each pair. The wool is also gone.

*   *   *

Yes, my brothers and sisters, I am very thankful for my situation. Only God can grant such a happy life. He alone. He gives all this to me in mercy. Not a day passes when I do not thank Him for His help and faithful love.

*   *   *

If the aged Mr. and Mrs. Jantzen could write me a few lines that would make me very happy. . . . How many times did I not play chess with you last year. . . . when you talk to the De Heus family, extend warm greetings to them from their family and from me. Tell them that, as hoped, things are going well.

[Closing]

November 17, 1856

Dear brothers and sisters,

I cannot tell you how much it pleased me when I went to the post office and found a letter from Holland lying there for me. I was also pleased to note that you are all well and that you continue to do as well as you desire with the exception of brother Willem.

And now, about other matters. First, I was surprised that you could not get the interest and even more that you could not get my money because, as you wrote, my power of attorney which Mr. Van den Berg, the notary at the Hague, made out for me . . . was not in order. I am sure I asked him whether this power of attorney covered everything. Whereupon he answered, "Yes." Did I have to list everything from A to Z? I conclude that he said "yes" without considering the matter carefully. Would you do me the favor of calling this to his attention. It can't be that I wrote for the money too soon. Certainly not.

Well, I have thought this over and have begun to do something about it myself. I hope it will turn out all right because I am pressed for time. This is what I have done. That same afternoon [when the letter arrived] I went to a lawyer here in Muscatine and explained the matter to him. He told me a great deal and gave me some advice. But it did not satisfy me so I went to one of the local banks and explained the situation. I have followed their advice.

They gave me three bills of exchange which I was to make out in your name and as you see this was done. Be so kind as to take this bill of exchange to the Netherlands bank in Amsterdam to receive the money there. You will receive the second bill of exchange and the third one the following week in case the second one is lost. . . . You will find the bill of exchange in *this* letter.

You must have received two letters in succession from me—those in which I wrote for the money. Ferdinand did not write anything about that. If you get my money deduct one hundred and twenty-five guilders and send it to the elderly Mr. Jantzen in Amsterdam. He knows what to do with it. But please, do not forget that. And because you have had to pay so much postage on my business, feel free to deduct the postage from the money you receive and also some for all of your trouble. I would send the postage from here, but that cannot be done. Do you understand now? Everything?

And now, another matter. It is difficult to answer all your questions because I am in a hurry to get this letter on its way. But let me begin by congratulating sister Roberdina on her marriage. I hope everything will go well for *both* of you and that you will always understand each other, for where there is no love things never go right. May God bless you in your new life.

*   *   *

I also congratulate Willem and sister Chris on the birth of a child. May heaven grant that she will grow up soon and give you much joy in the years to come. Kiss little Chrisje for me and also little Willem, that little angel. How clearly I can still see him lying in that cradle when I left you that morning to undertake this great journey. I was so sorry to learn that you were the only ones [mentioned in the letter] who could not rejoice in your situation—and that you could foresee only difficulties. Keep up your courage Willem. Much can happen in a year's time. I have experienced that myself. Who knows, you might be here yourself next year. I mean that. If I continue to be as successful as I am now, I will pay the travel expense of you, your wife, and children. Possibly I could come to get you.

Sister Anna, I also congratulate you on your engagement—and with a

brother of Ferdinand [Jantzen]. As far as I know he is a fine person—
and one with whose parents you are acquainted—yes, and with the entire
family. I rejoice with you that you have reached this point with someone.
Oh, if only I were fortunate enough to be able to write that I am engaged
now. But I can tell you this, there is every possibility that you will learn
something about it in my next letter. I have a fine—very fine—and good-
natured girl in mind. May this materialize! I am not giving you her name
yet. And for the time being I certainly do not want old Mr. Jantzen to
say anything about this to the De Heus family. Don't mention it. I beg
you.

Sister Cateau, I wish you a speedy delivery. Perhaps by the time you
receive this you will have given birth to your child.

* * *

Sister Alida, I'm happy you are so well satisfied [with your teaching
apprenticeship] at Alphen. Study well and do your best. If I ever return
to Holland with a wife and children, they will attend your school.

* * *

Brother Gerhard, what happened at Mr. Kosten's to make you leave
so suddenly? Tell me about that. How are you doing in Zutphen?[1] That
is a beautiful area, isn't it? If you are not satisfied there, just come to
America. I will help you. The trip is not as bad as you may think it is.
But if you decide to undertake it, be careful and alert. Don't think about
it too long—come. You are young and strong. With God's help I have
survived. Come in the spring, Gerhard. I advise it strongly. This is a
good place for everyone and there is still room for you in America.
Thousands of parcels of land, larger than all of Europe, are still unoccupied. You will not stub your big feet on the curbstones here because
people have not heard of pavement here. And you won't develop blisters
from walking. Gerhard, do you still remember our little evening with
wine on the last Sunday I was in Holland?

* * *

Now some miscellaneous items. There has been snow on the ground
here for eight days already. We have had light frost every day. The
winter evenings are much shorter here. It gets dark at five o'clock. December 21 is the shortest day here. In Holland it gets dark gradually,
but here it is dark suddenly.[2] That seemed strange to me at first but now
I am used to it. In the summer we have excessive heat. There is a great
deal of wildlife here—bedbugs by the millions, mosquitoes, and all kinds

of animals that are strange to Holland. Nature is also very different. At noon here [during the winter] it is like 7:30 in the evening in Holland.

They have an entirely different kind of horse and wagon here and no carriage at all. The Americans[3] are large of stature, long necked, with a prominent Adam's apple. They are lean, pale because of the heat, lively, fiery-eyed, and mostly rascals and cheats. Black people have thick red lips, curly hair, and are small of stature but very strong.

There are no birds here except canaries [probably goldfinches] and no sparrows. In a rainstorm you must picture the Americans wearing their boots over their trousers. Sometimes the boots get stuck in the mud. Our city is growing.

People here eat not with a fork but with a knife, which is very easy once you get used to it.

Turf [peat] is unknown here. People burn only wood, and no coal either. Steam engines are also fired with wood. There are no vegetables here—only a few turnips and some apples. Pella[4] is a Dutch colony. There, they grow a few vegetables and potatoes. Here people eat only pork and bread—sometimes beef.

There are hundreds of religious denominations here. There are many sick people here, especially among the Dutch and the Germans—mostly from the bloody flux and fevers [dysentery]. I also had the diarrhea but I'm over it. I did not have the bloody flux. That is all that I have had so far. Yes, I am exceptionally fortunate, and I must admit that I have received God's help in abundant measure. I am always in good spirits from the moment I get up until I go to bed. I lack nothing, have good food, good drink, enough money, good health, and strength. What more could I ask?

It is my wish that you may all get along as well as I have. Pray sincerely to God without ceasing that you will receive earthly as well as spiritual blessings. Do that and it will be well with you and, above all, resist sin and the temptations of the world. Do that with all that is in your power. God can and will hear and bless you abundantly. That is what I have experienced.

[Closing missing]

1. One of the old Hanseatic League cities located on the IJssel River in Gelderland.
2. Probably an impression caused by the sun's dropping behind forested hills which do not exist in Amsterdam.
3. Generally "American" can be interchanged with "Yankee" or "English."
4. Pella, Iowa, a Dutch settlement founded in 1847 by the Reverend Hendrik P. Scholte.

December 17, 1856

Dear brothers and sisters and esteemed Mr. and Mrs. Jantzen,[1]

I can imagine hearing you say "Well, what do you know. Another letter from Jan. He writes me one letter after another without waiting for an answer." Well, what can I say. I've not changed. When I have something on my mind I have to take care of it.

I discovered (brother Gysbert) that the bill of exchange I sent to you would be useless, so I thought I would write and tell you before you had gone through a lot of trouble for me. A number of people with whom I consulted here told me it would be useless. Then I spoke to an elderly Jew who frequently comes into our store. I did not know that this chap was so shrewd. He told me that I should have a power of attorney made out by the Dutch consul in St. Louis, about two hundred miles from here. Without that, he said, I would not get one cent. This, he said was the surest way. This seemed very understandable and acceptable to me, so now I have had an entirely new power of attorney made up. Thereupon I wrote to the Dutch consul asking him courteously to prepare a power of attorney and, of course, I explained the whole matter to him. He did that and I received it from him this morning with instructions to have it signed by a lawyer and two witnesses. As soon as I have done this I am instructed to send the power of attorney to you, Gysbert, by way of St. Louis. You may expect it, then, any day now. When you receive the power of attorney please take care of the matter and then be *very very careful* when you send the money. You know how Americans are— swindlers, pickpockets, etc., etc. But not all of them. Some are also good and honest. And yes, feel free to deduct all the postage and also the one hundred and twenty-five guilders for the De Heus family. Do not forget that. Now I trust that everything will work out satisfactorily.

Thank God everything has gone as well as I could wish until now. I have everything I need and see daily progress in my business. The De Heus family remain the same. You should not think that my contact with this family is just as it was in Amsterdam. No. They treat me like a brother. I go there whenever I wish. I keep my possessions in their home, except for the few things I need in my room. We are so close to each other that I can't imagine that they are not my family. We do business together. So you need not ask if I go there frequently.

I have again changed boardinghouses—this time to one of the most prominent families in Muscatine. These people wallow in money. Naturally, they are Americans but not blacks. You cannot imagine how pompously things are carried on here.

My partner is a fine fellow.

As for the winter here—if you were to imagine the most severe and biting cold, you would only imagine half of what it is. Oh! Oh! The winter here is something. For three days it froze so hard that the Mississippi River was not only covered with ice, but wagons crossed it loaded with wood. The Mississippi is on average a half mile wide in Muscatine and it flows through the whole country. For several days the snow has been four feet deep. Here people say this is only the beginning of winter—something like a light frost in Holland. It is a difficult task to walk to the De Heus family. They live amid the hills a quarter mile outside the city. When I wish to go there I must go over a hill that rises four hundred feet above the city. When I reach the top, believe me, I am tired. In addition I have to be on my guard against holes and dips that are invisible under the snow. Last Sunday, I tell you, I thought I would die going there. Several people here have had frozen ears, hands, and noses. There is no cure for that and they must be removed. Last winter Wynand de [Heus] had a finger removed. Several people have frozen to death.

As far as wild animals go, fortunately there are very few in Iowa. There are some bears, which appear only when there is snow on the ground. Last winter fourteen were caught here in one day, but that was an exceptionally large number. One hundred and forty men rode out on horses with the necessary gunpowder, shot, and lances to get them. Wynand was also with the hunters.

*   *   *

Three weeks ago we started the carpentry work here. The building has an entirely new front. It is now the best looking tobacco shop in the entire city. The painter is working on the inside but the rest is all finished.

*   *   *

The entire front of the building was taken off, and we had a temporary store in the baggage room. But because of that and the cold I developed diarrhea, which lasted four days. I am well again except that I lost some weight. I have become so heavy that I surely outdo Uncle Gysbert. People around here call me "that fat Dutchman." If you were to see me now you would not believe that I could have had the long lean legs that supported my body when I was among you.

Now you will probably ask, "What makes you decide to board with such a prominent family?" Well the reason is that since I am a complete stranger here, I want to become known among the decent and dignified people. That is the sort I wish to associate with.

* * *

Last week I almost bought sixty acres of land but changed my mind. I decided it was too far from the city and too small to begin farming or to rent out. Now you will probably say, "Now what? A tobacco merchant and a farmer at the same time?" But you see, here in America the situation is [that people do many things] to make money, regardless of how different they may be. Last week I lent someone one hundred and ten dollars for three months at twenty-five percent interest. Lending money is not unusual here. It is done every day here—a person receives a given percentage, depending on the circumstances, but twenty-five percent is not too much here. Banks can charge up to thirty. Some time ago I had some money on deposit at a bank and earned twelve and a half percent. . . . But the Americans have a saying, "All wood is not good wood." So you have to watch out.

* * *

In America the rich and poor eat three times a day—at 7:00 A.M., Noon and 6:00 P.M. Meals consist of meat, bread, potatoes, turnips, tarts, several varieties of baked goods, jellies, etc.—always the same in the morning, noon, and evening, except they eat turnips only in the morning. They also eat a great deal of Indian corn. This is fed to horses instead of oats. At first I could not eat it, but now I can. It is a white color when it is cooked and it is eaten with butter. Gysbert—you know all about it. You have raised it in your garden—a tall plant with pointed broad leaves.

But hold on a minute I just heard a tinkling of bells, looked up, and now I see Mr. De Heus in front of the store with his horse and sleigh. The horse is wearing a plume and bells which I took along from Holland. And how the Americans stare at it—and those poor black devils stand wondering if they have gone crazy or are thinking maybe that it is an idol appearing in makeup. Uncle Klaas [de Heus] has come to get me with the sleigh. But unfortunately, my partner will be gone for about an hour and I'll have to wait.

* * *

Gerhard, tell me if I am mistaken, but I think there are some people of the Zahn family living in Zutphen. If so, do you ever visit them? Who are they and what kind of people are they? If so, give them my regards.

I wish you could see what a mess things are here in America. You have no idea about it. Everyone does, acts, says, deals, and believes anyway he wishes or feels. There is no servant class here. Everything, whatever kind of dirt it is, goes into the street. It is never cleaned up. All kinds of animals roam through the city. You can't walk two steps without hearing someone shouting directions to some hogs, horses, oxen, other animals, and people. There are runaways every day—sometimes five or six. They don't even pay attention—if someone is run over they have to take care of themselves. That's the truth. You must never expect someone to be helpful unless he is well paid. No one will do anything here merely to be friendly. Gerhard, that is the rule. It smells to high heaven. The most recent report about immigration in the American newspaper stated that the annual total was 11,667.

Here in Muscatine the houses are larger than in Holland. I have not traveled throughout Holland, but that is what I think. Many houses here are built completely from wood, but now that the city is growing daily, that is no longer allowed. So throughout America people are beginning to build with brick.

*   *   *

Many pretty young ladies come to visit at my boardinghouse. There are more beautiful girls here than in Holland, but oh, what a difference. Their clothing is really beautiful. None of the women here go on errands. They don't go out to buy supplies—meat, potatoes, starch, etc. Women here have greater advantages than you can imagine in Holland. When meeting a women on the street a man is expected to step aside as soon as possible, making sure he allows her to pass on the inside. If a man does not do this, and if an older person notices, he has the right to give you a sound tap or even a slap. When I was in New York for those days I was almost tipsy from stepping aside for the women.

Broadway is the principal street in New York (three and a half miles long) where people ride and rush about in an almost unbelievable manner. Yes, I can tell you that an estimated six hundred omnibuses go by every day on that one street—that in addition to many hundreds and hundreds of other wagons and vehicles. In all of America there is only one canal and that one is in New York City. It is at least as wide as the river by Zuidzigt, and it runs through the entire city.

Yesterday I bought a cheap clock for five dollars, but it has no chimes.

And, now, Gerhard, I will stop writing. I think this is enough. If I had the time I could write enough to fill a book.

*   *   *

Young and old folks too, write to me! Write a great deal and often! You can depend on it that it is a festive day for me when I hear from

Holland. I go to the post office three times each day, but . . . there is never a letter from Holland. Then I walk back disappointedly.

[Closing]

1. The parents of Ferdinand Jantzen, who lived either with Ferdinand or nearby.

March 23, 1857

Dear brothers and sisters,

On January 18 I was finally able to rejoice after receiving a letter from Holland, which I read with pleasure—and also with some alarm. But, before going on I must thank Ferdinand and Gysbert heartily for their trouble on my behalf. Although I did not receive the money until March 13 the results were favorable.

* * *

A proverb says, "The mouth overflows with that which is in the heart," and so I cannot delay writing about the news included below. I have been engaged since the nineteenth of this month to a very beautiful, cute, good-hearted, and moral young woman by the name of Wynanda Wilhelmina de Heus, three and a half weeks short of twenty-four years of age. What do you have to say about that? Let me have your answer. My state of affairs allows for this because I make good money here in my store. Things are going well for me. I have such a good and pleasant life that I would not trade America for three Hollands. My fortunes improve literally from week to week—not only because I am engaged but because everything comes my way. If there is anyone on earth who experiences God's help and support, it is I. Oh, if I could only praise and thank Him fully, but I must confess that I fall far short in doing so.

I was ill from December 28 to mid-January. . . . I was extremely weak for 3 to 4 weeks and then tired so that I lost a great deal of weight. Last week I weighed one hundred and fifty-two pounds and last summer one hundred and eighty-five pounds—a big difference in such a short time. That little experience cost me fourteen Dutch guilders for medicine.

* * *

It grieved me to learn, Willem, that you are so unsuccessful. I often wish that you had come here with me. Gerhard, I am concerned about your future, so do what I have done. Leave your fatherland before it is too late. Look at Willem as an example. Here, an honest person who conducts himself well can make good progress. Have yourself declared to be of age and come here as soon as you can. Advance the travel money for Willem, his wife, and children and I dare to bet that you will be repaid with 4.25 percent interest within two years. If a person is willing and able he can get ahead here. America is so extensive that there are thousands and thousands of miles that are not yet inhabited. There is plenty of room for Gerhard, Willem, Chris, and two children. Oh, Gerhard, if only I could persuade you. What is to become of Willem? And of yourself?

Enclosed you will find a letter addressed to Mr. Scheernecker, cigar maker in the Tuinstraat. Ferdinand, will you do me the great favor of giving this to him as soon as possible? It is an order for fifty thousand cigars. On the cigars that I brought with me I made profit like water. But do not tell him that I wrote this because then he will probably think, "Now I can charge him more!" I wrote to him that I only wish what I can sell readily. For safety sake I am giving you herewith the address Scheernecker must use. It is Mr. Zahn and Scheernecker, Muscatine, Iowa, and at the bottom North America must be added.

* * *

Please answer my questions and write sometime. I write so often and so much. Ferdinand, you do the best with writing. Willem, keep up your courage. Just now I am not able [to help you] because of the many expenses required during the first year of taking over this business. Even though I am on another continent, I will do what I can for you.

[Closing]

September 14, 1857

Dear brothers and sisters,
[Most of this letter berates his siblings for writing so seldom.]

* * *

I recently received the letter from which I learned that I could not get the cigars. I am extremely sorry about that. I was also sorry to learn that sister Alida was very ill. . . . I am very eager to hear some news from you, but I will not ask a ninth time, for it is just so much wasted effort [eight previous letters went unanswered]. I must say I never thought you would treat me this way. You should realize that I am on a strange continent, separated from you by thousands of miles, and I'm eager to receive some news—especially about brother Gerhard's plans. I have, at least, heard from cousin Hector, who is living in St. Louis . . . and who plans to come here.

* * *

As for my situation, I am doing as well as I could desire. But I will not write anything more about this because I do not think you are very interested. I do wish to add this—I plan to be married soon.

[Closing]

P.S. I just received another letter from cousin Hector in which I learned that brother Gerhard has bid farewell to Uncle and Aunt in Zutphen and that he is probably on the way. By this time he could be a long way on the ocean. So I expect him in early November. You cannot imagine how it hurts me to be informed of this by others and not from my own family.

Jan George Zahn to Gerhard Zahn
Muscatine, Iowa, to Amsterdam
October 9, 1857

Dear brother Gerhard,
Yesterday I received your letter and I hasten to answer it as soon as possible. It was such a pleasure to hear some news from you. . . . Write me, honestly, what the reason is that not one of them [his siblings] will have anything more to do with me.

* * *

You wrote that you had written earlier that you would like to come here. I had never heard about this from anyone except from cousin Hector. You did write once to ask about the book business here, and I answered that it would not be advisable, absolutely no good. Do you know the best way you could sell books here? If you were to come with a collection of bad books—including, for example, books which would teach the best methods of picking pockets, stealing, cheating, swindling, etc.—you could sell them on the street. Or otherwise sell religious books. You may say that is a strange combination. Yes, true enough. But people here are wondrous creatures.

American religion consists of this: to acquire a great deal of knowledge, to dress attractively, and to commit no open sins but sin only in the dark and on the sly. Americans have one virtue which is this: if you take one thousand Americans, probably nine hundred will not be slaves to alcoholic beverages. Believe me, to find really good folk, one would have to search with a lantern. Just as large as the country here is, so great also is the evil of an evil person here. One is forced to that opinion and it seems to me that people are becoming worse as time goes by. Everyone conducts himself exactly as he pleases. In cases of dispute, people shoot one another in the head at the first chance and they break down or burn one another's houses. Poisoning? That is common here.

Is there no authority or discipline here? Oh, man, yes. [For example,] a couple of weeks ago the mayor got into a fight with his son in a brothel. They gave each other a good beating. The police came, and having heard what was going on, the ruling was a twenty-five-cent fine. [The options are] innocent or hanging and it all takes place in less than a half hour, but of one thousand murderers who are tried only one receives punishment.

Negroes are treated shamefully here. I cannot bear to see the way they are treated. I have defended them on several occasions, but that has cost me dearly. I always ask, in what way is a black person inferior to me? Is that right or not? Even if it were to cost me my life, I wish to support every Negro and will do so as much as I can. So you need not ask [be surprised] if I have all of them as customers. "Freedom, Liberty, and Equality" is the motto here in America, but a Negro may not consider himself to be included.

With all my writing, I am in danger of forgetting your questions and of not answering half of them. So I will proceed . . . as to whether or not you should come here. I don't know exactly what to write in regard to this—especially since you are in a position that surprises me. I wish to write you a few words to tell you how I feel about your future engagement. I trust you will not take it ill of me in view of the fact that I am writing because of my concern for you personally. I do not think it would be advisable at present for you to take such a step. What kind of future would you have? . . .

Consider the case of brother Willem. There he sits with a wife and two children in absolute poverty. Would it not be heartrending for you if, by being in such a hurry, you would involve yourself, to say nothing about your wife, in the most severe difficulties?

Now, Gerhard, this is not all that I wish to warn you against. See here, it may be that this is a good and courageous girl. I do not know her. But I pray of you that you will keep your eyes open. Oh! at first everything appears so lovely and rosy, and love can overcome absolutely all problems, but later a person often finds that he is mistaken. Then it is too late. Remember this is a step you take for life, and it is not to be taken lightly. I say again, Gerhard, I pray of you, look out. Do not consider it lightly. It would be worth a great deal to me if I could talk to you in person.

Now, regarding your coming here. If you wish to come here with a wife, I would say, no. You could better remain where you are. It is not possible for me to write and say that you should feel free to come here or to tell you how you can make a living immediately. I may not write that. Things are not simply dished up here any more than in Holland.

And what is more, even if you came here alone, I could not promise that you would find work at once and earn a living easily. It would take six pages to tell you exactly what the situation here is. Working here is completely different from working in Holland. That cannot be explained in a few words. This is certain, you should feel free to leave the fatherland and anyone who is able and willing to work can always find some work and make money. You cannot, however, play the gentleman and get by. If I had only taken that advice to heart, I would have made much more progress. At the beginning when I was here I did just what I am now advising you against. But I allowed myself to be misled with nice words and now it is too late.

I live here comfortably and well. I dress according to local customs and pay ten guilders [$4.00] for board without laundry or sleeping quarters. But I do not save a cent. I go to parties and [encounter] all kinds of filth, enough to cause me to gag, but I leave at the first opportunity. You may ask, "Aren't you crazy for going when you realize what it is like?" Well, what can I say? I have committed myself to certain things and cannot get away from it without difficulty. (Keep all of this to yourself.)

Believe me, in America the president and a manure shoveler are equal. So you need not be ashamed if you work with a shovel one day and go about dressed like a Parisian dandy the next. You can hold your head high. Meanwhile, if you pick a few pockets and steal, the American thinks, just go ahead—just so a person gets rich. How he does it doesn't matter.

Now, as to my business. As far as the amount of sales is concerned—that is very satisfactory. I have three men working for me and my partner and I also work all day.[1] We even worked until one o'clock the last two Sundays. I do not like to do that, but it was necessary. Now you probably will think, Jan is making money. But no. Tobacco is so high in price that we make practically nil. The tobacco I purchased at a high price last spring has almost doubled since that time. Two weeks ago my partner went to St. Louis to buy a new supply of tobacco and came back with the sad, sad news that we had to invest another 1,700 guilders [$680.00]. That is six and a half guilders [$2.60] per pound. But we had to have the tobacco. You can figure it out for yourself. After paying that much per pound, I need eighty-five guilders [$35.00] per week for wages, rent, and light. How much will be left over? After thinking it all over, I have plans to dispose of the business and look about for something else. Last year the tobacco crop was a complete failure.

Muscatine is the same as always except that humanity here is getting worse by the day. The wolves are also multiplying terribly in the woods here. Soon a wolf hunt will take place and I plan to join it. Last winter I encountered one in the woods. If I had not had a large dog with me, I might have become a victim, but I escaped with little difficulty. Oh, you get used to everything here. One time I got stuck in snow up to my stomach.

* * *

There are no fire engines here. When there is a fire people will outrun one another to steal everything in sight. Then, when everything has been taken, people still do not put out the fire. A hearse here is a black vehicle decorated with glass and drawn by two lively horses. Anyone who wishes follows the body. The cemetery is open to the public at all times because America is a free country. Nothing is locked here. If I wish to enter another person's house, I do so without asking and look things over. If anyone wishes to walk along the streets with drums and flags, with noise and shouting, he does so. Since I have been here, two houses have been battered down. I've seen the poisoning of dogs, cows, and horses. In a word, stealing cattle is the order of the day. If I can lay hands on such a thief, he can be hanged from the nearest tree without hesitation. Women, however, must be respected here—as if they were goddesses. You do not need to ask if the women wear the trousers here. (Gerhard, make sure you remain the boss.)

* * *

This winter I have had nine dogs. One was poisoned, one was stolen, and I sold the others. Now I have none left. Living expenses were terribly high last winter. Now they are inexpensive again. Four weeks ago we got our first gaslights. Living is really a joke here. Oh! I wish you were here. Believe me, we would have a good laugh.

Now, Gerhard, you know how things are here, and I leave it up to you. Please write back soon. Don't make me wait so long. I am oh so lonely here and so far from you. Believe me, I do not forget you or the other brothers and sisters.

[Closing]

1. See Johanna Nijenhuis to Family, July 30, 1865, which follows the Zahn letter series.

John Zahn to Ferdinand Jantzen
Muscatine, Iowa, to Amsterdam
September 20, 1858

Dear brothers and sisters,

I can hear you say it, Aha! A letter from America. I haven't seen one
for a long time. The reason is that there was no news to write and I did
not receive news from Holland. But now I have great news to tell you—
I have become the father of the cutest little girl on August 6. I wish you
could see her. She is such an angel. She is already beginning to smile.
Oh, but sometimes she cries enough to deafen me. Still, that is nothing
that will not turn out all right. The Zahn family is growing nicely. Cateau
almost has three already, Willem has four, Gysbert has two, Jan has
one—that makes a total of ten altogether. Since Gerhard is engaged, that
will add more. Sister Anna, what is your situation? Have you not just
about reached that stage? I think it is about time.

My darling Mina is now completely recovered. She has suffered a great
deal, but she is able to take care of housework again and she goes out
again.

I cannot compliment any of you on your good conduct—not a single
letter from any of you to my wife. At least one of you might have written
when we notified you about our wedding. What's more, my wife wrote
to you personally. Oh, well, we are thinking about coming to Holland
next year if we live and are well. It is such an easy thing to do now—
even being on the telegraph line.

*　*　*

I am very eager to have some news from Holland. Is everything still
the way it has always been? Will Willem III abdicate? What is the situation? Was a preacher almost killed at the main market in Amsterdam?
Are the Jews and Protestants becoming more antagonistic to each other?
Has the Lynbaan almost burned to the ground? Have you had a very
dry summer? Oh, I have many more questions. Even if you do not write
I know how to get the facts. Gerhard, have you been so ill? Have you
recovered? Today is September 20 and it is hot enough to melt. How is
the weather in Holland today?

America remains a really wonderful country. If you ever came here
you would gaze around in amazement. But I have become accustomed
to it and almost feel that this is the way things should be.

At the end of November we are going to move to Fourth Street, to a better and nicer house than the one we're living in now. I think you will know about where Fourth Street is located.[1]

And now my dear brothers and sisters, when will you write again?

[Closing]

1. Zahn may have drawn a map and sent it to Amsterdam.

Johanna Nijenhuis to Family
Muscatine, Iowa, to Winterswijk, Gelderland
July 30, 1865 [Selected Segment]

* * *

We were married July 25, 1855, and have three children, one girl and two boys. . . . My husband is J. H. Stemerdink, who is a cigar maker. At first he worked here for a Hollander named De Heus. He was a good boss and my husband worked for him at twenty-five dollars per month, which was good money. But that only lasted for a year. When De Heus became very sick he wanted to sell the cigar store to my husband and another person named Zahn—also a Hollander. And that was done. I was much against it. But after much talking the partnership was formed, and that Zahn, who is a real sweet-talker, deceived my husband very much. So we had the shop together for about nine months[1] and in that time it lost about four hundred dollars. That is no small thing for us. The Americans say that he [Zahn] stole the money because cigar shops make good money here. And all the Americans told us not to pay one more cent to Zahn. The Americans who know my husband like him very much and had much sympathy for him.

As you can imagine, that was a terrible blow for us. We began with nothing and saved almost one hundred dollars in the first year [of their marriage]. We put all that money in the cigar store and lost all of it. If this Zahn had not cheated us, we would have made good money. Then, that following summer, work was so scarce that my husband could not earn one cent in four months. We had to live on the little that I could earn.[2] So we have had disaster after disaster. Then I became so sick after my first child was born . . . that I had to call the English doctor. He came to see me three times every day so you can see how sick I was.

The worst problem is that ever since the loss of that money my husband's mind has been weakened. He is not entirely out of his mind, but it is bad enough so that he cannot work. My brothers [living around Muscatine] have all tried to find work for him.

1. The partnership was formed sometime around November 1856 and probably ended shortly after October 1857 because Zahn's letter that month indicates his intention to leave the business.
2. Probably as a domestic. She had no children at that time.

17 *Willem Hendrik de Lange*

Willem Hendrik de Lange, a clerk in the office of H. Houck, a notary public in Deventer, Overijssel, emigrated in 1873 and joined his wife's family, the Spanjers, in Grand Rapids, Michigan. A river city like Grand Rapids, Deventer was established before the tenth century, and it became a prominent walled town within the Hanseatic League. The city grew and prospered from both trade and administrative functions until the fifteenth century, when western coastal cities such as Amsterdam surpassed the IJssel River trading centers. Nonetheless, Deventer has remained a significant governmental and ecclesiastical center with magnificent restorations of its late medieval architecture. As his letters indicate, De Lange missed the culture and social routines of his native city. By contrast Grand Rapids was a place of dirt streets and wooden sidewalks in 1873.

White-collar immigrants like De Lange made up only about 10 percent of the Dutch emigration (1834–1880), and about 20 percent of these migrated within the Dutch colonial empire. Among America-bound immigrants white-collar professionals were only an 8 percent fragment, even though about 40 percent of the Netherlandic populace found livelihoods in both high- and low-paying white-collar occupations. Obviously, Willem de Lange represents a rather narrow strand of the general immigration.[1]

Like the other urbanites in this chapter, De Lange possessed writing skills sharply superior to the simpler compositional powers of most correspondents with rural backgrounds, and his perceptions are starkly different from theirs. But public demonstrations of urbanity and wit could

These letters were donated by the Provincial Archives of Overijssel, 1976, and first translated by G. H. Ligterink.

[1] Lambert, *The Making of the Dutch Landscape*, pp. 142–72; Swierenga, "Dutch International Labour Migration to North America in the Nineteenth Century," in *Dutch Immigration to North America*, ed. Ganzevoort and Boekelman, pp. 24–25.

Deventer, Overijssel, city center and market, no date. Courtesy of Calvin College Library Archives, photo collection.

easily interfere with an immigrant's social adaptation and acceptance. De Lange's judgment that he "would never feel at home in America" was probably accurate, and other professionals, including pastors and school-teachers, echoed his view that thorough Americanization would be possible only for their children. Well-educated white-collar professionals were especially vulnerable to social discontent. In 1872 the founder and leading citizen of Holland, Michigan, the Reverend Albertus van Raalte, noted that clerks and other office workers had poor prospects for success in America, particularly if they expected to find employment comparable to their work in the Netherlands. A factory job and the eventual acquisition of a skilled trade was, he thought, the best route to success in Grand Rapids. Van Raalte also noted that immigrants who exhibited socially superior attitudes based on their educational and occupational status in the Netherlands, "will be trampled under foot."[2]

In a manner of speaking De Lange was indeed "trampled under foot," but not because of his caustic comments. He was accidentally killed by an errant bobsled on January 28, 1874. Obviously, then, his adjustment to both mainstream American culture and the already Americanizing Dutch enclave in Grand Rapids was cut short.

The bobsled tragedy received considerable attention in the local press,

[2] Albertus C. van Raalte to Abraham Kuyper in the Abraham Kuyper Papers, Free University of Amsterdam, July 4, 1872.

which reported several other incidents in which the sleds caused injuries and were public nuisances. Reporting De Lange's collision on Bridge Street, the Grand Rapids *Daily Morning Democrat* noted that the city's youth had carried their sport to the limit, "having the audacity to stop teams of horses until the crews going down on their sleds could get by."[3]

In greater detail the *Daily Eagle* explained, "The boys had constructed a set of 'bobs'—two sleds connected by a long plank—long enough to carry a dozen or more of them at once. On this vehicle they would come down Bridge Street with tremendous speed and force—running across Canal Street and far out onto the bridge. About 9 o'clock, a Hollander named De Lange, a schoolteacher residing on or near Spring Street, was crossing Bridge Street at the junction of Ottawa just as the boys on the above-mentioned sleigh were coming swiftly down. They ran upon him, striking his legs and breaking both of them, we are informed. The services of Dr. Wood, whose offices are at that corner, were immediately secured. The wounded man was conveyed home with some difficulty in a hack, and all that was possible was done for him." But that "all" was not enough. De Lange died two days later, probably from a concussion.[4]

When Marten Schoonbeek, whose letters appear elsewhere in this book, learned of this dramatic event he wrote immediately to his son, a schoolteacher in Oude Pekela, "It would be impossible to count the times we have wished you were here this week. . . . you would have been able to become a teacher immediately in a Dutch school. The teacher there lost his life in a very sad way. . . . If you were here you could have taken over his position" (Marten Schoonbeek to Jacobus Schoonbeek, February 8, 1874).

Wisely, Jacobus Schoonbeek remained in the Netherlands, where his credentials sustained his lifelong career as an educator. In Grand Rapids his siblings achieved no similar status, and although always adequately housed and fed, they gained their livelihoods in work shoes with callused hands.

That, as Van Raalte suggested in 1872, was a reliable and normal pattern for success, and typically, Willem de Lange's boys found employment in the industrial sector. The eldest son toiled in the furniture industry. Two others were harness makers in their small shop in Sparta, Michigan, and Karl, the youngest, became a machinist in the local Alexander Dodge Company.

[3] Herbert J. Brinks, "Grand Rapids, an Immigrant's First Impressions," *Origins* 3, no. 2 (1985): 30–34.
[4] Ibid.

Whether or not these achievements would have satisfied Willem de Lange's expectations for his children cannot be known. Although not destitute, the De Langes were too poor when they arrived in 1873 to afford their own travel costs. As the letters disclose, Willem's death forced his widow and children to move in with her parents, the Spanjers. Such a narrowing of economic circumstances could only have restricted and complicated educational and career opportunities for the De Lange children.

At present the De Lange family is scattered across the continent from Michigan and Indiana to Texas, Oregon, and California. Their religious loyalties are diverse, and for the most part they have married outside of the ethnic community. Some are blue-collar workers; others are nurses, business managers, and one is a stockbroker. They have merged with mainstream American society to such an extent that the various strands of the extended family have lost meaningful relationships.[5]

Willem de Lange to H. Houck
Grand Rapids, Michigan, to Deventer, Overijssel
October 4, 1873

Esteemed sir:

Finally I am carrying out my promise to write you, even though it is difficult because of a cramp in my right hand. That, however, is no hindrance in my present employment, which requires little writing [compared to his office work in Deventer].

To begin, I hope that you and your esteemed family will receive this letter in the best of circumstances, both in body and spirit, which, thank God, is also true of me and mine.

Now I will give you a short, succinct account of my travels from Deventer to Grand Rapids. I had imagined that the trip would be very difficult, but it turned out even worse because my wife was blind for nearly three-quarters of the trip and thus all the irritations of travel fell upon my shoulders. I would not make such a trip again with a blind wife and four children for $1,000. We arrived in Rotterdam at midnight, and then it took forty-five minutes to find lodging. In Rotterdam it was nothing but hauling luggage around and getting my family on board the ship. All of which nearly killed me. From morning until evening I was literally soaked through and through with sweat.

[5] William de Lange, interview by author, October 16, 1977, and Mrs. William de Lange, interview by author, May 22, 1993, telephone notes, in W. H. de Lange Papers, Immigrant Letter Collection.

Saturday, on June 28, we left Rotterdam and had fine weather, but for the remaining days we had nothing but rain and mist so that the passage held no charm for me. Occasionally we encountered heavy dark clouds[1] that forecast approaching storms—gloomy comforters. We had a high percentage of childish companionship because 113 of the 263 passengers were children. Almost everyone was seasick. Fortunately, I was not, but on the other hand, because I was healthy, I became everyone's servant. The food was poor. For twelve days we ate moldy bread, and in July [a time for vegetables in Holland] we got only potatoes with sauerkraut or pea soup and both of these with spoiled American bacon. We had no better food because someone stole part of our luggage in Rotterdam, and it contained all the food that we packed for the trip. We did not miss the luggage until we were at sea and then had no opportunity to get more. So we experienced total poverty and could do nothing but eat the sour apple and hope for better. We were at sea for twenty-seven days and it was a happy moment when the Jersey coast came into view. At New York it was busy again because we had to gather up our luggage and present it for inspection. We were in New York for twenty-four hours but didn't see much because we were so busy with our luggage. But the city is large, dirty, and busy.

Castle Garden, the landing place, is a building arranged solely for immigrants. One thousand five hundred people can sleep there, but only on their own bedding. We did not stay there but looked for other quarters because we had had enough difficulty of that sort.

Finally, [by train] we raced across the country through tunnels, mountains, and valleys to reach Grand Rapids. We stopped at the Niagara Falls for ten minutes and they were astonishing. But for the most part, we had to be on guard against thieves and swindlers—including the conductor of one train, who drummed ten cents from each passenger with the promise of coffee in the morning and then disappeared when we changed trains. After forty-eight hours on the train we arrived in Grand Rapids. Meanwhile, my wife's eyes had become better while we were at sea. We were greeted joyfully and with a well-prepared meal. Seeing that people here are well off improved my outlook.

After resting a few days I took my membership papers to the consistory of the Spring Street Christian Reformed Church, and even though seven others had applied before me, they decided to make me their schoolteacher for ten dollars per week. I am required to teach the children well enough so they can read and write Dutch. They learn other subjects in the English [public] schools. I teach from Monday through Friday, 9:00 A.M.–4:00 P.M. The prospects are good because people can live well here

Williams Street Dutch-language school, Grand Rapids, 1870s. Courtesy of Calvin College Library Archives, photo collection.

on ten dollars per week. So, I opened the school with about 100 students on August 11, 1873—one day after my 48th birthday. Things were much more peaceful in your office. It was rather lively here at first and I doubted that I could hold out, but now, after eight weeks I am getting used to it. Even so, these "Yankees" are uncivilized rascals and not easy to control. When I begin to teach an evening class I will earn still more. My oldest son works for a tailor and earns one dollar per week.

These are the high points of my experiences and I will close now with a few of my impressions. There is still much uncultivated land here between Grand Rapids and New York. I saw many scrawny cows on the way although there are also many fat cows. Nature is not very beautiful here. You see hardly any flowers—except on Sundays in church, where the ladies' hats are decorated like flower gardens. You see few birds here and those I see don't sing. Out of one hundred cows, ninety-nine are red. [Dutch, i.e., Frisian cows are usually black and white.]

There are many horses and wagons here and they are also driven by women. The horses seem to be more gentle and tame than in the Netherlands. The traffic is heavy here. When I look outside I can easily see 12–14 carriages at a time. The streets are very wide here, with running fountains at various places. Wooden vats are also set out to water horses because it is very hot here in the summer. It can get up to 112 degrees, and in the winter the cold is similarly severe.

Grand Rapids is located in a valley and along its surrounding hills. Its boundaries are larger than Amsterdam, but it is not cramped. It has a population of about 30,000 from all nations. It contains forty-two churches and some cost up to $150,000. The Americans value worship highly. There are also many factories, large stores, and other expensive buildings. The many wooden houses are well planned. Currently I live on the second floor of such a house and pay rent of $2.00 per week.

It consists of two main rooms and two side rooms without windows and several closets. It stands directly across from my school. At first we lived a half hour away from the school. This location is more convenient.

The English here are very wasteful and bombastic, as is evident in their advertisements—sometimes they print their names across the whole fronts of their stores. The Dutchmen here are industrious and miserly. The Germans are the leading tradesmen. The Irish are lazy good-for-nothings. Poverty exists here only among the blacks, former slaves, but they are very industrious and highly honored when you greet them.

The Americans idolize their women, so much so that even the richest man would not think of asking his maid to polish his boots. The American woman is proud, lazy, dirty, and wasteful. If you acquired one with a $50,000 dowry, she would still be too expensive to keep.

Now, I must conclude this letter. If you wish to know more about America, you have only to write and I will try to answer your questions.

Believe me, I respect you and your family as highly as ever and am thankful for all the favors I received from you. Give my hearty greetings to your brothers and sisters and their children.

And now, once again, I wish you all the best. Your willing servant,

W. H. de Lange

1. He described these clouds as "boer met zijn varkens" (the so-called farmer with his pigs).

Grand Rapids city center, Division and Monroe, 1880. Courtesy of the Grand Rapids Public Library—Michigan and Family History Department.

December 22, 1873

Esteemed sir:

It was a pleasure to receive your valued letter of October 2, even though it was mislaid in the post office, for some time. This was caused by changes in the distribution of mail. Earlier everyone rented a numbered box in the post office, and we could pick up mail there weekly or as often as one wished. Now eight mail carriers have been appointed, and we no longer look for mail in the box. Because it had my earlier box number on it, your mail was misplaced. And now, on the day that I received it, I am writing to you, and I hope that this letter will arrive safely in your hands.

Conditions in America are not as favorable as they were. There is a great financial crisis, which has greatly reduced employment and trade. One business after another goes bankrupt and you hear about public auctions every day. People hope for better times next spring, but I don't know if that will happen. Even though the hard times have not yet affected me, I do not advise anyone to come here at present. Those who have the means are returning to the Netherlands. I don't know if that is wise either because, according to the newspapers, the Netherlands is also experiencing hard times—a number of businesses have gone bankrupt. I read that meat prices have dropped there, but they are still expensive compared to here, for we pay only six U.S. cents (12 Holland cents) per pound. Meat, sugar, and flour are very cheap here. The rest is about the same as in the Netherlands. Because the most essential products are so cheap, you do not see poverty here, and anyway, people would not admit it if they were poor.

We have had three cold snaps already this winter—sometimes it is so cold that you must cover your whole head. We had a heavy snowstorm here on December 3 and 4, and a kind of earthquake at the same time. I was shaking in bed like I was at sea on the ocean. My wife jumped out of bed in fear, but the cold drove her back quickly. The quake caused much damage both to churches and people.[1] Currently it is mild again. Frequently here I observe occurrences in the sky which I never noticed in the Netherlands—it is a wafting bank of green clouds which generally precedes snow.

Concerning your question about my becoming a schoolteacher so easily here—I must tell you that America is a free country and everyone does what they want! Even if I wished to declare myself a physician, no one would stop me. But it is also certain that those with evidence of training have the most credibility. It is difficult to find accredited teachers here, and those who have diplomas are often unable to keep these American rascals under control. I also feel too weak for that at times. When I can find a better job I am going to leave this school.

It was a pleasure to learn that Broekhuizen is doing so well [in my place], and I hope that it continues so.

Fortunately, we are all healthy here. I was never so healthy in the Netherlands. I have neither chest nor stomach pains anymore. My wife is fat and healthy. My oldest son goes to the English [public] school. The next one goes to my school, so he can learn to read Dutch first. Karl, the four-year-old, runs around with the English neighbor children and speaks a language that neither we nor his friends can understand. Henrick, after being sickly for a long time, is now better. As for me, I am and will always be a stranger here. I often say that I will never be able to forget my dear fatherland—no more than I can do without my right hand.

It would please me if you could give my greetings to your esteemed family—especially the widow, Mrs. Kronenberg.

Respectfully, I am your willing servant,

W. H. de Lange

139 Spring Street
Grand Rapids
State of Michigan
North America

1. Both the Grand Rapids *Daily Eagle*, December 4, 1873, and the Grand Rapids *Daily Democrat*, December 5, 1873, reported news of an unprecedented windstorm on the night of December 3, which toppled buildings, factory chimneys, and church steeples. Fallen trees stopped railroad traffic and wooden sidewalks were scattered about the streets.

T. Janssen to H. Houck
Grand Rapids, Michigan, to Deventer, Overijssel
February 14, 1874

Dear sir:

No doubt it will surprise you to receive a letter from a stranger, but the cause is that I am obliged to inform you of the terrible disaster which befell your former employee, W. H. de Lange. On the evening of January 28, 1874, while walking home from his wife's parents' house, he was unexpectedly hit by a sled that was charging down a hill. Both of his legs were smashed. The situation was horrible, but he did regain full consciousness. On the following morning your letter arrived and I read it to him. That evening, however, he fell into an unnatural sleep and never regained consciousness. He died calmly on January 30.

His widow's situation was desperate—first because of her sudden loss and, in addition, because it seemed that all her financial support was taken away. It is fortunate, however, that she is in America because under such circumstances lavish generosity is immediately evident here. Already more than $400 has been donated to support the widow, and it has been invested in the safest and most profitable manner. Obviously the passage of time will reduce such compassion, so, notwithstanding this momentary outpouring of good intentions, her future is clouded by a dark veil. I recommend this widow of your former employee to your kind sympathy and request some assistance. I ask this because it is evident from your letter that you are kindly disposed toward De Lange.

I hope that the letter explains the situation satisfactorily.

With great esteem, T. Janssen

The widow's address is 399 Ottawa Street.

Willem Spanjer to H. Houck
Grand Rapids, Michigan, to Deventer, Overijssel
April 7, 1874

Mr. Houck, Notary Public of Deventer
Dear sir:

I am writing these few lines on behalf of the widow De Lange. The first letter you received to inform you about the sad news of his death was written by Mr. T. Janssen, who was asked to write at that time. Although I have never had the pleasure of meeting you in person, it is an honor for me to thank you in the name of the widow for the liberal support of 125 guilders which came in your letter. It was like water to a weary and thirsty soul. She will be forever grateful for your good deed and blesses the memory of your family. She has no means to repay you but has learned to depend on the Lord who is a father to orphans and a husband to widows. The Lord is rich in mercy and also in providing benefits to such as you. He will certainly repay you.

The loss is great, both to the widow and also to us. We experienced continuously pleasant relationships with our son-in-law. On the evening of the accident he left our house in good spirits, but a half hour later we were cast into the deepest of sorrows. The place of the accident is a five-minute walk from our house. A doctor lives close to that place and De Lange was brought there unconscious.

Three sleds, each with six or eight boys, were coming down the hill, which is about 200 feet long. The sleds were coming down the hill at amazing speeds—as fast as a locomotive at top speed. De Lange saw two sleds go by. He watched them with surprise but did not imagine that a third sled was still coming. That sled shattered one of his legs and broke the other leg. It threw him into the air about eight feet and he landed on the ground unconscious. By the time we arrived, some people had taken him home in a covered carriage, and we were able to speak with him while he was still in the carriage. Six men brought him up into his home and a number of friends stayed with him until 4:00 P.M. the next day. Then he fell into a coma and died without pain on January 30.

We have taken the widow and children into our house. It is better for her to stay here than at home, where she must continually see the school where her husband worked. We, as her family, have decided to support her with our advice and necessities. I am not a wealthy man and I must work to support myself, but I had enough saved up to pay for their ocean passage last year.

With this, I have given you a short account of this tragedy. I hope that you receive this letter in good circumstances.

P.S.

Dear sir:

It is the wish of my husband and daughter that I close this letter with greetings from my daughter to you and your esteemed family. My daughter would be pleased to receive letters from you once in a while. Once again, I close with hearty thanks from my daughter for your friendship and good deeds.

From the Widow de Lange
written by Mrs. Spanjer [her mother]

V

Detached Immigrants

Introduction

Unlike the urbanities in Part IV, nearly all the "detached" immigrants in this part were unmarried and all of them avoided close connections with their ethnic fellows in America. Apart from Henri and Margo van Hall, all the detached immigrants were single and lived in urban America. Thus, their letters refer infrequently to other Dutch immigrants but focus instead on their private experiences and novel surroundings. William Smith, for example, wrote only about his poultry farm, hunting, fishing, and a major hurricane. Ignaats Bunnemeijer provided a detailed description of his work on Wards Island, New York, and H. Koopman was constantly fascinated by Chicago. Jan Willem Nijenhuis explained the details of his work and the benefits of labor union membership and, like the others in this chapter, he wrote almost nothing about interpersonal relationships.

Although none of these correspondents elected to live in Dutch immigrant communities, several (Anna Kuijt, Koopman, and Nijenhuis) were acquainted with them. Koopman was especially disaffected with Chicago's Dutch communities, and Kuijt, who worked briefly for a Dutch family in Maurice, Iowa, found that rural community unattractive. She had been a shopkeeper in Amsterdam before immigrating, and Chicago provided a more congenial setting. Nijenhuis, who deserted his family in Winterswijk, apparently preferred both anonymity and loneliness in Newark to risking the embarrassment of meeting acquaintances in Paterson or other Dutch communities.

The "detached" immigrants were more secular than their enclaved cohorts. Henri and Margo van Hall were devout Catholics, recently married. The others, however, wrote virtually nothing about their church affiliations, their pastors, their religious beliefs, or their pious feelings. Their salutations and closing lines, occasions where even moderately pious writers inserted a wish or word about God's favor, contained no religious reflections. H. Koopman who wrote much about religious hypocrisy in Chicago's Dutch subculture turned to American fundamentalism late in life. He was probably attending Dwight L. Moody's church in 1921 when he adopted a major strand of fundamentalist dispensationalism. However inadequately he may have understood this complex system of predicting Christ's return, Koopman was anxious to convince his relatives in Drenthe that 1926 would usher in the last days. By exchanging his own religious tradition for American fundamentalism, Koopman assimilated a piece of religious culture which the Dutch Reformed community usually avoided.

In general, the writings in this chapter reflect the rapid Americanization of those who did not join communities with strategies for retaining a measure of ethnic solidarity. Henri van Hall, for example, was already enmeshed in Anglo-American culture when he returned to the Netherlands and married Margo. Thereafter, because they settled amid a heterogeneous frontier population in Montana, neither of them were likely to retain much of their native culture apart from their commonly shared links with Catholic priests in the Netherlands. Anna Kuijt, by marrying Dudley Bates, committed herself to an Anglo-American family with no Dutch identity. The other correspondents reported nothing about their associations with Netherlanders in America, and if they married, in all probability they found spouses outside of the Dutch subculture. Thus, all these immigrants demonstrate patterns of acculturation significantly different from those of Dutch immigrants who settled in such enclaves as Grand Rapids, Paterson, or the small Dutch towns of the West and Midwest.

18   *Henri and Margo van Hall*

This curious double letter, written by newlyweds in Etchetah, Montana (Junction City was the postal address), reveals an especially atypical immigrant experience. Clearly Henri van Hall was not a recent immigrant. It appears obvious, though, that he traveled to the Netherlands to court and marry Margo Suermondt. His obvious command of English and his knowledge of American literature suggest that he may have returned to the Netherlands to find a spouse with a compatible religious affiliation and educational status. The prospects for that sort of marital compatability were slight anywhere in the United States and especially on the western Great Plains.

This letter was donated by Willibrord Rutten, 1990, and first translated by Herbert Brinks.

Junction City, located near the confluence of the Yellowstone and Horn rivers, prospered from riverboat trade in 1882. The construction of the Northern Pacific Railroad, which paralleled the Yellowstone River, probably brought a frenzy of activity to Junction City in 1882, but the town burned to the ground in 1883 and was never rebuilt. The Van Halls, no doubt, moved elsewhere, but their destination and subsequent experiences are unknown.[1]

Henri and Margo van Hall to Father Laurentius Suermondt
Junction City, Montana, to Huissen, Gelderland
November 2, 1882

Dear Laurentius!
You have, no doubt, expected a letter from me long ago. I often intended to write to you but time has been very limited ever since we left Holland. Margo often told me that I must write to you, for then we should also get a letter from you soon. I hope that you have read most of the letters that I wrote to Ravenstein. From them you may have learned all about our situation and our territory at large. We are both well and happy, enjoying good health and making money as fast as we can. The happiness of our married life has surpassed our most sanguine expectations. Margo is to me everything that I could wish—always ready to sacrifice her own comforts to mine if only she knows what she can do to make me happy. Indeed, she is in every respect a most loving wife. She helps me faithfully to make money, and by the grace of God, we hope to make a little fortune in a few years so that we may be able to spend a little time in Holland again among our relatives and fond friends.
I am teaching school and everything goes all right.
Montana is still wild country, it being only a few years since it was opened to settlers. It is very remarkable for its natural scenery and for the immense herds of buffalo which graze on the plains. The gold and silver mines of Montana yield great quantities of the best kind of ore. The climate is extremely healthful. The air is pure and dry, with an Italian sky. Margo always says that she feels much better here than she ever did in Holland.
The farmers generally complain about the want of water, it being too dry to raise good crops. Farming can be carried on successfully only by irrigation, and that is very expensive. The Northern Pacific Railroad now runs past this place. It is completed to about a hundred miles west of

[1] Roberta C. Cheney, *Names on the Face of Montana* (Missoula, Mont.: Mountain Press, 1983), pp. 143–44.

Etchetah. The road is now 1,000 miles long, and when completed to the Pacific Coast it will be over 2,000 miles.

We see a great many Indians here. Some time ago they went past our house for several days—thousands of them. They all went on a buffalo hunt.

Socially it is not as refined here as was where I have been before. Still, we have found some very nice families here—all English. They are the nicest. Margo speaks English very well already and understands almost everything she hears.

We often hear from Rev. Ignaat, who sends us newspapers every week and also the *Katholic Illustratie* which we like very much. Dear Mother has written us a nice letter and Margo was as happy as a child when she received it. Constantius also wrote us a little letter from Ravenstein. I will answer him to Rome in a few days.

Last week I sent Ignaat a picture of Longfellow and a view of his house and study. I asked Ignaat to send it to you as soon as possible. I found it here in a periodical and thought it might please you because it contained some personal recollections about the poet and his character. I know that you love Longfellow because we talked so often about his beautiful poetry. I was pleased when I saw . . . that armchair in the picture which he received as a present from the children of Cambridge and which is made from the chestnut tree described in "The Village Blacksmith." Please, dear Laurentius, let me know how you like it.

We hope to hear from you soon. Margo will be so happy when you write us a long letter. We often talk about you and wonder how you are. How are you getting along with your English? Do you study it yet?

If there is anything in this country that you would like to have, please let me know and I will send it to you. When I happen to find a volume of Longfellow's best works I will make a present of it to you.

Now, dear Laurentius, I will close my letter and hope to hear from you soon. With our best wishes for you we remain forever faithfully your brother and sister,

Henri and Margo

This letter was written in English. The following addendum by "Margo" is in Dutch.

Dear Laurentius,

I cannot let this letter go off without writing a few lines. We would certainly be pleased to have a letter from you too, Laurentius. Wasn't it nice that the esteemed fathers at Huissen informed us that you were coming to Ravenstein! You have not forgotten us in your prayers have you? I don't think so because we are very fortunate even though we are in such a rough country as we are here. We work as much as we can

Address:

N. America,
Mr. Henri van Hall,
Etchetah,
Custer Co.
Montana.

Waarde Laurentius

Margo Van Hall's November 2, 1882, letter to her brother, Father Laurentius
Suermondt, in Huissen, Gelderland

and make good money. It is, though, a bitter, bitter disappointment that we hear so little about God and worship. Most of the time Henri is our pastor on Sunday and he reads the Scripture in our house and the brothers and sisters-in-law also come when they can. Laurentius, now that I am married I have discovered firsthand how very fortunate I am to have a religious husband. You cannot imagine how much of a blessing it is when Henri prays with me. Without religious devotion we could not maintain our love for each other. Henri writes that I do all that I can for him, but he in the same way does all that he can for me. Continue to pray for us.

Receive hearty greetings from your always loving sister,

Margo

P.S. How fortunate I would be to receive a letter from you.

19   *Ignaats M. Ludovicus Bunnemeijer*

Family historian Th. Snitselaar wrote that I. M. L. Bunnemeijer, born 1862, deserted the Naarden garrison of the Dutch army in 1882. Apart from his 1882 letter, no additional information about Bunnemeijer has been discovered. The letterhead is that of the State Emigrant Hospital, Wards Island, New York City, but the hospital has no record of this young man's employment or treatment.[1]

Ignaats M. Ludovicus Bunnemeijer to Ludovicus Hulstkamp
New York City to Hillegersberg, Zuid Holland
May 8, 1882

Esteemed Uncle,

This is my first letter from this place and I hope to receive some favorable news from you in return. I do not claim that I deserve it, but I hope to win back your respect by my future conduct. I know I have been guilty of foolish behavior, but in some cases things that were bad have turned out all right. Indeed, I cannot say that I am sorry to have come here for one moment. On the contrary, even though it is a fact that the winds have not always been favorable, I do get along well, and America is just the right country for me. A person can do any kind of

This letter was donated by Th. Snitselaar, 1976, and first translated by Herbert Brinks.
[1] John F. Magoulahan to Th. Snitselaar, October 30, 1973, Th. Snitselaar to H. J. Brinks, April 17, 1976, in Immigrant Letter Collection, Calvin College Archives.

work that he is able to perform and not be ashamed of it. That is what I like. At least I can now keep my head above water and earn money without being dependent on strangers. In the meantime I can assure you that I am on the lookout for opportunities to make money. It was anything but comfortable last winter when I was without money. But that time is past and I have steady work now. I did have a difficult time when I came into this country with only $12.00 in my pocket and without speaking English.

As you can see from this letterhead I am now in the emigrant hospital. My work is not difficult. It consists mainly of this—I go with the doctor whenever he makes his rounds, and when he wishes to speak to Hollanders, Germans, or Frenchmen, I translate for him. They promise to pay me according to what they take in. That is not much because the hospital is poor. But I enjoy it here. The people do not seem to be so formal and restrained as was the case in Holland.

It is true that I do not earn much here—very little actually—but I enjoy such a pleasant life that I plan to remain here for at least one year. I have all the food I need. And for whatever a person really needs to buy, he is given a paper that is signed [by the store clerk], and everything is taken care of. The finest clothes are available and we go with a clerk who interprets for us to find what we want.

Our hospital is located on an island. It is like a beautiful garden and four of us live here now in the summer. We have a small garden house arranged conveniently. Our meals are brought to us from the kitchen and a maid takes care of our housekeeping.

We are required to begin work at 7:00 A.M. and we are finished by 5:00 P.M. If we are not needed, we can read or do as we please, but we must be available. I am here to translate from Dutch, Frisian, and German. Another fellow translates from Italian and Russian, a third does Slavic languages, and the fourth translates Spanish and Turkish. Among ourselves we speak English because I am a Hollander, another fellow is Spanish, the third is an Armenian, and the fourth is Italian. We live a life here such as I have not enjoyed for years—and at very low cost. We have few needs, and we are not only supplied with our necessities, but we are treated with consideration.

I have been offered better-paying positions two or three times, but I don't know if I would be more satisfied. At any rate, I would stay here until the summer next year even if I were offered $1,000 per year. By then I will be able to speak English more correctly and be able to obtain a better position than this one.

I wrote to Jozef last week. Please be so kind as to write me and tell me how things are with Maria and Johanna. I would also like to know how things are going for Jozef and Louisa. If they need anything, please write and tell me and I will try to give them as much as you gave to me. I thank you once again for the help you gave me. . . . You never know how the dice will roll.

I have never seen a city like New York—so big and beautiful. It was surprisingly cold this winter—colder than anything I experienced in Holland. . . . It was cold from January to April but now it has changed and it is as warm as June in Holland.

One sees little of America's so-called freedom[1]—only that you hear more about murders and deathly beatings here than in Europe. It is remarkable that you can see little difference between New York City and Europe, but thirty minutes outside of the city the real America comes to light. Woodlands and attractive roads. Beautiful scenery and great hospitality.

With a group of eleven people I walked to Philadelphia this winter. We marched for about three days, and we had meals with farmers every day. In Philadelphia I had the opportunity to earn enough to ride the train back home.

In America it is just as people say—you can be what you want to be. No one needs to be ashamed. On one day a man may wear rags and on the next he may be dressed up with a gold watch and no one asks him how this came about.

Do not forget to give my greetings to the whole family. And tell them that things are going better for me than I ever imagined. But that reminds me, Uncle, I lost my pocketbook with a letter of identification and Mother's picture. Please be so kind as to send another picture to me and, if possible, also one of Father. I mean the very small medallion size. I want them very much.

I am pleased that I don't have to write asking you for money as I did in the past. That was not pleasant for me and not for you either. Little Louis, no doubt, is growing bigger. I am sending him a few American postal stamps. If he wants more he only needs to ask me and I'll send him a whole batch.

I ask especially that you do not neglect to give my greetings to Aunt Bartje, Johanna, Louis, Aaltje, and the whole family. Give my heartfelt thanks to all of them. Please excuse my writing on these half sheets— this is the only paper I have in the hospital.

Thanking you once again, I remain your most respectful nephew,

M. L. Bunnemeijer

1. This literal translation may imply a contrasting lifestyle outside of New York City as described in the same paragraph.

20 H. Koopman

H. Koopman's birthplace, Borger, is located about midway along a low ridge, the Hondsrug, which traverses the whole province of Drenthe between the city of Groningen and Coevorden on the German border. Prehistoric grave sites, *hunebedden*, demonstrate that Borger has been settled at least since 4000 B.C., but it has always been thinly populated agricultural terrain. Sand-soil farms on the ridge and tillable soils created from surrounding peat lands required an agricultural strategy that balanced grazing land and animal husbandry to produce manure for field crops. Commercial fertilizers altered that formula after the 1870s, when Drenthe's sandy soils sustained commercial agriculture with surpluses of potatoes, dairy products, and hogs. Presently Borger and much of Drenthe has been reforested to create natural recreation areas.[1]

As his letters indicate, H. Koopman remembered the manure-dependent and labor-intensive farms around Borger as both minimally productive and heavily taxed. Despite his relative wealth in 1920, he had no desire to return home as a farmer. Chicago had also spoiled his taste for village life with its social stratification and narrow country roads. His native village had only eighty-eight dwellings and three hundred residents in 1840, and the population of the entire *gemeente* was only twenty-two hundred. As Koopman pointed out, however Borger had grown since his departure, Chicago's buildings, roads, and technological advances were beyond the imaginations of his relatives there.[2]

The misbegotten plans to establish a Dutch colony in Liverpool, Texas, of which Koopman wrote bitterly, probably stemmed from the land developer Theodore F. Koch, who, in conjunction with others, promoted several Texas colonies, including the short-lived Winnie, Texas, venture (1910–1915), which also attracted Dutch immigrants from Chicago. The Liverpool settlement is not mentioned in the standard histories.[3] Thus, Koopman's account may well be the only surviving narrative of this fiasco.

These letters were donated by Mrs. Koopman-Hofkamp, 1976, and first translated by Herbert Brinks.
[1] Lambert, *The Making of the Dutch Landscape*, pp. 240–44.
[2] Van der Aa, *Aardrijkskundig woordenboek* 2:392.
[3] Lucas, *Netherlanders in America*, pp. 436–40.

H. Koopman to Brother
Chicago, to Borger, Drenthe
August 27, 1892

Dear brother,

I have a job as a gardener, and it comes with a room for $30 per month. The room is too big for one person. I live 1,000 feet from the lake [Michigan] and 100 feet above sea level. A bridge that crosses the road nearby is 185 feet long.

I am happy that you have your own house and that your children are growing up well. But if you had come to America, you would find it ten times better here for the working man.

Chicago is a second Paris, and in another year we will have the World's Fair here. Many Europeans will visit Chicago then.

Life is free here. You have no one looking over your shoulder.

Heartfelt greetings,
H. Koopman

[1894, Fragment]

I would not come back to the Netherlands to work for someone. It does not pay. It is best to be an independent farmer, but that costs too much there. You have to keep two houses [one for a hired hand] and pay high taxes in addition to all the work. All the manure has to be brought out to the field in wagons and everything is too expensive there.

In America you can get good land that does not have to be fertilized for ten years. Little care is required to watch the animals. They put posts in the ground about every twenty feet and attach iron threads to them on all sides of the pasture. Such a place, with a wooden house for a family of four and with a barn and two houses, costs about 3,000 guilders. That is for a nice place. The land is all in one place and has 2–4 feet of black soil. In its natural state it is grassland and it can be bought for almost nothing [no doubt he means homestead land]. Some people buy woodland, but that makes for a lot of work because you must take all the trees and stumps out of the ground. And such land is more worn out.

In southern Texas most crops can be raised two times a year on the same land—even including potatoes. But farmers work the land poorly here. All they do is plow—digging into the ground like pigs—and then they flatten it out with harrows. Most farmers here are lazy. They only work two-thirds of the time. At harvest time a few farmers use just one machine and it mows and threshes the grain all at once. I believe they have up to thirty men working on that single machine and they go from one place to another until everything is finished. Then the grain is brought away directly and sold. The work is done mainly by farm laborers. They raise potatoes here much as they do in Stadskanaal [a town near Borger]. They do not raise much hay here because the cattle stay out in the fields year around. But in some of the northern states it is much colder than [the Netherlands]. Sometimes the cattle actually freeze to death in their stalls.

* * *

You wrote about your children and especially about Altje, that she is a capable girl and earns 50 guilders per year. And also that Roelof earns fifty guilders. That is rather good for Drenthe. And that Altje wears her hair loose I find much more attractive than an *oorijzer* [a traditional head ornament with specific regional designs]. But she must, of course, be on her guard while working in a hotel because there is much danger and treachery in the world. I wish that she were not so far away, because here she could easily earn $3.00 per week.[1] If your children were here, they would be far better off because those who start out as laborers in Borger remain laborers. Better possibilities are available here. But I don't want to urge anyone to come here because the surroundings are entirely different. But I have an American spirit and I like it much better than in the Netherlands. In the city I can enter a tavern and sit next to a lawyer to drink beer and smoke a cigar. We walk down the same streets. And at a public meeting I can go in and sit down with any gentleman and wear clothes that are as good and fine as his—including starched collars and fashions of that sort. But the first year in a new land is hard.

Altje has written about a gold medallion. I will send her one or the money to buy one. I am not changed because I left you. But I don't know if I will ever return. If so, I'm afraid that I will not stay, and then it is always so saddening to leave again. But just the same, write to me about the price of pastureland and cropland. Do you continue to live in the same house? And the books I am sending—they are in English, but I will see if I can find them in Dutch. I will let you know what my plans are, but I intend to see the mountains and valleys once. The [enclosed] pictures of the officials and the man that they are going to hang comes from the newspaper that I read here every day. Now I hope that you and your wife will receive this letter in good health.

[Closing]

1. Her Dutch wages of 50 guilders, or $20, certainly seemed a pittance compared to $150 in Chicago.

H. Koopman to Nephew
Chicago to Borger, Drenthe
July 14, 1917

Dear nephew,
    [Opening]
    It was comforting to read that your father died with complete faith in
Jesus Christ. Some day I hope to meet him. But for now I am in good
health. Some people who have known me for a long time are surprised
when I tell them how old I am. They think that I look ten years younger.
When America declared war on Germany, men up to forty-six years of
age were called for military service and they called me too. I had to swear
that I was sixty, but they did not actually believe me.
    You should not be disappointed about not passing the examination.
You are still young and you should always expect the best because there
is much good in life. In the beginning here I also had many disappointments and grief. I had no friends and did not know the language. And
the Hollanders that I did meet were treasonous, even including the
Dutch consul.
    [For example], two Dutch pastors sent many of their members to Texas
where there were 50,000 acres that belonged to a Holland land company.
It was, they said, a land flowing with milk and honey. So I went to have
a look. The distance was 1,000 miles from Chicago. But when I saw it I
said, "The land is at sea level—by the Gulf of Mexico. When the sea
comes up you will be flooded. You need a steam plow to break up the
land." The people were killing themselves with work. I lived for two days
on coffee and pancakes. They had no bread—not one piece of bacon or
meat. I went away famished. At Alvin I went to a hotel, asked for a good
dinner, and took the train back to Chicago.
    When I came back not many Hollanders would believe me. But within
less than a year they were all washed out by the sea. They lost everything.
A few came back begging but neither the Dutch consul nor the pastors
would help them. They didn't want to know anything about it. Then I
told the Hollanders what I told you. I should have had it printed in the
newspaper. That's the way the preachers and the consul people operate.
I never go to Holland churches or consulates anymore.
    But you should never give up. Don't trust anyone and don't tell anyone
your secrets. If you need money write to me and I will send some money.
Within a year I will have saved $2,000, i.e., 5,000 guilders. If you get
into difficulty write and I will help.

                                                              [Closing]

H. Koopman to Brother
Chicago to Borger, Drenthe
March 8, 1921

Dear brother,

This letter is to learn from you if you and your family are well and if sister Marchien is still alive. What are your present circumstances? The great war has caused a lot of oppression but I have not felt any of it. I am in good health. I live in pleasant circumstances.

I have a furnished room on the boulevard and I go wherever I wish for pleasure. I don't work anymore. If I were in the Netherlands, they would tax me heavily because I own more than 30,000 guilders [$12,000]. I wish some one of you would write to me and tell me about your situation. My time on earth cannot be very long anymore and I would not like to have my money divided by strangers when I die. I would like to be remembered by you or your children after my death, and hope that you will write back soon.

With esteem,
H. Koopman

May 2, 1921

Dear brother,

I enjoyed your letter of March 28 and I see from it that you are all well. I also received a pleasant letter from Harm Jan. . . . I hope that he will pass the civil service exam on May 6. If he does not pass, he should try again. It pleases me greatly that all goes well with Altje. But I don't hear anything about Roelof. I remember him but I don't hear anything from him. Is he still there?

* * *

Three years ago I was in the hospital and no one came to see me, but the doctor liked me very much. He knew that I was a good streetcar conductor because I drove through all the streets of Chicago. He gave me all kinds of privileges and I ate five times a day.

I had scarlet fever, which I got from the doctor's son. He was in the hospital with it, and when he was almost better I drove him and his father home in my streetcar. But two days later I and his father both had scarlet fever. Otherwise I have been healthy all the time, for which I thank God almighty, for I have experienced that we cannot trust anyone here on earth.

[Repeat of his experience with the Texas Land Company.] They pub-

Chicago march 8, 192

Waarde Broeder,

Deze brief is dienende om U te informeren of Gij en uw huisgezin nog altemaal wel zijt, en of zuster Marchien nog leeft, En in welke omstandigheden gij verkeert, Want die Groote Oorlog heeft veel verdrukking gebragt, Maar ik heb er niets van gevoeld, En ik ben goed gezond En verkeer in goede omstandigheden, Werken doe ik niet meer, Ik heb een gemeubeleerde kamer aan de Boulevard, En voor mijn Pleizier Ga ik waar ik wil, was ik in Nederland zij zouden mij goede belasting op leggen, want ik ben over dertig duizend Gulden waart, Nu zou ik graag hebben dat een van U mij schrijft, die of nog zijn en in welke omstandigheden zij verkeren mijn tijd kan niet lang meer zijn op deze aarde, Mijn Geld zou ik niet Graag door Vreemdelingen laten verdelen wanneer ik kom te Sterven, ik zou graag hebben dat U of uwe kinderen, mij na mijn dood Gedagtig waren in hope dat gij mij spoedig schrijft.

met Achting

H. Koopman

H. Koopman's March 8, 1921, letter to his brother in Borger, Drenthe lished booklets about it signed by four Dutch pastors and the manager of a large store. I myself went to Rev. Dykstra's[1] home and asked him many questions because he gave the impression that he had been there. But when I went [to Texas] and stayed overnight at the last railroad station hotel, I found that the settlement, Liverpool, was still twenty-five miles away and with no railroad. The next day I walked to Liverpool and saw large ranches with thousands of animals. I asked a lady at one of the [ranch] houses for a drink of water because you can't drink the ditch water. It is too warm there. She gave me all the information. The place is completely unsuitable for agriculture and only good for fattening cattle. When I arrived at Liverpool, I saw their little houses and was disappointed. . . . When I went back to Chicago I talked to Rev. Dykstra and the manager of the big store. I told them there was only one road to Liverpool and that you had to walk there because there was no railroad. They admitted that they had never been there and had gone no farther than the town of Alvin. Then they asked me about Liverpool—what kind of town it was. I told them it was bad for agriculture. . . . The people came back begging on the way. You must have heard about one of them—he was a veterinarian from Stadskanaal and he died soon after returning.

Since then I have had no contact with Dutch preachers or the Dutch newspapers. I say they are worse than Judas Iscariot because he repented and returned the money.

* * *

Now, you have written to me asking me to come back, but that is difficult. I own stocks in coal mines and in a factory and do not know if I can get rid of them. They pay 7–8 percent interest and are worth about 820,000 guilders [$328,000]. Otherwise, I would like to return and spend my last days in Holland. Still, I will try to find out if I can sell them without loss. If so, I want to spend my last days with you. And before the winter starts I want to send you some money for the winter months.

[Closing]

1. Lawrence Dykstra, pastor of Englewood, Chicago, RCA, 1893–1898.

October 12, 1921

Esteemed brother,

Your letter of September 28 arrived. I was worried that you did not receive my letter with a check for 163 guilders. Now I am happy that you received it.

Chicago, State and Washington Streets, looking west, 1920s. Courtesy of the Chicago Photographic Collection, Special Collections, the University Library, the University of Illinois at Chicago.

* * *

Harm Jan should not be too concerned about not passing [the civil service exam]. There are many disappointments in life. In my time I've had three or four, but I read a book that says "never give up."

A family from Drouwenerveen named Vander Kaap traveled with me to America. He was an enormous and strong man, but with no ability. He could not adapt himself and could not learn English. He went back to the Netherlands with his wife and seven or eight children. Two of them were full-grown but not one had courage. Harm Jan must not be disturbed about the talk of some people. Jealousy is always great. But he must never make his secrets known and always try to increase his knowledge.

You write about Borger being built up. But if you were in Chicago you would be all eyes. There are houses here, one next to another, up to twenty or thirty stories high. Some have three stories below ground, with doors to a tunnel that is thirty feet under the street. . . . Steel rails are laid in the tunnels and there is room enough for two trains to pass each other easily. Electric lights are on day and night. You must not think of streets like [those in] Holland—here, there are eighteen-foot-wide lanes on each side of the street, so that four vehicles can pass each other. You can also see the elevated train, which is built on steel posts. The trains fly past each other. They go to the north, south, and west. Lake Michigan is on the east.

Two years ago I read in a Chicago newspaper about some immigrants from Holland. The newspaper said there was a man from Holland walking with his head back. He shouted, "What high houses! What high houses!" . . . Later I will write you about the bigness of this land.

[Closing]

November 17, 1921

Esteemed brother,

*   *   *

You wrote that the crops have failed and that it will bring great poverty because potatoes and beans are eaten by many working people. It is completely different here because if there is a failure in one place, another area will have a surplus. But there is still a lot of cheating here because large conglomerates buy up everything and keep it in warehouses so long that there is great need. Sometimes they sell it for three times the original value. And the president doesn't bother to do anything about it. People fear that there may be a revolution some day because the people do not get their rights.

*   *   *

I don't go to any Dutch church anymore. I go to the American church where Bible students preach. They don't ask for money there, and they help those who are in need or poverty. I go there twice on Sundays, and they prove from the Bible that the end of time is near—no later than 1926. And then the millennium will dawn and all the kingdoms of the earth will be destroyed and Christ will rule as king. At that time there will be millions who will not die.[1]

I hope you will receive this in good health.

Greetings to all,
H. Koopman

1. This premillennarian interpretation of certain biblical passages was foreign to Reformed teachings in the Netherlands and in the immigrant churches. Koopman's espousal of such views indicates religious Americanization within fundamentalist circles—perhaps from the D. L. Moody Church in Chicago.

January 25, 1922

[Opening]
You wrote saying that the end of the earth is still far off. [You think that] because the Bible is not well understood among you. The Bible Society here does not add one word, nor does it omit any words from the Bible. Most of the preachers in the world are unacquainted with the Greek and Hebrew languages. The word "hell" means "Sheol" in Hebrew and "Hades" in Greek. But what does this really mean in Hebrew? The grave or tomb. Just ask an educated Jew about that.

* * *

You must examine all the Scripture passages I sent to you. God says that in the 70th Jubilee year the Jews will be sent back to their land. Now seventy times fifty is 3,500 years and that will come up in 1926. And if you read about Abraham in Genesis concerning the promise to receive the promised land, then the time cannot come any later than 1932. But not everyone will inherit the earth—only those who are considered worthy of the Jews. The Gentile governments will come to an end and the world's kingdoms will be no more. But instead Jesus Christ will reign as king, and no tears will flow nor will men prepare for war. You must read Matthew 24, and the second chapter of Daniel and then write to me about your thoughts.

[Closing]

March 14, 1922

Dear brother and wife,
    [Opening]
I have written about the Bible so you can look it up and read it yourself. You say that [the end of the world will not come] until there is faith.[1] But that is not so. . . . The blood will come up to the horses' bridles but not before that great and illustrious day when the Lord comes and Jesus will come on the clouds and reign over the world in righteousness. After this there will be faith. Read the fourteenth chapter of the Revelation of John. Then you can see for yourself. But read it with judgment and understanding. And look in Matthew 24, where Jesus says there will be destruction and oppression such as has never been on the earth. But after this the sun will be darkened and God will light up the

Jan Willem Nijenhuis,
about 1890. Courtesy of
Calvin College Library
Archives, photo collection.

earth and all tears and sadness will be taken away. But only for those
who have Jesus as their redeemer.

[Closing]

1. Koopman's brother seems to be suggesting the postmillennial view that Christ will
return when Christianity spreads to become the dominant faith on the globe.

21 *Jan Willem Nijenhuis*

Until 1984, when two letters from Jan Willem Nijenhuis were discovered in Winterswijk, Gelderland, Nijenhuis's descendants believed that
he had been lost at sea in 1907. Apparently, his immediate family had
no direct communication with him after he deserted them, and his two

These letters were donated by G. Wagendorp, 1990, and first translated by Herbert
Brinks.

correspondents in Winterswijk did not inform the Nijenhuis family of his whereabouts. Even if his wife, Gesiena Damkot, knew about her husband's safe arrival in Newark, she nonetheless perpetuated the tale that he died at sea. The recent discovery of these letters in Winterswijk has disproved this myth and spurred the curiosity of Jan Willem's descendants.

After G. Wagendorp, J. W. Nijenhuis's grandson, gained possession of these letters, he attempted to discover something about the unknown history of his grandfather in Newark, but to no avail. He continues to wonder if Jan Willem ever remarried, if he had children in America, and if these or other descendants are still living. And above all, he would like to make contact with American grandchildren of Jan Willem Nijenhuis, if any exist.[1]

Jan Willem Nijenhuis to L. Mulder
Newark, New Jersey, to Winterswijk, Gelderland
July 5, 1908

Family members and friends,

Here are a few words from me in America. I have experienced so much that it is not possible to write all of it. I have not heard one word from the land of my birth. I wrote to you last year but it may not have come to your address. I was sick for seven weeks and could not pay close attention to the mail. It is not good to get sick here because it cost me $1.00 per day in the hospital. Now I have a union card [trade union hospitalization insurance] and that frees you from paying, but you don't get the card free of charge—it costs $30. If you die the children get $150 from the union. Tradesmen should join the union. (I'll write more later.)

This place is entirely different from Holland—especially if you have no relatives here. And you can't trust friends and acquaintances. It is also different with respect to work, clothing, customs, room, and board. Work, if you have it or can find it with the union, is eight hours per day or forty-four hours per week. Passaic and Paterson have many Hollanders. All the people here are English, German, and Polish, but no Italians. This city has a population of 350,000. There is nothing to do here on Sunday. Millionaires rule the roost here. At the moment times are bad. The factories are working at half power and everything is expensive. That always happens here when they elect a new president. But people say it has never been so bad as this year and most of last year. They say

---

[1] G. Wagendorp, interview by author, November 12, 1990, notes in Jan Willem Nijenhuis Papers, Immigrant Letter Collection.

it was also bad in 1892–93, but not like this. I would not advise anyone to come to America at this time because there are 100,000 people out of work and the prospects are bad—so I have read. And then there is the problem of not knowing English on top of that. At the moment I can get along with talking at work and things like that.

And now a little about my trip, or this letter will get too long. I worked in Laren, near Hilversum, for fourteen days and then my leg became very swollen and I could not walk. Dr. Wittig treated me for fourteen days and then I made plans to come here immediately. I went to No. 23 Damrak, in Amsterdam to reserve a place on the boat, that was the 19th of April. Friday, the 20th, I left for Rotterdam. After rocking on the ocean for eleven days I took my first step on American soil in New York on May 1. Then, after ten days in New York I went to Elizabeth, New Jersey, and after that I came here.

I took only a few things along with me to Laren, and those I took with me here. That was fortunate because many things here are not made well.

I paid $96 for the trip. It was expensive then and costs only $60 now. I boarded the *Noordam* in Rotterdam with 2,500 persons and another 250 came aboard in Toulon [France]. With 250 of the ship's crew, we had 3,000 persons aboard. I will write more about the trip later.

It is currently very warm here, warmer than anything you have in Holland.

I will close this letter with the hope that you receive it in good health, and also that the children are well and healthy.

Sunday 7:00 P.M.
Willem

November 9, 1908

Family and acquaintances,

I am writing to respond to your letter of September 9 with its questions, and also to add some other information. At the moment I am in reasonably good health and I hope the same for you, for your family, the sisters and brothers-in-law and especially for the children. I am very pleased to know that they are learning well, and Bertus too. When I return, as I hope to do after a few years, he will be fully grown.

I had a letter from the Klein Poelhuis family last week and I was pleased to learn that they had a son who is already one and a half years old. He was born just about the time that I came here on April 30.

I have been working as a painter ever since I came here because tradesmen do not work outside of their trade here. . . . Union wages for a painter here are $3.28 per day, or 8 guilders in Dutch money. The hours are 8:00–12:00 and 1:00–5:00. So if you can work regularly you can earn a good wage.

But the economy has been poor since I came here. It's just beginning to improve a little. The election is now past and the new president, Taft, a Republican, was elected by a 1.5-million-vote majority. I am not getting union wages at this time but $2.50, or 6 guilders, per day. Wages are a little lower in the West but prices are lower too. At this time I am working in Maplewood. I had almost no work this summer. At the moment things are a little better and next year it will certainly be better. They are planning a building here with thirty-eight floors, six floors higher than the Singer Building in New York City.

I take the electric train to work at 7:00 A.M. tomorrow and return home by 5:30 P.M. Maplewood is three hours [walking] from Newark. I am working for this boss for the third time now. He is of Norwegian birth, but he speaks English. About three weeks ago, after working for him for fourteen days, I threw the paintbrush at his ears. Now, after eight days he came back and asked me to work for him because he knows that I am a good worker. I went to work for him because I was just out of work again. You don't have to be so afraid of the boss here. You learn that quickly in America.

Maplewood is a nice place, located entirely in a valley and surrounded by mountains. It has large wooden homes all painted white inside and outside, even including the floors. And they are building more there too.

Little building is going on in Newark, but everything must go quickly. Now, I have answered all of your questions truthfully. If you want to know more, just write and ask.

The Union questions I will answer more broadly at another time, because that could easily take half a day to answer. Union wages for carpenters are $4.00 per day, $4.50 for bricklayers, and $5.00 for plumbers—those who lay pipe for water and gas.

Herewith I enclose a [money order] for Egbert; it is a gift for Bertus [probably a nephew]. I think he is now old enough to go out with you on Sunday [that is, attend church].

Concerning my possessions in your care, I have yet to decide. The chest with my accounts you must preserve. You may keep the paint brushes, and Miene can use the sandpaper. If you happen to see the paint salesman, find out what he will give for the green [paint] in my two chests.

Last week I discovered that the postcard you sent me arrived at the address of my first boss, Dieterich, in Elizabeth, New Jersey. He could not find it, but he did not send it back to you.

I have some things in Doetinchem, at the Cafe Meeuwsen! I've not written to them. I am sorry that I so carelessly left my things behind. They did not want my bed because they have beds enough. I will inquire here about the cost of shipping over my suitcase.

With this I close and hope that Bertus and Miena will receive it in health and well-being.

With friendly greetings,
Willem

22 *Anna Kuijt*

In 1906 Anna Kuijt (1879–1961) immigrated to Chicago, where two of her siblings had preceded her. They had been born in Amsterdam, but they lived in an orphanage near Nijmegen from 1884 until about 1895 when they moved back to Amsterdam and lived with Gerrit Kuijt, their oldest brother. The youngest of the children, Anna, managed a small retail butter store on Nicolaas Beets Street until she emigrated. Thereafter she corresponded with brother Gerrit, who moved from Amsterdam to Hilversum, where he raised chickens. Anna suffered from a leg infection, which, however uncomfortable, did not prevent her from living to the age of eighty-two.

Coenraad Kuijt, Anna's brother, also corresponded with Gerrit Kuijt in Hilversum. His August 12, 1909, letter from Chicago reveals additional details about Anna's experiences as a housemaid.

> You write that you have not heard much from Anna. Well, we did not hear much from her when she lived in Holland either. We tell her often enough that she should write, and that's all we can do.
>
> Her leg is now healed. She has had a number of jobs—some for one or two weeks and others for one or two months. At the moment she is working for people who spend their summers in Aurora, Illinois (about fifty miles from Chicago), and from there she goes with them to Kankakee (also about fifty miles from here). These people bought a house there and Anna is going to live with them. She has been with them now for two months and we don't know how long she will remain there.

These letters were donated by J. C. Schoenmaker-Zeewuster, 1986, and first translated by Herbert Brinks.

By December 26, 1909, Anna had returned to Chicago and was then hospitalized for her ailing leg. Coenraad reported:

> Anna is still in the hospital but we expect to take her out in a few weeks. They have done everything they can for her and she can take her medicine at home. She has progressed to some degree but her restoration is far from complete. The big question is if she will ever be completely healed. For our part, we don't think so, and the doctors have differing views of the matter. Thus, it is a sad history, right?[1]

Nonetheless, Anna was able to move to Maurice, Iowa, in 1910 and return to Chicago the following year. By then she probably clerked in a downtown shop, much as she had done in Amsterdam. Her rather sudden marriage to Dudley Bates in 1918 was reported in the last of her surviving letters. But the Kuijt family historian indicates that she outlived Bates by thirty-four years and died in Momence, Illinois, on October 4, 1961.[2]

Anna Kuijt to Gerrit and Letha Kuijt
Chicago to Hilversum, Noord Holland
December 23, 1907

Dear Gerrit and Letha,

No doubt you are saying, "Well, finally a letter from Anna." I must admit that I have waited a long time, but I did not know if you were on the ocean or if you had a new address.[1] And I did not know your address, but enough of that. Who knows how long it may be until we see each other again. The time goes by so quickly, especially when you are busy, and that is the case for me at present.

You should know that I already have a job, but the jobs here are not so nice because they work differently here and on top of that I have to do the washing and everything along with that. In the beginning I didn't make much headway, but now Jeanette [another maid in the house] has been helping me. She arrived just a short while ago. She gets things done quickly. When she begins at 7:00 A.M. she has the whole wash hanging on the line by 10:30.

But now something else. You will want to know how I managed the trip. I was very sick for the five days before landing because we had bad weather and that was not very nice. And a word of wisdom to you. I suggest that you do not take too many things along—a wash basin, for

[1] Coenraad Kuijt Papers, 1908–1911, Immigrant Letter Collection.
[2] J. C. Schoenmaker-Zeewuster, Kuijt Family History, in Coenraad Kuijt Papers, Immigrant Letter Collection.

example—because all the apartments here have bathrooms with sinks. They do not have much furniture—only a few chairs and a bookcase. Sell your clothes, because the transportation cost for them is very high, and if you carry much, they open all your trunks. They did not look at my things very carefully. I just said that I could not understand. They did not see the cigars I had with me, so we smuggled in the tobacco. My luggage had already been inspected when Miss Neter gave me the tobacco. Thus I was able to bring that off quite well. And the nickel teapot that I had with me—I had to open my trunk, and they pulled out the teapot and looked at it from all sides. They asked me what I had paid for it. I only said I don't know and so I had to pay nothing [no duty] on it. Everything went according to plan. My goods came to rest at the letter "K" and those of your brother by the letter "R." Van Wijk[2] walks from one to the other and if you stand by the "K" he comes directly to you. You should ask him immediately if he will help you with your things because he will try to find someone who will not look so carefully at your things. If you eat lunch with Van Wijk, don't order any bread for the train because we had to throw out $4.00 worth of food. In the train someone comes often enough with everything you need to eat. Anyway, when you arrive in New York there are stores where you can buy a few rolls. That is better.

I saw Henk yesterday, Sunday. He arrived Saturday morning. William Goedhart took him through the city on Saturday night. He wanted to stay here rather than go to Colusa, [California]. And I believe it would be better for you to stay in Chicago for a few months too. The accommodations outside of the city are not so expensive. If you go to Colusa one at a time, it would not be so expensive as traveling with the whole household. There is not much going on in Colusa, and Gerrit might not be able to find work there. As your brother wrote to Coen, they have a false impression about this in Holland. Your brother also recommended that I not go there. And Chicago is also better for your boys. Of course, you must know too that groceries are less expensive here in Chicago. If you could start a store here or buy a house, they are not so expensive. They are all of one story and most of them have gas installed.

Your brother [Coen] is a painter. Perhaps he has already written to you, but he should write once at least to tell you how things are and how they were.

When Henk came over, a child died on the boat. They had given him too much to drink to combat seasickness. He was thrown into the sea at 11:00 in the evening. Henk saw it from close up.

When we arrived in New York your brother acted as a direct witness.[3] Henk must have written you that your brother had to pay 150 guilders on his luggage, and a whole bunch more for the organ. I don't think much was broken—only the milk can and the heart-shaped bowl—and the tray for the drinking glasses. I had too many things with me and I have stored them in Jeanette's cellar.

Now, Gerrit and Letha, I will end this and, if you want to know anything else, just write and I will write back sooner.

Anna Kuijt

1. Gerrit and Letha Kuijt were intending to emigrate but changed their plans when Gerrit was disqualified for immigration because of a chronic illness.
2. Probably a Dutch-speaking representative from an immigrant-aid society. There were two Dutch American agencies of this sort, one in New York City and another in Hoboken, New Jersey.
3. Probably for Anna Kuijt, who, as a single woman, needed verification of her independent status and good character to gain entrance.

August [1908]

Dear Gerrit and Letha,

Please excuse me for having waited so long to write you, but it has been so terribly warm here that I don't have the energy. Otherwise things are going well here. I work for very good people. At the moment they are out of Chicago for a month and I am alone in the house with their dog. I don't earn as much as many want to earn here, and I must work very hard here baking bread and all sorts of other things. I am not really strong enough because it is difficult work for me with my leg, which has started to bother me again. It is not as bad as it was in Holland because it pained me a great deal then. I went to a doctor here to get some information for an official paper. He said it was not dangerous, but that I was too young to have a leg like that.

From the letter that Christien wrote to your brother Coen, I understand that you stayed in Hilversum. I think that that is better for you at present than here. When one does not know the language, it is quite a burden and the wages are not as high as people in Holland think. It is better to come here when you are young and you can learn things easily.

Gerrit and Letha, how are you and the boys? Is Gerrit feeling better now that he works outside and you have gotten back all the money from the food? You never know what fate has in store for us. I never thought much about going to America and now I have been here for nearly a year. Time passes so quickly.

People here tend to go to church a lot. You are respected more if you go to the church. I don't go too much. I find it too warm. Jeanette, W. C., and Nellie go faithfully every Sunday, Jeanette two times every Sunday. They are doing well. Jeanette is terribly frugal and thus they can save a little. They have a piece of property but not yet enough money to build on it. It is difficult for them to save much with four boys. That is the same here as in Holland. My employers are off to New York. They say that they plan to visit Amsterdam in about five years and then I will go along with them. They would like to see Holland once.

Now Gerrit and Letha, I will close as there is not much news here. My best wishes to you from your loving sister, Anna. Give the boys a thousand kisses from Aunt Anna Kuijt.

[Closing]

Anna Kuijt to Gerrit and Letha Kuijt
Maurice, Iowa, to Hilversum, Noord Holland
November 27, 1910

Dear Gerrit and Letha,

I received your letter in good health, and I was pleased to receive it because it has been a while since we last wrote to one another. And anyway, I did not have your address. It is wonderful isn't it, that Gerrit has completely recovered and that the boys are making such progress. They will get very tall, won't they? How old are they now? I would like to see them so much, but nothing will come of that unless you come here once. I think that you could have done well here too. Where I am now, Hollanders are practically the only residents. It is not so difficult with the language here. Schoolteachers can hardly find a boarding place here, so if you came here you could easily keep boarders.

Most people here raise their own vegetables and potatoes. They also have many chickens here. I asked my employers if a person could make a living by raising chickens here. They said, yes, if you have a good understanding of the business. Eggs cost less here than in Holland. I think they are thirty cents a dozen. In the summer they are only ten cents. Not very expensive, is it? It's too bad that the soil where you are is so poor, right? It is very good here, and there is a place for sale near here. The Van Donselaars, near here, just bought five acres [they have other land that they cannot sell]. They thought about raising apples on that land but it takes five years to get enough apples. It is good apple land. That would be nice for your brother if he had come here and for his wife. They would not need to know English so well here, right?

I did not know that Gerrit from the Stoofsteeg was dead. I heard lots about it. I wonder if Christien will like living alone in the apartment.

It must cost a lot of money to send your boys to school. Do you still have to pay so much taxes? Here you don't have to pay any if you rent an apartment. But you do if you have your own home. Even then, it is not high.

I also received a letter from Cato and she said all was going very well for you, that for the present you will not come here because if you have it good in Holland you simply don't have to come here. If things had not gone well with the things you began there, then I would say come here. I don't know now if it is good for the boys here, but I would say yes because if one has a little training one can do well anywhere.

Things are about the same for me. I walk with a cane on the street, but not in the home. I will stay here in Maurice for the winter, but I'll see about the summer. Perhaps I can learn to sew well. You can earn quite a bit on the side here with that.

Now Gerrit and Letha, I will close hoping that you will write me back again soon. Send my best wishes to the boys and best wishes to you also. And a kiss from your sister,

Anna

Anna Kuijt to Uncle and Cato [Kuijt]
Chicago to Hilversum, Noord Holland
August 12, 1911

Dear Uncle and Cato,

I have waited a long time to write, haven't I? But I could not send you a proper address. At the moment I am putting the socks and underclothes through an ironing machine.

I rented a room which was too far away from my work, so I could not send you that address. Now I have a more expensive room only half a block from my work. It is quite nice.

I earn $6.00 for five days' work. I am usually free on Mondays and Saturdays and I work until 6 o'clock in the evening. I eat in a restaurant, so that's not too bad, right?

I can walk much better now than a few weeks ago. I was sick for a few days then, and the doctor thought that I had something wrong with my appendix, and that I had to go to the hospital immediately. (I think he thought that I would die if I did not go right away.) I said that I wanted to sleep on it first, and I am still alive. Doctors don't frighten me so much anymore and they like to operate a great deal here. Otherwise I have had quite a bit of luck here, don't you agree?

How are things with you and Uncle? I heard that you [Cato] made another trip to Germany. You all looked so well on the postcard. And it was nice that Henrij and Suze also could go along. No doubt Uncle was very happy when you came back. Who cooked the meals for Uncle? Could Meintje be doing that already? And who took over the store for Suze? How long were you in Germany?

Cato, in your last letter you wrote that you wanted to crochet a skirt for me. That would cost a great deal of money, and if you were not so far away I would like to have that skirt. But perhaps you can send me a pattern and tell me how I must do it. Then I can do it myself. I believe that Anna de Lang still has a crochet book, right? I could look at that.

Jeanette and Coen are doing very well. They both have fine houses and it is cool there. It hardly seems that they live in a big city there—it's almost like the country. When I go there I have to take four different streetcars.

I live only two blocks away from the lake. In the evening when I am finished working, I often go to the beach and sit there for a few hours.

Now, Cato, you can see how many mistakes I am making, but I am nearly asleep and must go to bed quickly.

I hope that you will get this letter in the best of health and with best wishes I remain your loving sis,

Anna

P.S. It is no longer so very warm here. We have had very warm weather. Now, goodbye.

Anna Kuijt Bates to Gerrit and Letha Kuijt
Morgan Park, Illinois, to Hilversum, Noord Holland
January 15, 1918

Dear Gerrit and Letha,

I received your letter in good health and thank you for the congratulations. You must have been surprised when you saw that, suddenly, I was married. Well, so far I don't have any complaints or regrets—even though it all happened quite quickly.

I only knew Dudley for five months and we did not see each other that often. He is an only son and we live with his mother. The house belongs to her and she rents out the first floor for $30 per month. We live above and I do not have to pay any rent. Dudley does not need to make much money, but I do everything myself. I bake bread and cake and pie, so that does not cost too much. I just bought ten pounds of sugar for 42 cents. That is a big difference from Holland, right? There it cost 25 cents for one pound.

I think you would be better off here in America, but I don't know for sure. It is best to just jump in. Can Herman speak English? Dudley cannot understand any Dutch. There are many places here where they speak Dutch, but that is the place where I was three years ago. It would not be good for Herman's work there. That would be better in the city.

I wish that I knew where it would be best for you and then you would certainly all want to come there. I am happy that Gerrit is so healthy now. He really suffered much in Haarlem.

I just received a letter from Suze saying she would like to come here too if it weren't for the English language.

We had a chicken for Christmas dinner. We paid so much for it and it was about five pounds. What do you get for a chicken, and what do eggs cost now in Holland?

We have had very nice weather here. Not much snow.

Now, Gerrit and Letha, I will close because I must finish making supper. Kindest regards to you and to Gerrit and Herman from your aunt and sister, Anna.

Gerrit and Herman must write Uncle Dudley a letter in English. Then he will write back too. I would love to see you again, but I'm afraid I would not be able to recognize you anymore because you are so big. Be good. You must come here too. Best wishes, OK.

Your Aunt and Uncle Dudley.

My address is:
Mr. Dudley Bates
1914 Grove Street
Morgan Park, Illinois

23   *Willem Smith*

Anna Tangenberg wrote that her uncle, Willem Siebrand Smith, corresponded with her when she was a young girl. At that time, about 1935, Willem Smith lived in Tampa, Florida, and raised chickens for a living. He was also involved in dog racing.

The letters published here (1935–1936), sent to his mother and his niece, Anna, reveal only a thin slice of Willem's life. Like all the correspondents in this chapter, he was separated from the major Dutch enclaves, and although Anna Tangenberg suggests that Willem may have lived briefly in Grand Rapids, Michigan, he made no reference to Dutch connections in his letters.[1]

These letters were donated by A. B. D. Tangenberg, 1987, and first translated by Herbert Brinks.

[1] A. B. D. Tangenberg to Herbert J. Brinks, October 26, 1987, Immigrant Letter Collection.

Willem Smith to Mother and Family
Tampa, Florida, to Finsterwolde, Groningen
September 15, 1935

Dear Mother and family,

I am well and hope you are too. I've been very busy this past week with rebuilding my house and chicken coops because we have had another hurricane. That is a terrible kind of storm. I had a lot of damage, but it could have been worse. I can repair most everything myself. I lost some chickens, but most of them survived. Whole houses were blown down here and trees were snapped off. Some people died and many were injured. Some may never be found. A whole train was blown off the track and a steamboat was blown onto the land with much damage. About 800 soldiers were camped here to help with the dead and the injured. It was not so terrible for me. I had all my windows boarded up tight. We knew beforehand that the storm was coming, and we could prepare for it to some degree. The storms come, for the most part, in September or October—just after the rainy season. Usually the storms are not so bad, but we have had three or four bad storms since I have been in Florida.

Storms occur the world over and they can be bad in Holland too, especially in the fall and winter. But this last storm here was very bad—at one place so many people died that they could not be properly buried. They were found three days after the storm and in such a decayed state that they could only pour oil over the bodies and burn them up. They could do nothing else.

The weather is nice again now and I am very busy cleaning up my property.

Greetings from your loving son, W. Smith

P.S.

Dear Annie,

I received your letter and photo and was very happy with them. You look very nice in the picture. I showed it to my friends and they all remarked that you looked very nice standing there. The picture came over in good condition. I should also have my picture taken again and then you can see me once again.

At the moment I am repairing my boat, which was damaged by the big storm we had here. Everything was blown around here and some boats were thrown far inland. So I am busy and a bit upset by all the things that need repairing. Some things are totally lost. Over half of the oranges were lost. . . . But after a few weeks you will not be able to notice the damage.

Hearty greetings from your loving uncle,

W. Smith

November 26, 1936

Dear Mother,

Apart from a bad cold I am in good health. I caught my cold when I went hunting. Usually we go deer hunting here with a group and stay in the woods for a few days. We make a big fire in the evening. But I think I'm getting a little too old for that now.

Well, today it is Thanksgiving Day, a general holiday that Americans celebrate by eating turkey and baked goods. I think I will be satisfied with eating a chicken—a very young hen which tastes very good.

There is not much news here. Things are about the same. In some places people are on strike from work. It's a strange world isn't it?

There are a great number of farms here with about 1,000 workers and they are on strike for no reason. There is also a work strike among the sea men [stevedores] and boats cannot be loaded or unloaded. A few days ago a strike began in a canning factory that was just recently opened for the season. They preserve vegetables and fruit here in the winter. Of course the farmers here are very angry because they will lose their crops without the workers. So it goes here.

The farmers have a good harvest. The first tomatoes are coming in and they are very good. They weren't very good in Holland when I lived there, and perhaps not now either. At first I did not like them but now I eat them like an apple. They are very healthful and they give you an appetite for more.

Well, my paper is full, so I send you my hearty greetings,

Your loving son, W. Smith

P.S.

Dear Annie,

When you receive this, it will be near your birthday, and I hope that you will celebrate it in good health and well-being. I would enjoy coming over to see you in person once but I am too far away and traveling costs too much money at present. Perhaps you can come to see me, because it is a nice world here. With the ocean nearby and always warm in the winter there is always something to do here.

I often take a boat out on the Gulf of Mexico and catch some fish. Do you ever eat fish? Well, today I am home with a cold. I was out hunting for a few days and we slept in the woods by a big fire. The nights are always cool here and then you can easily catch a cold.

Well, my letter is nearly full, *and again congratulated with your birth day and many more and plenty kisses from your unkle, W. Smith. good by Annie and be a good girl.*[1]

1. The material in italics was written in English.

APPENDIXES

Appendix A   *List of Translators*

STUDENTS, 1985–1994

Michele Boonstra
Jacqueline Eckmann
Anthony Hop

Elske Horchner
Marijke Jonker
Jan Peter van Seventer

Evert van Steenbergen
Hestien Vreugdenhil
Tjetske Vreugdenhil

VOLUNTEERS, 1990–1994

Floyd Antonides
Jack Appel
Harold Bossenbroek
Gerard Bouma
Sietske Bruinsma
Anja Buma
Gilmer Compaan
Dena Damsteegt
Peter de Gelder

Maria de Groot
Margaret Eshuis
Jacob Geuzebroek
Elizabeth Hietkamp
John Hofstee
Roland Hoogendoorn
D.P. Jongkind
Arie Klein
Louisa Kuiper

Grace Meetsma
Elco Oostendorp
Tineke Ouwinga
Louise Smit
Hillie Stoker
Calvin Van Lonkhuizen
Cornelis Van Nuis
Enno Wolthuis
John Yzenbaard
And one more.

Appendix B   *Dates and Places of Emigration*

Name	Emigration Date	Municipality of Last Residence	Total Number of Emigrants, 1835–1880
Avink	1869	Borculo, Gelderland	162
Bunnemeijer	1882	Naarden, Noord Holland	5
De Lange	1873	Deventer, Overijssel	192
Diemer	1893	Hoogeveen, Drenthe	44
Dunnink	1848	Staphorst, Overijssel	276
Eringa	1892	Spannum, Friesland*	99
Heller	1891	Ulrum, Groningen	512

Appendix B (*cont.*)

Name	Emigration Date	Municipality of Last Residence	Total Number of Emigrants, 1835–1880
Koopman	1892	Borger, Drenthe	52
Kuijt	1906	Amsterdam, Noord Holland	2,227
Lankester	1850	Middelburg, Zeeland	357
Mannee	1847	Zierikzee, Zeeland	670
Niemeijer	1904	Middelstum, Groningen	290
Nijenhuis	1907	Winterswijk, Gelderland	2,198
Plaisier	1910	Ridderkerk, Zuid Holland	31
Schoonbeek	1873	Nieuwolda, Groningen	48
Smith	[1920]	Finsterwolde, Groningen	1
Van den Hoek	1866	Noordeloos, Zuid Holland	106
Van der Bosch	1847	Gendringen, Gelderland	278
Van Hall	1882	Huissen, Gelderland	10
Verstegen	1850	Zeeland, Noord Brabant	115
Wonnink	1871	Geesteren, Gelderland**	162
Zahn	1856	Amsterdam, Noord Holland	2,227
Zondervan	1889	Firdgum, Friesland***	224

SOURCE: Data provided by Robert P. Swierenga, History Professor at Kent State University.

*Gemeente Hennaarderadeel
**Gemeente Borculo
***Gemeente Barradeel

Appendix C *Comparative Weights, Measures, and Currency*

Netherlands		United States
1 pond, 500 grams	=	1 pound, 454 grams
1 mud	=	2.75 bushels
1 hectare	=	2.47 acres
1 bunder	=	2.47 acres
1 shilling	=	12.5 cents
1 guilder	=	2.50 cents*

*This rate of exchange prevailed from 1850 to 1917 with little variation.

SELECTED BIBLIOGRAPHY

Algra, H. *Het wonder van de 19e eeuw: Van vrije kerken en kleine luyden.* Franeker, The Netherlands: T. Wever, 1976.

Barnow, A. J. *The Making of Modern Holland.* New York: Norton, 1944.

Beets, Henry. *De Chr. Geref. Kerk in N.A.* Grand Rapids, Mich.: Grand Rapids Printing, 1918.

Blink, H. *Opkomst van Nederland als economisch-geographisch gebied van de oudste tijden tot heden.* Amsterdam: De Wereldbibliotheek, 1925.

Bodnar, John. *The Transplanted: A History of Immigrants in Urban America.* Bloomington: Indiana University Press, 1985.

Bratt, James H. *Dutch Calvinism in Modern America: A History of a Conservative Subculture.* Grand Rapids, Mich.: Eerdmans, 1984.

Brinks, Herbert J. *Schrijf spoedig terug: Brieven van immigranten in Amerika, 1847–1920.* The Hague: Boekencentrum, 1978.

Brouwer, Arie R. *Reformed Church Roots.* Grand Rapids, Mich.: Reformed Church Press, 1977.

Brugmans, I. J. *De arbeidende klasse in Nederland in de 19e eeuw, 1813–1870.* The Hague: Martinus Nijhoff, 1925.

——. *Paardenkracht en mensenmacht: Sociaal-economische geschiedenis van Nederland, 1795–1940.* The Hague: Martinus Nijhoff, 1961.

Cheney, Roberta C. *Names on the Face of Montana.* Missoula, Mont.: Mountain Press, 1983.

Cook, Richard. *South Holland, Illinois, 1846–1966.* Privately printed, 1966.

Cuddy, Dennis L., ed. *Contemporary American Immigration: Interpretive Essays.* Boston: Twayne, 1982.

Deeleman, Th. *Opdat wij niet vergeeten.* Kampen, the Netherlands: J. H. Kok, 1949.

de Haas, Joh. *Gedenkt uw voorgangers.* 5 vols. Haarlem, Netherlands: Vijlbrief, 1984–89.

De Jong, Gerald F. *The Dutch in America, 1609–1974.* Boston: Twayne, 1975.

De Jong, Louis. *The Netherlands and Nazi Germany.* Cambridge: Harvard University Press, 1990.

De Jonge, J. A. *De industrialisatie in Nederland tussen 1850 en 1914.* Epe, The Netherlands: Scheltema en Holkema, 1968.

de Wolde, J. *Ontginning en verkavelingen in de gemeente Staphorst.* Staphorst, The Netherlands: Gemeentebestuur, 1980.

——. *Staphorst zoals het werkelijk Is*. Staphorst, The Netherlands: Gemeentebestuur, 1978.

Doezema, Linda Pegman. *Dutch Americans: A Guide to Information Sources*. Detroit: Gale Research, 1979.

Dolan, Jay P. *The American Catholic Experience: A History from Colonial Times to the Present*. Garden City, N.Y.: Doubleday, 1985.

Ernst, Robert. *Immigrant Life in New York City, 1825–1863*. Port Washington, N.Y.: Ira Friedman, 1965.

Eyck, F. Gunther. *The Benelux Countries: An Historical Survey*. New York: Van Nostrand, 1959.

Formsma, W. J., et al. *Historie van Groningen: Stad en land*. Groningen, The Netherlands: Wolters-Noordhoff, 1981.

Gabriel, Ralph H. *The Course of American Democratic Thought*. New York: Ronald Press, 1956.

Galema, A., B. Henkes, and H. te Velde, eds. *Images of the Nation: Different Meanings of Dutchness*. Amsterdam: Rodopi, 1993.

Ganzevoort, Herman, and Mark Boekelman, eds. *Dutch Immigration to North America*. Toronto: Multicultural History Society of Ontario, 1983.

Goldberg, David. *A Tale of Three Cities: Labor Organization and Protest in Paterson, Passaic, and Lawrence, 1916–1921*. New Brunswick: Rutgers University Press, 1989.

Gordon, Milton. *Assimilation in American Life: The Role of Race, Religion, and National Origins*. New York: Oxford University Press, 1964.

Grant Public Library Staff. *The Beginnings of Grant, Michigan*. Privately printed [1954].

Hall, Henry. *The History of Auburn*. New York: Dennis Brothers, 1869.

Herberg, Will. *Protestant, Catholic, Jew: An Essay in American Religious Sociology*. Garden City, N.Y.: Doubleday Anchor, 1960.

Horrisberger, Doris, et al. *Grant Area Yesterday, Today*. Grant, Mich.: Taylor, 1979.

Kirk, Gordon W. *The Promise of American Life: Social Mobility in a Nineteenth-Century Immigrant Community, Holland, Michigan, 1847–1894*. Philadelphia: American Philosophical Society, 1978.

Kroes, Rob. *The Persistence of Ethnicity: Dutch Calvinist Pioneers in Amsterdam, Montana*. Urbana and Chicago: University of Illinois Press, 1992.

Kroes, Rob, and Henk-Otto Neuschafer, eds. *The Dutch in North America: Their Immigration and Cultural Continuity*. Amsterdam: Free University Press, 1991.

Kromminga, John. *The Christian Reformed Church: A Study in Orthodoxy*. Grand Rapids, Mich.: Baker Books, 1949.

Lambert, Audrey M. *The Making of the Dutch Landscape: An Historical Geography of the Netherlands*. London: Academic Press, 1985.

Lemmen, Loren, and Swenna Harger. *The County of Bentheim and Her Emigrants to North America*. Holland, Mich.: Privately printed, 1990.

Ligterink, G. H. *De landverhuizers: Emigratie naar Noord-Amerika uit het Gelderse—Westfaalse grensgebied tussen de jaren, 1830–1850*. Zutphen, The Netherlands: De Walberg Pers, 1981.

Lucas, Henry. *Dutch Immigrant Memoirs and Related Writings*. 2 vols. Assen, The Netherlands: Van Gorcum, 1955.

——. *Netherlanders in America: Dutch Immigration to the United States and Canada, 1789–1950.* Ann Arbor: University of Michigan Press, 1955.

Motley, John L. *The Rise of the Dutch Republic: A History.* 2 vols. New York: A. L. Burt, 1864.

Niemeijer, Jan A. *Kroniek van het geslacht Niemeijer.* Groningen, The Netherlands: Niemeijer Press, 1971.

Nieuwenhuis, Nelson. "A History of Dutch Settlement in South Dakota to 1900." M.A. thesis, University of South Dakota, 1948.

Parker, Nathan H. *Iowa as It Is in 1855.* Chicago: Keen and Lee, 1855.

Reitsma, J. *Geschiedenis van de hervorming en de Hervormde Kerk der Nederland.* Groningen, Netherlands: J. B. Wolters, 1899.

Schakel, M. W. *Geschiedenis van de hoge en vrije heerlijkheden van Noordeloos en Overslingeland.* Gorinchem, the Netherlands: J. Noorduijn, 1955.

Scheanwald, Dick. *McBain Centennial, 1977.* Privately printed, 1977.

Schreuder, Yda. *Dutch Catholic Immigrant Settlement in Wisconsin, 1850–1905.* New York: Garland, 1989.

Shetter, William. *The Netherlands in Perspective: The Organization of Society and Environment.* Leiden: Martinus Nijhoff, 1987.

——. *The Pillars of Dutch Society: Six Centuries of Civilization in the Netherlands.* The Hague: Martinus Nijhoff, 1971.

Sinke, Suzanne. "Home Is Where You Build It: Dutch Immigrant Women in the United States, 1880–1920." Ph.D. diss., University of Minnesota, 1993. Ann Arbor, Mich.: University Microfilms International.

Smits, C. *De Afscheiding van 1834.* Vol. 1: Oudkarspel, the Netherlands: De Nijverheid, 1971. Vols. 2–7: Dordrecht, The Nethelands: J.P. van den Tol, 1974–1986.

Stokvis, P. R. D. *De Nederlandse trek naar Amerika, 1846–1847.* Leiden: Universitaire Pers, 1977.

Swierenga, Robert P. *Dutch Emigrants to the United States, South Africa, South America, and Southeast Asia, 1835–1880: An Alphabetical Listing by Household Heads and Independent Persons.* Wilmington, Del.: Scholarly Resources, 1983.

——. *Dutch Households in U.S. Population Censuses, 1850, 1860, 1870: An Alphabetical Listing by Family Heads.* Wilmington, Del.: Scholarly Resources, 1987.

——. *Dutch Immigrants in U.S. Passenger Manifests, 1820–1880: An Alphabetical Listing by Household Heads and Independent Persons.* Wilmington, Del.: Scholarly Resources, 1983.

——. *The Dutch Transplanting in Michigan and the Midwest.* Ann Arbor: Historical Society of Michigan, 1986.

——. *The Dutch Transplanting in the Upper Middle West.* Marshall, Minn.: Southwest State University Press, 1991.

——. *The Forerunners: Dutch Jewry in the North American Diaspora.* Detroit: Wayne State University Press, 1994.

——, ed. *The Dutch in America: Immigration, Settlement, and Cultural Change.* New Brunswick: Rutgers University Press, 1985.

Swierenga, Robert P., and Philip R. Vandermeer, eds. *Belief and Behavior: Essays in the New Religious History.* New Brunswick: Rutgers University Press, 1991.

Taylor, Lawrence J. *Dutchmen on the Bay: The Ethnohistory of a Contractual Community.* Philadelphia: University of Pennsylvania Press, 1983.

Thernstrom, Stephen, ed. *Harvard Encyclopedia of American Ethnic Groups*. Cambridge: Harvard University Press, 1980.

Van Dedem, W. J. *Staphorst 100 Jaar Geleden*. Staphorst, The Netherlands: Heinen van de Rollecate, 1984.

Van der Aa, A. J., *Aardrijkskundig woordenboek der Nederlanden*. 13 vols. Gorinchem, The Netherlands: Jacobus Noorduyn, 1839–51.

Vanderstel, David. "The Dutch of Grand Rapids, Michigan, 1848–1900." Ph.D. diss., Kent State University, 1984. Ann Arbor, Mich.: University Microfilms International.

Van Eerd, C., and K. Oppeland, eds. *Vrouwen in den Vreemde*. Zutphen, The Netherlands: De Walburg Pers, 1993.

Van Hinte, Jacob. *Netherlanders in America: A Study of Emigration and Settlement in the Nineteenth and Twentieth Centuries of the United States of America*. Ed. Robert P. Swierenga. Grand Rapids, Mich.: Baker Book House, 1985. Edited translation of a 1928 Dutch-language publication.

Van Houtte, J. A. *An Economic History of the Low Countries*. New York: St. Martin's Press, 1977.

Van Stekelenburg, Henri. *Landverhuizing als regionaal verschijnsel Van Noord-Brabant naar Noord-Amerika, 1820–1880*. Tilburg, The Netherlands: Stichting Zuidelijk Historisch Contact, 1991.

Van Stuijvenberg, J. H. *De economische geschiedenis van Nederland*. Groningen, The Netherlands: Wolters-Noordhoff, 1977.

Vecoli, Rudolph, and Suzanne Sinke, eds. *A Century of European Migrations*. Urbana: University of Illinois Press, 1991.

Wesseling, J. *De Afscheiding van 1834 in Friesland*. 2 vols. Groningen, The Netherlands: De Vuurbaak, 1980.

——. *De Afscheiding van 1834 in Groningerland*. 3 vols. Groningen, The Netherlands: De Vuurbaak, 1973–78.

——. *De Afscheiding van 1834 in Overijssel*. Groningen, The Netherlands: De Vuurbaak, 1984.

——. *De Afscheiding van 1834 in Zeeland*. Barneveld, The Netherlands: De Vuurbaak, 1987.

Wilterdink, Willem. *Winterswijkse pioniers in Amerika*. Winterswijk, The Netherlands: Vereniging "Het Museum," 1990.

Yans-McLaughlin, Virginia, ed. *Immigration Reconsidered: History, Sociology, and Politics*. New York: Oxford University Press, 1990.

Zwaanstra, Henry. *Reformed Thought and Experience in the New World*. Kampen, The Netherlands: J. H. Kok, 1973.

INDEX OF PERSONAL NAMES

INDEX OF PLACE-NAMES

TOPICAL INDEX

Accidents: bobsled kills teacher, 263–264, 409, 417–418; broken leg, 367; burns, 301; car wreck, 323; collapse of building, 101; collapse of school staircase, 376; construction-site accident, 86; to cow, 167; drowning, 104, 107, 209; injury at sea, 158; leg cut by barbed wire, 218; manure-spreader accident, 215; shipwreck, 245; train-trestle accident, 297. *See also* Fires

Act of Secession, 13

Adoption, 318

Advice to would-be immigrants, 217, 231. *See also* Assessments of America and American life

Afscheiding: birthplace of, 154; Lankester and, 339–340; pious isolation of, 10; rural character of, 16; in Staphorst, 25–26

Agricultural depression of 1920s, 86

Ailments/diseases/maladies: animal lice, 122; bad back, 318; blindness, 289, 411–412; cattle disease, 122, 137; cholera, 111, 115, 344, 371; cold/colic (horse), 168; colds, 162, 226, 272, 313, 366, 452; deafness, 8, 79, 81, 83; depression, 218; diarrhea, 166, 253, 258, 397; dysentery, 395; fever, 33; headaches, 80; heat prostration, 112, 142, 169, 178, 327 (horses); hog disease, 111, 186, 206, 303; hunger and thirst (cattle), 152; influenza (grippe), 100–101, 214–215, 218; *koperzuur*, 373; leg cramps, 53, 55; leg infection, 443–444, 446, 448; lung infection, 226, 233; lung and liver disease, 134; mental illness, 128–129, 162, 407–408; mental retardation, 253, 254–255, 270, 277, 279, 283, 284, 285, 288–289; nervous condition, 80, 203; pain, 58, 148; pneumonia, 316; poor eyes, 143, 207, 315; potato disease, 48; pregnancy problems, 37; rheumatism, 96; scarlet fever, 158, 433; seasickness, 30, 110, 245, 306, 385, 412, 445; sores, 67, 237; stomach problems, 124, 131, 299, 376; throat infection, 245, 277; "trouble

swallowing," 97; tuberculosis (consumption), 47, 57, 254, 318; vision disorder, 253; vomiting and fever (infant), 130; war wounds, 287

Alcohol/drinking/drunkenness, 189, 213, 239, 306, 402

Alexander Dodge Company (Grand Rapids), 410

Alpine Avenue Christian Reformed Church (Grand Rapids), 330

American family, 172, 178

American fundamentalism, 422

"Americans," 286, 392, 395–396, 407; generosity of, 343

Antirevolutionary Party, 20

Army, 50. *See also* Military service

Artesian wells, 154, 180, 184

Assassination of Lincoln, 43, 358–359

Assessments of America and American life: by Bunnemeijer, 426–428; by De Lange, 409, 413, 415–416; by Diemer, 86–87, 90–91, 101; by Eringa, 176, 180–181, 186, 188–189, 193, 195–196, 203, 210; by Koopman, 430–431; by Kuijt, 446, 448–449; by Lankester, 342–343, 360, 364; by Mannee, 365, 367, 368–369, 375; by Niemeijer 305, 310–312, 314; by Nijenhuis, 440–441; by Philipsen, 236–237, 240, 242; by Plaisier, 331; by Schoonbeck, 284, 287–288; by Smith, 452; by Van der Bosch, 229; by Van den Hoek, 109–111, 113, 115–116, 137, 141, 144–145, 149, 150–152, 154; by women, 46, 188, 381; by Wonnink, 249, 258–259, 266, 268, 270; by Zahn, 383, 402–406; by Zondervan, 296, 297

Assessment of Dutch immigrants, 432, 437

Assimilation into mainstream culture, 162; of De Langes, 411; of "detached" immigrants, 422; of Dunninks, 29–30; of Eringas, 174; of Hellers, 105, 156; immediate, 3n.3; of Lankesters, 340; of Plaisiers, 322; of Schoonbecks, 255; third-

Hunebedden, 429
Hunting, 36, 332, 380, 391, 452
Hymn singing, 12

Icebergs, 246
Immigrant-aid societies, 446n. 2
Independence of Jewish, Catholic, Protestant
  immigrant groups 19–20
Independent congregations, 279n.1, 280,
  282n.1
Indians, 18, 138, 196, 350, 424
Industrial Revolution in Netherlands, 223
Inflation, 354
Inheritance, 98, 106, 186, 210, 212, 238, 350
Insane asylum, 128
Interurban, 73, 325, 329
Iowa, 169
Irish, 414
Isabella, 326

Jews, 1, 9, 337, 363, 406, 438
Jobs, occupations, professions/wages: *in the
  Netherlands* before immigration: butter-
  store manager, 443; farmer, 23; field hand,
  23; notary public, 408; ship captain, 363;
  shopkeeper, 421; veterinarian, 435; weaver,
  23; *in America*: baker, 339, 343;
  blacksmith, 344; boarding-house owner,
  226, 301; bookkeeper and clerk, 107, 146,
  286, 288; brickmaker, 35; builder, 285;
  cabinet maker, 222, 320; carpenter, 69, 86,
  91–93, 95, 211, 218, 228, 231, 252;
  cheese-factory worker, 82–83; chicken
  raiser, 192, 450–451; cigar maker, 309–
  310, 316, 407; cigar-store employee, 389;
  clerk in shop, 79, 228, 233, 444; coal
  miner, 303; construction supervisor, 230;
  day laborer, 34, 222; ditch digger, 112;
  dog racing, 450; drugstore worker, 278;
  engraver, 288; factory worker, 7, 63, 70;
  82, 221, 250, 280, 297, 302, 323, 329, 410;
  farmer, 7, 14, 63, 222, 317–318, 320–321;
  farmhand, 6, 7, 91, 112, 114, 124, 159,
  221–222, 243, 256, 290, 302–303, 327–
  328, 344; flax farmer, 319–320; foreman in
  print shop, 358; fort worker, 167; garage
  worker, 81; gardener, 430; gasline layer,
  298; gentleman farmer, 14, 339, 342;
  gravel-mine laborer, 320; greenhouse
  worker, 320; grocer, 321; harness maker,
  410; horse breeder, 69; hog raiser, 303;
  hospital worker, 427; housekeeper, 172,
  448; housemaid, 7, 59, 124, 253, 302, 381,
  443–444; house mover, 255, 280, 282;
  investor, 339; land leaser, 339; laundress,
  257, 259, 268, 301–302, 313; logger, 84;
  machinist, 410; manager of wholesale
  grocery firms, 340; market gardener, 221–
222, 304, 320–321; mason, 7, 275, 297–
298, 344, 346; maternity nurse, 368;
midwife, 302, 368; miller, 134–345;
missionary, 207, 243; money lender, 398;
owner of business, 7, 10, 23, 47, 66, 158,
243, 339–340, 357, 364, 380, 383, 391,
407; painter, 218, 342, 441–442, 445;
paper–mill worker, 248; plasterer, 275,
297–298; racetrack worker, 297;
railroad-tie maker, 86; railroad worker, 74,
128, 218; reporter, 285; sales
representative, 340; sawmill worker, 41,
243, 248; seamstress, 202, 207; sewer
digger, 250, 298; sharecropper, 6; shingle
maker, 34; shoemaker, 10, 364; silk-
factory worker, 294, 295–296, 299; starch
maker, 340–341; steel worker, 297; stone
burier, 151–152; streetcar conductor, 433;
stump puller, 159; tailor, 72, 82–83, 223,
233–234, 413; teacher, 69, 107, 146, 174,
263, 412, 416, 423; tobacco dealer, 337,
401; tradesman, 14; trash hauler, 9, 304,
309, 313, 316; typesetter, 310; vegetable
salesman, 304, 318; well digger, 89;
wholesale produce dealer, 221; wood
worker, 222; woodcutter, 165, 170;
wooden-shoe maker/seller, 252–253, 262,
265
John Ball Park, 324

Kaapse Children's Bible, 193
Katholic Illustratie, 424
Kerosene, 360
Knights of Labor, 143
Kommie, 50
Kroonprins, 368
Kuyperian Calvinism, 16–18

Labor unions, 143, 287, 440–442
Land prices, 65, 72, 82–83, 106, 118, 125,
  129, 133; Beaverdam, 33, 36, 39; Chicago
  area, 121–122; Grand Rapids, 347; Little
  Chute, 46–47; Orange City, 133; South
  Blendon, 82; South Dakota, 138, 141, 146,
  195, 213; South Holland, 106, 129, 131;
  Three Oaks, Mich., 118
Languages: English, Dutch, Fries, 183;
  English eulogy, 227; English for RCA
  synod, 199; English for sermons, 266;
  "Language of Canaan," 29; learning
  Dutch, 66, 161, 193, 201; learning English,
  18, 31, 40, 43, 47, 51–52, 66, 113, 116,
  121, 175, 178–179, 195, 237, 246, 258–259,
  263, 266, 270–271, 277, 309, 313–314, 317,
  323, 325–326, 343, 367, 369, 386, 391, 412,
  424, 427, 441, 447, 450; learning Japanese,
  220; losing Dutch, 76, 101, 281, 377;
  ministers trained in English, 118

DOCUMENTS IN AMERICAN SOCIAL HISTORY

Edited by NICK SALVATORE

Their Lives and Numbers:
The Condition of Working People in Massachusetts, 1870–1900
edited by Henry F. Bedford

We Will Rise in Our Might:
Workingwomen's Voices from Nineteenth-Century New England
by Mary H. Blewett

Dutch American Voices:
Letters from the United States, 1850–1930
edited by Herbert J. Brinks

Peter Porcupine in America:
Pamphlets on Republicanism and Revolution
by William Cobbett, edited and with
an Introduction by David A. Wilson

Invisible Immigrants: The Adaptation of English and Scottish Immigrants
in Nineteenth-Century America
by Charlotte Erickson

Keepers of the Revolution: New Yorkers at Work in the Early Republic
edited by Paul A. Gilje and Howard B. Rock

News from the Land of Freedom: German Immigrants Write Home
edited by Walter Kamphoefner, Wolfgang Helbich, and Ulrike Sommer

History of My Own Times
by William Otter, edited by Richard B. Stott